CONTENTS

PREFACE

As you embark on the fascinating journey of studying child development, it is our hope that this workbook will help you master the material in your text. *Infants, Children, and Adolescents,* by Laura E. Berk. Our intention in preparing the workbook is to provide you with active practice in learning the content in your textbook and thought-provoking questions that help you clarify your own thinking. Each chapter in the workbook is organized into the following six sections.

BRIEF CHAPTER SUMMARY

We begin with a brief chapter summary of the material, mentioning major topics covered and general principles emphasized in text discussion. Each chapter of your textbook includes two additional summaries: an informal one at the beginning of the chapter, and a structured summary at the end of the chapter. Thus, the brief chapter summary in the workbook will be your third review of the information covered in each chapter. It is intended to remind you of major points in the text before you embark on the remaining activities in the workbook.

LEARNING OBJECTIVES

We have organized the main points in each chapter into a series of objectives that indicate what you should be able to do once you have mastered the material. We suggest that you look over these objectives before you read each chapter. You may find it useful to take notes on information pertaining to objectives as you read. When you finish a chapter, try to answer the objectives in a few sentences or a short paragraph. Then check your answers against the text and revise your responses accordingly. Once you have completed this exercise, you will have generated your own review of chapter content. Because it is written in your own words, it should serve as an especially useful chapter overview that can be referred to when you prepare for examinations.

STUDY QUESTIONS

The main body of each chapter consists of study questions, organized according to major headings in the textbook, that assist you in identifying main points and grasping concepts and principles. Text pages on which answers can he found are indicated next to each entry. The study question section can be used in a number of ways. You may find it helpful to answer each question as you read the chapter. Alternatively, try reading one or more sections and then testing yourself by answering the relevant study questions. Finally, use the study question section as a device to review for examinations. If you work through it methodically, your retention of chapter material will be greatly enhanced.

ASK YOURSELF . . .

In each chapter of your textbook, critical thinking questions that appear at the end of each major section. Answering these questions will help you analyze important theoretical concepts and research findings. Four types of questions are included: *Review* questions, which assist with recall and comprehension of information in the text; *Apply* questions, which encourage application of your knowledge to controversial issues and problems; *Connect* questions, which help you to integrate what you have learned across age periods and aspects of development, thereby building an image of the whole person; and *Reflect* questions, which make the study of child development personally meaningful by asking you to reflect on your own development and life experiences. Each question is answered on MyDevelopmentLab, where you may compare your reasoning to a model response. For directions on how to register and access MyDevelopmentLab, see p. ix.

SUGGESTED STUDENT READINGS

A list of three to five suggested readings compliments each text chapter. The readings have been carefully selected for their interest value and readability; the majority are recently published. A brief description of the content of each suggested reading is provided.

CROSSWORD PUZZLES

To help you master the central vocabulary of the field, we have provided crossword puzzles that test your knowledge of important terms and concepts. Answers can be found at the back of the workbook. If you cannot think of the term that matches a clue in the puzzles, your knowledge of information related to the term may be insecure. Reread the material in the text chapter related to each item that you miss. Also, try a more demanding approach to term mastery: After you have completed each puzzle, cover the clues and write your own definitions of each term.

PRACTICE TESTS

Once you have thoroughly studied a chapter, find out how well you know the material by taking the two multiple choice practice tests. Then check your answers using the key at the back of the workbook. If you answered more than a few items incorrectly, spend extra time rereading the chapter, writing responses to chapter objectives, and reviewing the study questions in this guide.

Now that you understand how the workbook is organized, you are ready to begin using it to master *Infants, Children, and Adolescents.* We wish you a rewarding and enjoyable course of study.

Laura E. Berk
Trisha Mann
Sara Harris
Judy Ashkenaz
Mark Seidl

STUDENT REGISTRATION & LOGIN
MyDevelopmentLab & MyDevelopmentLab CourseCompass

MyDevelopmentLab is a state of the art, interactive and instructive online solution for child and lifespan development. MyDevelopmentLab combines multimedia, tutorials, video, simulations, animations, tests and quizzes to make teaching and learning fun. Below you will find instructions to register and access MyDevelopmentLab or MyDevelopmentLab CourseCompass.

STUDENT REGISTRATION & LOGIN: MyDevelopmentLab

Before You Begin

To register for MyDevelopmentLab you will need:
- ☑ Your school zip code
- ☑ A MyDevelopmentLab student access code (packaged with your text)
- ☑ A valid email address

Registration

1. Enter **http://www.mydevelopmentlab.com** in your Web browser.
2. Under "First-time users," click **Students.**
3. Click the **Register** link.
4. If you have your access code, click the **Next** button.
5. Select "**No, I am a New User**."
6. Open your **Student Access Code Card** to reveal your unique **Access Code** and enter the code in the fields provided.
7. Enter your School **Zip Code**, select **United States** as your Country and click **Next.**
8. Enter your **Name** and **Email** and select **Your School.**
9. Create your **Login Name** and **Password**, answer the **Security Question** and click **Next.**

If successful, you will receive a **Confirmation Screen** with your information (this screen was also emailed to you).

Login and Accessing the Ask Yourself Questions

1. Enter **http://www.mydevelopmentlab.com** in your Web Browser.
2. Under "Returning users," click **MyDevelopmentLab.**
3. Enter the **Login Name** and **Password** you created and click **"Log In."**
4. Click on *Infants, Children, and Adolescents,* Sixth Edition, or *Infants and Children,* Sixth Edition (the title of your text), and then click **"Submit."**
5. From the Table of Contents page, select your **chapter**.
6. Under Chapter Topics, select your Topic to **open the E-Book**.
7. Next to the Ask Yourself box, select the **Explore** Icon.
8. Complete questions and choose **Submit for grading** or Clear answers to start over.

STUDENT REGISTRATION & LOGIN: MyDevelopmentLab CourseCompass

Before You Begin

To register for MyDevelopmentLab CourseCompass you will need:

- ☑ The "Course ID" provided by your instructor
- ☑ Your school zip code
- ☑ A MyDevelopmentLab CourseCompass student access code (packaged with your text)
- ☑ A valid email address

Registration

1. Enter **http://www.mydevelopmentlab.com** in your Web browser.
2. Under "First-time users," click **Students.**
3. Click the **Register** link.
4. If you have your access code and Course ID, click the **Next** button.
5. Select "**No, I am a New User.**"
6. Open your **Student Access Code Card** to reveal your unique **Access Code** and enter the code in the fields provided.
7. Enter your School **Zip Code**, select **United States** as your Country and click **Next.**
8. Enter your **Course ID** and click **Next.**
9. Enter your **Name** and **Email** and select **Your School.**
10. Create your **Login Name** and **Password**, answer the **Security Question** and click **Next.**

If successful, you will receive a **Confirmation Screen** with your information (this screen was also emailed to you).

Login and Accessing the Ask Yourself Questions

1. Enter **http://www.mydevelopmentlab.com** in your Web Browser.
2. Under "Returning users," click **MyDevelopmentLab CourseCompass**.
3. Enter the **Login Name** and **Password** you created and click **"Log In."**
4. You will see your **Course** listed under **Courses You Are Taking.**
5. Click on this Course and select the **Chapter Contents** from the left navigation menu.
6. From the Table of Contents page, select your **chapter**.
7. Under Chapter Topics, select your Topic to **open the E-Book.**
8. Next to the Ask Yourself box, select the **Explore** Icon.
9. Complete questions and choose **Submit for grading** or Clear answers to start over.

CHAPTER 1
HISTORY, THEORY, AND RESEARCH STRATEGIES

BRIEF CHAPTER SUMMARY

Child development is the study of all aspects of human growth and change in the first two decades of life, from conception through adolescence. It is part of a larger, interdisciplinary field, developmental science, which looks at all changes throughout the lifespan. Researchers often divide development into three broad domains—physical, cognitive, and emotional and social—while recognizing that each domain influences and is influenced by the others. Further, researchers usually divide the first two decades of life into five age periods. In addition, some researchers identify the transition from adolescence to adulthood as a distinct period: emerging adulthood. These divisions make the vast, interdisciplinary study of human constancy more orderly and convenient.

Theories are orderly, integrated ideas, based on scientific verification, that guide and give meaning to our observations and give us a basis for practical action. This chapter provides an overview of philosophical and theoretical approaches to child study from medieval to modern times. It also reviews major research strategies used to study child behavior and development.

All major theories of child development take a stand on three basic issues: (1) Is development continuous or discontinuous? (2) Is there one universal course of development or many possible courses? (3) Are genetic or environmental factors (nature or nurture) more important in development? Modern child development theories also pay attention to the various contexts in which children grow up. Further, theories differ in the degree to which they emphasize stability versus the potential for change. Modern theories generally take a balanced point of view on these issues, recognizing the merits of both positions.

Research methods commonly used to study children include systematic observation; self-reports; the clinical, or case study, method; and ethnography. Investigators of child development may use a correlational research design, which shows a relationship but does not allow inferences about cause and effect. Or they may use an experimental design, which permits cause-and-effect inferences. To study how their participants change over time, investigators use special developmental research strategies, including longitudinal, cross-sectional, sequential, and microgenetic designs. Each method and each design has both strengths and limitations.

Conducting research with children poses special ethical dilemmas. Guidelines have been developed that can be used to determine if the benefits of research outweigh the risks and to ensure that children's rights are protected.

LEARNING OBJECTIVES

After reading this chapter, you should be able to:

1.1 Explain the importance of the terms *applied* and *interdisciplinary* as they help to define the field of child development. (p. 4)

1.2 List the age periods researchers use to study child development, and cite the three domains in which development is often divided. (pp. 4–6)

1.3 Explain the role of theories in understanding child development, and describe the three basic issues on which major theories take a stand. (pp. 6–10)

1.4 Trace historical influences on modern theories of child development, from medieval times through the early twentieth century. (pp. 11–13)

1.5 Describe the theoretical perspectives that influenced child development research in the mid-twentieth century, and cite the contributions and limitations of each. (pp. 14–21)

1.6 Describe six recent theoretical perspectives of child development, noting the contributions of major theorists. (pp. 21–29)

1.7 Identify the stand that each modern theory takes on the three basic issues of child development presented earlier in this chapter. (pp. 29, 30)

1.8   Describe the methods commonly used to study children, and cite the strengths and limitations of each. (pp. 29, 31–35)

1.9   Contrast correlational and experimental research designs, and cite the strengths and limitations of each. (pp. 35, 37–39)

1.10   Describe research designs used to study development, noting the strengths and limitations of each. (pp. 40–43)

1.11   Discuss children's research rights, and explain why research involving children raises special ethical concerns. (pp. 43, 45–46)

STUDY QUESTIONS

The Field of Child Development

1.   True or False: Research on child development has been stimulated by both scientific curiosity and social pressures to better children's lives. (p. 4)

2.   Child development is an *interdisciplinary* field. Explain what this means. (p. 4)

_____

_____

_____

Domains of Development

1.   List the three broad domains in which development is often divided. (p. 4)

    A. _____

    B. _____

    C. _____

Periods of Development

1.   List the six age periods used to segment the first two-and-a-half decades of life. (pp. 5–6)

    A. _____   Age span: _____

    B. _____   Age span: _____

    C. _____   Age span: _____

    D. _____   Age span: _____

    E. _____   Age span: _____

    F. _____   Age span: _____

Basic Issues

1.   What are the three elements of a good theory? (p. 6)

    A. _____

    B. _____

    C. _____

2. Cite two reasons that theories are important to the study of child development. (pp. 6–7)

    A. _____

    B. _____

3. Explain how theories differ from opinions. (p. 7)

    _____

    _____

    _____

Continuous or Discontinuous Development?

1. Describe the two views theories use to explain the course of development. (pp. 7–8)

    A. _____

    _____

    B. _____

    _____

2. The (continuous / discontinuous) perspective maintains the belief that development occurs in stages. Explain what this means. (p. 8)

    _____

    _____

One Course of Development or Many?

1. Explain how distinct *contexts* can influence child development. (p. 8)

    _____

    _____

    _____

2. Describe both personal and environmental factors that shape the context of a child's development. (p. 8)

    Personal: _____

    Environmental: _____

    _____

    _____

Relative Influence of Nature or Nurture?

1. Briefly discuss the two views theories use to explain the underlying causes of development. (p. 8)

    A. _____

    _____

    B. _____

    _____

2. Describe how a theory's position on nature and nurture affects whether there is an emphasis on stability or change. (p. 9)

    A. _____

    _____

    B. _____

    _____

A Balanced Point of View

1. True or False: Theorists today regard heredity and environment as interwoven, each affecting the potential of the other to modify the child's traits and capacities. (p. 9)

Biology and Environment: Resilient Children

1. Define *resilience,* and explain why researchers are increasingly interested in this concept. (p. 10)

    A. _____

    _____

    B. _____

    _____

2. List and briefly describe the four broad factors that appear to offer protection from the damaging effects of stressful life events. (p. 10)

    A. _____

    _____

    B. _____

    _____

    C. _____

    _____

    D. _____

    _____

Historical Foundations

Medieval Times

1. In medieval times, childhood (was / was not) regarded as a distinct developmental period. Cite evidence to support your response. (p. 11)

    _____

    _____

The Reformation

1. True or False: Puritan doctrine stressed the innate goodness of all children. Briefly explain your response. (p. 11)

    _____

    _____

2. True or False: The Puritans placed a high value on the development of reasoning in children. (p. 11)

Philosophies of the Enlightenment

1. During the Enlightenment, the British philosopher John Locke regarded the child as a tabula rasa, which means
   _____. Explain his view. (pp. 11–12)

   _____

   _____

   _____

2. Summarize Locke's stance on each of the three basic issues of human development. (p. 12)

   Continuous or discontinuous development?

   _____

   _____

   _____

   One course of development or many?

   _____

   _____

   _____

   Relative influence of nature or nurture?

   _____

   _____

   _____

3. Jean-Jacques Rousseau, a French philosopher during the Enlightenment, introduced the notion of children as
   noble savages. Explain what he meant by this term. (p. 12)

   _____

   _____

   _____

4. Describe some of the key differences in the theories put forth by John Locke and Jean-Jacques Rousseau.
   (p. 11)

   _____

   _____

   _____

5. Cite two concepts included in Rousseau's theory that remain important to modern theories of child development.
   (p. 12)

   A. _____

   B. _____

Scientific Beginnings

1. Briefly describe the two principles emphasized in Darwin's theory of evolution. (p. 12)

   A. _____

   _____

   _____

   _____

   B. _____

   _____

   _____

   _____

2. Who is generally regarded as the founder of the child study movement? (p. 13)

   _____

3. The _____ *approach* to child development uses age-related averages to represent typical development. (p. 13)

4. Who constructed the first successful intelligence test? (p. 13)

   _____

5. Why did this test succeed, while previous efforts to create a useful intelligence test had failed? (p. 13)

   _____

   _____

6. A translated version of this test was developed for use with English-speaking children. What is the name of this instrument? (p. 13)

   _____

Mid-Twentieth-Century Theories

The Psychoanalytic Perspective

1. Summarize the basic concepts of the *psychoanalytic perspective.* (p. 14)

   _____

   _____

   _____

2. Freud's _____ *theory* emphasized that how parents manage their child's sexual and aggressive drives in the first few years of life is crucial for healthy personality development. (p. 14)

3. Name and briefly describe the three components of personality outlined in Freud's theory. (p. 14)

   A. _____

   _____

   B. _____

   _____

   C. _____

   _____

4. Match each of the following stages of psychosexual development with the appropriate description. (p. 15)

_____ Stage in which sexual instincts die down
_____ Stage in which the infant desires sucking activities
_____ Stage in which the Oedipal and Electra conflicts take place
_____ Stage marked by mature sexuality
_____ Stage in which toilet training becomes a major issue between parent and child

1. Oral
2. Anal
3. Phallic
4. Latency
5. Genital

5. Cite one contribution and three limitations of Freud's theory. (p. 14)

Contribution: _____

_____

_____

Limitation: _____

_____

Limitation: _____

_____

Limitation: _____

_____

6. In what ways did Erikson build upon and improve Freud's theory? (pp. 14–15)

_____

_____

_____

_____

7. Match each of Erikson's stages with the appropriate description. (p. 16)

_____ Successful resolution of this stage depends on the adult's success at caring for other people or productive work.
_____ The primary task of this stage is the development of a sense of self and a sense of one's place in society.
_____ Successful resolution of this stage depends on a warm, loving relationship with the caregiver.
_____ In this stage, children experiment with adult roles through make-believe play.
_____ Successful resolution of this stage depends on parents granting the child reasonable opportunities for free choice.
_____ Successful resolution of this stage involves reflecting on life's accomplishments.
_____ The development of close relationships with others helps ensure successful resolution of this stage.
_____ Children who develop the capacity for cooperation and productive work will successfully resolve this stage.

1. Basic trust vs. mistrust
2. Autonomy vs. shame and doubt
3. Initiative vs. guilt
4. Industry vs. inferiority
5. Identity vs. role confusion
6. Intimacy vs. isolation
7. Generativity vs. stagnation
8. Integrity vs. despair

8. Cite two contributions of psychoanalytic theory. (p. 15)

   A. _____

   B. _____

9. Discuss two reasons why psychoanalytic theory is no longer in the mainstream of child development research. (p. 16)

   A. _____

   _____

   B. _____

   _____

Behaviorism and Social Learning Theory

1. True or False: Behaviorism focuses on the inner workings of the mind. (p. 16)

2. True or False: Watson's study of little Albert, an 11-month-old baby who was taught to fear a white rat by associating it with a loud noise, supported Pavlov's concept of *classical conditioning*. (p. 17)

3. Summarize B. F. Skinner's *operant conditioning theory*. (p. 17)

   _____

   _____

   _____

4. Describe the concept of modeling, also known as *imitation* or *observational learning*, as emphasized in Bandura's *social learning theory*. (p. 17)

   _____

   _____

   _____

5. Summarize Bandura's revisions to his social learning theory, which stress the importance of *cognition* in the learning process. (pp. 17–18)

   _____

   _____

   _____

6. Behaviorism and social learning theory have had a major applied impact on the field of child development through the introduction of *behavior modification*. Explain this procedure. (p. 18)

   _____

   _____

   _____

7. Discuss two limitations of behaviorism and social learning theory. (p. 18)

   A. _____

   _____

   B. _____

   _____

Piaget's Cognitive-Developmental Theory

1. True or False: Piaget's *cognitive-developmental theory* is consistent with the principles of behaviorism; that is, Piaget believed that knowledge is imparted to children through the use of reinforcement. Briefly explain your response. (p. 18)

   _____

   _____

2. Define Piaget's concept of *adaptation*. (pp. 18–19)

   _____

   _____

3. Match each of Piaget's stages with the appropriate description. (p. 20)

   _____ During this stage, thought becomes more complex, and children develop   1. Sensorimotor
   the capacity for abstract reasoning.   2. Preoperational
   _____ This stage is characterized by the use of eyes, ears, hands, and mouth to   3. Concrete operational
   explore the environment.   4. Formal operational
   _____ During this stage, children use symbols and engage in make-believe play.
   _____ This stage is marked by the development of logical, organized reasoning
   skills.

4. What did Piaget use as his chief method for studying child and adolescent thought? (p. 19)

   _____

5. Discuss contributions of Piaget's theory. (pp. 19–20)

   _____

   _____

6. Cite three recent challenges to Piaget's theory. (p. 20)

   A. _____

   _____

   B. _____

   _____

   C. _____

   _____

Recent Theoretical Perspectives

Information Processing

1. Briefly describe the *information-processing* view of child development. (p. 21)

   _____

   _____

   _____

2. How are flowcharts used by information-processing researchers? (p. 21)

   _____

   _____

3. In what basic way are information processing and Piaget's theory alike? In what basic way are they different? (p. 22)

    Alike: _____

    Different: _____

4. Cite one strength and two limitations of the information-processing approach. (p. 22)

    Strength: _____

    Limitation: _____

    Limitation: _____

5. Briefly describe a new area of investigation, called *developmental cognitive neuroscience.* (pp. 22–23)

    _____

    _____

    _____

6. List three areas in which developmental cognitive neuroscientists are making rapid progress in the field of child development. (p. 23)

    A. _____

    B. _____

    C. _____

Ethology and Evolutionary Developmental Psychology

1. *Ethology* is the study of (p. 23)

    _____

    _____

2. Name the two European zoologists who laid the modern foundations of ethology. (p. 23)

    A. _____

    B. _____

3. Contrast the notion of a *critical period* with that of a *sensitive period.* (p. 23)

    Critical period: _____

    _____

    _____

    _____

    Sensitive period: _____

    _____

    _____

    _____

4. Explain how John Bowlby used the principles of ethology to understand the infant-caregiver relationship. (pp. 23–24)

    _____

    _____

    _____

5. Briefly explain the primary focus of *evolutionary developmental psychology,* and list a question that may be asked by an evolutionary developmental psychologist. (p. 24)

    A. _____

    _____

    B. _____

    _____

Vygotsky's Sociocultural Theory

1. Explain the importance of social interaction in Vygotsky's *sociocultural theory.* (p. 24)

    _____

    _____

    _____

2. Compare and contrast the theories of Piaget and Vygotsky. (pp. 24–25)

    _____

    _____

    _____

    _____

3. True or False: Because cultures select tasks for children's learning, children in every culture develop unique strengths not present in others. (p. 25)

4. Vygotsky's emphasis on culture and social experience led him to neglect _____ contributions to development. (p. 25)

Ecological Systems Theory

1. Summarize the core tenet of Bronfenbrenner's *ecological systems theory.* (p. 25)

    _____

    _____

2. To explain the contribution of both biological and environmental influences on development, Bronfenbrenner recently characterized his perspective as a _____ model. (p. 25)

3. Match each level of ecological systems theory with the appropriate description or example. (pp. 26–27)

    _____ Relationship between the child's home and school   1. Microsystem
    _____ The influence of cultural values   2. Mesosystem
    _____ The parent's workplace   3. Exosystem
    _____ The child's interaction with parents   4. Macrosystem

4. Provide examples of factors in each system that can enhance development. (pp. 26–27)

    Microsystem: _____

    Mesosystem: _____

    Exosystem: _____

    Macrosystem: _____

5. Bronfenbrenner's _____ system refers to temporal changes that affect development, such as the timing of the birth of a sibling. (p. 27)

6. In ecological systems theory, development is controlled by (environmental circumstances / inner dispositions / the interaction of environmental circumstances and inner dispositions). (p. 27)

New Directions: Development as a Dynamic System

1. Describe the *dynamic systems perspective.* (p. 27)

    _____

    _____

    _____

2. Based on the dynamic systems perspective, explain how individuals develop both universal traits and individual abilities. (p. 28)

    Universal traits: _____

    _____

    Individual abilities: _____

    _____

Comparing Child Development Theories

1. Identify the stances that the following modern theories take on the three basic issues of childhood and child development: (p. 30)

Theory	Continuous or Discontinuous Development?	One Course of Development or Many?	Nature or Nurture as More Important?
Psychoanalytic perspective	_____	_____	_____
Behaviorism and social learning theory	_____	_____	_____
Piaget's cognitive-developmental theory	_____	_____	_____
Information processing	_____	_____	_____
Ethology and evolutionary developmental psychology	_____	_____	_____
Vygotsky's sociocultural theory	_____	_____	_____
Ecological systems theory	_____	_____	_____
Dynamic systems perspective	_____	_____	_____

Studying the Child

1. Research usually begins with a _____, or a prediction about behavior drawn from a theory. (p. 29)

Common Methods of Gathering Information

1. Compare and contrast *naturalistic* and *structured* observation techniques, noting one strength and one limitation of each approach. (pp. 31–33)

Naturalistic: _____

_____

Strength: _____

_____

Limitation: _____

_____

Structured: _____

_____

Strength: _____

_____

Limitation: _____

_____

2. Explain how *clinical interviews* differ from structured interviews, and note the benefits and limitations of each technique. (pp. 33–34)

Clinical: _____

_____

Benefits: _____

_____

Limitations: _____

_____

Structured: _____

_____

Benefits: _____

_____

Limitations: _____

_____

3. Cite the primary aim of the *clinical, or case study, method,* and note the procedures often used to achieve this goal. (p. 34)

Aim: _____

_____

Procedures: _____

_____

4. What are the drawbacks of using the clinical method? (p. 34)

    _____

    _____

5. _____ is a research method aimed at understanding a culture or distinct social group. This goal is achieved through _____, a technique in which the researcher lives with the cultural community and participates in all aspects of daily life. (p. 34)

6. Cite two limitations of the ethnographic method. (p. 35)

    A. _____

    B. _____

Cultural Influences: Immigrant Youths: Amazing Adaptation

1. True or False: Students who are first-generation (foreign-born) and second-generation (American- or Canadian-born, with immigrant parents) achieve in school as well as or better than students of native-born parents. (p. 36)

2. On average, adolescents from immigrant families are (more / less) likely to commit delinquent and violent acts, to use drugs and alcohol, or to have early sex. (p. 36)

3. Discuss two ways in which family and ethnic community influence the academic achievement of adolescents from immigrant families. (p. 36)

    A. _____

    _____

    B. _____

    _____

General Research Designs

1. Explain the basic features of the *correlational design*. (pp. 35, 37)

    _____

    _____

2. True or False: The correlational design is preferred by researchers because it allows them to infer cause and effect. Explain your response. (p. 37)

    _____

    _____

    _____

3. Investigators examine the relationships among variables using a(n) _____ , a number that describes how two measures, or variables, are associated with one another. (p. 37)

4. A *correlation coefficient* can range from _____ to _____. The magnitude of the number shows the (strength / direction) of the relationship between the two variables, whereas the sign indicates the (strength / direction) of the relationship. (p. 37)

5. For a correlation coefficient, a positive sign means that as one variable increases, the other (increases / decreases); a negative sign indicates that as one variable increases, the other (increases / decreases). (p. 37)

6. A researcher determines that the correlation between warm, consistent parenting and child delinquency is −.80. Explain what this indicates about the relationship between these two variables. (p. 37)

_____

_____

_____

7. If the same researcher had found a correlation of +.45, what would this have indicated about the relationship between warm, consistent parenting and child delinquency? (p. 37)

_____

_____

_____

8. What is the primary distinction between a *correlational design* and an *experimental design*? (p. 37)

_____

9. Describe the difference between an *independent* and a *dependent* variable. (p. 37)

Independent: _____

_____

Dependent: _____

_____

10. What is the feature of an experimental design that enables researchers to infer a cause-and-effect relationship between the variables? (p. 37)

_____

_____

11. Researchers engage in _____ *assignment* of participants to treatment conditions. Why is this important in experimental studies? (p. 38)

_____

_____

12. In _____ *experiments,* researchers randomly assign people to treatment conditions in natural settings. (p. 38)

13. True or False: Natural experiments differ from correlational research in that groups of participants are carefully chosen to ensure that their characteristics are as much alike as possible. (p. 39)

Designs for Studying Development

1. In a _____ *design,* participants are studied repeatedly at different ages, and changes are noted as the participants get older. (p. 40)

2. List two advantages of the longitudinal design. (p. 40)

A. _____

_____

B. _____

_____

3. Describe three problems in conducting longitudinal research. (p. 40)

   A. _____

   _____

   B. _____

   _____

   C. _____

   _____

4. In what way do *cohort effects* threaten the accuracy of longitudinal research findings? (pp. 40–41)

   _____

   _____

   _____

5. Describe the *cross-sectional design.* (p. 41)

   _____

   _____

   _____

6. In cross-sectional designs, researchers (do / do not) need to worry about participant dropout and practice effects. (p. 41)

7. Summarize two drawbacks of the cross-sectional design. (pp. 41–42)

   A. _____

   _____

   B. _____

   _____

8. In _____ *designs*, researchers conduct several similar cross-sectional or longitudinal studies at varying times. List three advantages of this design. (p. 42)

   A. _____

   _____

   B. _____

   _____

   C. _____

   _____

9. In a _____ design, researchers present children with a novel task and follow their mastery over a series of closely spaced sessions. (p. 43)

10. Microgenetic research is especially useful for studying (physical / cognitive / emotional and social) development. (p. 43)

11. List three reasons why microgenetic studies are difficult to carry out. (p. 43)

    A. _____

    _____

    B. _____

    _____

    C. _____

    _____

Social Issues: Education: Can Musical Experiences Enhance Intelligence?

1. True or False: The "Mozart effect" has a long-lasting influence on intelligence. (p. 44)

2. To produce lasting gains in mental test scores, interventions must have the following two features: (p. 44)

    A. _____

    _____

    B. _____

    _____

3. Explain how enrichment activities, such as music or chess lessons, can aid a child's developing intelligence. (p. 44)

    _____

    _____

    _____

Ethics in Research on Children

1. Why are ethical concerns especially complex when children take part in research? (p. 43)

    _____

    _____

    _____

2. Briefly describe the following children's research rights. (p. 45)

    A. Protection from harm:

    _____

    B. Informed consent:

    _____

    C. Privacy:

    _____

    D. Knowledge of results:

    _____

    E. Beneficial treatments:

    _____

3. For children _____ years and older, their own informed consent should be obtained in addition to parental consent prior to participation in research. (pp. 45–46)

4. What is *debriefing,* and why does it rarely work well with children? (p. 46)

   A. _____

   _____

   B. _____

   _____

ASK YOURSELF . . .

For *Ask Yourself* questions for this chapter, along with feedback on the accuracy of your answers, please log on to MyDevelopmentLab (for registration and access, please visit mydevelopmentlab.com or follow the directions on p. ix).

1) Select the Chapter of the *Ask Yourself.*
2) Open the E-Book and select the Explore icon next to the *Ask Yourself.*
3) Complete questions and choose "Submit answers for grading" or "Clear Answers" to start over.

SUGGESTED STUDENT READINGS

Boyden, J., de Berry, J. (Eds.). (2004). *Children and youth on the front lines: Ethnography, armed conflict, and displacement.* New York: Berghahn Books. Presents fascinating, ethnographic accounts of children's experiences with violence, war, and trauma.

Bronfenbrenner, U. (Ed.). (2005). *Making human beings human.* Thousand Oaks, CA: Sage. An excellent resource for anyone interested in psychology, sociology, education, family studies, or related fields, this book examines the complexity of human development, including one's ability to influence and be influenced by many layers of the environment.

Greene, S., & Hogan, D. (Eds.). (2005). *Researching children's experiences: Approaches and methods.* Thousand Oaks: Sage. Examines the various methods and designs for conducting research with children, including strengths, limitations, and ethical concerns.

Schoon, I. (2006). *Risk and resilience: Adaptations in changing times.* New York: Cambridge University Press. Using findings from Britain's National Child Development and British Cohort Studies, this book examines factors that promote and undermine resilience in childhood and during the transition to adulthood.

PUZZLE 1.1 TERM REVIEW

Across

2. Genetically determined, naturally unfolding course of growth
3. Information-_____ approach: views the human mind as a symbol-manipulating machine
7. Freud's theory focusing on early sexual and aggressive drives
9. Erikson's stage theory of development entailing resolution of psychological conflicts
10. Social _____ theory: emphasizes the role of observational learning in the development of behavior
11. In ecological systems theory, temporal changes in a child's environment
14. Theory that focuses on how social interaction contributes to development
16. Theory concerned with the adaptive value of behavior
20. _____ developmental psychology seeks to understand the adaptive value of species-wide cognitive, emotional, and social competencies as those competencies change with age

21. _____ savages: view of children as possessing an innate plan for healthy growth
23. Development as a process in which new ways of understanding and responding to the world emerge at specific times
25. Nature-_____ controversy
26. In ecological systems theory, social settings that do not contain the child but that affect their experiences in immediate settings

Down

1. Unique combinations of personal and environmental circumstances that can result in different paths of change
4. _____ development: field of study devoted to understanding constancy and change from conception through adolescence and emerging adulthood
5. Theory that emphasizes the unique developmental history of each child
6. View of the child as a blank slate: tabula _____
8. In ecological systems theory, activities and interaction patterns in the child's immediate surroundings

12. In ecological systems theory, cultural values, laws, customs, and resources that influence experiences and interactions at inner levels of the environment
13. _____ systems theory: view of the child as developing within a complex system of relationships
15. Emphasizes the study of directly observable events
17. In ecological systems theory, connections between the child's immediate settings
18. Ability to adapt effectively in the face of threats to development
19. Piaget's _____-developmental theory suggests that children actively construct knowledge as they manipulate and explore their world
22. Development as gradually adding on more of the same types of skills that were there to begin with
23. _____ systems perspective: the child's mind, body, and physical and social worlds form an integrated system
24. Qualitative change characterizing a particular time period of development

PUZZLE 1.2 TERM REVIEW

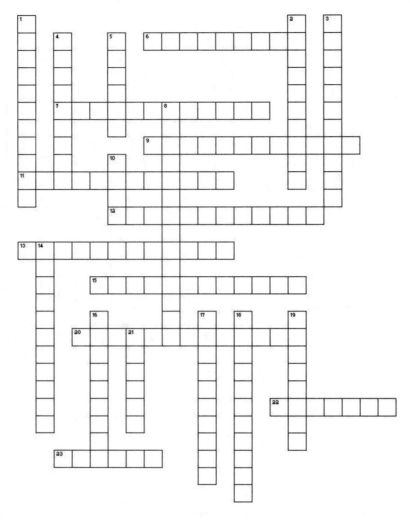

Across

6. _____ period: a time that is optimal for certain capacities to emerge
7. Developmental cognitive _____ is the study of relationships between changes in the brain and the developing child's cognitive processes and behavior
9. Design in which the same participants are studied repeatedly, at different ages
11. _____ observation: observing a behavior of interest in the natural environment
12. Design that permits inferences about cause and effect
13. Behavior _____: procedures that combine conditioning and modeling to eliminate undesirable behaviors and increase desirable responses
15. Design in which researchers present children with a novel task and follow their mastery over a series of closely spaced sessions

20. Design in which researchers gather information without altering the participants' experience
22. Developmental _____: an interdisciplinary field that includes all changes throughout the lifespan
23. Describes, explains, and predicts behavior

Down

1. Variable manipulated by the researcher
2. _____ designs allow researchers to conduct several similar cross-sectional or longitudinal studies at varying times
3. Participant observation of a culture
4. Variable expected to be influenced by the experimental manipulations
5. _____ effects refer to the impact of cultural historical change on the accuracy of findings
8. Design in which groups of people differing in age are studied at the same point in time

10. The clinical method or _____ study approach
14. Structured _____: the researcher sets up a situation that evokes a behavior of interest and observes that behavior in a laboratory setting
16. Approach that uses age-related averages to represent typical development
17. _____ interview: each participant is asked the same questions in the same way
18. A number describing how two variables are related is called a correlation _____
19. In a _____ interview, the researcher uses a flexible, conversational style to probe for a participant's point of view
21. _____ assignment helps researchers control characteristics of participants that could reduce the accuracy of their findings

PRACTICE TEST #1

1. Our knowledge of child development is interdisciplinary. What does this mean? (p. 4)
   a. Our knowledge of child development is based exclusively on research conducted by people in the field of child development.
   b. Child development is not recognized as a distinct field of study.
   c. It has grown through the combined efforts of people from many fields.
   d. Child development is part of a larger discipline known as developmental psychology.

2. The domains in which children develop (p. 4)
   a. involve only cognitive skills.
   b. occur sequentially.
   c. pertain to infants and toddlers alone.
   d. combine in an integrated, holistic fashion.

3. The period of infancy and toddlerhood lasts from (p. 6)
   a. conception to birth.
   b. birth to 2 years.
   c. 2 to 6 years.
   d. 6 to 11 years.

4. Researchers have posited a developmental period called emerging adulthood because (p. 6)
   a. most societies encourage prolonged immaturity.
   b. younger adults have moved beyond adolescence but not yet assumed adult roles.
   c. they no longer consider adolescence a useful category.
   d. young people now tend to defer exploration of love, career, and personal values.

5. A good theory is a useful tool of research because it (p.7)
   a. stands outside cultural values and belief systems.
   b. is not subject to further testing.
   c. describes, explains, and predicts behavior.
   d. distills complex observations into a single statement.

6. Researchers who view development as continuous would maintain that the difference between immaturity and maturity is essentially (p. 7)
   a. longer developmental periods.
   b. stages.
   c. a sense of morality.
   d. amount or complexity.

7. A researcher who emphasizes the role of nature in development would examine the effects of (p. 8)
   a. inborn biological givens.
   b. a single theory of development.
   c. the physical and social world.
   d. stages.

8. Research shows that resilient children tend to (p. 10)
   a. come from broken families.
   b. bond with grandparents.
   c. have biologically endowed characteristics that help them cope with stressful events.
   d. change their environments often to reduce their exposure to risk.

9. During medieval times, (p. 11)
   a. religious writings presented contradictory depictions of children's natures.
   b. the concept of childhood was shaped by the notion of original sin.
   c. children were regarded as small adults.
   d. children were viewed as essentially angelic innocents.

10. John Locke encouraged parents to (p. 12)
    a. use physical punishment to foster obedience.
    b. allow children to follow their own inclinations.
    c. use praise and approval as rewards.
    d. keep their children's minds a tabula rasa for as long as possible.

11. G. Stanley Hall and Arnold Gesell are best known for (p. 13)
    a. reintroducing the idea of original sin into the study of child development.
    b. launching the normative approach, in which measures of behavior are taken on large numbers of individuals and computed to represent typical development.
    c. developing a more sophisticated theory of the mind as a tabula rasa.
    d. challenging Darwin's theory.

12. Psychoanalytic theorists accept the clinical, or case study, method because (p. 15)
    a. without it, psychoanalytic theories are too vague to be tested empirically.
    b. it is the best way to chart how experience imprints the blank mind.
    c. it allows them to avoid the constraints of mental testing.
    d. it accords with their view that the individual's unique life history must be studied.

13. According to Piaget, children move from the preoperational stage to concrete operational stage when (p. 19)
    a. they begin to use their senses and movement to explore the world.
    b. their action patterns become symbolic though illogical.
    c. their cognition transforms into more organized reasoning.
    d. they develop powers of abstract, systematic reasoning.

14. Like Piaget's theory, the information-processing approach regards children as (p. 22)
    a. struggling to accommodate their sexual and aggressive drives to the needs of society.
    b. active, sense-making beings who modify their thought in response to environmental demands.
    c. involved in a process of increasingly selective imitation.
    d. largely influenced by culture.

15. Developmental cognitive neuroscience has made rapid progress in (p. 23)
    a. identifying the types of experiences that support or undermine brain development.
    b. clearing away the lingering influence of psychoanalysis.
    c. analyzing thought into components and reassembling those into a comprehensive theory.
    d. demonstrating with greater nuance the effects of operant conditioning.

16. Ethological theory proposes that during the critical period, the child needs appropriate stimulation in order to (p. 23)
    a. undergo the brain changes that enable various behavior patterns.
    b. begin the process of psychosocial development.
    c. acquire certain adaptive behaviors.
    d. conform to social norms.

17. Vygotsky viewed cognitive development as a (p. 25)
    a. process that occurs within a large organism-environment system.
    b. socially mediated process in which children depend on assistance from adults.
    c. process free of social or cultural contexts.
    d. process that occurs rapidly during the critical period.

18. According to Bronfenbrenner, relationships at the level of the microsystem (p. 26)
    a. are more important than those at the mesosystem level.
    b. involve only parents.
    c. shield children from forces that originate in the exosystem.
    d. are bidirectional.

19. The dynamic systems view proposes that children (p. 27)
    a. undergo the most profound changes when the microsystem clashes with the macrosystem.
    b. reorganize their behavior in response to changes in the organism-environment relationship.
    c. learn primarily through social interaction.
    d. actively code, transform, and organize information.

20. The greatest limitation of naturalistic observation is that (p. 31)
    a. not all individuals will be able to display a particular behavior in everyday life.
    b. it does not distinguish between human and animal behavior.
    c. it relies too heavily on self-reports.
    d. too often parents intervene to make children perform a particular behavior.

21. Researchers employing the ethnographic method try to minimize their influence on the culture they are studying by (p. 34)
    a. confining themselves to systematic observation.
    b. observing only one or two aspects of children's experience in that culture.
    c. describing, rather than interpreting, cultural meanings.
    d. becoming part of the culture.

22. According to ethnographies, one of the reasons that children of immigrant parents often succeed in school is that the (p. 36)
    a. children inherited high intelligence from their parents.
    b. parents often studied with them.
    c. parents believe that education is the surest way to improve life chances.
    d. children have thoroughly assimilated the values of their new homeland.

23. The correlational design enables researchers to (p. 35)
    a. eliminate the influence of the correlation coefficient.
    b. examine relationships between participants' characteristics and their behavior or development.
    c. infer cause and effect.
    d. understand the interactions among independent and dependent variables.

24. The major problem with the cross-sectional design is that it (p. 41)
    a. can be influenced by cohort effects.
    b. relies too heavily on quasi-experiments.
    c. does not provide evidence of change at the individual level.
    d. too often yields results that cannot be assembled into general theories.

25. Microgenetic studies are difficult to conduct because (p. 43)
    a. the time required for children to change their behavior is hard to anticipate.
    b. combining longitudinal and cross-sectional designs is very difficult.
    c. such studies require a large number of random assignments.
    d. researchers must control so many independent variables.

PRACTICE TEST #2

1. In the period of middle childhood, (p. 6)
   a. language begins to develop.
   b. make-believe play blossoms.
   c. the child masters basic literacy skills.
   d. the young person establishes autonomy from the family.

2. The existence of many theories of child development (p. 7)
   a. helps advance knowledge by engaging the efforts of many researchers.
   b. prevents researchers from developing coherent explanations.
   c. suggests that development is always discontinuous.
   d. inhibits researchers' efforts to improve the welfare and treatment of children.

3. Theories of discontinuous development propose that development (p. 8)
   a. concludes in middle childhood.
   b. is a process of gradually augmenting skills present since birth.
   c. proceeds through five domains.
   d. occurs through sudden and rapid periods of transformation.

4. A theorist who argues that personality is shaped by intellectual stimulation from teachers holds which of the following views of development? (pp. 8–9)
   a. nature
   b. nurture
   c. continuous
   d. discontinuous

5. In America, the efforts to teach children self-reliance and self-control led Puritan parents to (p. 11)
   a. adopt a moderate balance between severity and permissiveness.
   b. use extremely harsh, repressive measures.
   c. reject the idea of original sin.
   d. put children to work as soon as they could walk.

6. According to Rousseau, (p. 12)
   a. child development is very similar to the evolution of other species.
   b. children can be ranked on an intelligence scale.
   c. parents should be receptive to children's needs at each of four stages of development.
   d. children have little influence on their own development.

7. Darwin's theory influenced theories of child development as researchers (p. 12)
   a. borrowed his conception of children as angelic.
   b. applied his emphasis on the adaptive value of physical and behavioral characteristics to child development.
   c. adapted his techniques of mental testing to children.
   d. came to view play as an example of survival of the fittest.

8. Freud proposed that children develop through stages in which they (p. 14)
   a. confront conflicts between biological drives and social expectations.
   b. become active, contributing members of society.
   c. conform to a greater or lesser extent to statistical norms.
   d. respond to reinforcers.

9. Erikson's psychosocial theory departed from Freud's theory by emphasizing (p. 15)
   a. the limited role of the superego.
   b. the case study method.
   c. the lifespan nature of development.
   d. empirically verifiable concepts.

10. According to Albert Bandura, (p. 18)
    a. development must be understood in relation to each culture's life situation.
    b. behavior can be shaped with operant conditioning.
    c. children develop a superego as they strive to meet parental and social expectations.
    d. children gradually become more selective in which behaviors they imitate.

11. A major limitation of Piaget's theory is that it (p. 20)
    a. discounts the role of the child's social world in its development.
    b. rests on limited use of clinical interviews.
    c. underestimates the competencies of infants and preschoolers.
    d. overemphasizes the effects of reinforcers on behavior.

12. The information-processing approach views development as a process of continuous change because it (p. 22)
    a. regards thought processes as similar at all ages but present to a greater or lesser extent.
    b. views environment as the supreme force in development.
    c. emphasizes stages through which children acquire new skills.
    d. assumes that personality emerges through maturation.

13. One criticism of the information-processing approach is that it (p. 22)
    a. fails to account sufficiently for the influence of unconscious drives.
    b. relies too heavily on intelligence tests.
    c. pays too much attention to nonlinear and illogical aspects of children's cognition.
    d. is better at analyzing thinking into its components than at reassembling them into a comprehensive theory.

14. Which of the following approaches draws upon diverse disciplines to study the relationship between changes in the brain and the child's cognitive processing and behavior patterns? (pp. 22–23)
    a. the normative approach
    b. behaviorism
    c. developmental cognitive neuroscience
    d. the information-processing approach

15. John Bowlby originated the ethological theory of attachment, pointing out that (pp. 23–24)
    a. infant smiling and babbling are built-in social signals that encourage caregivers to interact with them.
    b. facelike stimuli play a crucial role in infants' survival.
    c. children are most ready to develop important capacities during sensitive periods.
    d. imprinting is less important than previously thought.

16. An evolutionary developmental psychologist would seek to answer which of the following questions? (p. 24)
    a. What happens to the brain to enable imaginative play?
    b. What does play tell about children's sexual and aggressive drives?
    c. How can play be shaped by the application of reinforcers?
    d. What do children learn from play that might lead to adult gender-typed behaviors?

17. Unlike Vygotsky's sociocultural theory, Bronfenbrenner's ecological systems theory considers (p. 25)
    a. the effects of imprinting during the critical period.
    b. the child's biologically influenced dispositions.
    c. children's cooperative dialogues with more experienced elders.
    d. the adaptive value of species-wide competencies.

18. The dynamic systems perspective (p. 28)
    a.   draws upon every field of science except physics.
    b.   rejects the ecological systems emphasis on the effects of the chronosystem.
    c.   draws upon information-processing and contextual theories.
    d.   had been applied mainly to the study of language acquisition.

19. Structured observation deals with the limitation of naturalistic observation by (p. 31)
    a.   establishing a laboratory situation that evokes the behavior of interest.
    b.   employing clinical interviews.
    c.   studying parents as well as children.
    d.   rewarding children who display the behavior of interest.

20. The major advantage of the clinical, or case study, method is that it (p. 34)
    a.   allows people to express their thoughts in terms as close as possible to the way they think in everyday life.
    b.   isolates the subject of study from the effects of culture.
    c.   fits with nearly all research designs.
    d.   yields detailed narratives that offer insights into the array of factors affecting development.

21. Immigrant adolescents who had arrived in Canada often described their first year as very difficult because (p. 36)
    a.   they did not speak English or French.
    b.   their parents did not immediately establish close ties to an ethnic community.
    c.   they could not get into good schools.
    d.   their parents had to work too many hours to supervise them.

22. Experimental design enables researchers to (p. 37)
    a.   gauge the effects of subtle changes in dependent variables.
    b.   minimize their cultural influence.
    c.   perceive cause-and-effect relationships by controlling the independent variable.
    d.   free themselves from the constraints of laboratory experiments.

23. Researchers can minimize the influence of cohort effects by employing _____ designs. (p. 42)
    a.   longitudinal
    b.   sequential
    c.   cross-sectional
    d.   ethnographic

24. Research into the effect of music on children's intelligence suggests that (p. 44)
    a.   sustained musical experiences can lead to small increases in intelligence.
    b.   both music and drama lessons produced the same intelligence gains.
    c.   listening to classical music will increase intelligence.
    d.   music lessons can lead to gains in social maturity.

25. One of the most important ethical issues in research on children is (p. 43)
    a.   parental involvement in the research design.
    b.   the role of the federal government in the research process.
    c.   the lack of guidelines from research-oriented associations.
    d.   children often cannot evaluate for themselves what participation in research will mean.

CHAPTER 2
BIOLOGICAL AND ENVIRONMENTAL FOUNDATIONS

BRIEF CHAPTER SUMMARY

This chapter examines the foundations of development: heredity and environment. The principles of genetic transmission determine the characteristics that make us human and contribute to individual differences in appearance and behavior. Inheritance of harmful recessive genes and abnormalities of the chromosomes are major causes of serious developmental problems. Genetic counseling and prenatal diagnosis help people at risk for transmitting hereditary disorders assess their chances of giving birth to a healthy baby.

Environmental influences on development are no less complex than hereditary factors. The family has an especially powerful impact. It operates as a complex, dynamic social system in which members exert direct, indirect, and third-party effects on one another. Socioeconomic status influences child-rearing practices: Poverty and homelessness undermine effective family functioning and children's well-being, while affluence may lead to overscheduling and lack of emotional closeness, which also have negative effects. The quality of community life, from neighborhoods and schools to small towns and cities, is another influence on children's development. Cultural values—for example, the degree to which a society emphasizes collectivism versus individualism—combine with public policies, laws, and government programs to shape experiences in all of these contexts.

Some child development specialists believe that it is useful and possible to determine "how much" heredity and environment contribute to individual differences. Others think that the effects of heredity and environment cannot be clearly separated. Instead, they want to discover "how" these two major determinants of development work together in a complex, dynamic interplay.

LEARNING OBJECTIVES

After reading this chapter, you should be able to:

2.1 Distinguish between genotypes and phenotypes. (p. 51)

2.2 Describe the structure and function of chromosomes and DNA molecules. (p. 52)

2.3 Explain the process of mitosis. (pp. 52–53)

2.4 Describe the process of meiosis, and explain how it leads to genetic variability. (pp. 53–54)

2.5 Describe the genetic events that determine the sex of the new organism. (pp. 54–55)

2.6 Identify two types of twins, and explain how each is created. (pp. 55–56)

2.7 Explain how alleles influence the inheritance of traits, such as through dominant–recessive inheritance, incomplete dominance, X-linked inheritance, polygenic inheritance, mutation, and genetic imprinting. (pp. 56–60)

2.8 Describe the origins and consequences of Down syndrome and abnormalities of the sex chromosomes. (pp. 60–62)

2.9 Discuss reproductive choices available to prospective parents, noting the pros and cons of reproductive technologies. (pp. 63–68)

2.10 Describe family functioning from the ecological systems perspective, citing direct and indirect family influences and explaining the view of the family as a dynamic, changing system. (pp. 69–71)

2.11   Discuss the impact of socioeconomic status, including affluence and poverty, on family functioning. (pp. 71–75)

2.12   Summarize the role of neighborhoods and schools in the lives of children. (pp. 75–77)

2.13   Discuss how cultural values and public policies influence the well-being of children. (pp. 77–82)

2.14   Explain the various ways heredity and environment may combine to influence complex human traits. (pp. 82–89)

STUDY QUESTIONS

1.   _____ are directly observable characteristics that depend in part on the _____, the complex blend of genetic information that determines our species and also influences all of our unique characteristics. (p. 51)

Genetic Foundations

1.   Rodlike structures in the nuclei of cells that store and transmit genetic information are called _____. (p. 52)

2.   Humans have (23 / 46) pairs of chromosomes in each cell. (p. 52)

The Genetic Code

1.   Chromosomes are made up of a chemical substance called _____. It looks like a twisted ladder and is composed of segments called _____. (p. 52)

2.   The process through which DNA duplicates itself so that each new body cell contains the same number of chromosomes is called _____. (p. 52)

The Sex Cells

1.   Sex cells, or _____, are formed through the process of (mitosis / meiosis). (p. 53)

2.   True or False: Sex cells contain only half the number of chromosomes normally present in body cells. (p. 53)

3.   When the sperm and ova unite at conception, the cell that results is called a _____. (p. 53)

4.   During meiosis, the process of _____, in which chromosomes next to each other break at one or more points and exchange segments, creates new hereditary combinations unique to the individual. (p. 53)

5.   Explain why the genetic variability produced by meiosis is important in an evolutionary sense. (p. 53)

_____

_____

Boy or Girl?

1.   The twenty-two matching pairs of chromosomes are called _____. (p. 54)

2.   The twenty-third pair of chromosomes, also called the sex chromosomes, determine the sex of the child. In females, this pair is called _____, whereas in males it is called _____. (p. 54)

Multiple Births

1. Match each of the following terms with the appropriate description. (p. 55)

_____ This type of twinning may result from environmental influences like temperature changes, variations in oxygen levels, or late fertilization of the ovum.

_____ This is the most common type of multiple birth.

_____ Older maternal age and use of fertility drugs and in vitro fertilization are major causes of this type of twinning.

_____ These twins are genetically no more alike than ordinary siblings.

_____ These twins share the same genetic makeup.

1. Fraternal, or dizygotic, twins
2. Identical, or monozygotic, twins

2. True or False: During the early years of life, children of single births are often healthier and develop more rapidly than twins. (p. 55)

Patterns of Genetic Inheritance

1. Each of two forms of a gene located at the same place on the autosome is called a(n) _____. (p. 56)

2. If the alleles from both parents are alike, the child is _____ and will display the inherited trait. If the alleles inherited from the mother and father are different, then the child is _____, and the relationship between the alleles will determine the trait, or phenotype. (p. 56)

3. Describe *dominant–recessive inheritance*, and provide one example of this type of inheritance. (pp. 56–57)

A. _____

_____

B. _____

_____

4. One of the most common recessive disorders is _____, which affects the way the body breaks down proteins contained in many foods. (p. 56)

5. _____ *genes* enhance or dilute the effects of other genes. (p. 56)

6. True or False: Serious diseases typically result from dominant alleles. Briefly explain your response. (p. 57)

_____

_____

7. Describe *incomplete dominance*, and name one condition that results from this pattern of inheritance. (p. 57)

A. _____

_____

B. _____

_____

8. (Males / Females) are more likely to be affected by *X-linked inheritance*. Why is this the case? (p. 57)

_____

_____

9. Name one X-linked disorder. (pp. 57, 58)

_____

10. True or False: In recent decades, the proportion of male births has declined in many industrialized countries. Explain your answer. (p. 59)

_____

_____

_____

11. _____ occurs when alleles are chemically marked in such a way that one pair member is activated, regardless of its makeup. (p. 59)

12. List three conditions or diseases that are caused by *genetic imprinting.* (pp. 59–60)

A. _____   B. _____

C. _____

13. Explain how harmful genes are created. (p. 60)

_____

_____

14. Describe *polygenic inheritance*, and give an example of a trait that is determined by this pattern of inheritance. (p. 60)

A. _____

_____

B. _____

_____

Chromosomal Abnormalities

1. Most chromosomal defects are the result of mistakes during _____, when the ovum and sperm are formed. (p. 60)

2. _____, the most common chromosomal abnormality, often results from a failure of the twenty-first pair of chromosomes to separate during meiosis. For this reason, the disorder is sometimes called Trisomy 21. (p. 60)

3. List the physical and behavioral characteristics of Down syndrome. (p. 61)

Physical: _____

_____

Behavioral: _____

_____

4. True or False: The risk of Down syndrome rises with maternal age. (p. 61)

5. Disorders of the sex chromosomes result in (more / less) serious consequences than do disorders of the autosomes. (p. 61)

6. Identify whether the following myths about individuals with sex chromosome disorders are true or false. (pp. 61–62)

A. Males with XYY syndrome are more aggressive and antisocial than XY males.   True or False

B. Most children with sex chromosome disorders suffer from mental retardation.   True or False

C. Girls with Turner syndrome have trouble with spatial relationships, such as drawing pictures and noticing changes in facial expressions.   True or False

D. Children with sex chromosome disorders have intellectual problems that are usually very specific.   True or False

Reproductive Choices

Genetic Counseling

1. What is the purpose of genetic counseling, and who is most likely to seek this service? (p. 63)

_____

_____

_____

Biology and Environment: The Pros and Cons of Reproductive Technologies

1. Briefly describe the following reproductive technologies: (p. 66)

Donor insemination: _____

_____

_____

_____

In vitro fertilization: _____

_____

_____

_____

Surrogate motherhood: _____

_____

_____

_____

2. True or False: Children conceived through in vitro fertilization typically exhibit a variety of behavioral and adjustment problems and have insecure attachments to their parents. (p. 66)

3. Discuss some of the concerns surrounding the use of donor insemination and in vitro fertilization. (p. 66)

_____

_____

_____

4. Describe some of the risks involved with surrogate motherhood. (p. 66)

    _____

    _____

    _____

5. Briefly describe several new reproductive technologies, and note ethical dilemmas associated with each. (pp. 66–67)

    A. _____

    _____

    B. _____

    _____

Prenatal Diagnosis and Fetal Medicine

1. _____ are medical procedures that permit detection of developmental problems before birth. (p. 63)

2. Cite six types of prenatal diagnostic methods. (p. 64)

    A. _____

    B. _____

    C. _____

    D. _____

    E. _____

    F. _____

3. True or False: The techniques used in fetal medicine rarely result in complications like premature labor or miscarriage. (p. 64)

4. Summarize the goals of the Human Genome Project, and explain why this program offers hope for correcting hereditary defects. (pp. 64–65)

    _____

    _____

    _____

5. Describe three steps that prospective parents can take before conception to increase their chances of having a healthy baby. (p. 68)

    A. _____

    B. _____

    C. _____

The Alternative of Adoption

1. Why has the availability of healthy babies declined in North America and Western Europe? (p. 65)

    _____

    _____

2. Adopted children and adolescents have (fewer / more) learning and emotional difficulties than other children. Cite two possible reasons for this trend. (pp. 65, 67)

A. _____

B. _____

3. Discuss research findings on international adoptees' development in comparison to birth siblings or agemates who stay behind. (pp. 67–68)

_____

_____

_____

4. True or False: Most adoptees have serious, long-term adjustment problems that are evident well into adulthood. (p. 68)

Environmental Contexts for Development

The Family

1. Distinguish between direct and indirect familial influences. (pp. 69–70)

Direct: _____

_____

Indirect: _____

_____

2. Discuss some ways in which the family system must adapt over time. (pp. 70–71)

_____

_____

_____

Socioeconomic Status and Family Functioning

1. List the three variables that determine a family's *socioeconomic status (SES)*. (p. 71)

A. _____   B. _____

C. _____

2. Compare child characteristics emphasized in lower-SES families with those emphasized in higher-SES families. (pp. 71–73)

Lower-SES: _____

_____

Higher-SES: _____

_____

3. Describe the influence of SES on parenting practices and parent-child interaction. (pp. 71–73)

_____

_____

_____

4. Summarize the factors that explain SES differences in family interaction. (pp. 71–73)

_____

_____

_____

5. True or False: Higher-SES children show more advances in cognitive development and tend to perform better in school than their lower-SES peers. (p. 73)

Social Issues: Education: Worldwide Education of Girls: Transforming Current and Future Generations

1. Cite two ways that educating girls benefits the welfare of families, societies, and future generations. (p. 72)

A. _____

_____

B. _____

_____

2. How does education influence family health? (p. 72)

_____

_____

_____

3. True or False: The empowerment that education provides women is associated with more equitable husband-wife relationships and a reduction in harsh disciplining of children. (p. 72)

Affluence

1. Discuss two factors that contribute to poor adjustment in affluent youths. (p. 73)

A. _____

_____

B. _____

_____

2. What simple routine does research associate with a reduction in adjustment difficulties for both affluent and low-SES youths? (p. 73)

_____

Poverty

1. What subgroups of the population are hardest hit by poverty? (p. 74)

A. _____   B. _____

C. _____   D. _____

2. The poverty rate is (higher / lower) among children than any other age group. (p. 74)

3. Describe how the constant stresses that accompany poverty gradually weaken the family system. (pp. 74–75)

_____

_____

_____

4. Summarize the developmental risks that homeless children face. (p. 75)

_____

_____

_____

Beyond the Family: Neighborhoods and Schools

1. Neighborhood resources have a greater impact on children growing up in (disadvantaged / well-to-do) areas. Why is this the case? (pp. 75–76)

_____

_____

2. Summarize features of the Better Beginnings, Better Futures Project of Ontario, Canada, and note major outcomes of the program. (p. 76)

Features: _____

_____

_____

Outcomes: _____

_____

_____

3. List four broad features of the school environment that impact students' developmental outcomes. (pp. 76–77)

A. _____

B. _____

C. _____

D. _____

4. Why are higher-SES parents more likely to have regular contact with teachers than lower-SES parents? (p. 77)

_____

_____

The Cultural Context

1. What are _subcultures_? (p. 77)

_____

_____

2. The African-American _____ _household_, in which one or more adult relatives live with the parent-child nuclear family unit, is a vital feature of black family life. (p. 77)

3. Distinguish the characteristics of collectivist versus individualistic societies. (pp. 77–78)

    Collectivist: _____

    _____

    Individualistic: _____

    _____

4. What are *public policies*? (p. 79)

    _____

5. True or False: Among developed nations, the United States and Canada have served as forerunners in the development of public policies to safeguard children. (p. 79)

6. List some of the areas in which American and Canadian public policies regarding children are deficient. (pp. 79–80)

    _____

    _____

    _____

7. Cite three reasons why attempts to help children and youth in the United States and Canada have been difficult to realize. (p. 80)

    A. _____

    B. _____

    C. _____

8. The _____ is a legal agreement that commits each cooperating country to work toward guaranteeing environments that foster children's development, protect them from harm, and enhance their community participation and self-determination. The United States (is / is not) one of the two countries in the world that has not yet ratified this agreement. (p. 80)

9. How are researchers helping to improve public policies that enhance child development? (p. 82)

    _____

    _____

Cultural Influences: The African-American Extended Family

1. Cite characteristics of the African-American extended family that help reduce the stress of poverty and single parenthood. (p. 78)

    _____

    _____

    _____

2. How does the African-American extended family help transmit cultural values? (p. 78)

    _____

    _____

    _____

Social Issues: Health: Welfare Reform, Poverty, and Child Development

1. Briefly summarize features of welfare-to-work programs. (p. 81)

_____

_____

_____

_____

2. True or False: To date, the welfare-to-work programs have been successful in making all welfare recipients financially independent. (p. 81)

3. True or False: A welfare-work combination, in which individuals retain some welfare support while working, seems to have the greatest benefit for children and families. Explain your answer. (p. 81)

_____

_____

_____

4. Explain how welfare policies in other Western nations, such as France and Canada, attempt to protect children from the damaging effects of poverty. (p. 81)

France: _____

_____

_____

Canada: _____

_____

_____

Understanding the Relationship Between Heredity and Environment

1. _____ is a field devoted to uncovering the contributions of nature and nurture as they relate to individual differences in human traits and abilities. (p. 83)

The Question, "How Much?"

1. Name the two methods used by behavioral geneticists to infer the role of heredity in complex human characteristics. (p. 83)

   A. _____   B. _____

2. What are *heritability estimates*? (p. 83)

_____

_____

_____

3. Heritability estimates are obtained from _____ *studies*, which compare characteristics of family members. (p. 83)

4. True or False: Heritability estimates for intelligence and personality are approximately .50, indicating that genetic makeup can explain half of the variance in these traits. (p. 83)

5. What is a *concordance rate*? (p. 84)

_____

_____

6. What do concordance rates of 0 and of 100 mean? (p. 84)

0: _____

100: _____

7. When a concordance rate is much higher for (identical / fraternal) twins, then heredity is believed to play a major role. (p. 84)

8. Discuss three limitations of heritability estimates and concordance rates. (pp. 84–85)

A. _____

_____

B. _____

_____

C. _____

_____

The Question, "How?"

1. In *range of reaction*, heredity (limits / increases) responsiveness to varying environments. In *canalization*, heredity (restricts / expands) the development of certain behaviors. (pp. 85–86)

2. Range of reaction highlights two important points. List them. (pp. 85–86)

A. _____

_____

B. _____

_____

3. Describe the concept of *canalization*. (p. 86)

_____

_____

_____

4. Which is more strongly canalized: infant perceptual and motor development or intelligence and personality? (p. 86)

5. According to the concept of _____, our genes influence the environments to which we are exposed. (p. 86)

6. Match the following types of genetic-environmental correlations with the appropriate descriptors. (p. 86)

_____ Children increasingly seek out environments that fit their genetic tendencies (niche-picking).

_____ A child's style of responding influences other's responses, which then strengthens the child's original style.

_____ Parents provide an environment consistent with their own heredity.

1. Passive correlation
2. Evocative correlation
3. Active correlation

7.   The tendency to choose environments that complement our heredity is called _____. (p. 86)

8.   _____ means development resulting from ongoing, bidirectional exchanges between heredity and all levels of the environment. Researchers call this view of the relationship between heredity and the environment the _____ framework. (p. 88)

9.   Provide an example of *epigenesis*. (p. 88)

_____

_____

ASK YOURSELF . . .

For *Ask Yourself* questions for this chapter, along with feedback on the accuracy of your answers, please log on to MyDevelopmentLab (for registration and access, please visit mydevelopmentlab.com or follow the directions on p. ix).

1)   Select the Chapter of the *Ask Yourself*.
2)   Open the E-Book and select the Explore icon next to the *Ask Yourself*.
3)   Complete questions and choose "Submit answers for grading" or "Clear Answers" to start over.

SUGGESTED STUDENT READINGS

Lindsey, D. (2007). *Future of children: Wealth, poverty, and opportunity in America.* New York: Oxford University Press. Presents an overview of child and family poverty in the United States, including the role of public policy in child development.

Mundy, L. (2007). *Everything conceivable: How assisted reproduction is changing men, women, and the world.* New York: Knopf. A compelling look at reproductive technologies, this book examines current research, as well as controversies, surrounding assisted reproduction. The author also includes personal narratives, myths, and the social consequences of assisted reproduction.

Peters, R. D., Leadbeater, B., & McMahon, R. J. (Eds.). (2005). *Resilience in children, families, and communities: Linking context to practice and policy.* New York: Kluwer Academic. An ecological approach to the study of resilience, this book examines empirical research, intervention efforts, and the role of public policy in fostering resilience in children and families.

Segal, N. L. (2005). *Indivisible by two: Lives of extraordinary twins.* Cambridge, MA: Harvard University Press. A fascinating look into the lives of multiples, this book follows 12 sets of twins, triplets, and quadruplets. The author not only describes the unique experiences of multiples, but she also highlights the many challenges faced by the parents, friends, and spouses of these extraordinary individuals.

PUZZLE 2.1 TERM REVIEW

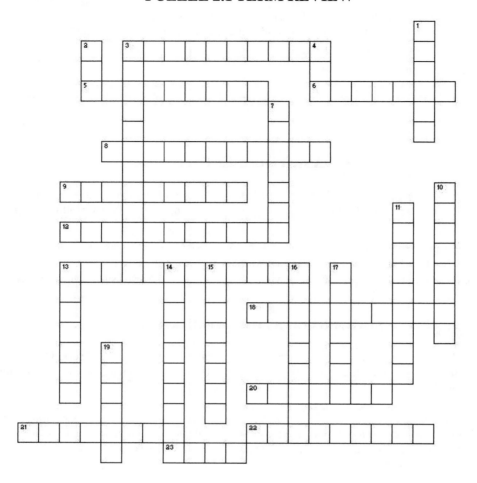

Across

3. Having two identical alleles at the same place on a pair of chromosomes
5. The 22 matching chromosomes pairs in each human cell
6. _____ inheritance: the recessive gene is carried on the X chromosome
8. _____ twins have the same genetic makeup
9. Fraternal, or _____, twins
12. Rodlike structures in the cell nucleus that store and transmit genetic information
13. An exchange of genes between chromosomes next to each other during meiosis (2 words)
18. _____ dominance: a pattern of inheritance in which both alleles are expressed in the phenotype
20. The process of cell division
21. A sudden but permanent change in a segment of DNA
22. Directly observable characteristics
23. A segment of a DNA molecule that contains hereditary instructions

Down

1. Each of two forms of a gene located at the same place in the autosomes
2. Long, double-stranded molecules that make up chromosomes (abbr.)
3. Having two different alleles at the same place on a pair of chromosomes
4. _____ chromosomes: The 23rd pair of chromosomes; XX in females, XY in males
7. The process of cell duplication
10. Genes that enhance or dilute the effects of other genes
11. _____ inheritance: Many genes determine a characteristic
13. A heterozygous individual who can pass a recessive trait to his or her children
14. Genetic _____: alleles are chemically marked in such a way that one pair member is activated, regardless of its makeup
15. The genetic makeup of an individual
16. Dominant-_____ inheritance: in heterozygous pairings, only one allele affects the child's traits
17. Human sperm and ova
19. Cell formed by the union of the sperm and the ovum at conception

PUZZLE 2.2 TERM REVIEW

Across

2. _____-environmental correlation: the notion that heredity influences the environments to which an individual is exposed
6. Genetic _____ is designed to help couples assess their chances of giving birth to a baby with a hereditary disorder.
7. Group of people with beliefs and customs that differ from those of the larger culture
11. A measure of a family's social position and economic well-being (abbr.)
14. In _____ societies, people think of themselves as separate entities and are largely concerned with their own personal needs
15. _____ policies: laws and government programs designed to improve the condition of children and families
16. _____ studies compare the characteristics of family members to obtain heritability estimates.
17. _____ diagnostic methods are medical procedures that permit detection of problems before birth.

Down

1. Development resulting from ongoing, bidirectional exchanges between heredity and environment
3. Range of _____: a person's genetically determined response to a range of environmental conditions
4. In _____-family households, parent and child live with one or more adult relatives
5. Tendency for individuals to actively choose environments that complement their heredity (2 words; hyph.)
8. In _____ societies, people define themselves as part of a group and stress group over individual goals
9. _____ rate: percentage of instances in which both members of a twin pair show a trait when it is present in one pair member
10. _____ genetics: field devoted to uncovering the contributions of nature and nurture to individual differences in human traits and abilities
12. _____ estimate: measure of the extent to which individual differences in complex traits in a specific population are due to genetic factors
13. Tendency of heredity to restrict the development of some characteristics to just one or a few outcomes

PRACTICE TEST #1

1. The paired bases of the DNA molecule (p. 52)
   a. take shapes that are determined by phenotypes.
   b. can occur in any order along its sides.
   c. join in various ways across the ladder rungs.
   d. determine how nurture will affect the individual.

2. Of the following factors, which is responsible for the complexity of human beings? (p. 53)
   a. the number of human genes
   b. the richness of human cytoplasm
   c. the length of human chromosomes
   d. the variety of proteins made by human genes

3. In the male, meiosis produces (p. 53)
   a. one ovum.
   b. several gametes.
   c. four sperm.
   d. two zygotes.

4. In industrialized nations, older maternal age, fertility drugs, and in vitro fertilization are major causes of (p. 55)
   a. the rise in fraternal twinning.
   b. slowed cell mitosis after conception.
   c. a decline in the production of autosomes.
   d. late fertilization of the ovum.

5. In heterozygous children, (p. 56)
   a. traits inherited from both parents dominate.
   b. gametes often combine to produce zygotes that twin.
   c. Y chromosomes are more common than X chromosomes.
   d. relationships between the alleles determine the phenotype.

6. Serious diseases rarely result from dominant alleles because (p. 57)
   a. modifier genes are more likely to cancel out the gene carrying the disease.
   b. children who develop the disease often die before they reproduce, thus eliminating the harmful allele from the family's heredity.
   c. heterozygous individuals often carry the dark hair gene that also makes them more resistant to certain diseases.
   d. using in vitro fertilization helps parents avoid producing harmful combinations of alleles.

7. Males are more likely to suffer from X-linked disorders because (p. 57)
   a. they are less likely to die in infancy than females.
   b. the proportion of male births is rising in many industrialized countries.
   c. they are more prone to patterns of incomplete dominance.
   d. their sex chromosomes do not match.

8. After germline mutation occurs, (p. 60)
   a. a DNA defect appears in every cell derived from the affected body cell.
   b. an individual is more likely to develop a serious illness as a result of smoking.
   c. the defective DNA is passed on to the next generation when the individual mates.
   d. the range of possible polygenetic inheritance decreases.

9. Individuals with Down syndrome who live past age 40 often show symptoms of (p. 61)
   a. Alzheimer's disease.
   b. trisomy 21.
   c. fragile X syndrome.
   d. hemophilia.

10. The pedigree that results from genetic counseling (p. 63)
    a. traces the descent of X-linked inheritance.
    b. predicts the outcome of polygenetic inheritance.
    c. determines traits, such as hair and eye color, that a child will get from his or her parents.
    d. uses fundamental genetic principles to estimate the likelihood that parents will have an abnormal child.

11. New reproductive technologies have caused many to worry that (p. 67)
    a. surrogate motherhood will no longer be available to financially needy women.
    b. too much genetic information will be widely available.
    c. those methods could lead to selective breeding of babies with particular traits.
    d. governments' restrictions on their use will become too stringent.

12. Amniocentesis can help identify genetic defects by (p. 64)
    a. removing a small plug of tissue from the end of one or more chorionic villi.
    b. obtaining a sample of fluid from the uterus.
    c. beaming high-frequency sound waves at the uterus.
    d. obtaining a sample of fetal blood.

13. By middle childhood, international adoptees placed in homes in infancy (p. 68)
    a. have mental test scores similar to those of their nonbiological siblings.
    b. fare about as well in development as their birth siblings who stayed behind.
    c. are more prone to emotional difficulties.
    d. tend to have problems trusting their adoptive parents.

14. According to Bronfenbrenner's theory, forces that comprise the chronosystem confront a family with (p. 71)
    a. powerful social values.
    b. different and sometimes conflicting parenting styles.
    c. constant change to which each other must adapt.
    d. isolation, alienation, and the beha ms that can result from those.

15. For both affluent and low-SES youths, adjustment can be reduced by (p. 73)
    a. longer school days.
    b. a simple routine like eating dinner with parents.
    c. more social activities with friends outside the home.
    d. stronger discipline.

16. According to a United Nations report, the education of girls (p. 72)
    a. has declined slightly in the developed world.
    b. is most effective in one-room rural schools.
    c. has made little headway in Latin America.
    d. is the most effective means of combating maternal and child mortality.

17. Of the following Western nations, which has the highest percentage of extremely poor children? (p. 74)
    a. the United States
    b. Canada
    c. France
    d. Switzerland

18. The Better Beginnings, Better Futures Project of Ontario, Canada, has (p. 76)
    a. done little to alleviate the effects of poverty on children.
    b. focused particularly on neighborhood recreation facilities, such as playgrounds.
    c. yielded gains in family functioning, effective parenting, and children's reading skills.
    d. yet to reduce the overall frequency of emotional and behavior problems.

19. Of the following indicators, both Canada and the United States rank higher than Ireland and Singapore in (p. 79)
    a. childhood poverty.
    b. infant deaths in the first year of life.
    c. teenage pregnancy rates.
    d. expenditures on health care as a percentage of gross domestic product.

20. Compared with nuclear-family households, extended-family arrangements (p. 78)
    a. add to the stress of childrearing.
    b. weaken children's relationships with people outside the family.
    c. prepare girls more effectively than boys for the work of managing a separate household.
    d. place more emphasis on cooperation and moral and religious values.

21. Most heritability estimates come from kinship studies that compare (p. 83)
    a. parents and children.
    b. identical and fraternal twins.
    c. brothers and sisters.
    d. children and their cousins.

22. Researchers generally use concordance rates to (p. 84)
    a. study the contribution of heredity to emotional and behavioral disorders.
    b. compare heritability estimates.
    c. quantify the effects of parental stress on children's learning.
    d. demonstrate the extremely powerful influence of heredity on criminality.

23. The most serious criticism of heritability estimates and concordance rates is that (p. 85)
    a. twin studies cannot necessarily be applied to the general population.
    b. they tell us too much about nature and not enough about nurture.
    c. the statistics they produce give no precise information about how intelligence and personality develop.
    d. they tend to overestimate the influence of environmental factors on intelligence and behavior.

24. Intelligence and personality are less strongly canalized because (p. 86)
    a. they are shaped by passive correlation.
    b. they vary significantly with changes in the environment.
    c. they display a narrow reaction range.
    d. the process of niche-picking changes them very little.

25. The concept of epigenesis can help researchers (p. 88)
    a. make sense of how internal stimulation triggers gene activity.
    b. to extend an individual's range of reaction.
    c. trace the effects of evocative correlation.
    d. understand development as a series of complex changes between nature and nurture.

PRACTICE TEST #2

1. Humans share most of their DNA with (p. 52)
   a. bacteria.
   b. reptiles.
   c. pigs.
   d. primates.

2. The essential function of meiosis is to (p. 53)
   a. ensure that each generation receives a constant quantity of genetic material.
   b. stimulate the production of zygotes.
   c. prevent damaged genes from crossing over to the next generation.
   d. regulate the process of mitosis.

3. Gametes that form in females carry (p. 55)
   a. either an X or a Y chromosome.
   b. only short chromosomes.
   c. an X chromosome.
   d. all the genetic material the human organism needs.

4. The frequency of identical twins is (p. 55)
   a. much higher in industrialized nations.
   b. slightly lower in Asia than elsewhere.
   c. the same around the world.
   d. steadily rising in North America.

5. The example of PKU illustrates the fact that (p. 56)
   a. conditions once thought to be due to dominant-recessive inheritance actually result from multiple genes.
   b. heterozygous individuals are not always carriers of recessive traits.
   c. hair color and facial features are reasonably accurate predictors of inherited disabilities.
   d. inherited recessive disorders do not always lead to untreatable conditions.

6. The sickle cell carrier rate is believed to be higher in Canada than in the United States because (p. 57)
   a. the risk of malaria is slightly higher in Canada.
   b. more African Canadians are recent immigrants than African Americans.
   c. incomplete dominance patterns are more common throughout the entire Canadian population.
   d. more African Canadians live at higher altitudes than African Americans.

7. The concept of genetic imprinting helps to explain why (p. 59)
   a. children inherit certain parent-specific diseases.
   b. the rate of sickle cell anemia is rising among North Americans of European descent.
   c. females are more likely to suffer the effects of X-linked inheritance.
   d. fragile X syndrome results in 2 to 3 percent of autism cases.

8. Most chromosomal defects result from (p. 60)
   a. radiation.
   b. mistakes during meiosis.
   c. somatic mutation.
   d. Prader-Willi syndrome.

9. Adding or subtracting from the usual number of X chromosomes results in (p. 62)
   a. Down syndrome.
   b. facial abnormalities.
   c. incomplete dominance.
   d. particular intellectual deficits.

10. Candidates for genetic counseling typically are (p. 63)
    a.   women who have had three or more pregnancies.
    b.   men with XYY syndrome.
    c.   women of advanced maternal age.
    d.   individuals with Down syndrome.

11. The overall success rate of in vitro fertilization is 30 percent, but (p. 66)
    a.   it often requires more ova than most women produce.
    b.   success declines steadily with age.
    c.   that rate is far lower when the man has fertility problems.
    d.   it can increase the risk of X-linked disease.

12. More people in North America and Western Europe are adopting from other countries because (p. 65)
    a.   the availability of healthy babies in those regions has declined.
    b.   adoptable children in their own countries are often past infancy.
    c.   adopted children tend to have fewer learning and emotional difficulties.
    d.   they can select children like themselves in personality and background.

13. The family is the most powerful context of development because it (p. 69)
    a.   constitutes a macrosystem.
    b.   protects children from environmental stressors.
    c.   introduces children to the physical world, creates unique bonds, and teaches fundamental skills and values.
    d.   guards children from most indirect influences.

14. Compared to low-SES parents, high-SES parents tend to (p. 71)
    a.   expect their children to be polite and obedient before all else.
    b.   talk to and stimulate their infants and preschoolers more.
    c.   encourage their female children more than their male children.
    d.   pass on higher levels of stress to their children.

15. In North America, poverty is highest among (p. 74)
    a.   Native-American children.
    b.   Hispanic children.
    c.   African-American children.
    d.   Canadian-Aboriginal children.

16. Most homeless families consist of (p. 75)
    a.   women with children under age 5.
    b.   ethnic minorities.
    c.   one or more members with mental illness.
    d.   people turned away from government-supported housing.

17. Studies have shown that children whose families moved into low-poverty neighborhoods (p. 75)
    a.   had trouble adjusting to their new surroundings.
    b.   showed little change in their behavior.
    c.   showed substantially better health and school achievement.
    d.   improved more in social interaction than in academic performance.

18. Higher-SES parents tend to interact frequently with their children's teachers because (p. 77)
    a.   they generally live in small towns.
    b.   their backgrounds and values are often similar to those of the teachers.
    c.   their children and the teachers' children often go to the same schools.
    d.   they can more easily take time off work than lower-SES parents.

19. U.S. opponents of the United Nations Convention on the Rights of the Child maintain that it (p. 80)
    a. would shift the burden of child rearing from the family to the state.
    b. is insufficiently collectivist.
    c. does not go as far toward protecting children as U.S. policies already in place.
    d. forces the United States to adopt principles that few other nations observe.

20. The results of welfare reform in Canada and the United States suggest that (p. 81)
    a. the faster parents leave welfare for work, the faster their children's lives will improve.
    b. work requirements should be more stringent.
    c. welfare reform promotes children's development only when it results in a more adequate standard of living.
    d. both countries' commitment to providing affordable child care helped to decrease their welfare roles.

21. Currently, most kinship studies find that heredity (p. 83)
    a. plays hardly any role in intelligence.
    b. has a strong influence on intelligence.
    c. cannot be conclusively linked to many traits.
    d. plays a moderate role in intelligence.

22. Heritability estimates are controversial because they (p. 84)
    a. are too dependent on the extent to which twin pairs reflect genetic and environmental variation.
    b. can easily be misapplied to suggest dubious genetic bases for certain traits.
    c. employ simplistic statistical procedures.
    d. tell us nothing about personality traits.

23. Reaction range highlights that (p. 86)
    a. strongly canalized behavior develops similarly in diverse environments.
    b. concordance rates are likely to exaggerate the role of heredity.
    c. different genetic-environmental combinations can make two people look the same.
    d. despite our highly varied genetic makeups, we tend to respond in similar ways to different environments.

24. In older children, active genetic-environmental correlation becomes common because (p. 86)
    a. as they gain more freedom, they seek environments that fit their genetic tendencies.
    b. their heredity evokes stronger responses that, in turn, prompt them to display certain behaviors even more.
    c. their hereditary traits become less strongly canalized.
    d. they cease to engage in niche-picking.

25. Theorists who emphasize the effects of canalization and range of reaction would most likely believe that (p. 87)
    a. unfavorable genetic-environmental correlations can be uncoupled.
    b. active correlation has little bearing on genetic tendencies.
    c. heritability estimates are the most accurate predictors of intelligence.
    d. genetic-environmental correlation is driven largely by genetics.

CHAPTER 3
PRENATAL DEVELOPMENT

BRIEF CHAPTER SUMMARY

This chapter begins with a discussion of motivations for parenthood and current changes in birth patterns. Today, men and women are more likely to weigh the pros and cons of having children than they were in previous generations. The American family has declined in size over time, a trend that has benefits for child rearing. Births to women over age 30 have increased, a change associated with both advantages and disadvantages for children.

At no other time is change as rapid as it is before birth. Prenatal development takes place in three phases: (1) the period of the zygote, during which the newly fertilized ovum travels down the fallopian tube and attaches itself to the uterine wall; (2) the period of the embryo, during which the groundwork for all body structures is laid down; and (3) the period of the fetus, the "growth and finishing" phase.

The prenatal period is a vulnerable time. The developing organism can be endangered by teratogens, including drugs, cigarettes, alcohol, radiation, and environmental pollution, as well as infectious disease, inadequate exercise and nutrition, maternal stress, Rh blood incompatibility, and maternal age. Prenatal health care is vitally important to ensure the health of mother and baby.

For most expectant parents, however, the prenatal period is not a time of medical hazard. Rather, it is a time of major life change in which mothers and fathers prepare for parenthood.

LEARNING OBJECTIVES

After reading this chapter, you should be able to:

3.1 Cite advantages and disadvantages of parenthood mentioned by modern North American couples. (pp. 93–95)

3.2 Review current trends in family size and childbearing age, and discuss their impact on child development. (pp. 95–97)

3.3 List the three phases of prenatal development, and describe the major milestones of each. (pp. 97–104)

3.4 Define the term *teratogen*, and summarize the factors that affect the impact of teratogens. (pp. 104–107)

3.5 List agents known to be or suspected of being teratogens, and discuss evidence supporting the harmful effects of each. (pp. 107–115)

3.6 Discuss maternal factors other than exposure to teratogens that can affect the developing embryo or fetus. (pp. 115–119)

3.7 Discuss the importance of prenatal health care, and cite some of the barriers to seeking such care. (pp. 119–122)

3.8 Explain the factors that contribute to personal adjustment as expectant mothers and fathers prepare for parenthood. (pp. 122–124)

STUDY QUESTIONS

Motivations for Parenthood

Why Have Children?

1. List five advantages and five disadvantages of parenthood mentioned by North American couples. (p. 95)

    Advantages:

    A. _____

    B. _____

    C. _____

    D. _____

    E. _____

    Disadvantages:

    A. _____

    B. _____

    C. _____

    D. _____

    E. _____

How Large a Family?

1. List two major reasons that family size has declined in industrialized nations. (p. 95)

    A. _____

    B. _____

2. Describe the benefits of growing up in a small family. (p. 95)

    _____

    _____

    _____

3. True or False: Children's mental test performance tends to decline with later birth order. (pp. 95–96)

4. Describe factors that contribute to lower intelligence scores for children in large families. (p. 96)

    _____

    _____

    _____

5. Discuss some of the pros and cons of living in a one-child family, including perspectives of both parents and children. (p. 96)

    Pros (children): _____

    _____

    Cons (children): _____

    _____

Pros (parents): _____

_____

Cons (parents): _____

_____

Is There a Best Time During Adulthood to Have a Child?

1. Cite reasons why many modern couples are delaying childbearing into their thirties and beyond. (pp. 96–97)

_____

_____

2. True or False: Both males and females experience a decline in reproductive capacity with age. (p. 97)

Prenatal Development

Conception

1. Approximately once every 28 days, an ovum is released from one of a woman's two _____, and it travels through one of the two _____, which are long, thin structures that lead to the uterus. (p. 98)

2. The male produces vast numbers of sperm in the _____, two glands located in the scrotum. (p. 98)

3. True or False: Sperm live for up to 10 days and can lie in wait for the ovum, which survives for 3 days after being released in the fallopian tube. (p. 98)

The Period of the Zygote

1. The period of the zygote lasts about _____ weeks, from fertilization until the tiny mass of cells drifts down and out of the fallopian tube and attaches itself to the wall of the uterus. (p. 99)

2. Match each term with the appropriate definition. (p. 99)

    _____ Will become the structures that provide protective covering and nourishment to the new organism
    _____ Hollow, fluid-filled ball that is formed by a tiny mass of cells four days after fertilization
    _____ Will become the new organism

    1. Blastocyst
    2. Embryonic disk
    3. Trophoblast

3. List two functions of the *amniotic fluid*. (p. 99)

    A. _____

    B. _____

4. True or False: As many as 30 percent of zygotes do not make it through the first two weeks. (p. 99)

5. The _____ permits food and oxygen to reach the developing organism and waste products to be carried away. (p. 99)

6. The *placenta* is connected to the developing organism by the _____. (p. 100)

The Period of the Embryo

1. The period of the *embryo* lasts from implantation through the _____ week of pregnancy. (p. 101)

2. True or False: The most rapid prenatal changes take place during the period of the embryo. (p. 101)

3. Why is the embryo especially vulnerable to interference with healthy development? (p. 101)

    _____

    _____

4. List the organs and structures that will be formed from each of the three layers of the embryonic disk. (p. 100)

    Ectoderm: _____

    Mesoderm: _____

    Endoderm: _____

5. Briefly summarize the events that take place during the second month of pregnancy. (p. 101)

    _____

    _____

    _____

The Period of the Fetus

1. True or False: The period of the *fetus* is the longest prenatal period. (p. 102)

2. Prenatal development is divided into _____, or three equal time periods. (p. 102)

3. The white, cheeselike substance that protects the skin from chapping in the amniotic fluid is called _____. (p. 102)

4. _____ is a white, downy hair that covers the entire body of the fetus. (p. 102)

5. The age at which the baby can first survive if born early is called the *age of* _____. When does this typically occur? (p. 102)

    _____

6. Summarize research findings on the relationship between fetal activity patterns and temperament in early childhood. (p. 103)

    _____

    _____

    _____

7. True or False: During the third trimester, fetuses are able to distinguish the tone and rhythm of different voices and sounds. Briefly explain your response. (p. 103)

    _____

    _____

    _____

8. Describe major changes in the fetus during the final three months of pregnancy. (pp. 103–104)

    _____

    _____

    _____

Prenatal Environmental Influences

Teratogens

1. Define the term *teratogen,* and describe four factors that affect the impact of teratogens on prenatal development. (p. 105)

   Teratogen: _____

   _____

   A. _____

   B. _____

   C. _____

   D. _____

2. A _____ *period* is a limited time span in which a part of the body or a behavior is biologically prepared to develop rapidly and is especially sensitive to its surroundings. (p. 105)

3. True or False: The period of the zygote is the time when teratogens are most likely to cause serious defects. (p.106)

4. When taken by mothers four to six weeks after conception, _____, a sedative widely available in some countries during the early 1960s, produced deformities of the embryo's developing arms and legs, and less frequently, caused damage to the ears, heart, kidneys, and genitals. (p. 107)

5. True or False: Heavy caffeine intake during pregnancy is associated with low birth weight, miscarriage, and newborn withdrawal symptoms. (p. 108)

6. Describe the difficulties faced by babies who are prenatally exposed to cocaine, heroine, or methadone. (pp. 108, 110)

   _____

   _____

   _____

7. Explain why it is difficult to isolate the precise damage caused by prenatal drug exposure. (p. 110)

   _____

   _____

   _____

8. Summarize physical and behavioral effects of maternal smoking during the prenatal period. (p. 110)

   _____

   _____

   _____

   _____

9. True or False: If the mother stops smoking at any time during her pregnancy, even during the last trimester, she reduces the chances that her baby will be negatively impacted. (p. 110)

10. Explain the mechanisms through which smoking harms the fetus. (p. 111)

    _____

    _____

    _____

11. Why should expectant mothers, even those who do not smoke, avoid smoke-filled environments? (p. 111)

_____

_____

12. Infants who have a range of physical and behavioral abnormalities and whose mothers drank heavily throughout most or all of pregnancy are said to have _____ . (p. 111)

13. Match the following characteristics with the proper diagnosis. (p. 111)

_____ At least three areas of mental functioning are impaired, despite typical physical growth and absence of facial abnormalities

_____ Characterized by two of the three facial abnormalities and brain injury

_____ Distinguished by slow physical growth, a pattern of three facial abnormalities, and brain injury

A. Fetal alcohol syndrome (FAS)
B. Partial fetal alcohol syndrome (p-FAS)
C. Alcohol-related neurodevelopmental disorder (ARND)

14. Describe physical and mental impairments associated with fetal alcohol spectrum disorders that persist from the preschool years through early adulthood. (pp. 111–112)

Preschool and school years: _____

_____

Adolescence and early adulthood: _____

_____

15. Describe two ways in which alcohol produces its devastating effects. (p. 112)

A. _____

_____

B. _____

_____

16. True or False: Mild drinking, less than one alcoholic drink, is associated with poor outcomes for the child. Therefore, no amount of alcohol is safe to drink during pregnancy. (p. 112)

17. True or False: Low doses of radiation exposure, such as through medical x-rays, are believed to be safe for the developing fetus and have not been linked to any negative outcomes. (p. 112)

18. Match each of the following environmental pollutants with its effect on development. (p. 113)

_____ This teratogen, commonly found in paint chippings from old buildings and other industrial materials, is related to low birth weight, prematurity, brain damage, and physical defects.

_____ In the 1950s, children prenatally exposed to this teratogen in a Japanese community displayed mental retardation, abnormal speech, and uncoordinated movements.

_____ Women who ate fish contaminated with this substance gave birth to babies with slightly reduced birth weights, smaller heads, more intense physiological reactions to stress, less interest in their surroundings, and later memory and intellectual deficits.

1. Mercury
2. PCBs
3. Lead

19. Describe the outcomes associated with embryonic and fetal exposure to *rubella*. (p. 114)

Embryonic: _____

_____

_____

Fetal: _____

_____

_____

20. When women carrying the AIDS virus become pregnant, they pass on the disease to their baby approximately _____ to _____ percent of the time. (p. 114)

21. True or False: Most infants prenatally exposed to the AIDS virus survive eight to ten years after the appearance of symptoms. (p. 114)

22. Pregnant women can become infected with _____, a parasitic disease found in many animals, from eating raw or undercooked meat or from contact with the feces of infected cats. (p. 115)

Biology and Environment: The Prenatal Environment and Health in Later Life

1. True or False: Numerous studies have identified a link between low birth weight and serious health problems later in life, including heart disease, stroke, and diabetes. (p. 107)

2. List the consequences of high birth weight on adult health. (p. 107)

_____

_____

3. What can individuals do to prevent prenatal risks from becoming a reality? (p. 107)

_____

_____

Social Issues: Health: Can a Thalidomide-Like Tragedy Occur Again? The Teratogenic Effects of Accutane

1. What is Accutane? (p. 109)

_____

_____

2. Summarize pregnancy complications and birth defects associated with Accutane use. (p. 109)

Pregnancy complications: _____

_____

Birth defects: _____

_____

3. Describe barriers to preventing prenatal exposure to Accutane. (p. 109)

_____

_____

_____

4. Cite three strategies for preventing prenatal Accutane exposure. (p. 109)

A. _____

B. _____

C. _____

Other Maternal Factors

1. Regular, moderate exercise during pregnancy is associated with (increased / decreased) birth weight. (p. 115)

2. Summarize the behavioral and health problems of prenatally malnourished babies. (p. 116)

    _____

    _____

3. List the vitamin and mineral supplements that have been found to reduce prenatal complications and birth defects. (pp. 116–117)

    A. _____   B. _____

    C. _____   D. _____

    E. _____   F. _____

4. True or False: Prenatal malnutrition is currently limited to developing countries, and it has been entirely eradicated in the United States through government programs for low-income pregnant women. (p. 117)

5. Describe the mechanisms through which maternal stress affects the developing organism, and note outcomes associated with severe emotional stress during pregnancy. (pp. 117–118)

    Mechanisms: _____

    _____

    _____

    Outcomes: _____

    _____

    _____

6. Under what conditions can *Rh factor incompatibility* cause problems for the developing fetus? (p. 118)

    _____

    _____

    _____

7. Problems resulting from the Rh factor are more likely to affect (first-born / later-born) children. (p. 118)

8. True or False: Healthy women in their thirties experience far more prenatal difficulties than women in their twenties. (p. 118)

9. The physical immaturity of teenage mothers (does / does not) lead to pregnancy complications. (p. 119)

The Importance of Prenatal Health Care

1. Describe two potential complications that can arise during pregnancy. (p. 119)

    A. _____

    _____

    B. _____

    _____

2. Name two groups of women who often do not receive adequate prenatal care, and note the consequences for their babies. (p. 119)

    A. _____   B. _____

    Consequences: _____

    _____

3. Discuss some of the barriers to obtaining prenatal health care mentioned by expectant mothers who delay or never seek such care. (p. 119)

_____

_____

_____

Cultural Influences:
Culturally Sensitive Prenatal Care Promotes Healthy Pregnancies

1. Why is the lack of patient-sensitive prenatal care particularly disturbing to many ethnic minority women? (p. 121)

_____

_____

2. Describe the benefits of group prenatal care for minority expectant mothers. (p. 121)

_____

_____

_____

Preparing for Parenthood

1. Over _____ percent of pregnancies in industrialized nations result in healthy newborn babies. (p. 122)

Seeking Information

1. Pregnant mothers regard _____ as an extremely valuable source of information, second in importance only to their doctors. (p. 122)

The Baby Becomes a Reality

1. What changes and experiences help expectant parents come to view the baby as a reality? (p. 123)

_____

_____

_____

Models of Effective Parenthood

1. True or False: Men and women who have had good relationships with their own parents are more likely to develop positive images of themselves as parents during pregnancy. (p. 123)

2. Cite three benefits of participating in special intervention programs for expectant mothers and fathers. (p. 124)

   A. _____

   B. _____

   C. _____

The Parental Relationship

1. True or False: Having a baby typically improves a troubled marital relationship. (p. 124)

2. Describe some of the ways in which pregnancy changes a marital relationship. (p. 124)

_____

_____

_____

ASK YOURSELF . . .

For *Ask Yourself* questions for this chapter, along with feedback on the accuracy of your answers, please log on to MyDevelopmentLab (for registration and access, please visit mydevelopmentlab.com or follow the directions on p. ix).

1)   Select the Chapter of the *Ask Yourself.*
2)   Open the E-Book and select the Explore icon next to the *Ask Yourself.*
3)   Complete questions and choose "Submit answers for grading" or "Clear Answers" to start over.

SUGGESTED STUDENT READINGS

Curtis, G. B., & Schuler, J. (2005). *Your pregnancy for the father-to-be.* New York: Perseus Publishing. Written for a general audience, this book provides information to expectant fathers about physical changes during pregnancy, medical tests and procedures, and the importance of providing the mother with social support during pregnancy and after the baby arrives. Other topics include: costs of having a baby, child-care expenses, planning for the future, and the impact of pregnancy on a couple's relationship.

Hopkins, B., & Johnson, S. P. (Eds.). (2005). *Prenatal development of postnatal functions.* Westport, CT: Praeger. Examines the link between prenatal and postnatal development, including brain development, the effects of maternal stress, the importance of nutrition, and learning experiences before and after birth.

Miller, M. W. (2006). *Brain development: Normal processes and the effects of alcohol and nicotine.* New York: Oxford University Press. Examines the effects of alcohol and nicotine on the developing nervous system. The author explores the immediate and long-term consequences of prenatal exposure to alcohol and nicotine, including research on brain plasticity and resilience.

PUZZLE 3.1 TERM REVIEW

Across

2. The _____ cord connects the prenatal organism to the placenta
5. Zygote four days after fertilization, when it forms a hollow, fluid-filled ball
6. _____ fluid: keeps the temperature in the womb constant and provides a cushion against jolts
7. Age of _____: age at which the fetus can first survive if born early
11. The prenatal organism from two to eight weeks after conception
12. Ring of cells which will become the structures that provide protective covering and nourishment to the new organism
13. White, cheeselike substance that covers the fetus and prevents chapping
14. Membrane that encloses the developing organism in amniotic fluid
15. White, downy hair that covers the fetus

Down

1. _____ tube: primitive spinal chord
3. The blastocyst burrows deep into the uterine lining during _____
4. Embroynic _____: cluster of cells inside the blastocyst which will become the new organism
8. The prenatal organism from the ninth week to the end of pregnancy
9. Outer membrane that forms a protective covering and sends out villi from which the placenta emerges
10. Separates the mother's bloodstream from that of the fetus while permitting the exchange of nutrients and waste products

PUZZLE 3.2 TERM REVIEW

Across

2. Environmental agent that causes damage during the prenatal period
3. Fetal Alcohol _____: Mental retardation, slow growth, and facial abnormalities resulting from maternal alcohol consumption during pregnancy
4. German measles; causes a variety of prenatal abnormalities
5. Fetal alcohol _____ disorder: A range of physical, mental, and behavioral outcomes caused by prenatal alcohol exposure
6. Illness marked by increased maternal blood pressure and swelling of the face, hands, and feet
7. Sedative available in the early 1960s that caused deformities of the arms and legs when taken between the fourth and sixth week after conception
9. Three equal periods of time in prenatal development
10. Parasitic disease caused by eating raw or undercooked meat or through contact with the feces of infected cats

Down

1. Alcohol-related _____ disorder: The least severe form of fetal alcohol spectrum disorders that involves brain injury, but with typical physical growth and absence of facial abnormalities
4. When present in the fetus's blood but not in the mother's, the _____ factor may cause the mother to build up antibodies that destroy the fetus's red blood cells
8. _____ fetal alcohol syndrome: A form of fetal alcohol spectrum disorder characterized by facial abnormalities and brain injury, but less severe than fetal alcohol syndrome; usually seen in children whose mothers drank alcohol in smaller quantities during pregnancy
11. Viral infection that destroys the immune system (abbr.)

PRACTICE TEST #1

1. Today, in Western industrialized nations, the issue of whether to have children is a(n) (p. 94)
   a. unavoidable cultural demand.
   b. individual choice.
   c. biological given.
   d. religious imperative.

2. Today, to rear a child from birth to age 18, new parents in the United States will have to spend about (p. 95)
   a. $150,000.
   b. $170,000.
   c. $190,000.
   d. $210,000.

3. Between 1960 and the present, the average number of children per North American couple declined because of (p. 95)
   a. fewer marriages.
   b. cultural prohibitions on larger families.
   c. people marrying at later ages.
   d. more effective birth control, a woman's decision to work, and marital instability.

4. In the past quarter century, births have greatly increased to women in their (p. 96)
   a. teens.
   b. twenties.
   c. thirties.
   d. forties.

5. About once every 28 days, in the middle of the menstrual cycle, an ovum bursts from one of the woman's (p. 98)
   a. ovaries.
   b. fallopian tubes.
   c. corpus luteum.
   d. uterine linings.

6. The male produces sperm in the (p. 98)
   a. cervix.
   b. penis.
   c. embryonic disk.
   d. testes.

7. How long can sperm live in the fallopian tubes waiting for an ovum? (p. 98)
   a. no more than 6 hours
   b. 3 days
   c. up to 6 days
   d. as much as 2 weeks

8. The placenta starts to develop (p. 99)
   a. when the yolk sac emerges to produce blood cells.
   b. when villi emerge from the chorion and burrow into the uterine wall.
   c. when the blastocyst develops into the trophoblast.
   d. within 24 hours after implantation occurs.

9. Early in the period of the embryo, the embryonic disk develops the ectoderm, which will become the (p. 101)
   a. nervous system.
   b. muscles.
   c. urinary tract.
   d. circulatory system.

10. By the end of the second trimester, (p. 102)
    a. the placenta has been replaced by the vernix.
    b. the organs, muscles, and nervous system have begun to connect.
    c. most of the brain's billions of neurons are in place.
    d. the growth of glial cells slows and gradually stops.

11. By 28 weeks, fetuses (p. 103)
    a. are awake about 20 percent of the time.
    b. are no longer irritated by sudden loud noises.
    c. make tiny flutters that are still too light to be felt by the mother.
    d. blink their eyes in reaction to nearby sounds.

12. Defects resulting from teratogens can affect emotional and social development because they (p. 106)
    a. often cause malformations of the arms and legs.
    b. can damage critical parent-child interactions, peer relations, and opportunities to explore.
    c. strike during sensitive periods.
    d. tend to cluster during the embryonic period.

13. Researchers suspect that high birth weight may promote which of the following conditions in adult women?
    (pp. 106–107)
    a. breast cancer
    b. diabetes
    c. heart disease
    d. stroke

14. Several studies suggest that regular aspirin use during pregnancy is linked to (p. 108)
    a. erythema nodosum in children.
    b. high rates of vaginal cancer in daughters of mothers who used it.
    c. low birth weight and infant death around the time of birth.
    d. newborn withdrawal symptoms.

15. To help prevent Accutane-related fetal malformations, doctors often counsel women to (p. 109)
    a. refrain from taking other vitamin A-derived drugs.
    b. abstain from sex or use two forms of birth control.
    c. monitor their vitamin A levels closely.
    d. reduce their doses of Accutane.

16. The principal difference between fetal alcohol syndrome (FAS) and alcohol-related neurodevelopmental disorder
    (ARND) is that (p. 111)
    a. FAS involves two, rather than three, facial abnormalities.
    b. ARND involves only short eyelid openings.
    c. FAS involves no brain injuries.
    d. ARND involves at least three areas of mental functioning despite typical physical growth and absence of
        facial abnormalities.

17. Of the following environmental teratogens, which is responsible for prematurity and brain damage? (p. 113)
    a. mercury
    b. PCBs
    c. lead
    d. carbon dioxide

18. If a pregnant woman catches rubella, her child (p. 114)
    a. risks developing eye cataracts, organ defects, and mental retardation.
    b. may be especially sensitive to herpes simplex 2.
    c. has a better chance of being born with the rubella antibody.
    d. will be more vulnerable to toxoplasmosis.

19. Most prenatal AIDS babies survive only (p. 114)
    a. a few hours after birth.
    b. 3 to 5 days.
    c. 4 to 6 weeks.
    d. 5 to 8 months.

20. Maternal stress can cause a variety of problems, including miscarriage, because (p. 118)
    a. it can suppress the mother's production of folic acid.
    b. stress hormones crossing the placenta can dramatically increase the fetal heart rate.
    c. it can cause the mother to exercise too vigorously.
    d. stress has been linked to increased risk of viral infection.

21. Inadequate prenatal care is most common among (p. 119)
    a. women age 50 to 55.
    b. white, middle-class women.
    c. women who suffer from preeclampsia.
    d. adolescent, low-income, and ethnic minority women.

22. Evaluations of group prenatal care have revealed that the participants (p. 121)
    a. prefer the group leaders to be men from the participants' culture.
    b. engage in fewer health-damaging behaviors.
    c. tend to be young mothers.
    d. are less likely to ask questions for fear of embarrassment.

23. Men and women are more likely to develop positive images of themselves as parents when they (p. 123)
    a. have had more than one child.
    b. have experience caring for children prior to having one of their own.
    c. have had good relationships with their own parents.
    d. wait to have children until they feel secure in their careers.

24. Research suggests that in a troubled marriage, pregnancy (p. 124)
    a. adds to rather than lessens family conflict.
    b. can help the parents improve their relationship.
    c. often prompts the mother and father to seek out models of effective parenting.
    d. causes the parents to turn from their troubles and focus on preparing for the changes that will occur as soon as the baby is born.

25. During pregnancy, women typically look to their partners for (p. 124)
    a. expressions of masculine strength and protectiveness.
    b. deeper commitment to providing a steady income.
    c. emotional calm and reserve.
    d. demonstrations of affection and interest in the pregnancy.

PRACTICE TEST #2

1. Between 1958 and the present, the percentage of North American couples that bear children declined from 78 percent to (p. 94)
   a.   62 percent.
   b.   65 percent.
   c.   70 percent.
   d.   74 percent.

2. Of the following factors, which is a cause of declining family size in industrialized nations? (p. 95)
   a.   earlier marriage
   b.   marital instability
   c.   sexual abstinence
   d.   government policy

3. According to the U.S. National Longitudinal Survey of Youth, in general, the larger the family, the lower the mental test scores of the all the siblings, because (p. 96)
   a.   mothers who are low in intelligence tend to give birth to more children.
   b.   the parents of such families are more likely to divorce.
   c.   mothers tend to be too busy to foster their children's education.
   d.   the homes of large families tend to be full of noise and other distractions.

4. Male reproductive capacity gradually declines after age (p. 97)
   a.   15.
   b.   20.
   c.   25.
   d.   30.

5. The largest cell in the human body is the (p. 98)
   a.   fallopian tube.
   b.   ovum.
   c.   zygote.
   d.   sperm.

6. Most conceptions result from intercourse (p. 98)
   a.   within 6 hours before or after ovulation.
   b.   during the week of ovulation.
   c.   on the day of or during the 2 days preceding ovulation.
   d.   during the 2 hours before or after ovulation.

7. During the period of the zygote, implantation occurs when the (p. 99)
   a.   blastocyst burrows into the uterine lining.
   b.   sperm penetrates and fertilizes the ovum.
   c.   trophoblast forms the chorion.
   d.   amnion encloses the developing organism.

8. In the second month of the period of the embryo, the (p. 101)
   a.   organism develops the endoderm.
   b.   neural tube and neurons develop.
   c.   heart begins to pump blood.
   d.   liver and spleen assume production of blood cells.

9. During the last three months of pregnancy, (p. 103)
   a. the genitals form so that the sex of the fetus becomes evident.
   b. grooves and convolutions form in the surface of the cerebral cortex.
   c. the fetus tends to rest quietly because of decreasing space in the womb.
   d. the lanugo grows over the fetus's body.

10. During the eighth month of pregnancy, a layer of fat develops to assist with (p. 104)
   a. temperature regulation.
   b. antibody production.
   c. blood circulation.
   d. waste filtration.

11. The effects of teratogens (p. 106)
   a. usually kill the fetus in the womb.
   b. mostly cause malformations of the limbs.
   c. can be subtle and delayed for years.
   d. tend to concentrate during the first two weeks after conception.

12. Research indicates that high birth weight is associated with (p. 107)
   a. excessive weight gain in adulthood.
   b. lower maternal estrogen during pregnancy.
   c. greatly increased risk of cardiovascular disease in adulthood.
   d. increases in digestive and lymphatic cancer in both men and women.

13. Throughout the first year, infants who were exposed to heroine and methadone are (p. 108)
   a. less attentive to the environment than nonexposed babies.
   b. more likely to develop respiratory distress than nonexposed babies.
   c. likely to develop genital abnormalities during adolescence.
   d. more prone to irritability and vomiting than nonexposed babies.

14. Of the following, which factor accounts for continued prenatal exposure to the teratogenic drug Accutane? (p. 109)
   a. Manufacturers have failed to provide adequate warnings.
   b. The drug's teratogenic effects have only recently been established.
   c. The pregnancies were unplanned, and women who become pregnant without planning are often less responsive to teratogen counseling.
   d. The pregnant women smoked while taking the drug.

15. Newborns of smoking mothers (p. 110)
   a. tend to have smaller head sizes than newborns of mothers who do not smoke.
   b. are less attentive to sounds.
   c. often have facial abnormalities.
   d. have abnormally high birth weights.

16. Low levels of radiation, such as those resulting from medical X-rays, can increase the risk of (p. 112)
   a. adult diabetes.
   b. a smooth or flattened philtrum.
   c. smaller head size.
   d. childhood cancer.

17. In industrialized nations, how many commonly used chemicals are potentially dangerous to the developing organism?
   (p. 113)
   a. less than 20,000
   b. about 50,000
   c. more than 75,000
   d. nearly 1,000,000

18. Pregnant women may become infected with toxoplasmosis (p. 115)
    a.   from contact with the urine of infected dogs.
    b.   by eating raw or undercooked meat.
    c.   through unprotected sex with an infected person.
    d.   through drug abuse.

19. In addition to adequate quantities of food, which of the following nutritional factors is crucial to the health of newborns? (p. 116)
    a.   vitamin-mineral enrichment
    b.   reduced consumption of dairy products
    c.   food that has been thoroughly irradiated
    d.   foods that are low in folic acid

20. Women age 50 to 55 experience high rates of pregnancy complications because (p. 118)
    a.   they and the fetus tend to develop Rh factor incompatibility.
    b.   their systems often produce high levels of cortisol.
    c.   their bodies have had more time to absorb environmental teratogens.
    d.   menopause and aging reproductive organs often prevent them from conceiving naturally.

21. If untreated, toxemia in pregnant women can cause (p. 119)
    a.   extreme facial malformations in babies.
    b.   high birth weight.
    c.   convulsions in the mother and fetal death.
    d.   higher levels of stress hormones crossing the placenta.

22. Lack of patient-sensitive prenatal care is particularly disturbing to women from cultures that (p. 121)
    a.   value large families.
    b.   emphasize warm, personalized styles of interaction and a relaxed sense of time.
    c.   encourage them to begin bearing children early.
    d.   stress indirect discussion of intimate matters like pregnancy.

23. Of the following factors, which is especially likely to spark negative or ambivalent feelings about parenthood? (p. 122)
    a.   an unplanned pregnancy
    b.   if the mother is over age 35
    c.   the parents' levels of education
    d.   a pregnancy in the third trimester

24. Expectant mothers tend to rank which of the following sources of information as second only to their doctors? (p. 122)
    a.   friends who have already had children
    b.   nurses
    c.   mothers and grandmothers
    d.   books

25. During their partner's pregnancy, men typically look for (p. 124)
    a.   interest in the pregnancy.
    b.   help with household chores.
    c.   expressions of warmth from their partner.
    d.   willingness to put aside career and other personal goals for motherhood.

CHAPTER 4
BIRTH AND THE NEWBORN BABY

BRIEF CHAPTER SUMMARY

Childbirth takes place in three stages: (1) dilation and effacement of the cervix, (2) delivery of the baby, and (3) birth of the placenta. Production of stress hormones helps the infant withstand the trauma of childbirth. The Apgar Scale permits assessment of the baby's physical condition immediately after birth.

Natural, or prepared, childbirth and delivery in a birth center are increasingly popular alternatives to traditional hospital delivery in Western industrial societies; some women choose home birth as a noninstitutional option. Social support during labor and delivery can promote a successful childbirth experience. However, various medical interventions are commonly a part of childbirth in the United States. These procedures help save the lives of many babies but can introduce new problems when used routinely.

Although most births proceed normally, serious complications sometimes occur. The most common complications result from oxygen deprivation and prematurity. Fortunately, many babies who experience severe birth trauma recover with the help of favorable child-rearing environments, which can be supported by high-quality intervention. Infant mortality rates are higher in the United States than in many other industrialized nations. Affordable, available prenatal care is a key factor in reducing infant mortality.

Infants begin life with a remarkable set of skills for relating to the surrounding world. Newborns display a wide variety of reflexes—automatic responses to specific forms of stimulation. In the early weeks, babies move in and out of different states of arousal (degrees of sleep and wakefulness) frequently but spend the most time in either rapid-eye-movement REM sleep, during which the brain stimulates itself, and non-REM (NREM) sleep.

Crying is the first way that babies communicate their needs. With experience, parents become better at interpreting the meaning of the infant's cries. Newborns' senses of touch, taste, smell, and sound are well developed. Vision is the least mature sensory capacity. Tests such as the Neonatal Behavioral Assessment Scale (NBAS) have been developed to assess the newborn's reflexes, state changes, responsiveness to stimuli, and other reactions.

The baby's arrival brings profound changes for the family system, which do not significantly strain a happy marriage but may cause distress in a troubled marriage. Special interventions exist to ease the transition to parenthood. Couples who support each other in their new roles typically adjust well.

LEARNING OBJECTIVES

After reading this chapter, you should be able to:

4.1   Describe the events leading up to childbirth and the three stages of labor. (pp. 130–131)

4.2   Discuss the baby's adaptation to labor and delivery, and describe the newborn baby's appearance. (pp. 131–132)

4.3   Explain the purpose and main features of the Apgar Scale. (pp. 132–133)

4.4   Discuss the concept of natural childbirth, noting the typical features of a natural childbirth program, the benefits of the natural childbirth experience, and the importance of social support. (pp. 133–135)

4.5   Discuss the benefits and concerns associated with home delivery. (p. 135)

4.6   List common medical interventions used during childbirth, circumstances that justify their use, and any dangers associated with each. (pp. 136–138)

4.7   Discuss the risks associated with oxygen deprivation, preterm, small-for-date, and low-birth-weight births, and review the developmental outlook for infants born under such circumstances. (pp. 138–141)

4.8   Describe several interventions for preterm infants, including infant stimulation and parent training. (pp. 141–143, 144)

4.9   Summarize the findings of the Kauai Study relating to the long-term consequences of birth complications. (pp. 143, 145)

4.10   Discuss parents' feelings of involvement with their newborn babies, noting research on bonding and rooming in. (pp. 146–147)

4.11   Name and describe major newborn reflexes, noting the functions served by each, and discuss the importance of assessing newborn reflexes. (pp. 147–149)

4.12   Summarize the five infant states of arousal, with particular attention to sleep and crying. (pp. 149–150)

4.13   Describe the newborn baby's responsiveness to touch, taste, smell, sound, and visual stimulation. (pp. 150–156)

4.14   Describe Brazelton's Neonatal Behavioral Assessment Scale (NBAS), and explain its usefulness. (pp. 156–157)

4.15   Discuss typical changes in the family system after the birth of a new baby, along with interventions that foster the transition to parenthood. (pp. 157–161)

STUDY QUESTIONS

The Stages of Childbirth

1. Describe three signs that indicate that labor is near. (p. 130)

   A. _____

   B. _____

   C. _____

Stage 1: Dilation and Effacement of the Cervix

1. Describe the events that take place during Stage 1 of childbirth. (p. 131)

   _____

   _____

   _____

2. The climax of Stage 1 is called _____, in which the frequency and strength of contractions are at their peak and the cervix opens completely. (p. 131)

Stage 2: Delivery of the Baby

1. True or False: Stage 2 lasts about 50 minutes for the first child and 20 minutes in later births. (p. 131)

2. Describe the events that take place during Stage 2 of childbirth. (p. 131)

   _____

   _____

   _____

Stage 3: Birth of the Placenta

1. What happens during Stage 3 of childbirth? (p. 131)

    _____

    _____

    _____

The Baby's Adaptation to Labor and Delivery

1. True or False: The infant's production of stress hormones is especially harmful during childbirth. Explain your answer. (pp. 131–132)

    _____

    _____

The Newborn Baby's Appearance

1. The average newborn baby is _____ inches long and weighs _____ pounds. (p. 132)

2. Explain why the newborn's head is large in comparison to the trunk and legs. (p. 132)

    _____

    _____

Assessing the Newborn's Physical Condition: The Apgar Scale

1. List the five characteristics assessed by the Apgar Scale. (pp. 132–133)

    A. _____

    B. _____

    C. _____

    D. _____

    E. _____

2. On the Apgar Scale, a score of _____ or better indicates that the infant is in good physical condition; a score between _____ and _____ indicates that the baby requires special assistance; a score of _____ or below indicates a dire emergency. (p. 132)

Approaches to Childbirth

1. True or False: In many village and tribal cultures, expectant mothers know very little about the childbirth process. (p. 133)

2. Explain how childbirth practices have changed over time in Western societies. (p. 133)

    _____

    _____

Natural, or Prepared, Childbirth

1. What is the goal of *natural childbirth*? (p. 134)

    _____

2. List and describe three features of a typical natural childbirth program. (p. 134)

A. _____

_____

B. _____

_____

C. _____

_____

3. Mothers who go through natural childbirth have (more / less) favorable attitudes toward the childbirth experience than those who do not. (p. 134)

4. Summarize the benefits of social support during childbirth. (p. 134)

_____

_____

_____

5. Name the childbirth position favored by research findings, and cite the benefits of using this position. (pp. 134–135)

Position: _____

Benefits: _____

_____

6. Describe some benefits of water birth. (p. 135)

_____

_____

Home Delivery

1. Home births are typically handled by certified _____, who have degrees in nursing and additional training in childbirth management. (p. 135)

2. True or False: For healthy women assisted by a trained professional, it is just as safe to give birth at home as in a hospital. (p. 135)

Medical Interventions

Fetal Monitoring

1. Explain the purpose of *fetal monitoring.* (p. 136)

_____

_____

2. Cite four reasons why fetal monitoring is a controversial procedure. (p. 136)

A. _____

B. _____

C. _____

D. _____

Labor and Delivery Medication

1. True or False: Some form of medication is used in more than 80 percent of North American births. (p. 136)

2. The most common approach to controlling pain during labor is _____ analgesia, in which a regional pain-relieving drug is delivered continuously through a catheter into a small space in the lower spine. (p. 136)

3. Discuss three problems with the routine use of labor and delivery medication. (pp. 136–137)

   A. _____

   _____

   B. _____

   _____

   C. _____

   _____

Instrument Delivery

1. In what circumstance is delivery with *forceps* or a *vacuum extractor* appropriate? (p. 137)

   _____

   _____

2. Summarize the risks associated with instrument delivery using forceps and vacuum extraction. (p. 137)

   Forceps: _____

   _____

   Vacuum extractor: _____

   _____

Induced Labor

1. Briefly describe an induced labor. (p. 137)

   _____

   _____

2. Describe two ways that an induced labor differs from a naturally occurring labor. (p. 137)

   A. _____

   _____

   B. _____

   _____

Cesarean Delivery

1. What is a *cesarean delivery*? (p. 138)

   _____

   _____

2.   In what circumstances is a cesarean delivery warranted? (p. 138)

_____

_____

3.   A natural labor after a cesarean is associated with slightly (decreased / increased) rates of rupture of the uterus and infant death. (p. 138)

Birth Complications

Oxygen Deprivation

1.   Describe the physical difficulties associated with *cerebral palsy*. (p. 139)

_____

_____

2.   _____ refers to inadequate oxygen supply during the birth process. (p. 139)

3.   Placenta _____ refers to a premature separation of the placenta, whereas placenta _____ refers to a detachment of the placenta resulting from implantation of the blastocyst low in the uterus so that the placenta covers the cervical opening. (p. 139)

4.   Discuss techniques used to prevent secondary damage after the initial brain injury from anoxia. (p. 139)

_____

_____

_____

5.   True or False: The vast majority of children who experience anoxia display life-long impairments in cognitive and linguistic skills. (p. 139)

6.   Infants born more than six weeks early are at risk for _____, a condition in which the baby's lungs are so poorly developed that the air sacs collapse, causing serious breathing difficulties. (p. 140)

Preterm and Low-Birth-Weight Infants

1.   Babies are considered premature if they are born _____ weeks or more before the end of a full 38-week pregnancy or if they weigh less than _____ pounds. (p. 140)

2.   True or False: Birth weight is the best available predictor of infant survival and healthy development. (p. 140)

3.   List the problems associated with low birth weight that persist through childhood and adolescence and into adulthood. (p. 140)

_____

_____

_____

_____

4.   Distinguish between *preterm* and *small-for-date* babies. (p. 140)

Preterm: _____

_____

Small-for-date: _____

_____

5. Of the two types of babies, (preterm / small-for-date) infants usually have more serious problems. (p. 140)

6. Describe the characteristics of preterm infants, and explain how those characteristics may influence the behavior of parents. (p. 141)

   A. _____

   _____

   B. _____

   _____

7. Discuss several interventions for preterm infants. (p. 142)

   _____

   _____

   _____

   _____

8. Briefly describe the concept of kangaroo care, and discuss the benefits associated with this type of infant stimulation. (p. 142)

   A. _____

   _____

   B. _____

   _____

9. True or False: Research suggests that all preterm children, regardless of family characteristics, require continuous, high-quality interventions well into the school years in order to maintain developmental gains. (p. 143)

Social Issues: Health: A Cross-National Perspective on Health Care and Other Policies for Parents and Newborn Babies

1. _____ *mortality* refers to the number of deaths in the first year of life per 1,000 live births. (p. 144)

2. True or False: African-American and Native-American infants are more than twice as likely as white infants to die in the first year of life. (p. 144)

3. _____ *mortality*, the rate of death in the first month of life, accounts for 67 percent of the infant death rate in the United States and 80 percent in Canada. (p. 144)

4. List the two leading causes of neonatal mortality. (p. 144)

   A. _____

   B. _____

5. Discuss the factors largely responsible for the relatively high rates of infant mortality in the United States. (p. 144)

   _____

   _____

   _____

6. Discuss factors linked to lower infant mortality rates. (pp. 144–145)

_____

_____

_____

Birth Complications, Parenting, and Resilience

1. In the Kauai longitudinal study, what factors predicted long-term difficulties following birth trauma? What factors predicted favorable outcomes? (pp. 143, 145)

   A. _____

   _____

   _____

   B. _____

   _____

   _____

2. True or False: In the Kauai study, children with serious birth complications and troubled family environments developed severe mental health problems, despite social support. (p. 145)

Precious Moments After Birth

1. True or False: Fathers provide their infants with as much stimulation and affection as mothers do. (p. 146)

2. True or False: The parent–infant relationship is highly dependent on close physical contact in the hours after birth in order for bonding to develop. (p. 146)

3. _____ is an arrangement in which the infant stays in the mother's hospital room all or most of the time. (p. 147)

The Newborn Baby's Capacities

Reflexes

1. What is a _reflex_? (p. 147)

   _____

2. Match each reflex with the appropriate response or function. (p. 148)

_____ Spontaneous grasp of adult's finger	1. Eye blink
_____ When the sole of the foot is stroked, the toes fan out and curl	2. Rooting
_____ Helps infant find the nipple	3 Sucking
_____ Prepares infant for voluntary walking	4 Swimming
_____ Permits feeding	5. Moro
_____ Infant lies in a "fencing position"	6. Palmar grasp
_____ Protects infant from strong stimulation	7. Tonic neck
_____ In our evolutionary past, may have helped infant cling to mother	8. Stepping
_____ Helps infants survive if dropped in water	9. Babinski

3. Briefly explain the adaptive value of three newborn reflexes. (p. 147)

   A. _____

   B. _____

   C. _____

4. Explain how some reflexes form the basis for complex motor skills that will develop later. (p. 147)

_____

_____

_____

_____

5. When do most newborn reflexes disappear? (p. 148)

_____

6. Explain the importance of assessing newborn reflexes. (p. 149)

_____

_____

_____

States

1. Name and describe the five infant *states of arousal.* (p. 150)

    A. _____

    B. _____

    C. _____

    D. _____

    E. _____

2. Describe the characteristics of *REM* and *NREM sleep.* (p. 150)

    REM: _____

    _____

    NREM: _____

    _____

3. Why do infants spend so much time in REM sleep? (p. 150)

    _____

    _____

4. What is the most effective way to soothe a crying baby when feeding and diaper changing do not work? (p. 152)

    _____

5. True or False: Rapid parental responsiveness reduces infant crying. Explain your answer. (pp. 152–153)

    _____

    _____

6. How do the cries of brain-damaged babies and those who have experienced prenatal and birth complications differ from those of healthy infants, and how might this difference affect parental responding? (pp. 152–153)

    _____

    _____

    _____

7. Persistent crying, or _____, is a fairly common problem in newborns characterized by intense crying and difficulty calming down, which generally subsides between ___ to ___ months of age. Describe an intervention aimed at reducing colic. (p. 152)

_____

_____

_____

Social Issues: Health: The Mysterious Tragedy of Sudden Infant Death Syndrome

1. What is *Sudden Infant Death Syndrome (SIDS)*? (p. 151)

_____

_____

2. True or False: In industrialized countries, SIDS is the leading cause of infant mortality between one week and twelve months of age. (p. 151)

3. True or False: Researchers have recently determined the precise cause of SIDS. (p. 151)

4. Describe some early physical problems that are common among SIDS victims. (p. 151)

_____

_____

_____

5. Explain how impaired brain functioning might cause SIDS. (p. 151)

_____

_____

_____

6. Describe four environmental factors associated with SIDS. (p. 151)

A. _____

_____

B. _____

_____

C. _____

_____

D. _____

_____

7. List three ways to reduce the incidence of SIDS. (p. 151)

A. _____

B. _____

C. _____

Sensory Capacities

1. True or False: Infants are born with a poorly developed sense of touch, and consequently, they are not sensitive to pain. (p. 153)

2. True or False: Infants not only have taste preferences, but they are also capable of communicating these preferences to adults through facial expressions. (p. 154)

3. True or False: Certain odor preferences are innate. (p. 154)

4. Explain the survival value of a newborn's sense of smell. (pp. 154–155)

   _____

   _____

5. At birth, infants prefer (pure tones / complex sounds). (p. 155)

6. True or False: Infants can discriminate almost all of the speech sounds of any human language. (p. 155)

7. Cite the characteristics of human speech preferred by infants. (p. 155)

   _____

   _____

8. Vision is the (most / least) mature of the newborn baby's senses. (p. 155)

9. Describe the newborn baby's *visual acuity*. (pp. 155–156)

   _____

   _____

10. True or False: Infants have well-developed color vision at birth, and they are immediately capable of discriminating colors. (p. 156)

Neonatal Behavioral Assessment

1. Which areas of behavior does the Neonatal Behavioral Assessment Scale (NBAS) evaluate? (p. 156)

   _____

   _____

2. What is the Neonatal Intensive Care Unit Network Neurobehavioral Scale (NNNS) specifically designed to evaluate? (p. 156)

   _____

   _____

3. Since the NBAS is given to infants all around the world, researchers have been able to learn a great deal about individual and cultural differences in newborn behavior and the ways in which various child-rearing practices affect infant behavior. Briefly discuss these findings. (pp. 156–157)

   _____

   _____

   _____

4. Why is a single NBAS score not a good predictor of later development, and what should be used in place of a single score? (p. 157)

   A. _____

   B. _____

5. How are NBAS interventions beneficial for the early parent–infant relationship? (p. 157)

_____

The Transition to Parenthood

1. Discuss several changes in the family system following the birth of a new baby. (p. 157)

_____

_____

_____

_____

Changes in the Family System

1. True or False: For most new parents, the arrival of a baby causes significant marital strain. (p. 158)

2. Describe changes in the division of labor in the home following childbirth. (p. 158)

_____

_____

_____

3. In what ways does postponing childbearing until the late twenties or thirties ease the transition to parenthood? (p. 158)

_____

_____

_____

4. Explain how a second birth affects the family system. (p. 158)

_____

_____

Biology and Environment: Parental Depression and Child Development

1. Differentiate between postpartum blues and postpartum depression, noting the prevalence rate of each. (p. 160)

    Postpartum blues: _____

    _____

    Postpartum depression: _____

    _____

2. Describe how the mother's depressed mood affects her newborn infant in the first months of life. (p. 160)

    _____

    _____

3. Describe parenting practices associated with persistent maternal depression, and note how these parenting behaviors impact the development of the child. (p. 160)

    Parenting practices: _____

    _____

    _____

Impact on child: _____

_____

_____

4. True or False: Persistent paternal depression is a strong predictor of child behavior problems. (p. 160)

5. Briefly summarize interventions for postpartum depression. (p. 160)

_____

_____

Single-Mother Families

1. True or False: Planned births and adoptions by single 30- to 45-year-old women are increasing. (p. 158)

2. The majority of nonmarital births are (planned / unplanned) and to women in their _____. (p. 159)

3. Describe common stressors associated with being a single mother. (p. 159)

_____

_____

_____

Parent Interventions

1. Describe five strategies that couples can use to ease the transition to parenthood. (p. 159)

    A. _____

    _____

    B. _____

    _____

    C. _____

    _____

    D. _____

    _____

    E. _____

    _____

2. Discuss how interventions for low-risk parents differ from interventions for high-risk parents. (pp. 159, 161)

    Low-risk: _____

    _____

    _____

    High-risk: _____

    _____

    _____

ASK YOURSELF . . .

For *Ask Yourself* questions for this chapter, along with feedback on the accuracy of your answers, please log on to MyDevelopmentLab (for registration and access, please visit mydevelopmentlab.com or follow the directions on p. ix).

1) Select the Chapter of the *Ask Yourself*.
2) Open the E-Book and select the Explore icon next to the *Ask Yourself*.
3) Complete questions and choose "Submit answers for grading" or "Clear Answers" to start over.

SUGGESTED STUDENT READINGS

Mifflin, P. C. (2004). *Saving very premature babies: Ethical issues.* London, UK: Butterworth-Heinemann. Examines the ethical and legal issues surrounding medical interventions for extremely premature babies. The author also addresses the challenges faced by parents of these babies, including the emotional and financial toll of long-term care.

Reed, R. K. (2005). *Birthing fathers: The transformation of men in American rites of birth.* New Brunswick, NJ: Rutgers University Press. Presents a historical overview of men's involvement in pregnancy and childbirth, including personal experiences and the transition to fatherhood.

Simonds, W., Rothman, B. K., Norman, B. M. (2006). *Laboring on: Birth in transition.* New York: Taylor & Francis. Examines a variety of issues concerning pregnancy and labor, including approaches to childbirth, medical interventions, debates over midwifery, and women's healthcare reform.

PUZZLE 4.1 TERM REVIEW

Across

4. A strong pain-killing drug that blocks sensation
6. Inadequate oxygen supply
7. Climax of the first stage of labor; the frequency and strength of contractions peak and the cervix opens completely
14. _____ labor: a labor started artificially by breaking the amnion and giving the mother a hormone that stimulates contractions
15. General term for a variety of problems that result from brain damage before, during, or just after birth (2 words)

Down

1. A mild pain-relieving drug
2. Positioning of the baby in the uterus such that the buttocks or feet would be delivered first
3. _____ and effacement of the cervix: widening and thinning of the cervix during the first stage of labor
5. Infants whose birth weight is below normal when length of pregnancy is taken into account (3 words)

6. The _____ Scale is used to assess the newborn immediately after birth
8. _____ distress syndrome: disorder of preterm infants in which the lungs are so immature that the air sacs collapse, causing breathing difficulties
9. _____ extractor: a plastic cup attached to a suction tube; used to assist in delivering the baby
10. Natural, or _____, childbirth: approach designed to overcome the idea that birth is a painful ordeal requiring extensive medical intervention
11. _____ delivery: a surgical delivery in which the doctor makes an incision in the mother's abdomen and lifts the baby out of the uterus
12. Metal clamps placed around the baby's head; used to pull the baby from the birth canal
13. _____ monitors: electronic instruments that track the baby's heart rate during labor

PUZZLE 4.2 TERM REVIEW

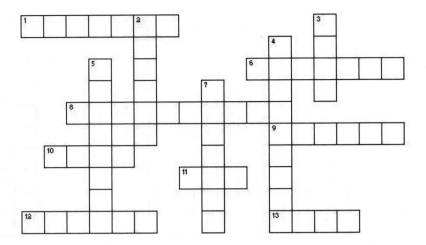

Across

1. States of _____: different degrees of sleep and wakefulness
6. Parents' feelings of affection and concern for the newborn baby
8. _____ depression: feelings of sadness and withdrawal that appear shortly after childbirth and continue for weeks or months
9. _____ mortality: the number of deaths in the first year of life per 1,000 live births
10. Test developed to assess the behavior of the infant during the newborn period (abbr.)
11. An "irregular" sleep state in which brain wave activity is similar to that of the waking state (abbr.)
12. An inborn, automatic response to a particular form of stimulation
13. A "regular" sleep state in which the heart rate, breathing, and brain wave activity are slow and regular (abbr.)

Down

2. Visual _____: fineness of visual discrimination
3. The unexpected death of an infant younger than one year of age that remains unexplained after thorough investigation (abbr.)
4. Arrangement in which the baby stays in the mother's hospital room all or most of the time (2 words)
5. _____ mortality: the number of deaths in the first month of life per 1,000 live births
7. Infants born several weeks or months before their due date

PRACTICE TEST #1

1. Early contractions of the upper part of the uterus are often called prelabor because they (p. 130)
   a. draw the baby's head into the uterus in preparation for labor.
   b. remain brief and unpredictable for several weeks.
   c. force out the bloody show.
   d. soften the cervix just before labor begins.

2. During the transition phase, before the cervix has completely dilated and effaced, the mother must relax and refrain from bearing down because she might (p. 131)
   a. bruise the cervix and slow her labor.
   b. prevent lightening from occurring.
   c. induce false labor.
   d. reharden the cervix.

3. Healthy babies adapt to the stress of childbirth by (p. 131)
   a. dropping their heads low in the uterus to hasten their passage out.
   b. curling into the so-called fetal position that protects their delicate organs.
   c. reducing the amount of blood passing to the brain and heart.
   d. producing cortisol and other stress hormones.

4. An Apgar score of between 4 and 6 means that the baby (p. 132)
   a. is in good physical condition.
   b. requires assistance in establishing vital signs.
   c. needs emergency medical attention.
   d. is close to death.

5. In Western nations, before the late 1800s, birth usually took place (p. 133)
   a. at home.
   b. in primitive hospitals.
   c. with the help of a "head helper."
   d. under a doctor's supervision.

6. Grantly Dick-Read and Fernand Lamaze (p. 134)
   a. established the first freestanding birth centers in the 1950s.
   b. introduced natural childbirth to North America.
   c. argued that natural childbirth is dangerous for women.
   d. developed the methods from which most natural childbirth programs draw.

7. Since 1970, the number of North American women who choose home birth has (p. 135)
   a. risen dramatically and now exceeds the number of women in Europe.
   b. remained constant at about 5 percent.
   c. risen but remains small, at about 1 percent.
   d. declined as doctors and hospitals have worked to discourage the practice.

8. In Canada, continuous fetal monitoring is (p. 136)
   a. used in all home births.
   b. usually reserved for babies at risk for birth complications.
   c. required in most hospitals.
   d. usually not recommended by certified nurse-midwives.

9. The most common labor-pain medication, the epidural analgesia, (p. 136)
   a.   allows the mother to feel contraction pressure and move her trunk and legs.
   b.   numbs the entire lower half of the mother's body.
   c.   strengthens uterine contractions.
   d.   has no effect on the infant's Apgar score.

10. A major reason for the rise in induced labors in North America is (p. 137)
   a.   the increasing rate of birth complication in older mothers.
   b.   that instrument deliveries have declined in popularity.
   c.   that many doctors and patients find them convenient.
   d.   improvements in delivery drugs.

11. A cause of anoxia, placenta abruptio, occurs when the (p. 139)
   a.   umbilical cord wraps around the baby's neck.
   b.   blastocyst implants so low that the placenta covers the cervical opening.
   c.   baby, just after birth, fails to start breathing.
   d.   placenta separates prematurely.

12. Compared with preterm infants, small-for-date infants are more likely to (pp. 140–141)
   a.   have been born at 34 to 35 weeks.
   b.   be well below average in physical growth during early childhood.
   c.   have lower intelligence scores by middle childhood.
   d.   experience moderately delayed cognitive development.

13. Kangaroo care can promote preterm babies' survival and recovery by (p. 142)
   a.   keeping the babies upright.
   b.   enabling parents to serve as human incubators through skin-to-skin touch.
   c.   regulating the babies' oxygen intake.
   d.   allowing parents to feed their babies through isolettes.

14. Which of the following factors is largely responsible for the high neonatal mortality rate in the United States? (p. 144)
   a.   widespread poverty and weak health-care programs for mothers and young children
   b.   the steady rise in maternal age
   c.   the high mortality rate of Inuit babies
   d.   increasing levels of harmful pollution

15. Several studies report that around the time of birth, first-time fathers (p. 146)
   a.   begin producing oxytocin.
   b.   produce less estrogen.
   c.   experience a drop in androgens.
   d.   produce less prolactin than mothers.

16. Babies display the rooting reflex when they (p. 147)
   a.   place a finger in their mouths.
   b.   are held under the arms.
   c.   face a bright light.
   d.   are hungry and are touched by another person.

17. Babies' sleep-wake cycles are affected largely by (p. 149)
   a.   fullness-hunger.
   b.   their parents' emotional state.
   c.   the time of day.
   d.   their sensitivity to external stimuli.

18. The incidence of SIDS peaks between ages (p. 151)
    a. 7 days to three weeks.
    b. 1 to 3 months.
    c. 2 to 4 months.
    d. 6 to 8 months.

19. In Western nations, the most common and effective method of soothing a crying baby is (p. 152)
    a. swaddling.
    b. taking the baby for a short car ride.
    c. massaging the baby's body.
    d. lifting the baby to the shoulder and rocking or walking.

20. Newborns show through _____ that they can distinguish several basic tastes. (p. 154)
    a. facial expressions
    b. sounds that indicate preferences
    c. hand and foot movements
    d. sucking and pushing out with the tongue

21. Allowing newborns to endure severe pain may result in (p. 154)
    a. the release of endorphins.
    b. sleep disturbances and feeding problems.
    c. decreased responsiveness to touch.
    d. reflexive fear.

22. The NBAS test has enabled researchers to (p. 156)
    a. predict intelligence into the preschool years with a high rate of success.
    b. measure how newborns discriminate colors.
    c. learn how different cultures' child-rearing practices can change or maintain a baby's reactions.
    d. draw conclusions about how babies link certain smells to particular bodies or objects.

23. Researchers believe that most newborn reflexes disappear during the first six months as (p. 149)
    a. the baby's weight exceeds its muscle strength.
    b. voluntary control over behavior increases with the development of the cerebral cortex.
    c. parental interaction stimulates more advanced motor skills.
    d. the child learns to block out certain kinds of stimuli.

24. Postponing parenthood until the late twenties or thirties can ease the transition to parenthood because waiting (p. 158)
    a. reduces the chance of emotionally devastating birth complications.
    b. helps to ensure that the new parents will not suffer violated expectations.
    c. women have time to withdraw from their careers gradually.
    d. permits couples to pursue occupational goals and gain life experience.

25. About what percent of babies in the United States and Canada are born to single mothers? (p. 158)
    a. 22
    b. 37
    c. 39
    d. 42

PRACTICE TEST #2

1. During Stage 1 of childbirth, the uterine contractions begin (p. 131)
   a.   2 to 3 minutes apart.
   b.   7 to 8 minutes apart.
   c.   10 to 20 minutes apart.
   d.   30 to 40 minutes apart.

2. During Stage 2 of childbirth, the mother
   a.   feels a natural urge to squeeze and push with her abdominal muscles. (p. 131)
   b.   pushes out the placenta.
   c.   has contractions 8 to 10 minutes apart.
   d.   transitions as her cervix opens completely.

3. The combination of small body and large head means that the infant (p. 132)
   a.   received too little oxygen during the birthing process.
   b.   has a well-developed brain that enables quick learning in the first few months.
   c.   bruised the mother's cervix.
   d.   produced the proper amount of cortisol.

4. The Apgar scale measures which of the following signs? (p. 133)
   a.   mental alertness and hand-eye coordination
   b.   the speed with which the infant begins nursing
   c.   breathing, blinking, and kicking
   d.   heart rate, respiratory effort, reflex irritability, muscle tone, and color

5. The purpose of the natural childbirth movement that arose during the 1950s and 1960s was to (p. 133)
   a.   make hospital birth as comfortable and rewarding as possible.
   b.   introduce European-style freestanding birth centers to North America.
   c.   remove doctors entirely from the birthing experience.
   d.   persuade women to have their babies at home.

6. Research indicates that mothers who are supported during labor (p. 134)
   a.   are more likely to have an episiotomy.
   b.   prefer lying flat on their backs with their feet in stirrups.
   c.   are less likely to have cesarean births.
   d.   tend to be more nervous and, therefore, experience more birth complications. (p. 135)

7. Most home births are handled by (p. 136)
   a.   doctors.
   b.   certified nurse-midwives.
   c.   experienced family members.
   d.   childbirth managers.

8. Fetal monitoring is controversial because it (p. 136)
   a.   can cause the baby to produce too many stress hormones.
   b.   is extremely painful for the mother.
   c.   may identify babies as being in danger, when, in fact, they are not.
   d.   disrupts the home birth experience.

9. Low-forceps delivery is associated with risk of (p. 137)
   a.   bleeding beneath the baby's skin and external to the skull.
   b.   low Apgar scores in infants.
   c.   neck and torso deformities.
   d.   injury to the baby's head and the mother's tissues.

10. The rise in cesarean births in Western industrialized nations is largely due to (p. 138)
    a. an increase in Rh incompatibility between mothers and their babies.
    b. medical control over childbirth.
    c. complications during natural childbirth.
    d. an increase in the number of babies in breech position.

11. Research suggests that oxygen deprivation just before, during, or just after birth can result in (p. 139)
    a. poor cognitive and language skills in early and middle childhood.
    b. respiratory distress syndrome.
    c. placenta previa.
    d. Apgar scores low in heart rate but high in color.

12. Research indicates that preterm babies stimulated with attractive mobiles, special waterbeds, and other means achieved (p. 142)
    a. few significant developmental gains.
    b. greater mental advancement by the end of their first year.
    c. faster weight gain, more predictable sleep patterns, and greater alertness.
    d. slower weight gain than preterm babies cared for in an isolette.

13. Research findings suggest that both preterm and economically disadvantaged babies need (pp. 142–143)
    a. kangaroo care.
    b. intensive intervention to achieve necessary developmental gains.
    c. help developing the rooting and sucking reflexes.
    d. more time in an isolette than economically advantaged babies.

14. Research indicates that six weeks or less of childbirth leave (p. 145)
    a. is linked to maternal depression, anxiety, and sense of role overload.
    b. can help new parents establish essential bonds with their child.
    c. is the norm in the United States and Canada.
    d. is especially detrimental to middle-SES parents.

15. The Kauai study, begun in 1955, reveals that children's personal characteristics and social experiences (pp. 143, 145)
    a. vary in their impact according to ethnic background.
    b. have a measurable impact on the neonatal mortality rate.
    c. reveal the significant effects of universal, high-quality health care and generous parental leave.
    d. increasingly contribute to the successful functioning of children who suffer serious birth problems.

16. Reflexes can help parents comfort their baby because they (p. 147)
    a. put infants to sleep.
    b. function as a shared language between parent and child.
    c. help infants control distress and amount of stimulation.
    d. enable parents to manage their own anxieties.

17. Newborns spend most of their sleep time in (p. 150)
    a. quiet alertness.
    b. the REM state.
    c. drowsiness.
    d. regular sleep.

18. A strong predictor of SIDS is (p. 151)
    a. extremely deep NREM sleep.
    b. abnormally high birth weight.
    c. abnormalities in the brain center than controls heart rate.
    d. smoking by mothers and other caregivers.

19. According to many researchers, crying peaks around 6 weeks, and then declines because (p. 152)
    a. normal readjustments of the central nervous system occur during that period.
    b. babies begin to learn more mature ways of expressing their desires.
    c. after 6 weeks, babies sleep more.
    d. around that time, parents generally feel more confident in their soothing techniques.

20. Newborns most susceptible to colic are those who (p. 152)
    a. have brain damage.
    b. cannot achieve normal REM sleep.
    c. react strongly to unpleasant stimuli.
    d. experienced anoxia at birth.

21. The least developed of the senses at birth is (p. 155)
    a. taste.
    b. vision.
    c. hearing.
    d. smell.

22. Marriages most likely to be distressed after a baby is born are those (p. 158)
    a. in which gender roles become more traditional than they were before.
    b. confronted with a baby who has severe birth defects.
    c. of older parents.
    d. troubled before the birth of the child.

23. Babies of depressed mothers often (p. 160)
    a. show delays in mental development.
    b. develop a heightened sensitivity to pain.
    c. get low NNNS scores.
    d. become unusually attached to their parents.

24. The majority of nonmarital births are (p. 159)
    a. to older women with secure careers.
    b. to couples who are ethnic minorities.
    c. unplanned and to women in their twenties.
    d. to teenage mothers.

25. Programs in which a trained intervener visits the home of high-risk parents have (p. 161)
    a. had greater success in Canada than in the United States.
    b. resulted in improved parent-infant interaction.
    c. been generally less effective than counselor-led parenting groups.
    d. done little to improve children's cognitive and social development.

CHAPTER 5
PHYSICAL DEVELOPMENT
IN INFANCY AND TODDLERHOOD

BRIEF CHAPTER SUMMARY

During the first two years, body size increases dramatically, following organized patterns of growth. The skull also grows rapidly, accommodating large increases in brain size. Neurons in the brain form an elaborate communication system, sending messages to one another by releasing neurotransmitters across the synapses. Myelination—the coating of neural fibers with myelin—improves the efficiency of message transfer. Neurophysiological methods that detect brain-wave activity allow researchers to identify relationships between the brain and psychological development.

The cerebral cortex surrounding the rest of the brain is the largest and most complex brain structure. Each hemisphere specializes in different functions, but brain plasticity allows some recovery of abilities lost to damage in one hemisphere. During sensitive periods in brain development, the rapidly growing brain must receive appropriate stimulation in order to reach its full potential. Rapid brain growth also causes substantial changes in organization of sleep and wakefulness during the first two years.

Various factors affect early physical growth. Heredity contributes to height, weight, and rate of physical maturation. Nutrition is crucial: Rapidly growing babies need extra calories to keep their developing organs functioning properly. Breast milk, which is ideally suited to meet infants' needs, is especially important in promoting infant survival and health in poverty-stricken regions. Rapid weight gain in infancy appears to be related to later overweight and obesity; malnutrition in the early years can lead to permanent stunting of physical growth and of brain development. Affection and stimulation are also essential for healthy physical growth.

Babies are born with built-in learning capacities that allow them to benefit from experience immediately after birth. Classical conditioning, operant conditioning, habituation and recovery, and imitation are important early learning capacities that infants use to explore their physical and social worlds.

Motor development, like physical growth, follows an organized sequence, with large individual differences in rate of motor progress. According to dynamic systems theory, mastery of motor skills involves acquiring increasingly complex systems of action in which each new skill is a joint product of central nervous system development, the body's movement possibilities, the goals the child has in mind, and environmental supports for the skill. Cultural variations in infant rearing practices also influence motor development. Of all motor skills, reaching may play the greatest role in infant cognitive development because it opens up a new way of exploring the environment. Reaching improves as depth perception advances and infants gain control of body movements. Early experience also plays a role.

Hearing and vision undergo major advances in the first year. Babies begin to organize sounds into complex patterns, detecting regularities that facilitate later language learning. Newborns prefer human speech to nonspeech sounds, and infants have a remarkable ability to extract regularities from complex, continuous speech, which prepares them to utter their first words around age 12 months. Visual development is supported by maturation of the eye and visual centers in the cerebral cortex. Depth perception develops gradually, helping infants avoid falling. Pattern perception begins at birth; newborns prefer to look at patterned rather than plain stimuli. Babies' tendency to look for structure in a pattern stimulus also applies to face perception; they quickly learn to prefer their mother's face to that of an unfamiliar woman. Size constancy and object constancy also begin in the first week of life. Through intermodal perception, babies perceive input from different sensory systems in a unified way. Perception is guided by the discovery of affordances—the action possibilities that a situation affords.

LEARNING OBJECTIVES

After reading this chapter, you should be able to:

5.1   Describe changes in body size, body proportions, and muscle–fat makeup during the first two years of life. (pp. 166–167)

5.2   Discuss skeletal growth during the first two years of life, including the growth of the skull and the appearance of teeth. (pp. 167–168)

5.3   Describe brain development during infancy and toddlerhood at the level of individual brain cells and at the level of the cerebral cortex. (pp. 168–172)

5.4   Summarize research on brain lateralization and brain plasticity. (pp. 172–173)

5.5   Describe research findings related to the existence of sensitive periods in brain development, and note the evidence of brain growth spurts and need for appropriate stimulation. (pp. 173–176)

5.6   Describe current methods of measuring brain functioning, and identify which measure is most appropriate during infancy and toddlerhood. (pp. 170–171)

5.7   Explain how the organization of sleep and wakefulness changes over the first two years. (pp. 176–178)

5.8   Discuss the impact of heredity on early physical growth. (p. 178)

5.9   Discuss the nutritional needs of infants and toddlers, the advantages of breastfeeding, and the extent to which chubby babies are at risk for later overweight and obesity. (pp. 178–180)

5.10   Discuss the impact of severe malnutrition on the development of infants and toddlers, and cite two dietary diseases associated with this condition. (pp. 180–182)

5.11   Describe the growth disorder known as nonorganic failure to thrive, noting common symptoms and family circumstances surrounding the disorder. (p. 182)

5.12   Explain how infants learn through classical conditioning, operant conditioning, habituation and recovery, and imitation. (pp. 183–187)

5.13   Describe the general course of motor development during the first two years, along with factors that influence it. (pp. 187–188)

5.14   Explain the dynamic systems theory of motor development, highlighting cultural variations in motor development. (pp. 189–190)

5.15   Describe the development of reaching and grasping, and explain how early experiences affect these skills. (pp. 190–193)

5.16   Summarize the development of hearing in infancy, giving special attention to speech perception. (pp. 193–194)

5.17   Summarize the development of vision in infancy, with particular attention to depth perception and pattern perception. (pp. 195–200)

5.18   Discuss the development of object perception during the first year of life. (pp. 200–201)

5.19   Explain the concept of intermodal perception. (p. 202)

5.20   Explain the Gibsons' differentiation theory of perceptual development. (pp. 202–203)

STUDY QUESTIONS

Body Growth

Changes in Body Size and Muscle–Fat Makeup

1. Infant and toddler growth is marked by (steady gains / little spurts). (p. 166)

2. Summarize changes in muscle–fat makeup during the first two years of life. (p. 167)

   _____

   _____

   _____

3. Describe sex and ethnic differences in body size and muscle–fat makeup during infancy. (p. 167)

   A. _____

   _____

   B. _____

   _____

Changes in Body Proportions

1. According to the two patterns of body growth, the (cephalocaudal / proximodistal) trend refers to growth from "head to tail," while the (cephalocaudal / proximodistal) trend refers to growth from the center of the body outward. (p. 167)

Skeletal Growth

1. The best way of estimating a child's physical maturity is to use _____, a measure of the development of the bones of the body. Explain how this estimate is obtained. (p. 167)

   _____

   _____

   _____

2. True or False: African-American children tend to be slightly behind Caucasian-American children in skeletal age. (p. 168)

3. Describe sex differences in skeletal age and body size during infancy and toddlerhood. (p. 168)

   _____

   _____

   _____

4. At birth, the bones of the skull are separated by six gaps, or soft spots, called _____. Explain their function. (p. 168)

   _____

   _____

   _____

5. At approximately what age do infants get their first tooth? What does early appearance of teeth reveal about physical maturity? (p. 168)

   A. _____

   B. _____

Brain Development

Development of Neurons

1. The human brain has 100 to 200 billion _____, or nerve cells, that store and transmit information. Between them are tiny gaps, or _____, across which messages pass. (p. 168)

2. Explain the process of *synaptic pruning.* (p. 169)

_____

_____

_____

3. About one-half the brain's volume is made up of _____, which are responsible for _____, the coating of neural fibers with an insulating fatty sheath that improves the efficiency of message transfer. (pp. 169–170)

Neurophysiological Methods

1. Match each of the following methods of measuring brain functioning to the appropriate description. (p. 170)

_____ Electroencephalogram (EEG)
_____ Event-related potentials (ERPs)
_____ Functional magnetic resonance imaging (fMRI)
_____ Positron Emission Tomography (PET)
_____ Near-Infrared Optical Topography (NIROT)

1. Thin, flexible optical fibers are attached to the scalp and infrared light is beamed at the brain. Absorption by areas of the cerebral cortex varies with changes in blood flow and oxygen metabolism.
2. Using the EEG, the frequency and amplitude of brain waves in response to particular stimuli are recorded in specific areas of the cerebral cortex.
3. Electrodes are taped to the scalp to record the stability and organization of electrical brain-wave activity in the brain's outer layers—the cerebral cortex.
4. After injection or inhalation of a radioactive substance, the individual lies inside a tunnel-shaped apparatus with a scanner that emits fine streams of X-rays, which detect increased blood flow and oxygen metabolism in the brain while a person processes particular stimuli.
5. A scanner magnetically detects increased blood flow and oxygen metabolism in areas of the brain as the individual processes particular stimuli. The result is a computerized moving picture of activity anywhere in the brain.

2. True or False: Near-Infrared Optical Topography (NIROT) works well in infancy and early childhood because the child can sit on the parent's lap and move during testing, unlike other methods of measuring brain functioning. (p. 171)

Development of the Cerebral Cortex

1. True or False: The cerebral cortex is the largest, most complex brain structure, accounting for 85 percent of the brain's weight and containing the greatest number of neurons and synapses. (p. 171)

2. Name the regions of the cerebral cortex, and describe the function of each. (p. 172)

A. _____

B. _____

C. _____

D. _____

3. Describe the different functions controlled by the left and right hemispheres of the brain. (p. 172)

Left: _____

_____

Right: _____

_____

4. Explain the concepts of *lateralization* and *brain plasticity*. (pp. 172–173)

Lateralization: _____

_____

Brain plasticity: _____

_____

_____

5. The brain is (more / less) plastic during the first few years than at any later time in life. (p. 173)

Biology and Environment: Brain Plasticity: Insights from Research on Brain-Damaged Children and Adults

1. Adults who suffered brain injuries in infancy and early childhood show (fewer / more) cognitive impairments than adults with later-occurring injuries. (p. 174)

2. Describe the impact of brain injury on childhood language development and spatial skills, noting how this relates to brain plasticity. (p. 174)

Language: _____

_____

Spatial skills: _____

_____

3. True or False: Recovery after early brain injury is greater for language than for spatial skills. (p. 174)

4. Describe the negative consequences of high brain plasticity. (p. 174)

_____

_____

5. True or False: Brain plasticity is restricted to childhood and is no longer evident by the time individuals reach adulthood. Provide research evidence to support your response. (p. 174)

_____

_____

_____

Sensitive Periods in Brain Development

1. Why is it difficult to study the effects of early deprivation in human infants? (p. 175)

    _____

2. What is cognitive catch-up? What does research on orphanage children reveal about cognitive catch-up? (p. 175)

    A. _____

    _____

    B. _____

    _____

3. Summarize evidence that appropriate stimulation is essential for healthy brain development. (pp. 173, 175)

    _____

    _____

    _____

4. True or False: Overstimulation of infants and toddlers threatens their interest in learning and may create conditions similar to those of stimulus deprivation. (p. 175)

5. Distinguish between *experience-expectant* and *experience-dependent* brain growth, and provide an example of each. (p. 176)

    Experience-expectant: _____

    _____

    _____

    Experience-dependent: _____

    _____

    _____

6. Evidence (does / does not) exist for a sensitive period in the first few years of life for mastering skills that depend on extensive training, such as musical performance or gymnastics. (p. 176)

Changing States of Arousal

1. In general, newborn babies sleep a total of ___ to ___ hours per day. The total sleep time of an infant declines (quickly / slowly); the average 2-year-old sleeps ___ to ___ hours per day. (p. 176)

2. Discuss how the social environment affects infants' changing arousal patterns. (pp. 176, 178)

    _____

    _____

    _____

Cultural Influences: Cultural Variations in Infant Sleeping Arrangements

1. True or False: Parent–infant cosleeping is the norm for approximately 90 percent of the world's population. (p. 177)

2. Explain how cultural values—specifically, collectivism versus individualism—influence infant sleeping arrangements. (p. 177)

   Collectivism: _____

   _____

   Individualism: _____

   _____

3. True or False: Research suggests that cosleeping evolved to protect infants' survival and health. Briefly explain your answer. (p. 177)

   _____

   _____

4. How do infant sleeping practices affect other aspects of family life? (p. 177)

   _____

   _____

   _____

5. Discuss the criticisms and concerns surrounding infant cosleeping. (p. 177)

   _____

   _____

   _____

Influences on Early Physical Growth

Heredity

1. True or False: When diet and health are adequate, height and rate of physical growth are largely determined by heredity. (p. 178)

2. When are children and adolescents likely to show catch-up growth? (p. 178)

   _____

   _____

Nutrition

1. List four nutritional and health benefits of breast milk. (p. 179)

   A. _____

   B. _____

   C. _____

   D. _____

2. Discuss the benefits of breastfeeding as they relate to mothers and infants in poverty-stricken regions of the world. (p. 179)

    _____

    _____

    _____

3. Rapid weight gain in infancy (is / is not) related to obesity at older ages. (p. 180)

4. Cite four ways in which parents can prevent infants and toddlers from becoming overweight at later ages. (p. 180)

    A. _____

    B. _____

    C. _____

    D. _____

Malnutrition

1. Describe the causes of *marasmus* and *kwashiorkor,* two dietary diseases associated with severe malnutrition, and summarize the developmental outcomes associated with these extreme forms of malnutrition. (pp. 181–182)

    Marasmus: _____

    _____

    _____

    _____

    Kwashiorkor: _____

    _____

    _____

    _____

    Outcomes: _____

    _____

    _____

    _____

2. True or False: Inadequate nutrition is largely confined to developing countries and recent surveys indicate that it is almost nonexistent in the United States and Canada. (p. 182)

3. What is food insecurity, and in what two populations is food insecurity especially high? (p. 182)

    A. _____

    B. _____   C. _____

Emotional Well-Being

1. What is *nonorganic failure to thrive,* and what are some common symptoms? (p. 182)

    A. _____

    _____

    B. _____

    _____

2. Discuss the family circumstances surrounding nonorganic failure to thrive. (p. 182)

_____

_____

_____

Learning Capacities

1. Define *learning,* and identify two basic forms of learning in which infants are equipped. (p. 183)

   A. _____

   B. _____   C. _____

Classical Conditioning

1. Briefly explain how learning takes place through *classical conditioning.* (p. 183)

   _____

   _____

   _____

2. Why is classical conditioning of great value to infants? (p. 183)

   _____

   _____

3. Match the following terms to the appropriate definitions. (pp. 183–184)

   _____ A neutral stimulus that leads to a new response once learning has occurred
   _____ A learned response exhibited toward a previously neutral stimulus
   _____ A reflexive response
   _____ A stimulus that automatically leads to a reflexive response

   1. Unconditioned stimulus (UCS)
   2. Unconditioned response (UCR)
   3. Conditioned stimulus (CS)
   4. Conditioned response (CR)

4. Using the above definitions as a guide (see question 3), outline the three steps involved in classical conditioning. (pp. 183–184)

   A. _____

   _____

   B. _____

   _____

   C. _____

   _____

5. In classical conditioning, if the CS is presented alone enough times, without being paired with the UCS, the CR will no longer occur. This is referred to as _____. (p. 184)

6. Some responses, such as _____, are very difficult to classically condition in young babies. Explain why. (pp. 183–184)

   _____

   _____

Operant Conditioning

1. Briefly explain how learning takes place through *operant conditioning*. (p. 184)

    _____

    _____

    _____

2. Define the terms *reinforcer* and *punishment* as they relate to operant conditioning. (p. 184)

    Reinforcer: _____

    _____

    _____

    Punishment: _____

    _____

    _____

3. Describe how operant conditioning plays a role in the development of social relationships. (p. 184)

    _____

    _____

    _____

Habituation

1. Define the terms *habituation* and *recovery*. (p. 185)

    Habituation: _____

    _____

    Recovery: _____

    _____

2. As infants get older, they habituate to stimuli more (slowly / quickly). What does this indicate about their cognitive development? (p. 185)

    _____

Imitation

1. Summarize what infants are able to learn through the process of *imitation*. (p. 186)

    _____

    _____

    _____

2. Explain the role of mirror neurons in relation to imitation and learning. (p. 186)

    _____

    _____

    _____

Motor Development

The Sequence of Motor Development

1. Distinguish between *gross* and *fine motor development,* and provide two examples of each. (pp. 187–188)

   Gross: _____

   _____

   Examples: _____

   Fine: _____

   _____

   Examples: _____

2. True or False: Although the *sequence* of motor development is fairly uniform, large individual differences exist in the *rate* of development. (p. 188)

3. Discuss the organization and direction of motor development in relation to the cephalocaudal and proximodistal trends. (p. 188)

   _____

   _____

   _____

   _____

Motor Skills as Dynamic Systems

1. According to the *dynamic systems theory of motor development,* mastery of motor skills involves acquisition of increasingly complex systems of action. Explain what this means. (p. 189)

   _____

   _____

   _____

2. List four factors that contribute to the development of each new motor skill. (p. 189)

   A. _____

   B. _____

   C. _____

   D. _____

3. True or False: Dynamic systems theory regards motor development as a genetically determined process. Briefly explain your response. (p. 189)

   _____

   _____

   _____

Dynamic Motor Systems in Action

1. What did Galloway and Thelen's microgenetic studies reveal about infant motor development? (pp. 189–190)

   _____

   _____

   _____

Cultural Variations in Motor Development

1.   In Wayne Dennis's orphanage research, what effects did lying on their backs have on babies' motor development? (p. 190)

_____

_____

2.   Give at least one example of how cultural variations in infant-rearing practices affect motor development. (p. 190)

_____

_____

Fine Motor Development: Reaching and Grasping

1.   Match each of the following terms to the appropriate definition. (pp. 190–191)

_____ Well-coordinated movement in which infants use the thumb and forefinger   1.   Prereaching
opposably   2.   Ulnar grasp
_____ Poorly coordinated swipes or swings toward an object   3.   Pincer grasp
_____ Clumsy motion in which the fingers close against the palm

2.   Explain how reaching and depth perception are related. (p. 191)

_____

_____

3.   Reaching (is / is not) affected by early experience. (p. 192)

4.   Does heavy enrichment lead to advanced motor development in infancy? Explain. (p. 192)

_____

_____

Bowel and Bladder Control

1.   At what age should parents typically begin toilet training their children, and why is this the case? (pp. 192–193)

Age: _____

Reason: _____

_____

2.   Name three effective toilet training techniques. (p. 193)

A. _____

B. _____

C. _____

Perceptual Development

Hearing

1. What is the greatest change in hearing that takes place over the first year of life? (p. 193)

   _____

2. Describe the changes in auditory perception over the first year of life that prepare infants for language acquisition. (pp. 193–194)

   Around 6 months: _____

   _____

   _____

   6–12 months: _____

   _____

   _____

3. Research shows that infants are impressive statistical analyzers of sound patterns. Explain what this means. (p. 199)

   _____

   _____

Biology and Environment: "Tuning in" to Familiar Speech, Faces, and Music: A Sensitive Period for Culture-Specific Learning

1. Describe changes in the ability to perceive familiar speech and familiar faces over the first year of life. (p. 195)

   Familiar speech: _____

   _____

   Familiar faces: _____

   _____

2. How do research findings on musical rhythm perception support the notion of a sensitive period for culture-specific learning? (p. 195)

   _____

   _____

   _____

Vision

1. What is *depth perception,* and why is it important in infant development? (p. 196)

   A. _____

   _____

   B. _____

   _____

2. Describe Gibson and Walk's studies using the visual cliff, and cite the limitations of this approach for studying infant depth perception. (p. 196)

    A. _____

    _____

    B. _____

    _____

3. Name and describe the three cues for depth. (p. 196)

    A. _____

    _____

    B. _____

    _____

    C. _____

    _____

4. Explain what infants learn from crawling that promotes sensitivity to depth information. (p. 197)

    _____

    _____

    _____

    _____

5. Provide an example from adult experience that helps to explain why crawling plays such an important role in the infant's knowledge and understanding of the three-dimensional world. (p. 197)

    _____

    _____

6. The principle of _____, which accounts for early pattern preferences, states that if infants can detect a difference in contrast between two or more patterns, they will prefer the one with more contrast. (p. 197)

7. True or False: By the end of the first year, a suggestive image of a pattern is all that babies need to recognize a familiar form. (p. 199)

8. Summarize the development of face perception across the first year of life. (pp. 199–200)

    Birth–1 month: _____

    _____

    2–4 months: _____

    _____

    5–12 months: _____

    _____

9. Cite factors that contribute to infants' refinement of face perception. (p. 197)

    _____

    _____

Social Issues: Education: Development of Infants with Severe Visual Impairments

1. True or False: Children with severe visual impairments show delays in motor, cognitive, and social development. (p. 198)

2. Discuss how severe visual impairments impact motor exploration and spatial understanding. (p. 198)

    _____

    _____

    _____

    _____

3. How do severe visual impairments affect the caregiver–infant relationship? (p. 198)

    _____

    _____

    _____

4. Cite four intervention techniques that can help infants with severe visual impairments become aware of their physical and social surroundings. (p. 198)

    A. _____

    _____

    B. _____

    _____

    C. _____

    _____

    D. _____

    _____

Object Perception

1. True or False: Size and shape constancy appear to emerge gradually over time as infants acquire more advanced knowledge of objects in the environment. (p. 201)

2. True or False: When two objects are touching, whether moving in unison or standing still, infants younger than 4 months of age do not perceive the boundary between the two objects, and therefore, cannot distinguish them. (p. 201)

Intermodal Perception

1. What is *intermodal perception*? (p. 202)

    _____

    _____

2. Explain the concept of *amodal sensory properties*. (p. 202)

    _____

    _____

    _____

3. True or False: From birth, infants are capable of combining information from multiple sensory systems. Cite research to support your response. (p. 202)

_____

_____

_____

4. Explain how intermodal perception facilitates processing of the infant's social world. (p. 202)

_____

_____

_____

Understanding Perceptual Development

1. Explain Gibsons' *differentiation theory.* (p. 202)

_____

_____

_____

2. Explain how acting on the environment plays a vital role in perceptual differentiation. (p. 203)

_____

_____

_____

ASK YOURSELF . . .

For *Ask Yourself* questions for this chapter, along with feedback on the accuracy of your answers, please log on to MyDevelopmentLab (for registration and access, please visit mydevelopmentlab.com or follow the directions on p. ix).

1) Select the Chapter of the *Ask Yourself.*
2) Open the E-Book and select the Explore icon next to the *Ask Yourself.*
3) Complete questions and choose "Submit answers for grading" or "Clear Answers" to start over.

SUGGESTED STUDENT READINGS

Brazelton, T. B., & Sparrow, J. D. (2006). *Touchpoints: 0 to 3*. Cambridge, MA: Da Capo Press. Written by leading experts in the field of child development, this book examines a variety of topics on infant and toddler development, including brain development, early learning capacities, toilet training, and child health and safety.

Coch, D., Dawson, G., & Fischer, K. W. (Eds.). (2007). *Human behavior, learning, and the developing brain: Typical development.* New York: Guilford Press. An interdisciplinary examination of brain and behavior relations, this book highlights the relationship between brain development, cognition, and social/emotional development. The chapters also reveal insights into the expanding field of cognitive neuroscience.

Zigler, E. F., Finn-Stevenson, M., & Hall, N. W. (2004). *The first three years and beyond: Brain development and social policy.* New Haven, CT: Yale University Press. Taking an interdisciplinary approach to understanding brain development, this book presents up-to-date research on the importance of early experiences for favorable development. Other topics include appropriate stimulation, the importance of breastfeeding and nutrition, and public policies for children and families.

PUZZLE 5.1 TERM REVIEW

Across

2. In classical conditioning, an originally reflexive response that is produced by a CS after learning has occurred (abbr.)
7. Experience-_____ brain growth: early organization of the brain depends on ordinary experiences with the environment
9. In operant conditioning, a stimulus that increases the occurrence of a response
10. _____ conditioning: form of learning that involves associating a neutral stimulus with a stimulus that leads to a reflexive response
11. Brain _____: ability of other parts of the brain to take over functions of damaged regions
13. Process in which neural fibers are coated with an insulating fatty sheath that improves the efficiency of message transfer
15. In operant conditioning, a stimulus that decreases the occurrence of a response
18. Cells that serve the function of myelination
19. The gaps between neurons across which messages are sent
21. _____ conditioning: form of learning in which spontaneous behavior is followed by a stimulus that changes the probability that the behavior will occur again
22. In classical conditioning, a neutral stimulus that through pairing with an UCS leads to a new response (abbr.)

Down

1. The largest, most complex brain structure is the _____ cortex
3. In classical conditioning, a reflexive response that is produced by an UCS (abbr.)
4. Specialization of functions of the two hemispheres of the cerebral cortex
5. An increase in responsiveness to a new stimulus following habituation
6. Experience-_____ brain growth: growth and refinement of brain structures result from specific learning experiences
8. In classical conditioning, a stimulus that leads to a reflexive response (abbr.)
12. Soft spots that separate the bones of the skull at birth
14. Growth centers in the bones
16. Nerve cells that store and transmit information
17. _____ age: an estimate of physical maturity based on development of the bones of the body
20. Synaptic _____: loss of connective fibers by seldom-stimulated neurons

PUZZLE 5.2 TERM REVIEW

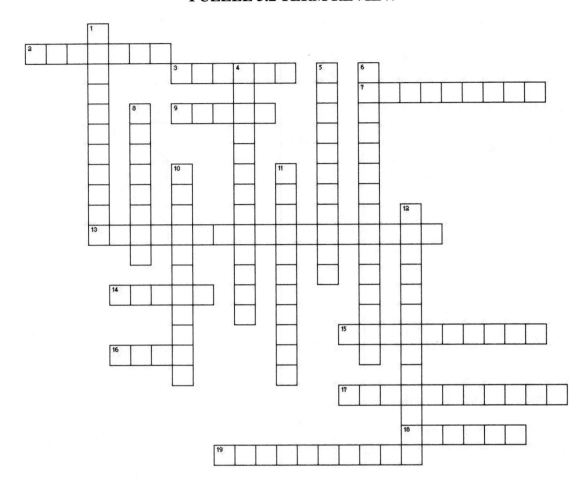

Across

2. _____ systems theory of motor development: views new motor skills as a reorganization of previously mastered skills that lead to more effective ways of exploring and controlling the environment
3. Well-formed grasp involving thumb and forefinger opposition
7. Learning by copying another person
9. _____ constancy: perception of an object's shape as the same, despite changes in the shape projected on the retina
13. Chemicals released by neurons that cross the synapse to send messages to other neurons
14. Clumsy grasp in which the fingers close against the palm
15. _____ failure to thrive: growth disorder caused by a lack of affection and stimulation
16. _____ constancy: perception of an object's size as the same, despite changes in the sizes of its retinal image
17. Contrast _____: if babies can detect a difference in contrast between two or more patterns, they will prefer the one with more contrast
18. _____ sensory properties: information that overlaps two or more sensory systems, resulting in perception of such input as an integrated whole
19. _____ perception combines information from more than one sensory system

Down

1. A gradual reduction in the strength of a response as a result of a repeated stimulation
4. _____ trend: pattern of physical growth that proceeds from head to tail
5. The poorly coordinated, primitive reaching movements of newborn infants
6. _____ theory: view that perceptual development involves detection of increasingly fine-grained, invariant features of the environment
8. A disease usually appearing in the first year of life that is caused by a diet low in all essential nutrients
10. The action possibilities that a situation offers an organism with certain motor capabilities
11. A disease usually appearing between 1 and 3 years of age that is caused by a diet low in protein
12. _____ trend: pattern of physical growth that proceeds from the center of the body outward

PRACTICE TEST #1

1. During the first 9 months, babies develop "baby fat" in order to (p. 167)
   a. maintain a constant body temperature.
   b. ensure a consistent source of nourishment.
   c. engage adults' affectionate attention.
   d. cushion the vital organs from violent trauma.

2. Examination of the epiphyses can determine the age of a child's skeleton because (pp. 167–168)
   a. the older the skeleton, the more fontanels at the epiphyses.
   b. older epiphyses show a greater proximodistal trend.
   c. the older the skeleton, the thinner the cartilage cells at the plates of the epiphyses.
   d. the younger the epiphyses, the more sutures there are across the plates.

3. Skull growth is especially rapid between birth and age 2 because (p. 168)
   a. the skull is developing many new fontanels.
   b. all of the bones are producing epiphyses.
   c. the birth sutures are disappearing.
   d. brain size is increasing.

4. The major limitation of neurophysiological methods is that they (p. 171)
   a. are unsuitable for infants and young children, since they require that the child remain as motionless as possible.
   b. cannot show that the research participant has processed a stimulus in a certain way.
   c. depend on X-ray photography.
   d. can determine only the stability and organization of brain-wave patterns.

5. The fact that damage to either hemisphere of the young brain affects early language competence indicates that (p. 174)
   a. language and spatial skills develop in the frontal lobes.
   b. the crowding effect slows the processing of verbal stimuli.
   c. the brain is less plastic than researchers once thought.
   d. language functioning is broadly distributed in the brain.

6. Rapid brain growth means that by age 2, most children (p. 176)
   a. no longer nap.
   b. need 12 to 13 hours of sleep.
   c. nap between 16 and 18 hours.
   d. take two daytime naps.

7. Breastfed infants become hungry quite often because (p. 180)
   a. breast milk is so easily digestible.
   b. they tend to be more active than bottle-fed infants.
   c. mothers of such babies tend to introduce them to solid food later.
   d. some of the nutrients in breast milk trigger hunger so that babies will consume more of it.

8. Infants can develop the signs of marasmus from (p. 182)
   a. excessive bottle-feeding.
   b. prolonged kwashiorkor.
   c. nonorganic failure to thrive resulting from lack of parental love.
   d. a diet too heavy in starch.

9. In classical conditioning, for learning to occur, (p. 184)
   a.   a conditioned stimulus must produce an unconditioned response.
   b.   a neutral stimulus that does not lead to the reflex must be presented just before, or at about the same time as, the unconditioned stimulus.
   c.   extinction must cancel out all unconditioned responses.
   d.   the conditioned response must lead to a new reflex.

10. By focusing on how infants shift from a novelty preference to a familiarity preference, researchers use habituation to assess infants' (p. 185)
   a.   recent memory.
   b.   recall.
   c.   remote memory.
   d.   attention.

11. Ninety percent of infants achieve the motor skill of scribbling vigorously at about age _____ months. (p. 188)
   a.   9-16
   b.   9-17
   c.   10-19
   d.   10-21

12. According to dynamic systems theory, motor development cannot be genetically determined because it (p. 189)
   a.   is motivated by exploration and the desire to master new tasks.
   b.   results from instabilities in the system.
   c.   is too complex for human genetic patterning to encode.
   d.   is hardwired.

13. Among the Kipsigis of Kenya, babies tend to hold their heads up, sit alone, and walk earlier than North American babies because Kipsigi mothers (p. 190)
   a.   give babies more tummy time than North American mothers do.
   b.   deliberately teach these skills by seating very young babies in holes in the ground, with rolled blankets to keep them upright.
   c.   leave babies lying on their backs in cribs for long hours, while the mothers are doing their work.
   d.   encourage babies to scoot on their bottoms rather than crawl.

14. By 5 to 6 months, infants can reach for and grasp objects in a room that has been darkened during the reach. This skill suggests that (p. 191)
   a.   infants aim their reaching motions at an object through prereaching.
   b.   reaching is largely controlled by proprioception.
   c.   infants of that age have reached a higher level of cephalocaudal development.
   d.   reaching is a softly assembled skill.

15. Toilet training should be delayed until the months following the second birthday because (p. 192)
   a.   prior to that time, the stimulation of training could undermine the development of motor skills.
   b.   younger children are generally uninterested in bowel and bladder control.
   c.   after age 2, children have the motor development to manipulate their own diapers.
   d.   at that time, children can consistently identify signals from a full bladder and rectum.

16. ERP brain-wave recordings indicate that around 5 months, infants (p. 194)
   a.   prefer rhythmically distinct foreign languages as much as sounds of their native tongue.
   b.   become sensitive to syllable stress patterns in their own language.
   c.   start to screen out sounds not used in their native language.
   d.   cannot yet distinguish most sounds in their own language.

17. Statistical analysis helps babies learn language by enabling them to (p. 194)
    a. extract regularities from complex, continuous speech.
    b. learn rules of grammar.
    c. detect words that start with strong syllables.
    d. distinguish between their own language and a foreign one.

18. Motion provides important information about depth because it (p. 196)
    a. gives children binocular depth cues.
    b. enhances children's sensitivity to pictorial depth.
    c. helps children learn that objects are not flat but three-dimensional.
    d. enables children to perceive the visual cliff.

19. Not until around the middle of the first year can blind infants (p. 198)
    a. initiate meaningful contact with peers and caregivers.
    b. use sound as a precise clue to object location.
    c. explore their world through reaching and crawling.
    d. produce definite emotional expressions.

20. At 12 months, infants' pattern perception has developed to the point that they (p. 199)
    a. are more contrast sensitive than they were at 6 months.
    b. stare at a single, high-contrast feature in a pattern.
    c. can perceive subjective boundaries in patterns that are not really present.
    d. detect objects represented by incomplete drawings.

21. Habituation research has revealed that young infants (p. 201)
    a. possess only size constancy.
    b. see only two-dimensional objects.
    c. have both size and shape constancy at birth.
    d. perceive only the constantly shifting images that objects cast on their retina.

22. Intermodal perception engages our capacity for (p. 202)
    a. assembling varied sensory information into integrated wholes.
    b. object unity.
    c. size and shape constancy.
    d. depth perception.

23. Intermodal sensitivity advances perceptual development by (p. 202)
    a. helping infants to develop contrast sensitivity.
    b. making amodal properties stand out.
    c. enabling children to ignore distracting social cues.
    d. making infants' statistical speech analysis more precise.

24. According to the Gibsons' differentiation theory, infants search for invariant features because those (p. 202)
    a. have the greatest object unity.
    b. offer the richest array of intermodal relationships.
    c. have the simplest patterns.
    d. are the stable features in a constantly shifting perceptual world.

25. A baby's sensitivity to affordances makes his or her exploratory actions (p. 203)
    a. future oriented and largely successful.
    b. less likely to be overwhelmed by complex intermodal stimuli.
    c. more sensitive to invariant features.
    d. reactive and blundering until around age 18 months.

PRACTICE TEST #2

1. After birth, the cephalocaudal trend changes, so that by age 2 the (p. 167)
   a. arms and legs have grown faster than the hands and feet.
   b. head accounts for one-fifth of total body length.
   c. chest and trunk have grown faster than any other part of the body.
   d. legs account for one-third of total body length.

2. Beginning in the sixth week of pregnancy, (p. 167)
   a. the embryonic skeleton forms out of cartilage.
   b. epiphyses develop on the ends of the fetus' long bones.
   c. cartilage cells harden into bone.
   d. the growth of the skeleton gradually slows and does not begin again until after birth.

3. During the prenatal period, the neural tube produces more neurons than the brain will need because (p. 169)
   a. when synapses are formed, many surrounding neurons die to make room for the final structure.
   b. stimulation kills off many of the delicate fetal neurons.
   c. synaptic pruning returns many neurons to undifferentiated brain tissue.
   d. neurons not coated during the myelination process die.

4. The frontal lobes undergo the most extended period of development because they (p. 172)
   a. specialize through lateralization.
   b. are the least plastic areas of the cerebral cortex.
   c. become the region of the "left-brained" functions.
   d. are responsible for consciousness, reasoning, and other thought.

5. fMRI studies reveal that the left hemisphere of the cerebral cortex is better at (p. 172)
   a. composing complex speech.
   b. processing information in a holistic, integrative manner.
   c. dealing with information in a sequential, analytic way.
   d. recovering from severe trauma.

6. Researchers speculate that attempts to hasten experience-dependent brain growth with intensive early learning (p. 176)
   a. can, in some instances, produce smarter babies.
   b. may accelerate experience-expected brain growth.
   c. could overwhelm neural circuits, thereby reducing the brain's sensitivity to everyday experiences.
   d. would do little to change patterns of development established by millions of years of evolution.

7. Studies of cosleeping have revealed that the practice (p. 177)
   a. often leads to emotional dependence in children.
   b. does not reduce mothers' total sleep time.
   c. has declined dramatically in North America.
   d. is largely unrelated to culture.

8. When diet and health are adequate, rate of physical growth is largely determined by (p. 178)
   a. heredity.
   b. the pace of catch-up growth.
   c. cultural variations.
   d. environment.

9. Marasmus usually appears in the first year of life when (p. 181)
   a. the baby's diet is very low in protein.
   b. too much starch is introduced too early.
   c. a baby's mother is too malnourished to produce enough breast milk and bottle-feeding is also inadequate.
   d. the baby suffers prolonged iron-deficiency anemia.

10. In newborns, reinforcement of the sucking response occurs (p. 184)
    a. only in response to milk or another sweet liquid.
    b. in response to stimuli that produce interesting sights and sounds, as well as to food.
    c. in response to loud, sudden noises.
    d. in response to deprivation of food.

11. Many scientists believe that mirror neurons (p. 186)
    a. are the biological basis of certain complex social abilities, including imitation.
    b. produce automatic responses that decline with age.
    c. are what distinguishes humans from other primates, such as chimpanzees.
    d. cause infants to turn their heads in response to sounds.

12. In the acquisition of motor skills, large individual differences exist in the (p. 188)
    a. cephalocaudal trend.
    b. rate of progress.
    c. proximodistal trend.
    d. sequence of development.

13. The research of James Galloway and Esther Thelen confirms that the order in which motor skills develop depends on (p. 190)
    a. a predetermined proximodistal pattern.
    b. each baby's inherited traits.
    c. the rate of early gross motor development.
    d. the anatomy of the body part used, the surrounding environment, and the baby's efforts.

14. Infants' prereaching declines around age 7 weeks because at that point, (p. 190)
    a. experience teaches babies how to control their hand movements.
    b. the mirror neurons necessary for finer reaching have grown.
    c. babies begin to improve the eye movements involved in tracking and fixing on objects.
    d. babies gain greater control over their fingers.

15. By the end of the first year, infants shift from ulnar grasp to pincer grasp when they (p. 191)
    a. begin to coordinate their thumbs and index fingers.
    b. can reach for objects in a darkened room.
    c. close their fingers against their palms.
    d. start coordinating both hands to explore objects.

16. Around 6 to 7 months, infants (p. 193)
    a. develop a sense of musical phrasing.
    b. recognize the same melody when it is played in different keys.
    c. can make more discriminations in music than in human speech.
    d. can distinguish musical tunes on the basis of rhythmic patterns.

17. Studies of infants' discriminations of speech, faces, and music suggest that between 6 and 12 months, (p. 195)
    a. babies retain their sensitivity to virtually all speech sounds but narrow their focus to familiar faces and music.
    b. babies experience a sensitive period during which they are biologically prepared to focus on socially meaningful perceptual distinctions.
    c. learning slows across the domains of vision and hearing.
    d. these areas of perception are largely unaffected by experience or other environmental factors.

18. Depth perception is especially important for (p. 196)
    a. enhancing scanning.
    b. tracking moving objects.
    c. understanding the layout of the environment and guiding motor activity.
    d. developing mature color vision.

19. Crawling promotes sensitivity to depth information because (p. 197)
    a.   it keeps babies in a single posture so that they can master particular spatial relations.
    b.   it enhances babies' confidence and, therefore, further exploration of their world.
    c.   babies quickly learn that the visual cliff is an illusion.
    d.   babies gradually figure out how to use depth cues to detect the danger of falling.

20. Children with limited or no vision show impressive developmental rebounds when (p. 198)
    a.   language emerges.
    b.   they achieve "reaching on sound."
    c.   their gross motor skills permit crawling.
    d.   they learn to interpret the meaning of others' reactions through touch.

21. Between 2 and 4 months, infants' face perception develops to the point that they (p. 200)
    a.   can perceive emotional expressions as meaningful wholes.
    b.   become sensitive to pictorial cues.
    c.   prefer a complex facial pattern over other, equally complex patterns.
    d.   prefer photos of faces with eyes open and a direct gaze.

22. Infants master object unity before perception of an object's continuous path because (p. 200)
    a.   the former requires only size constancy.
    b.   the latter is a more challenging task.
    c.   to achieve the latter, the child must have achieved a high level of pattern perception.
    d.   infants' contrast sensitivity improves with age.

23. When babies detect amodal sensory properties, they (p. 202)
    a.   acquire information that overlaps two or more sensory systems.
    b.   focus on information from a single modality.
    c.   succeed in perceiving an object's continuous path of movement.
    d.   take in scattered sensory information that is difficult to assemble into a whole.

24. At 3 to 4 months, infants' intermodal perception is such that they can (p. 202)
    a.   make sense of complex amodal relationships.
    b.   reach for an object in a room that has been darkened during their reach.
    c.   reach for a sounding object in the dark.
    d.   match faces with voices on the basis of lip-voice synchrony.

25. According to the Gibsons' differentiation theory, babies detect complex patterns when they (p. 202)
    a.   focus on invariant features.
    b.   explore internal features by noticing stable relationships.
    c.   assemble amodal properties into coherent wholes.
    d.   achieve both size and shape constancy.

CHAPTER 6
COGNITIVE DEVELOPMENT
IN INFANCY AND TODDLERHOOD

BRIEF CHAPTER SUMMARY

According to Piaget, from earliest infancy, children actively build psychological structures, or schemes, as they manipulate and explore their world. The vast changes that take place in Piaget's sensorimotor stage are divided into six substages. By acting on the world, infants make strides in intentional behavior, mastery of object permanence, and physical reasoning. In the final substage, they transfer their action-based schemes to a mental level, and representation appears.

Alternative explanations for babies' amazing cognitive accomplishments include the core knowledge perspective, which holds that babies are born with a set of innate knowledge systems, or core domains of thought—"prewired" understandings that permit a ready grasp of new, related information and therefore support early, rapid development. However, this approach has not offered greater clarity than Piaget's theory on how biology and environment jointly produce cognitive change.

Research findings have yielded broad agreement that many cognitive changes of infancy are gradual and continuous, not abrupt and stagelike, and that various aspects of infant cognition change unevenly. These ideas form the basis for another major approach to cognitive development—information processing, which focuses on the development of mental strategies for storing and interpreting information. With age, infants' attention becomes more efficient and flexible, and memory improves and is supported by a capacity for mental representation. Findings on infant categorization indicate that young babies structure experience in adultlike ways.

Vygotsky's sociocultural theory emphasizes that cognitive development is socially mediated as adults help infants and toddlers master challenging tasks. More specifically, skilled partners aid the child in carrying out tasks within their zone of proximal development.

A variety of infant intelligence tests have been devised to measure individual differences in early mental development. Most predict later performance poorly, but tests that focus on speed of habituation and recovery to visual stimuli and on object permanence are better predictors because they assess factors, such as memory and quickness and flexibility of thinking, that underlie intelligent behavior at any age. Other powerful influences on intellectual progress are the home environment, child care, and early intervention for at-risk infants and toddlers.

Behaviorist and nativist theories provide sharply contrasting accounts of language development. The interactionist view emphasizes that innate abilities and environmental influences combine to produce children's extraordinary language achievements. During the first year, infants prepare for language in many ways. First words appear around 12 months, two-word utterances between 18 and 24 months. Substantial individual differences exist in rate and style of early language progress. Conversational give-and-take and the use of child-directed speech (a simplified form of parental language) support infants' and toddlers' efforts to become competent speakers.

LEARNING OBJECTIVES

After reading this chapter, you should be able to:

6.1 Describe Piaget's view of development, noting how schemes change over the course of development. (pp. 208–209)

6.2 Describe the major cognitive achievements of Piaget's sensorimotor stage. (pp. 209–212)

6.3 Discuss follow-up research on sensorimotor development and its implications for the accuracy of Piaget's theory. (pp. 212–216)

6.4   Describe the alternate views of cognitive development, including the core knowledge perspective. (pp. 216–219)

6.5   Describe the general structure of the information-processing system, explain how this approach differs from Piaget's perspective, and review the strengths and limitations of the information-processing theory of cognitive development. (pp. 220–221)

6.6   Discuss changes in attention, memory, and categorization that take place over the first two years. (pp. 221–226)

6.7   Explain how Vygotsky's concept of the zone of proximal development expands our understanding of early cognitive development. (pp. 227–228)

6.8   Describe the mental testing approach, the meaning of intelligence test scores, and the extent to which infant tests predict later performance. (pp. 228–231)

6.9   Discuss environmental influences on early mental development, including home, child care, and early interventions for at-risk infants and toddlers. (pp. 231–235)

6.10 Describe three theories of language development, indicating the emphasis each places on innate and environmental influences. (pp. 236–240)

6.11 Describe major milestones of language development in the first two years, individual differences, and ways adults can support infants' and toddlers' emerging capacities. (pp. 240–242)

6.12 Describe the characteristics of infants' first words and two-word phrases, and explain why language comprehension develops ahead of language production. (pp. 242–243)

6.13 Describe individual and cultural differences in early language development, including factors that influence these differences. (p. 244)

6.14 Explain how child-directed speech and conversation support early language development. (pp. 244–246)

STUDY QUESTIONS

Piaget's Cognitive-Developmental Theory

1.   During Piaget's _____ stage, which spans the first 2 years of life, infants and toddlers "think" with their eyes, ears, and hands. (p. 208)

Piaget's Ideas About Cognitive Change

1.   According to Piaget, specific psychological structures, or organized ways of making sense of experience called _____, change with age. (p. 208)

2.   Match the following terms with the appropriate description. (pp. 208–209)

_____ Creating new schemes or adjusting old ones to produce a better fit with the environment

_____ Taking new schemes, rearranging them, and linking them with other schemes to create an interconnected cognitive system

_____ Using current schemes to interpret the external world

_____ Building schemes through direct interaction with the environment

1. Adaptation
2. Assimilation
3. Accommodation
4. Organization

The Sensorimotor Stage

1. True or False: Piaget believed that infants already know a great deal about their world from the time they are born. (p. 209)

2. Match each of the following sensorimotor substages with its appropriate description. (pp. 209–212)

   _____ Infants' primary means of adapting to the environment is through reflexes   1. Substage 1
   _____ Infants engage in goal-directed behavior and begin to attain object permanence   2. Substage 2
   _____ Toddlers repeat behaviors with variation, producing new effects   3. Substage 3
   _____ Infants' adaptations are oriented toward their own bodies   4. Substage 4
   _____ Infants' attention begins to turn outward toward the environment   5. Substage 5
   _____ Toddlers gain the ability to create mental representations   6. Substage 6

3. Explain the differences between primary, secondary, and tertiary circular reactions. (pp. 210–211)

   Primary: _____

   _____

   Secondary: _____

   _____

   Tertiary: _____

   _____

4. The ability to coordinate schemes deliberately to solve simple problems is called _____.
   (p. 210)

5. The understanding that objects continue to exist when out of sight is called _____.
   (p. 210)

6. Describe the *A-not-B search error.* (p. 211)

   _____

   _____

7. Our most powerful mental representations are of two kinds: (p. 211)

   A. _____

   B. _____

8. Describe three new capacities that result from the ability to create mental representations. (pp. 211–212)

   A. _____

   _____

   B. _____

   _____

   C. _____

   _____

Follow-Up Research on Infant Cognitive Development

1. Many studies show that infants understand concepts (earlier / later) than Piaget believed. (p. 211)

2. Explain the *violation-of-expectation method,* which is often used by researchers to identify infants' grasp of object permanence and other aspects of physical reasoning. (p. 212)

_____

_____

_____

_____

3. Explain why the violation-of-expectation method is controversial. (p. 212)

_____

_____

_____

4. Briefly summarize the controversial new evidence on object permanence in infancy, including Renée Baillageon's studies, as well as those seeking to confirm or refute her findings. (pp. 212–213)

_____

_____

_____

_____

5. True or False: Around 14 months, toddlers demonstrate a thorough understanding of hidden objects. (p. 213)

6. True or False: Infants demonstrate the A-not-B search error because of memory deficits; that is, they cannot remember an object's new location after it has been hidden in more than one place. (pp. 213–214)

7. Mastery of object permanence is a (gradual / sudden) achievement. (p. 214)

8. True or False: Laboratory research on deferred imitation supports Piaget's conclusion that infants cannot mentally represent experience until about 18 months of age. Provide evidence to support your response. (pp. 214–215)

_____

_____

_____

9. By 10 to 12 months of age, infants can solve problems by _____, meaning that they take a strategy from one problem and apply it to other relevant problems. (p. 215)

Evaluation of the Sensorimotor Stage

1. True or False: Recent research indicates that the cognitive attainments of infancy do, in fact, follow the neat, stepwise progression that Piaget postulated. (p. 216)

2. According to the _____ perspective, babies are born with a set of innate knowledge systems, or core domains of thought. (p. 217)

3. Cite four domains of thought studied by core knowledge theorists. (p. 217)

A. _____   B. _____

C. _____   D. _____

4. Summarize criticisms of the core knowledge perspective. (p. 217)

_____

_____

_____

5. True or False: The core knowledge perspective acknowledges that experience is essential for children to extend their initial knowledge. (p. 217)

6. Follow-up research on Piaget's sensorimotor stage yields broad agreement on two issues. Describe them. (p. 217)

A. _____

_____

B. _____

_____

Biology and Environment: Do Infants Have Built-In Numerical Knowledge?

1. According to the core knowledge perspective, what factors help infants advance their inherited foundation of knowledge? (p. 218)

_____

_____

2. What do research findings on infants' knowledge of numbers reveal? Why are these findings controversial? (p. 218)

A. _____

_____

B. _____

_____

Information Processing

1. In what ways do *information-processing* researchers agree with Piaget's theory? (p. 220)

_____

Structure of the Information-Processing System

1. Describe the three basic parts of the information-processing system, noting ways in which mental strategies can facilitate storage and retrieval at each level. (pp. 220–221)

Sensory Register: _____

_____

_____

Working Memory: _____

_____

_____

Long-term Memory: _____

_____

_____

2.   Explain the role of the *central executive* in managing the complex activities of the working memory system. (p. 221)

_____

_____

3.   *Long-term memory* has a(n) (limited / unlimited) capacity. (p. 221)

4.   Information-processing researchers believe that the (structure / capacity) of the human mental system is similar throughout life. (p. 221)

Attention

1.   List three ways in which attention improves during infancy. (pp. 221–222)

   A.   _____

   B.   _____

   C.   _____

2.   Cite one change in attention that occurs during the toddler years. (p. 222)

_____

3.   Explain how adults can foster sustained attention during infancy and toddlerhood. (p. 222)

_____

_____

Memory

1.   Explain how researchers use operant conditioning to study infant memory. (p. 222)

_____

_____

_____

2.   True or False: From the first few months of life, infant memory for operant responses is independent of context, meaning that infants apply learned responses to relevant new situations. (p. 222)

3.   True or False: Habituation/recovery research confirms that infants need to be physically active to acquire new information. Briefly explain your response. (p. 223)

_____

_____

4.   Distinguish between *recognition* and *recall* memory. (p. 223)

   Recognition: _____

   Recall: _____

5.   Can infants engage in recall? Explain, citing at least one example. (p. 223)

   A.   _____

   B.   _____

Biology and Environment: Infantile Amnesia

1. What is *infantile amnesia*? (p. 224)

   _____

   _____

2. Recall of personally meaningful one-time events from both the recent and distant past is called _____ *memory*. (pp. 224)

3. Provide two explanations for infantile amnesia. (p. 224)

   A. _____

   _____

   B. _____

   _____

4. Explain how the phenomenon of infantile amnesia can be reconciled with infants' and toddlers' remarkable memory skills. (p. 224)

   _____

   _____

   _____

5. Discuss two developments that contribute to the end of infantile amnesia. (pp. 224–225)

   A. _____

   _____

   B. _____

   _____

Categorization

1. Explain how categorization helps infants make sense of experience. (p. 224)

   _____

   _____

2. The earliest categories are _____, or based on similar overall appearance or prominent object part. By the second half of the first year, more categories are _____, or based on common function and behavior. (p. 225)

3. Briefly explain how the perceptual-to-conceptual change takes place. (pp. 225–226)

   _____

   _____

   _____

Evaluation of Information-Processing Findings

1. Information-processing research underscores the (continuity / discontinuity) of human thinking from infancy into adulthood. (p. 226)

2. In what way does information-processing research challenge Piaget's view of early cognitive development? (p. 226)

   _____

   _____

3. What is the greatest drawback of the information-processing approach to cognitive development? (p. 226)

   _____

   _____

The Social Context of Early Cognitive Development

1. According to Vygotsky's sociocultural theory, how do children learn to master activities and think in culturally meaningful ways? (p. 227)

   _____

   _____

2. Explain Vygotsky's concept of the *zone of proximal development,* emphasizing the role of adults in fostering children's cognitive development. (p. 227)

   _____

   _____

   _____

3. Explain how cultural variations in social experiences influence children's mental strategies. (pp. 227–228)

   _____

   _____

   _____

Cultural Influences: Social Origins of Make-Believe Play

1. Briefly summarize Vygotsky's view of make-believe play. (p. 229)

   _____

   _____

2. Explain why adults' participation in toddlers' make-believe play is so important. (p. 229)

   _____

   _____

   _____

3. True or False: In some cultures, such as Indonesia and Mexico, make-believe play is more frequent and complex with older siblings than with mothers. (p. 229)

Individual Differences in Early Mental Development

1. How does the mental testing approach differ from the cognitive theories discussed earlier in this chapter? (p. 228)

_____

_____

_____

Infant Intelligence Tests

1. What types of responses are tapped by most infant intelligence tests? (pp. 228–229)

_____

_____

_____

2. One commonly used infant test is the _____ *Scales of Infant Development,* designed for children between 1 month and 3 ½ years. (p. 230)

3. Intelligence tests are scored by computing a(n) _____, which indicates the extent to which the raw score deviates from the typical performance of same-age individuals. (p. 230)

4. In constructing intelligence tests, designers engage in _____, giving the tests to a large, representative sample and using the results as the standard for interpreting scores. (p. 230)

5. What is a *normal distribution*? (p. 230)

_____

_____

6. When intelligence tests are standardized, the mean IQ is set at _____. (p. 230)

7. True or False: Scores on infant intelligence tests are excellent predictors of later intelligence. Why or why not? (pp. 230–231)

_____

_____

_____

8. Due to concerns that infant test scores do not tap the same dimensions of intelligence measured at older ages, they are labeled _____, or _____, rather than IQs. (p. 231)

9. For what purpose are infant intelligence tests largely used? (p. 231)

_____

_____

10. Why do habituation and recovery and Piagetian object-permanence tasks predict later IQ more effectively than traditional infant intelligence tests? (p. 231)

_____

_____

Early Environment and Mental Development

1. What is the *Home Observation for Measurement of the Environment* (HOME)? What factors does the HOME measure? (pp. 231–232)

    A. _____

    _____

    B. _____

    _____

2. Regardless of SES and ethnicity, what aspects measured by HOME predict better language and IQ scores in toddlerhood and early childhood? (p. 231)

    _____

    _____

    _____

3. Cite ways in which both heredity and home environment contribute to mental test scores. (pp. 231–232)

    Heredity: _____

    _____

    Home environment: _____

    _____

4. Today, more than _____ percent of North American mothers with children under age 2 are employed. (p. 232)

5. Discuss the impact of low- versus high-quality child care on mental development. (pp. 232–233)

    Low-quality: _____

    _____

    High-quality: _____

    _____

6. Describe the overall condition of child care for infants and toddlers in the United States and Canada. (p. 233)

    _____

    _____

    _____

7. In the United States, child-care settings that serve (low-SES / middle-SES) families provide the very worst care. Briefly explain your response. (p. 233)

    _____

    _____

8. List and briefly describe at least four signs of *developmentally appropriate practice* in infant and toddler child care. (p. 234)

    A. _____

    B. _____

    C. _____

    D. _____

Early Intervention for At-Risk Infants and Toddlers

1. Describe center- and home-based interventions for infants and toddlers. (p. 234)

   Center-based: _____

   _____

   _____

   Home-based: _____

   _____

   _____

2. Discuss the effectiveness of early intervention programs with relation to infant and toddler mental development. (pp. 234–235)

   _____

   _____

3. Briefly describe the Carolina Abecedarian Project, and summarize the outcomes of this program. (p. 235)

   A. _____

   _____

   B. _____

   _____

4. What is Early Head Start? Cite three services available through Early Head Start. (p. 235)

   A. _____

   B. _____

   C. _____

   D. _____

Language Development

1. On average, children say their first word at _____ months of age. (p. 236)

Three Theories of Language Development

1. According to the behaviorist perspective, what two processes account for early language acquisition, and how do they do so? (pp. 236–237)

   A. _____

   _____

   B. _____

   _____

2. Why is the behaviorist perspective an incomplete explanation of early language development? (p. 237)

   _____

   _____

3. Discuss Chomsky's nativist perspective of language acquisition, noting how this approach differs from the behaviorist perspective. Be sure to explain the *language acquisition device* (LAD) in your response. (p. 237)

_____

_____

_____

_____

4. Provide evidence supporting Chomsky's view that human infants are biologically primed to acquire language. (p. 237)

_____

_____

_____

5. Name the two language-specific areas of the brain, and cite the function of each. (pp. 237–238)

   A. _____

   _____

   B. _____

   _____

6. True or False: If the left-hemispheric region is injured in the early years, other regions of the brain take over its language function. Briefly explain your response. (p. 238)

   _____

   _____

7. True or False: Research supports the idea that there is a biologically based sensitive period for language development. (p. 238)

8. Is acquiring a second language harder after a sensitive period has passed? Explain. (p. 239)

   _____

   _____

   _____

9. List two challenges to Chomsky's theory. (p. 239)

   A. _____

   B. _____

10. Summarize two views of the interactionist perspective of language development. (pp. 239–240)

   Information-processing perspective: _____

   _____

   Social-interaction perspective: _____

   _____

Getting Ready to Talk

1. At around 2 months of age, infants begin to make vowel-like noises called _____. At around 4 months of age, _____ appears, in which infants repeat consonant–vowel combinations in long strings. (p. 240)

2. What does research on deaf-born infants reveal about an early sensitive period for language development? (pp. 240–241)

_____

_____

_____

3. Describe *joint attention,* and indicate how it contributes to early language development. (p. 241)

A. _____

_____

B. _____

_____

4. Explain how caregivers can support conversational give-and-take in babies. (p. 241)

_____

_____

5. At the end of the first year, infants use _____ gestures to attract attention and interest of adults and to influence their behavior. How do these gestures contribute to language development? (p. 242)

_____

_____

First Words

1. Briefly describe the nature of toddlers' first words (for example, to which subjects do these words commonly refer?) (p. 242)

_____

_____

_____

2. True or False: Emotion influences early word learning. (p. 242)

3. When young children learn new words, they tend to make two types of errors. Name and describe each error, and provide an example of each. (p. 242)

A. _____

_____

_____

B. _____

_____

_____

The Two-Word Utterance Phase

1. List three developments that support rapid vocabulary growth during toddlerhood. (pp. 242–243)

A. _____

B. _____

C. _____

2. Explain the nature of *telegraphic speech*. (p. 243)

_____

_____

_____

Comprehension versus Production

1. Distinguish between language *comprehension* and language *production*. (p. 243)

Comprehension: _____

_____

Production: _____

_____

2. (Comprehension / Production) requires that children *recognize* only the meaning of a word, but for (comprehension / production) children must *recall* not only the word, but also the concept for which it stands. (p. 243)

Individual and Cultural Differences

1. True or False: Early vocabulary development proceeds at about the same rate for boys and girls. (p. 244)

2. Explain how a child's environment influences language development. (p. 244)

_____

_____

_____

3. Distinguish between *referential* and *expressive* styles of early language learning. (p. 244)

Referential: _____

_____

Expressive: _____

_____

4. (Expressive / Referential) style is associated with faster vocabulary development. (p. 244)

5. Cite factors that influence the development of referential and expressive styles. (p. 244)

_____

_____

Supporting Early Language Development

1. Describe three ways in which caregivers can support early language learning. (p. 245)

A. _____

B. _____

C. _____

2. Describe the characteristics of *child-directed speech*, noting how it promotes language development. (p. 245)

    _____

    _____

    _____

3. True or False: Parent–toddler conversation strongly predicts early language development and academic success during the school years. (p. 245)

**Social Issues: Education: Parent–Child Interaction:
Impact on Language and Cognitive Development of Deaf Children**

1. True or False: Over 90 percent of deaf children have hearing parents who are fluent in sign language. (p. 246)

2. Describe outcomes for children who have hearing parents not fluent in sign language. (p. 246)

    _____

    _____

    _____

3. Discuss differences in parent–child communication experienced by deaf children of hearing parents and deaf children of deaf parents. (p. 246)

    _____

    _____

    _____

ASK YOURSELF . . .

For *Ask Yourself* questions for this chapter, along with feedback on the accuracy of your answers, please log on to MyDevelopmentLab (for registration and access, please visit mydevelopmentlab.com or follow the directions on p. ix).

1) Select the Chapter of the *Ask Yourself*.
2) Open the E-Book and select the Explore icon next to the *Ask Yourself*.
3) Complete questions and choose "Submit answers for grading" or "Clear Answers" to start over.

SUGGESTED STUDENT READINGS

Goldin-Meadow, S. (2005). *Hearing gesture: How our hands help us think*. Cambridge, MA: Harvard University Press. Presents up-to-date research on the meaning and importance of nonverbal behaviors in learning and communication. The author maintains that understanding children's gestures has significant implications for supporting their language development and other aspects of learning.

Lombardi, J., & Bogle, M. M. (Eds.). (2004). *The promise of Early Head Start for American's youngest children*. Washington, DC: Zero to Three. Provides a thorough overview of Early Head Start, including services offered to children and families, the importance of early learning experiences for infants and toddlers, and current research on early intervention.

Posner, M. I., & Rothbart, M. K. (2006). *Educating the human brain*. Washington, DC: American Psychological Association. Presents 25 years of research on early cognitive development, including attention, self-regulation, the relationship between emotion and cognition, and ways parents and educators can foster early learning.

PUZZLE 6.1 TERM REVIEW

Across

1. _____ distribution: a bell-shaped distribution that results when individual differences are measured in large samples

4. Mental _____: procedures that operate on and transform information, thereby increasing the efficiency of thinking and the chances that information will be retained

5. _____, or short-term, memory: conscious part of memory where we actively work on a limited amount of information

6. _____, or goal-directed, behavior is a sequence of actions in which schemes are deliberately combined to solve a problem

7. The _____ register is the part of the mental system in which sights and sounds are held until they decay or are transferred to short-term memory

8. In Piaget's theory, a specific structure, or organized way of making sense of experience, that changes with age

11. The ability to remember and copy the behavior of a model who is not immediately present is known as _____ imitation

12. Object _____: understanding that objects still exist even when they are out of sight

16. A special part of working memory that directs the flow of information (2 words)

17. When infants stumble onto a new experience caused by their own motor activity and then try to repeat the event again and again, they are exhibiting a _____ reaction

18. Process of building new schemes through direct contact with the environment

19. _____-_____ memory: contains our permanent knowledge base

20. Infantile _____: the inability of most people to recall events that happened to them before age 3

21. Type of memory that involves noticing whether a new experience is identical to or similar to a previous one

22. _____-_____-_____ search error: if an object is moved from hiding place A to hiding place B, 8- to 12- month-old infants will search only in the first hiding place

23. _____ knowledge perspective: babies are born with a set of innate knowledge systems

Down

2. The external world is represented in terms of current schemes

3. The practice of giving an intelligence test to a large, representative sample, which serves as the standard for interpreting individual scores

9. Violation-of-_____ method: researchers habituate infants to an event and then determine whether they recover to a possible event or an impossible event

10. Mental _____: internal image of an absent object or past event

13. The internal arrangement and linking together of schemes so that they form a strongly interconnected cognitive system

14. New schemes are created and old ones adjusted to produce a better fit with the environment

15. Piaget's first stage, during which infants and toddlers "think" with their eyes, ears, and hands

21. Type of memory that involves remembering something in the absence of perceptual support

PUZZLE 6.2 TERM REVIEW

Across

1. In language development, the words and word combinations that children use
3. _____ attention: the child attends to the same object or event as the caregiver, who offers verbal information
6. Zone of _____ development: range of tasks that a child cannot yet handle independently but can accomplish with the help of more skilled partners
10. Pleasant vowel-like noises made by infants
12. Early language error in which words are applied too narrowly
13. _____ quotient: a score on an infant intelligence test; based primarily on perceptual and motor responses
15. Early language error in which words are applied too narrowly, to a wider collection of objects and events than is appropriate
16. Repetition of consonant-vowel combinations in long strings
17. Type of play in which children pretend, acting out everyday and imaginary images
18. Form of speech marked by high-pitched, exaggerated expression, clear pronunciations, and distinct pauses between speech segments (2 words, hyph.)
19. In language development, the words and word combinations that children understand

20. Standards devised by NAEYC that specify program characteristics that meet the developmental and individual needs of young children are called _____ appropriate practice

Down

2. _____ quotient: a score that permits an individual's performance on an intelligence test to be compared to the performances of other same-age individuals
4. _____ speech: toddlers' two-word utterances that leave out smaller and less important words
5. Style of early language learning in which toddlers use language mainly to talk about feelings and needs
7. Style of early language learning in which toddlers use language mainly to label objects
8. Area of the brain responsible for interpreting language
9. Checklist for gathering information about the quality of children's home lives (abbr.)
11. _____ memory: narrative accounts of significant, one-time events that are long-lasting because they are imbued with personal meaning
14. Area of the brain that controls language production
21. Innate system that permits children to speak in a rule-oriented fashion as soon as they learn enough words (abbr.)

PRACTICE TEST #1

1. According to Piaget, at times when children are not changing much, they (p. 208)
   a. adapt through equilibrium.
   b. assimilate more than they accommodate.
   c. shift from assimilation to accommodation.
   d. accommodate to disequilibrium.

2. According to Piaget, in the second year, the circular reaction (p. 209)
   a. enters the tertiary substage.
   b. centers around the child's body.
   c. declines because it is no longer adaptive.
   d. becomes experimental and creative.

3. Because infants in Piaget's Substage 4 can better anticipate events, they (p. 211)
   a. try to use their capacity for intentional behavior to change those events.
   b. no longer make the A-not-B search error.
   c. repeat events caused by their own behaviors.
   d. repeat behaviors with variation.

4. Some critics of the violation-of-expectation method of research believe that it (p. 212)
   a. does not take make-believe play into account.
   b. reveals babies' limited capacity to assimilate many new experiences.
   c. indicates only limited awareness of physical events.
   d. merely confirms the effects of deferred imitation.

5. Recent studies of deferred imitation and problem solving reveal that (p. 214)
   a. toddlers do not imitate rationally until about 18 months.
   b. deferred imitation is present as early as 6 weeks of age.
   c. infants lead purely sensorimotor lives.
   d. babies use representational thought at birth.

6. Contrary to Piaget, core knowledge theorists argue that (p. 217)
   a. babies construct all mental representations through sensorimotor activity.
   b. the violation-of-expectation method reveals very little about babies' cognitive abilities.
   c. babies begin life with a limited set of biases for attending to certain information.
   d. babies are born with a set of innate knowledge systems that permit a ready grasp of new, related information.

7. Follow-up studies of Piaget's sensorimotor stage have led researchers to (p. 217)
   a. reaffirm Piaget's basic model.
   b. agree that many cognitive changes in infancy are gradual and continuous.
   c. reject Piaget's description of the later sensorimotor substages.
   d. propose that various aspects of infant cognition develop together.

8. To aid retrieval of information from long-term memory, we (p. 221)
   a. categorize information as it is taken in.
   b. use the central executive to direct the flow of information.
   c. practice using it.
   d. associate it with particular mental strategies.

9. Information-processing researchers believe that the human mental system (p. 221)
   a. changes its structure through each stage of life.
   b. gradually comes to prefer long-term memory to working memory.
   c. enlarges its capacity throughout life.
   d. is due almost entirely to brain development.

10. In toddlerhood, sustained attention typically improves because (p. 222)
    a.   attraction to novelty declines.
    b.   children attend to more aspects of the environment.
    c.   habituation time rises to 3 or 4 minutes.
    d.   children become long lookers.

11. Habituation research on infants' memory of actions confirms that (p. 223)
    a.   novelty preference is stronger than familiarity preference.
    b.   Piaget's model of sensorimotor development is essentially correct.
    c.   memory is context dependent.
    d.   infants need not be physically active to acquire new information.

12. Categorization allows infants to (p. 224)
    a.   reduce the huge amount of new information they encounter and thus make sense of experience.
    b.   successfully solve object permanence tasks.
    c.   increase the huge amount of new information they encounter and thus make sense of experience.
    d.   accurately sort objects by name, color, size, and function.

13. Vygotsky believed that complex mental activities, such as voluntary attention and deliberate memory, originate in (p. 227)
    a.   conditioning.
    b.   dynamic systems.
    c.   social interaction.
    d.   conceptual categories.

14. Of the following Bayley-III scales, which depends on parental report? (p. 230)
    a.   Adaptive Behavior
    b.   Cognitive
    c.   Language
    d.   Motor

15. Intelligence test designers reach the standard for interpreting scores by (p. 230)
    a.   computing how much the raw score deviates from the typical performance.
    b.   determining how scores cluster around the mean.
    c.   establishing the number of scales to be measured.
    d.   giving the test to a large, representative sample and using the results.

16. According to research findings, one of the best infant predictors of IQ from early childhood into adolescence is (p. 231)
    a.   developmental quotients.
    b.   habituation and recovery to novel visual stimuli.
    c.   the rate at which the infant becomes fatigued during testing.
    d.   the amount of fluctuation in IQ between infancy and toddlerhood.

17. The HOME correlational findings must be treated with caution because they (p. 231)
    a.   make too little of the genetic-environment correlation.
    b.   are based on too narrow of a sample.
    c.   do not account sufficiently for the association between home environment and mental test scores.
    d.   rely on developmental quotients that are too vague to be useful.

18. In the United States, children of middle-SES families tend to receive the poorest quality child care because (p. 233)
    a. their parents are especially likely to place them in for-profit centers where the quality of care is often low.
    b. very few U.S. child-care centers offer high-quality care.
    c. most of the families that use child care are in that socioeconomic category.
    d. these families are most likely to take advantage of underfunded public centers.

19. Children who participate in center-based interventions and home-based interventions (p. 234)
    a. showed greater intelligence gains in Canada than in the United States.
    b. tend to come from more organized homes than children who do not participate.
    c. mostly remain in the same SES as their parents.
    d. score higher on mental tests by age 2 than children who do not participate.

20. According to the behaviorist perspective, children acquire language (p. 237)
    a. through application of the universal grammar.
    b. by imitation and reinforcement.
    c. through the work of specialized language areas in the brain.
    d. at a sensitive period during childhood.

21. Social-interactionist theorists of language development argue that children (p. 240)
    a. learn language as their efforts to communicate cue caregivers to provide appropriate language experiences.
    b. make sense of complex language environments by applying general cognitive capacities.
    c. master intricate grammatical structures with little experimentation.
    d. learn language with the brain regions that also control social interaction.

22. Young children sometimes overextend words to groups of similar experiences because (p. 242)
    a. they are still learning to assimilate adults' intermodal perceptual cues.
    b. their understanding of word meanings is too narrow.
    c. they have difficulty recalling, or have not acquired, a suitable word.
    d. emotion still influences their word learning more than cognitive achievements.

23. Young children's comprehension of language precedes production because (p. 243)
    a. they can retrieve from their memories either the word or the concept for which it stands, but not both.
    b. they still rely on adults' perceptual cues.
    c. until about 18 months, underextension limits production.
    d. comprehension requires only that they recognize the meanings of words.

24. Effective CDS can stimulate children's language development by (p. 245)
    a. employing utterance length just ahead of the of the child's.
    b. urging the child to overextend and thus learn by error.
    c. moving the child beyond his or her zone of proximal development.
    d. discouraging joint attention while encouraging use of more complex sentences.

25. Ninety percent of deaf children experience delayed language development and have poor social skills in toddlerhood through middle childhood because (p. 246)
    a. schools are not sensitive to their needs.
    b. their parents are not fluent in sign language.
    c. they tend to develop extremely expressive styles to compensate for communication difficulties.
    d. caregivers tend to only communicate with them visually.

PRACTICE TEST #2

1. According to Piaget, schemes reach true equilibrium when they (p. 209)
   a. enter a period of rest, during which they do not adapt to the environment.
   d. shift from organization to accommodation.
   c. become part of a network of structures applicable to the surrounding world.
   d. connect with sensorimotor functions.

2. In Piaget's model, children move from primary circular reaction to secondary circular reaction when they (p. 210)
   a. begin trying to repeat interesting events caused by their own actions.
   b. move from actions unrelated to experience to repeating chance behaviors largely motivated by their basic needs.
   c. start forming goal-directed schemes.
   d. learn to master object permanence.

3. According to Piaget, children in Substage 6 (p. 211)
   a. repeat behaviors with variation.
   b. arrive at solutions suddenly through apparent mental representation.
   c. use invisible displacement to solve problems of deferred imitation.
   d. fully grasp everyday activities so that they no longer need to act them out.

4. Recent studies of infants and object permanence suggest that mastery of the skill (p. 214)
   a. occurs suddenly at Substage 3.
   b. is not clearly linked to physical changes in the brain.
   c. happens at a rate determined by the frequency of external stimulation.
   d. is a gradual achievement.

5. Recent studies of babies' problem solving (p. 215)
   a. suggest that children form flexible mental representations by the middle of the second year.
   b. confirm Piaget's argument that infants develop intentional means-end sequences around 7 to 8 months.
   c. reveal that by 10 to 12 months, infants can solve problems by analogy.
   d. indicate that children do not move beyond trial-and-error experimentation until the end of the second year.

6. Core knowledge theorists base their conclusions about built-in numerical knowledge on babies' (p. 218)
   a. ability to deal with less-than and greater-than relationships.
   b. looking preferences.
   c. sensorimotor responses to quantities of toys.
   d. cerebral cortex development.

7. Because the capacity of working memory is relatively restricted, (p. 221)
   a. we must use mental strategies to increase our chances of retaining information.
   b. it can process only limited amounts of information from the sensory register.
   c. it cannot connect more than a few pieces of information.
   d. we cannot automatically use information gathered through it.

8. Very young babies have long habituation times because they (p. 221)
   a. take in information almost exclusively through the sensory register.
   b. thoroughly scan complex designs.
   c. cannot yet anticipate events.
   d. have difficulty disengaging their attention from interesting stimuli.

9. Operant conditioning research has revealed that as babies grow older, their memory becomes increasingly (p. 223)
   a. linked to novel experience.
   b. free of the central executive.
   c. context free.
   d. dependent on the ability to repeat previously learned behavior.

10. During the second year, children become capable of long-term recall because (p. 223)
   a. they have achieved the capacity for recognition.
   b. new neural connections have grown among multiple regions of the cerebral cortex.
   c. their memory has become increasingly context dependent.
   d. they have acquired so much information through physical engagement with their environment.

11. Nearly all studies of infantile amnesia agree that the acquisition of autobiographical memory depends on the child's (p. 224)
   a. implicit memory.
   b. self-image.
   c. social experience.
   d. language development.

12. Language both builds on and fosters categorization by (p. 226)
   a. enlarging the infants' store of perceptual categories.
   b. making the process largely context-free.
   c. calling infants' attention to commonalities among objects.
   d. expanding infants' recognition of familiar experiences.

13. To overcome the weakness of the information-processing approach, researchers have (p. 226)
   a. applied the dynamic systems view to early cognition.
   b. detached it from Piaget's system of sensorimotor stages.
   c. analyzed recall into even smaller components.
   d. tried to trace stronger links between perception and attention.

14. A child approaching a task within his or her zone of proximal development needs (p. 227)
   a. fewer perceptual categories than a child not working within that zone.
   b. to create new schemes by acting on the physical world.
   c. the help of a more skilled partner.
   d. to represent his or her experiences as efficiently and meaningfully as possible.

15. Vygotsky's theory suggests that to promote children's make-believe play, parents and teachers should (p. 229)
   a. provide a stimulating environment.
   b. emulate the practices of collectivist societies.
   c. allow children complete freedom to pursue their inclinations.
   d. participate with children and guide them through such play.

16. Which of the following items would be included in the Bayley-III Cognitive Scale? (p. 230)
   a. Attention to familiar and unfamiliar objects
   b. Recognition of objects and people following simple directions
   c. Naming of objects and pictures
   d. Grasping, sitting, and stacking blocks

17. A child who does better than 50 percent of his or her agemates on an intelligence test has an IQ of (p. 230)
   a. 60.
   b. 85.
   c. 100.
   d. 130.

18. The quality of child care in the United States and Canada is affected by a macrosystem of (p. 233)
    a. high taxation and poor financial management.
    b. individualistic values and weak regulation.
    c. excessive government oversight.
    d. an overemphasis on the needs of immigrant children.

19. One criticism of Chomsky's nativist theory is that (p. 239)
    a. the assumption of innate grammatical knowledge does not fit with some important observations of actual language development.
    b. it does not take sufficient account of the effects of reinforcement.
    c. the idea of a universal grammar is based on the structures of Western languages so it does not actually apply universally.
    d. the grammatical rules are too general to provide sufficient explanations.

20. Interactionist theories of language development emphasize both (p. 239)
    a. brain development and Piaget's idea of deferred imitation.
    b. imitation and reinforcement.
    c. language areas in the brain and a sensitive period for language development.
    d. inner capacities and environmental influences.

21. Babies move from cooing to babbling when they (p. 240)
    a. recognize that adults respond favorably.
    b. want to make more unpleasant sounds.
    c. add consonants to vowels.
    d. reach age 2 months.

22. By the end of the first year, infants use preverbal gestures to (p. 242)
    a. establish joint attention with adults.
    b. attract adults' attention and interest and influence their behavior.
    c. make greater sense of babbling.
    d. avoid give-and-take with adults.

23. When children's vocabulary permits telegraphic speech, they (p. 243)
    a. focus on high-content words and omit smaller, less important ones.
    b. display a remarkable grasp of subtle grammatical rules.
    c. organize experience into simple categories.
    d. tend to use nouns more than verbs.

24. Children who develop referential-style language tend to (p. 244)
    a. be unusually shy.
    b. utter compressed phrases that sound like single words.
    c. have an especially active interest in exploring objects.
    d. be speakers of Asian languages.

25. Young children tend to prefer CDS over other kinds of adult talk because it (p. 245)
    a. helps them to develop expressive-style language.
    b. involves pleasant cooing and babbling.
    c. holds their interests with long sentences.
    d. builds on communication strategies such as joint attention, to which they already respond.

CHAPTER 7
EMOTIONAL AND SOCIAL DEVELOPMENT
IN INFANCY AND TODDLERHOOD

BRIEF CHAPTER SUMMARY

Erikson's psychosocial theory, which builds on Freud's psychoanalytic theory, provides an overview of the emotional and social tasks of infancy and toddlerhood. For Erikson, trust and autonomy grow out of warm, supportive parenting in the first year, followed by reasonable expectations for impulse control during the second year.

Emotions play an important role in the organization of relationships with caregivers, exploration of the environment, and discovery of the self. Infants' ability to express basic emotions, such as happiness, anger, sadness, and fear, and respond to the emotions of others expands over the first year. As toddlers become more self-aware, self-conscious emotions, such as shame, embarrassment, and pride, begin to emerge. Emotional self-regulation improves as a result of brain maturation, gains in cognition and language, and sensitive child rearing.

Children's unique temperaments, or styles of emotional responding, are already apparent in early infancy. Heredity influences early temperament, but child-rearing and other experiences determine whether a child's temperament is sustained or modified over time. The goodness-of-fit model helps explain the bidirectional relationship between children's temperaments and parents' child-rearing styles.

Ethological theory is the most widely accepted view of the development of attachment—the strong affectionate tie that develops between infants and caregivers. According to this perspective, attachment evolved over the history of our species to promote survival. Research shows that responding promptly, consistently, and appropriately to infant signals supports secure attachment, whereas insensitive caregiving is linked to attachment insecurity. Because children and parents are embedded in larger contexts, family circumstances and cultural factors influence attachment patterns. Parents' internal working models—their view of their own attachment experiences—also play a role. Infants form attachment bonds not only with their mothers but also with other familiar people, including fathers, and siblings. When grandparents serve as primary caregivers for children, strong attachment ties develop between them.

Though limited, peer sociability is already present in the first two years, and it is fostered by the early caregiver–child bond. Continuity of caregiving seems to play a role in the relationship between early attachment security or insecurity and later development.

Once self-awareness develops over the first and second year, it supports a diverse array of social and emotional achievements. Empathy, the ability to categorize the self, compliance, and self-control are all by-products of toddlers' emerging sense of self.

LEARNING OBJECTIVES

After reading this chapter, you should be able to:

7.1 Discuss the first two stages of Erikson's psychosocial theory, noting the personality changes that take place at each stage. (pp. 252–253)

7.2 Describe the development of basic emotions, including happiness, anger, sadness, and fear, over the first year, noting the adaptive function of each. (pp. 253–256)

7.3 Summarize changes that occur during the first two years in understanding others' emotions. (pp. 256–257)

7.4 Discuss the nature of self-conscious emotions, explaining why they emerge during the second year and indicating their role in development. (pp. 257–258)

7.5 Trace the development of emotional self-regulation during the first two years. (pp. 258–259)

7.6   Discuss the three underlying components of temperament, and identify three types of children described by Thomas and Chess. (pp. 260–261)

7.7   Explain how temperament is measured. (p. 262)

7.8   Summarize the role of heredity and environment in the stability of temperament, including the goodness-of-fit model. (pp. 262–267)

7.9   Describe the unique features of ethological theory of attachment. (pp. 268–270)

7.10   Describe the Strange Situation and the Attachment Q-sort procedures for measuring attachment, and cite the four patterns of attachment assessed by the Strange Situation. (pp. 270–272)

7.11   Discuss the factors that affect attachment security. (pp. 273–276)

7.12   Discuss infants' formation of multiple attachments, and indicate how attachment paves the way for early peer sociability. (pp. 276–281)

7.13   Describe and interpret the relationship between secure attachment in infancy and cognitive, emotional, and social competence in childhood. (pp. 281–283)

7.14   Trace the emergence of self-awareness in infancy and toddlerhood, along with the emotional and social capacities it supports. (pp. 283–287)

STUDY QUESTIONS

Erikson's Theory of Infant and Toddler Personality

Basic Trust versus Mistrust

1.   How did Erikson expand upon Freud's view of development during infancy? (p. 252)

_____

_____

2.   Based on Erikson's theory, summarize the psychological conflict of the first year, *basic trust versus mistrust*, and explain how it can be positively resolved. (p. 252)

Conflict: _____

_____

Resolution: _____

_____

Autonomy versus Shame and Doubt

1.   In what way did Erikson expand upon Freud's view of development during toddlerhood? (p. 252)

_____

_____

2.   Explain how the psychological conflict of toddlerhood, *autonomy versus shame and doubt,* is resolved favorably. (pp. 252–253)

_____

_____

Emotional Development

1. In line with the dynamic systems perspective, emotional expressions are (flexibly / rigidly) organized; they vary with the person's developing capacities, goals, and contexts. (p. 254)

2. What is the MAX system, and how does it help researchers analyze the range of infant emotions? (p. 254)

   A. _____

   B. _____

Development of Basic Emotions

1. Define the term *basic emotions,* and provide several examples. (p. 254)

   Definition: _____

   _____

   Examples: _____

   _____

2. True or False: Infants come into the world with the ability to express all of the basic emotions. (p. 254)

3. How does the dynamic systems perspective help us understand how basic emotions become clear and well-organized? (p. 254)

   _____

   _____

   _____

4. Explain how caregiver communication affects an infant's emotional development. (p. 254)

   _____

   _____

   _____

   _____

5. At approximately what age do infants' emotional expressi n   organized? (p. 254)

   _____

6. What is a *social smile,* and when does it develop? (p. 255)

   A. _____

   B. _____

7. Laughter, which appears around ____ to ____ months, reflects (faster / slower) processing of information than does smiling. (p. 255)

8. How do expressions of happiness change between early infancy and the end of the first year? (p. 255)

   _____

   _____

9. The frequency and intensity of infants' angry reactions (increase / decrease) with age. Why does this happen? (p. 255)

   _____

   _____

   _____

10. Describe the circumstances in which infants are likely to express sadness. (p. 255)

_____

_____

11. Fear reactions (increase / decrease) during the second half of the first year. (p. 256)

12. The most frequent expression of fear in infancy is to unfamiliar adults, a response called
    _____ *anxiety.* (p. 256)

13. Cite several factors that influence infants' and toddlers' reactions to strangers. (p. 256)

_____

_____

_____

_____

14. How does a *secure base* aid infants' exploration of the environment? (p. 256)

_____

_____

_____

Understanding and Responding to the Emotions of Others

1. Early on, babies respond to others' emotions through the fairly automatic process of emotional
   _____, in which they match the feeling tone of the caregiver in face-to-face communication.
   (p. 256)

2. Define *social referencing,* and explain its role in infant development. (p. 257)

   Definition: _____

   _____

   Role: _____

   _____

   _____

3. At what age do infants understand that others' emotional reactions may differ from their own? (p. 257)

   _____

Emergence of Self-Conscious Emotions

1. What are *self-conscious emotions*? (p. 257)

   _____

   _____

2. Cite several examples of self-conscious emotions. (p. 257)

   _____

3. Besides self-awareness, what ingredient is required in order for children to experience self-conscious emotions?
   (p. 257)

   _____

4. True or False: The situations in which adults encourage children's expressions of self-conscious emotions vary
   from culture to culture. (p. 258)

Beginnings of Emotional Self-Regulation

1. Define *emotional self-regulation.* (p. 258)

   _____

   _____

2. Explain how caregivers contribute to children's style of emotional self-regulation. (pp. 258–259)

   _____

   _____

3. By the end of the second year, gains in representation and language lead to new ways of regulating emotion. Explain how this occurs. (p. 259)

   _____

   _____

   _____

Development of Temperament

1. Define *temperament,* and provide an example of a temperamental trait. (p. 260)

   A. _____

   _____

   B. _____

2. Cite two important findings from the New York longitudinal study of temperament. (p. 260)

   A. _____

   _____

   B. _____

   _____

The Structure of Temperament

1. List and describe five of the nine dimensions of personality outlined in Thomas and Chess's model of temperament. (p. 261)

   A. _____

   _____

   B. _____

   _____

   C. _____

   _____

   D. _____

   _____

   E. _____

   _____

2. List and describe the three types of children identified by Thomas and Chess. (p. 260)

   A. _____

   _____

   B. _____

   _____

   C. _____

   _____

3. True or False: All children fit into one of the three temperament categories described above. (p. 260)

4. Of the three styles of temperament, the _____ pattern places children at highest risk for adjustment problems. (p. 260)

5. Cite six dimensions of temperament identified by Mary Rothbart. (p. 261)

   A. _____

   B. _____

   C. _____

   D. _____

   E. _____

   F. _____

6. Define *effortful control,* and explain why it is important. (p. 261)

   A. _____

   _____

   B. _____

   _____

Measuring Temperament

1. Discuss the advantages and disadvantages of using parent reports to assess children's temperament. (p. 262)

   Advantages: _____

   _____

   _____

   Disadvantages: _____

   _____

   _____

2. Most physiological assessments of temperament have focused on _____ children, who react negatively to and withdraw from novel stimuli, and _____ children, who display positive emotion to and approach novel stimuli. (p. 262)

Biology and Environment: Development of Shyness and Sociability

1. What percentage of children identified as displaying extremes in shyness and sociability retain their temperamental style as they get older? (p. 263)

_____

2. What area of the brain does Kagan believe contributes to individual differences in arousal? (p. 263)

_____

_____

3. Discuss four physiological correlates of approach–withdrawal behavior. (p. 263)

A. _____

B. _____

C. _____

D. _____

4. Heritability research indicates that genes contribute (modestly / substantially) to shyness and sociability. (p. 263)

5. Explain how child-rearing practices affect the chances that an emotionally reactive baby will become a fearful child. (p. 263)

_____

_____

_____

Stability of Temperament

1. True or False: Temperamental stability from one age period to the next is generally low to moderate. (p. 262)

2. Long-term predictions about early temperament are best achieved after age _____, when styles of responding are better established. (p. 262)

3. True or False: Child rearing plays an important role in modifying biologically based temperamental traits. (p. 264)

Genetic Influences

1. Research shows that identical twins (are / are not) more similar than fraternal twins in temperament and personality. (p. 264)

2. Describe ethnic and sex differences in early temperament. (p. 264)

Ethnic: _____

_____

Sex: _____

_____

Environmental Influences

1. Explain how child rearing contributes to ethnic and sex differences in temperament. (p. 265)

_____

_____

_____

2. Explain how children reared in the same family develop distinct temperamental styles. (pp. 265–266)

_____

_____

_____

3. Both identical and fraternal twins tend to become (increasingly / decreasingly) similar from one another over time. (p. 266)

Temperament and Child Rearing: The Goodness-of-Fit Model

1. Describe the *goodness-of-fit* model. (p. 266)

_____

_____

2. How does the goodness-of-fit model help to explain why children with difficult temperaments are at high risk for future adjustment problems? (p. 266)

_____

_____

_____

3. Explain how cultural values and life conditions affect the fit between parenting and child temperament. (pp. 266–267)

_____

_____

_____

Development of Attachment

1. Define *attachment*. (p. 268)

_____

_____

2. True or False: Both psychoanalytic and behaviorist theories emphasize feeding as an important context in which infants and caregivers build a close emotional bond. (p. 268)

3. How did research on rhesus monkeys challenge the idea that attachment depends on hunger satisfaction? (p. 268)

_____

_____

Bowlby's Ethological Theory

1. True or False: The *ethological theory of attachment*, which recognizes attachment as an evolved response that promotes survival, is the most widely accepted view of the infant's emotional tie to the caregiver. (p. 269)

2. Match each phase of attachment with the appropriate description. (pp. 269–270)

   _____ Attachment to the familiar caregiver is evident, and infants display separation anxiety.

   _____ Infants are not yet attached to their mother and do not mind being left with an unfamiliar adult.

   _____ Separation anxiety declines as children gain an understanding of the parent's comings and goings and can predict his/her return.

   _____ Infants start to respond differently to a familiar caregiver than to a stranger.

   1. Preattachment phase
   2. "Attachment-in-the-making" phase
   3. "Clear-cut" attachment phase
   4. Formation of a reciprocal relationship

3. What is an *internal working model,* and how does it relate to personality? (p. 270)

   A. _____

   _____

   B. _____

   _____

Measuring the Security of Attachment

1. The _____, designed by Mary Ainsworth, is the most widely used laboratory technique for measuring the quality of attachment between 1 and 2 years of age. (p. 270)

2. Provide a brief description of the *Strange Situation.* (p. 270)

   _____

   _____

   _____

   _____

3. Match each of the following attachment classifications with the appropriate description. (pp. 270–271)

   _____ Before separation, these infants seek closeness to the parent and fail to explore. When she returns, they display angry behaviors, may continue to cry after being picked up, and cannot be easily comforted.

   _____ Before separation, these infants use the parent as a base from which to explore. They are upset by the parent's absence, and they seek contact and are easily comforted when she returns.

   _____ Before separation, these infants seem unresponsive to the parent. When she leaves, they react to the stranger in much the same way as to the parent. Upon her return, they are slow to greet her.

   _____ When the parent returns, these infants show confused, contradictory behaviors, such as looking away while being held.

   1. Secure
   2. Avoidant
   3. Resistant
   4. Disorganized/ disoriented

4. The *Attachment* _____ is an alternative to the Strange Situation for measuring attachment in children between 1 and 5 years of age. Briefly describe this method. (p. 271)

   _____

   _____

   _____

Stability of Attachment

1. Describe the link between SES and children's attachment security. (p. 272)

    _____

    _____

    _____

2. (Securely / Insecurely) attached babies are more likely to maintain their attachment status. Cite one exception to this trend. (p. 272)

    _____

Cultural Variations

1. Cite at least one example of how cultural variations in child rearing affect attachment security. (p. 272)

    _____

    _____

Factors That Affect Attachment Security

1. List four important influences that affect attachment security. (p. 273)

    A. _____

    B. _____

    C. _____

    D. _____

2. True or False: Adoption research shows that children can develop a first attachment bond as late as 4 to 6 years of age. (p. 273)

3. True or False: *Sensitive caregiving*—responding promptly, consistently, and appropriately to infants and holding them tenderly—is moderately related to attachment security in both biological and adoptive mother-infant pairs and in diverse cultures and SES groups. (p. 273)

4. Describe differences in caregiving experienced by securely attached and insecurely attached infants. (p. 273)

    Securely attached: _____

    _____

    _____

    Insecurely attached: _____

    _____

    _____

5. Describe *interactional synchrony*. (p. 274)

    _____

    _____

    _____

6. True or False: Moderate adult-infant coordination is a better predictor of attachment security than "tight" coordination, in which the adult responds to most infant cues. Briefly explain your response. (p. 274)

_____

_____

7. Among maltreated infants, _____ attachment is especially high. (p. 274)

8. Explain why children's characteristics do not show strong relationships with attachment security. (p. 275)

_____

_____

_____

9. Explain how family circumstances, such as job loss, a failing marriage, or financial difficulties, affect infant attachment. (pp. 275–276)

_____

_____

_____

10. Summarize the relationship between parents' childhood experiences and the quality of attachment with their own children. Based on this information, do our early rearing experiences destine us to become sensitive or insensitive parents? Explain. (p. 276)

A. _____

_____

B. _____

_____

Social Issues: Health: Does Child Care in Infancy Threaten Attachment Security and Later Adjustment?

1. True or False: American infants placed in full-time child care before 12 months of age are more likely than home-reared infants to display insecure attachments. (p. 277)

2. Summarize three factors that influence the relationship between child care and attachment quality. (p. 277)

A. _____

_____

B. _____

_____

C. _____

_____

3. Based on findings from the NICHD Study of Early Child Care, describe factors that contribute to higher rates of attachment insecurity. (p. 277)

A. _____

B. _____

C. _____

4. List three ways child-care settings can foster attachment security. (p. 277)

    A. _____

    B. _____

    C. _____

Multiple Attachments

1. Describe how mothers and fathers differ in the way they relate to and interact with babies, and discuss how these patterns are changing due to the revised work status of women. (p. 278)

    Mothers: _____

    _____

    Fathers: _____

    _____

    Work status: _____

    _____

2. Explain how fathers' involvement with babies affects family attitudes and relationships. (p. 278)

    _____

    _____

3. In which ethnic groups are grandparents most likely to assume the parenting role? Explain why. (pp. 278–279)

    _____

    _____

4. True or False: Grandparents tend to assume the parenting role under highly stressful life circumstances. Explain your answer. (pp. 278, 280)

    _____

    _____

    _____

5. When a new baby arrives, how is a preschool-age sibling likely to respond? Include both positive and negative reactions in your answer. (p. 280)

    Positive: _____

    _____

    Negative: _____

    _____

6. Discuss four ways in which mothers can promote positive relationships between infants and their preschool-age siblings. (p. 281)

A. _____

_____

B. _____

_____

C. _____

_____

D. _____

_____

Cultural Influences: The Powerful Role of Paternal Warmth in Development

1. True or False: Fathers' warmth toward their children predicts later cognitive, emotional, and social competencies as strongly as does mothers' warmth. (p. 279)

2. Describe two factors that promote paternal warmth. (p. 279)

A. _____

_____

B. _____

_____

From Attachment to Peer Sociability

1. How does culture predict the onset of peer sociability? (pp. 280–281)

_____

_____

_____

2. Explain the link between attachment to a sensitive caregiver and early peer relationships. (pp. 280–281)

_____

_____

_____

Attachment and Later Development

1. In a longitudinal study conducted by Sroufe and his collaborators, how did teachers rate preschoolers who were securely attached as babies? (p. 281)

_____

_____

2. Which attachment pattern is consistently related to fear, anxiety, anger, and aggression during the preschool and school years? (pp. 281–282)

_____

3. Some researchers have suggested that *continuity of caregiving* determines whether attachment is linked to later development. Briefly explain this relationship. (p. 282)

_____

_____

_____

Self-Understanding

Self-Awareness

1. True or False: Over the first few months, an infant's self-awareness is limited and is expressed only in perception and action. (p. 283)

2. Provide an example illustrating how by age 2, self-recognition is well under way. (pp. 283–284)

_____

_____

3. How does sensitive caregiving promote early self-development? (p. 284)

_____

_____

_____

4. Describe two ways in which self-awareness is associated with early emotional and social development. (pp. 284–285)

   A. _____

   _____

   B. _____

   _____

Categorizing the Self

1. Describe categorizations of the self that appear in toddlerhood, and cite an example of how children use this knowledge to organize their behavior. (p. 285)

_____

_____

_____

_____

Self-Control

1. List three developmental milestones that are essential for the development of self-control. (p. 285)

   A. _____

   B. _____

   C. _____

2. Once toddlers become capable of *compliance,* do they always obey requests and demands? Explain. (p. 285)

    _____

    _____

3. True or False: Toddlers who experience parental warmth and gentle encouragement are more likely to be cooperative and advanced in self-control. (p. 285)

4. Explain how attention and language contribute to *delay of gratification.* (p. 285)

    _____

    _____

5. List several ways adults can help toddlers develop compliance and self-control. (p. 286)

    _____

    _____

    _____

    _____

ASK YOURSELF . . .

For *Ask Yourself* questions for this chapter, along with feedback on the accuracy of your answers, please log on to MyDevelopmentLab (for registration and access, please visit mydevelopmentlab.com or follow the directions on p. ix).

1) Select the Chapter of the *Ask Yourself.*
2) Open the E-Book and select the Explore icon next to the *Ask Yourself.*
3) Complete questions and choose "Submit answers for grading" or "Clear Answers" to start over.

SUGGESTED STUDENT READINGS

Grossmann, K. E., Grossmann, K., & Walters, E. (Eds.). (2006). *Attachment from infancy to adulthood: The major longitudinal studies.* New York: Guilford. Presents findings from some of the most well-known longitudinal studies of attachment. Each chapter highlights the importance of early relationships for favorable development throughout the lifespan.

Kagan, J., & Snidman, N. (2004). *The long shadow of temperament.* Cambridge, MA: Harvard University Press. Using results from over two decades of longitudinal research, this book explores the relationship between temperament and psychological development.

Lamb, M. E. (Ed.). (2004). *The role of the father in child development* (4th ed.). Hoboken, NJ: Wiley. Examines the diverse and enduring contributions of father involvement to child development. An excellent resource for students, educators, mental health professionals, and anyone interested in working with children and families.

PUZZLE 7.1 TERM REVIEW

Across

5. Attachment style characterizing infants who remain close to the parent prior to separation but display angry behavior upon reunion
9. Model of attachment which states that an effective match between child-rearing practices and a child's temperament leads to favorable adjustment (3 words, hyph)
10. _____ caregiving involves prompt, consistent, and appropriate responses to infant signals
11. The _____ smile is evoked by the stimulus of the human face
12. Positive outcome of Erikson's psychological conflict of toddlerhood
14. The strong, affectionate tie that humans feel toward special people in their lives
16. Infants use the caregiver as a secure _____ from which to explore, returning for emotional support

Down

1. Negative outcome of Erikson's psychological conflict of infancy
2. Interactional _____: a sensitively-tuned emotional dance, in which the caregiver responds to infant signals in a well-timed, appropriate fashion, and both partners match emotional states

3. _____ Situation: procedure involving brief separations from and reunions with the parent that assesses the quality of the attachment bond
4. Social _____: relying on a trusted person's emotional reaction to decide how to respond in an uncertain situation
6. Attachment style characterizing infants who respond in a confused, contradictory fashion when reunited with the parent
7. The _____ theory of attachment views the infant's emotional tie to the caregiver as an evolved response that promotes survival
8. Attachment _____: method for assessing the quality of the attachment bond in which a parent sorts a set of descriptors of attachment-related behaviors on the basis of how well they describe the child
10. Attachment style characterizing infants who are distressed at parental separation and are easily comforted upon parental return
13. _____ working model: set of expectations derived from early caregiving experiences; guides all future close relationships
15. Positive outcome of Erikson's psychological conflict of toddlerhood

PUZZLE 7.2 TERM REVIEW

Across

2. Emotional self-_____: strategies for adjusting one's emotional state to a comfortable level of intensity
4. Stranger_____: an infant's expression of fear in response to unfamiliar adults
5. Stable individual differences in quality and intensity of emotional reaction, activity level, attention, and emotional self-regulation
6. A child who reacts negatively to and withdraws from novel stimuli
8. Voluntary obedience to adult request and commands
9. Temperament style characterized by inactivity; mild, low-key, reactions to environmental stimuli; negative mood; and slow adjustment to new experiences
10. _____ self: classification of the self according to prominent ways in which people differ, such as age, sex, physical characteristics, and competencies that develops between 18 and 30 months
11. Emotions involving injury or enhancement to the sense of self (2 words, hyph.)
15. Temperament style characterized by establishment of regular routines in infancy, general cheerfulness, and easy adaptation to new experiences

16. Temperament style characterized by irregular daily routines, slow acceptance of new experiences, and negative, intense reactions

Down

1. The capacity to understand another's emotional state and to feel with that person
3. Delay of _____ is the ability to wait for an appropriate time and place to engage in a tempting act
7. _____ emotions can be directly inferred from facial expressions
12. The self-regulatory dimension of temperament, called _____ control, involves voluntary suppression of a dominant, reactive response in order to plan and execute a more adaptive response
13. A child who reacts positively to and approaches novel stimuli
14. _____ anxiety: infant's distressed reaction to the departure of a familiar caregiver

PRACTICE TEST #1

1. Expanding Freud's theory, Erikson believed that a healthy outcome during infancy depends on the (p. 252)
   a. amount of food and oral stimulation offered.
   b. frequency and severity of punishment.
   c. continual presence of the mother.
   d. quality of caregiving.

2. According to Erikson, the toddler's conflict of autonomy versus shame and doubt is resolved favorably when parents (pp. 252–253)
   a. enforce strict toilet-training rules to bring the child's impulses in line with social requirements.
   b. encourage the superego's control over the ego and id.
   c. provide young children with suitable guidance and reasonable choices.
   d. allow children to toilet train themselves.

3. According to the dynamic systems view, emotional expressions (p. 254)
   a. are flexibly organized, varying with the person's developing capacities, goals, and contexts.
   b. are determined primarily by a person's gender.
   c. directly correspond to degree of brain development.
   d. reflect a person's experiences in infancy, with little influence from later events.

4. Infants' earliest emotional life consists of (p. 254)
   a. only two emotions, anger and happiness.
   b. the struggle for oral satisfaction.
   c. attraction to pleasant stimuli and withdrawal from unpleasant stimuli.
   d. fear of unfamiliar persons and events.

5. At about 18 to 24 months, children typically begin to (p. 257)
   a. identify emotions expressed during face-to-face communication.
   b. engage in emotional self-regulation by shifting attention and self-soothing.
   c. laugh at events with subtle elements of surprise.
   d. experience self-conscious emotions of shame, embarrassment, guilt, and pride.

6. The faster processing of information that begins around 3 to 4 months of age distinguishes (p. 255)
   a. social smiling from newborn smiling.
   b. laughter from smiling.
   c. true happiness from biological satisfaction.
   d. autonomy from trust.

7. The gradual rise in infants' anger from 4 to 6 months is adaptive in that (p. 255)
   a. new motor capacities enable an angry infant to defend herself or overcome an obstacle.
   b. anger serves as a bridge between the young infant's crying and the toddler's single-word expressions of need or desire.
   c. anger occurs in a smaller range of situations as infants realize that they cannot always affect their environment.
   d. it prepares the infant for separation from the caregiver.

8. In the second half of the first year, the infant's most frequent expression of fear is to (p. 256)
   a. heights.
   b. separation from parents.
   c. unfamiliar adults.
   d. the threat of pain.

9. The rise in fear after 6 months of age serves to (p. 256)
    a. balance the infant's approach and avoidance tendencies.
    b. keep the newly mobile baby's enthusiasm for exploration in check.
    c. place necessary limits on the parent's interactions with the infant.
    d. prepare the infant to respond to discipline during toddlerhood.

10. Around the middle of the second year, toddlers begin to use social referencing to (p. 257)
    a. establish richer joint attention.
    b. block out mixed signals in vocal communication.
    c. know when to laugh at a stimulus.
    d. compare their own and others' assessments of events.

11. Self-conscious emotions generally appear in the middle of the second year because 18- to 24-month-olds (p. 257)
    a. become firmly aware of the self as a separate, unique individual.
    b. feel less stranger anxiety than before.
    c. are less motivated by basic emotions.
    d. are cognitively ready to move beyond social referencing.

12. By 4 to 6 months, infants are generally better able to control their emotions because (p. 258)
    a. they have reached a higher level of self-consciousness.
    b. their more regular sleep patterns enable them to cope more effectively with stress.
    c. they have gained in ability to shift attention and engage in self-soothing.
    d. they can crawl away from emotionally disturbing situations.

13. Studies have revealed that infant boys have a harder time than infant girls in (p. 259)
    a. responding to caregivers' lessons in socially approved expression.
    b. regulating negative emotion.
    c. developing a vocabulary for talking about feelings.
    d. understanding themselves and others as emotional beings.

14. The results of the New York Longitudinal Study showed that (p. 260)
    a. temperament may protect a child from the negative effects of a stressful home life.
    b. girls are more reactive than boys.
    c. parenting practices have little effect on children's fundamental emotional styles.
    d. temperament is influenced primarily by environmental rather than biological factors.

15. Unlike the difficult child, the slow-to-warm-up child (p. 260)
    a. is generally cheerful.
    b. has irregular daily routines.
    c. adapts more quickly to new experiences.
    d. shows mild, low-key reactions to environmental stimuli.

16. As a method of studying temperament, home or laboratory observation (p. 262)
    a. enables inhibited children to accept novel stimuli.
    b. avoids the subjectivity of parent reports.
    c. is always more accurate than parental reports.
    d. tends to calm sociable children who might "act out" in an unfamiliar setting.

17. Long-term predictions from early temperament are best made after age 3 because (p. 262)
    a. saliva concentrations of cortisol fall after age 3.
    b. older children are better able to follow caregiver directions that regulate behavior.
    c. at that point, the child's system of emotion, attention, and action is better established.
    d. older children have greater skill at effortful control.

18. Unlike North American mothers, Japanese mothers tend to believe that babies (p. 265)
    a. come into the world as independent beings who must learn to rely on parents.
    b. must be weaned away from dependence to autonomy.
    c. should be encouraged to express strong emotion.
    d. must be free to develop individualistic qualities.

19. A limitation of the psychoanalytic and behaviorist accounts of attachment is that they (p. 268)
    a. overemphasize the infant's characteristics.
    b. underestimate the importance of toilet training.
    c. underemphasize emotional bonding between children and adults who are not their parents.
    d. overemphasize the role of hunger satisfaction.

20. In response to the Strange Situation, resistant babies tend to (p. 270)
    a. use the parent as a secure base and, when the parent returns after separation, actively seek contact.
    b. be unresponsive to the parent when she is present and show no distress when she leaves.
    c. seek closeness to the parent before separation and, after the parent returns, combine clinginess with angry, resistive behavior.
    d. show confused, contradictory behaviors at reunion, such as approaching the parent with flat, depressed emotion.

21. The fact that about two-thirds of siblings establish similar attachment patterns with their parents, although the siblings often differ in temperament, suggests that (p. 275)
    a. the heritability of attachment is very high.
    b. the heritability of attachment is virtually nil.
    c. the parents established appropriate interactional synchronies with all of the siblings.
    d. the siblings probably share a few characteristics that result in similar levels of attachment security.

22. Studies have shown that paternal availability to children is (p. 278)
    a. fairly similar across SES and ethnic groups.
    b. slightly higher in Canada than in the United States.
    c. dramatically different across cultures.
    d. higher in dual-earner families.

23. Between 1 and 2 years, coordinated interaction between agemates largely takes the form of (p. 280)
    a. smiling and reaching when they see one another.
    b. mutual imitation involving jumping, chasing, or banging a toy.
    c. using words to talk about and influence a peer's behavior.
    d. playing games with rules.

24. Around age 2, children display self-recognition by (p. 284)
    a. matching facial expressions with their caregivers.
    b. looking longer at images of their own leg positions than at those of other children.
    c. empathizing with others' emotional states.
    d. pointing to themselves in photos and referring to themselves by name or with a personal pronoun.

25. A toddler's use of consciencelike verbalizations ("No, can't!") to correct herself shows that she has become capable of (p. 285)
    a. independent thinking.
    b. self-awareness.
    c. compliance.
    d. resilience.

PRACTICE TEST #2

1. According to Erikson, basic trust versus mistrust is resolved favorably by (p. 252)
   a. a balance of care that tends toward love and sympathy.
   b. the triumph of the ego over the id.
   c. frequent oral satisfaction.
   d. separation between child and mother.

2. In Erikson's view, adults who have difficulty establishing intimate ties or who doubt their ability to meet new challenges (p. 253)
   a. have an overdeveloped superego.
   b. had too much autonomy as children.
   c. did not toilet train early enough or with sufficiently consistent rules.
   d. may not have fully mastered the tasks of basic trust and autonomy during infancy and toddlerhood.

3. Basic emotions, such as happiness and surprise, are (p. 254)
   a. imprinted as the infant establishes trust.
   b. universal in humans and other primates.
   c. not as flexibly organized as higher emotions.
   d. the result of unrestrained biological drives.

4. At about 3 to 5 months, infants' emotions have developed to the point that they (p. 256)
   a. are attracted primarily to neutral stimuli.
   b. begin to engage in social smiling.
   c. expect others to respond similarly to their gaze, smile, or vocalization.
   d. become angry more often and in a wider range of situations.

5. By the end of the first month, babies start to smile (p. 255)
   a. in response to gentle touches and sounds.
   b. at dynamic, eye-catching sights.
   c. when they hear the mother's soft, high-pitched voice.
   d. in response to parents' complex expressions and sentences.

6. Angry reactions increase as infants grow older because they (p. 255)
   a. want to control their own actions and the effects they produce.
   b. get hungry more often.
   c. can perceive, but not yet interpret, caregivers' complex emotional expressions.
   d. feel increasingly frustrated by their parents' contingent control over their movements.

7. Infants most often express sadness in response to (p. 255)
   a. pain.
   b. removal of an object.
   c. hunger.
   d. deprivation of a familiar caregiver.

8. Of the following situations, which is the most likely to cause stranger anxiety? (p. 256)
   a. An unfamiliar adult speaks to the baby's parents in a loud voice.
   b. An unfamiliar adult sits still and stares at the baby.
   c. An unfamiliar adult picks up the baby in a new situation.
   d. An unfamiliar adult approaches the baby slowly.

9. Studies have revealed that a caregiver's voice is more effective in social referencing than a facial expression alone because (p. 257)
   a. the voice conveys both emotional and verbal information.
   b. facial expressions often confuse young children.
   c. young children's hearing is better developed than their vision.
   d. hearing the voice does not require joint attention.

10. In collectivist cultures like those of China and Japan, calling attention to personal success often evokes the self-conscious emotion of (p. 258)
    a. pride.
    b. communal satisfaction.
    c. embarrassment.
    d. envy.

11. Because young infants have only a limited capacity to regulate their emotions, they (p. 258)
    a. engage in effortful control.
    b. depend on soothing for distraction and reorientation of attention.
    c. use social referencing to calm themselves.
    d. generally cannot tolerate face-to-face play.

12. Studies have revealed that when caregivers fail to regulate stressful experiences for infants, (p. 259)
    a. the development of self-conscious emotions is delayed.
    b. infants compensate by using effortful control.
    c. infants have trouble understanding social referencing.
    d. brain structures that buffer stress may fail to develop properly.

13. Self-regulation strategies help children to modify their (p. 260)
    a. temperament.
    b. self-consciousness.
    c. reactivity.
    d. autonomy.

14. In the Thomas and Chess model of temperament, a child with high rhythmicity (p. 261)
    a. has a very regular schedule for bodily functions, such as sleep, hunger, and excretion.
    b. is extremely distractible.
    c. tends to laugh, cry, or engage in gross motor activity with great energy.
    d. requires little stimulation to evoke a strong response.

15. According to Mary Rothbart, individuals differ not just in their reactivity on each dimension of temperament, but also in their (p. 261)
    a. threshold of responsiveness to stimuli.
    b. effortful capacity to manage that reactivity.
    c. level of activity or inactivity.
    d. frequency of negative mood.

16. Jerome Kagan's research has revealed that a comparatively high heart rate and saliva concentration of cortisol are common physiological responses of (p. 263)
    a. sociable children.
    b. children with a poorly developed amygdala.
    c. children who show greater EEG activity in the left frontal lobe.
    d. shy children.

17. The role of heredity in determining temperament is (p. 265)
    a. highest during infancy, when environmental influences have not had enough time to shape temperament.
    b. virtually impossible to measure because of the complex interaction of genetic and environmental influences.
    c. higher in childhood and beyond, when temperament becomes more stable.
    d. stronger in boys than in girls.

18. In Thomas and Chess's goodness-of-fit model, an effective match between rearing conditions and child temperament is best accomplished (p. 267)
    a. early, before unfavorable temperament–environment relationships produce maladjustment.
    b. at the point when adjustment problems become evident enough for caregivers to identify them.
    c. after the child has developed pragmatic skills.
    d. at birth, when infants typically display strong temperamental traits.

19. According to John Bowlby, during the "attachment in the making" phase, (p. 269)
    a. built-in signals, such as smiling and crying, help bring newborns into close contact with other humans who comfort them.
    b. infants begin to develop a sense of trust in caregivers' responses but still do not protest when separated from them.
    c. babies display clear-cut separation anxiety.
    d. rapid growth in representation and language enables toddlers to understand and predict a caregiver's behavior.

20. Research into stability of attachment indicates that (p. 272)
    a. the attachments of low-SES babies tend to be stronger than those of middle- or high-SES babies.
    b. children often show short-term instability in attachment quality during middle childhood.
    c. stability patterns tend to be the same across cultures.
    d. secure babies are more likely than insecure babies to maintain their attachment status.

21. Recent studies suggest that sensitive caregiving is _____ related to attachment security. (p. 273)
    a. not
    b. slightly
    c. moderately
    d. highly

22. Research into the relationship between child care and attachment quality suggests that we should (p. 277)
    a. increase the availability of high-quality child care.
    b. reject the Western European model of state-funded child care.
    c. regularly monitor children's cortisol levels.
    d. encourage caregivers to foster children's independence so that they adapt more favorably to nonparental care.

23. Studies have shown that in Western cultures, paternal warmth (p. 279)
    a. is highest in middle-SES families.
    b. yields greater benefits for boys than for girls.
    c. predicts little about children's later development.
    d. protects children against a wide range of difficulties, including childhood emotional problems.

24. The sensitivity to variations in caregivers' emotional messages that comes with self-awareness sets the stage for (p. 284)
    a. self-recognition.
    b. social referencing and the emergence of self-conscious emotions.
    c. emotional resilience.
    d. complex intermodal perception that, in turn, leads to self-awareness.

25. Language enables the development of the categorical self because it (p. 285)
    a. promotes self-recognition.
    b. replaces effortful control as the main determinant of self-awareness.
    c. permits children to represent the self and others more clearly.
    d. helps children become more consciously aware of their physical distinctness from their surroundings.

CHAPTER 8
PHYSICAL DEVELOPMENT IN EARLY CHILDHOOD

BRIEF CHAPTER SUMMARY

During early childhood, the rapid increase in body size tapers off and the child's shape becomes more streamlined, leading to improvements in posture and balance. The skeletal changes of infancy continue throughout early childhood. At the end of this period, children start to lose their primary teeth.

The brain continues to grow faster than any other part of the body. The cerebral cortex, especially, shows gains in myelination and formation of synapses, followed by synaptic pruning. Hand preference strengthens, a sign of greater brain lateralization. In addition, connections between different parts of the brain increase. These changes support improvements in a wide variety of physical and cognitive skills.

Both heredity and environmental factors continue to influence physical growth and health in early childhood. Heredity affects physical growth by regulating the production of hormones necessary for development of body tissues and of the brain. Extreme emotional deprivation can interfere with the production of growth hormone, causing a growth disorder called psychosocial dwarfism. Sleep difficulties, mostly in the form of night waking and nightmares, are common during the preschool years. Appetite declines, reflecting a slower rate of physical growth. Since caloric intake is reduced, preschoolers need a high-quality diet. Infectious disease interacts with malnutrition to seriously undermine children's growth, an effect that is especially common in developing countries. Although widespread immunization has led to dramatic declines in childhood diseases in the industrialized world, many children in the United States are not fully immunized.

Unintentional injuries are the leading cause of childhood death in industrialized nations. Preventive efforts are necessary at several levels, including laws that promote safety, improvement of community environments, and efforts to change parents' and children's behavior.

During the preschool years, children continue to integrate motor skills into dynamic systems. Gross motor skills, such as running, jumping, galloping, throwing, and catching appear and become better coordinated. Gains in fine motor development can be seen in preschoolers' ability to dress themselves, draw representational pictures, and print letters of the alphabet. As in other areas, heredity and environment combine to influence early childhood motor development.

LEARNING OBJECTIVES

After reading this chapter, you should be able to:

8.1 Describe changes in body size, body proportions, and skeletal maturity during early childhood. (pp. 293–296)

8.2 Explain the general growth curve, and discuss asynchronies in physical growth. (p. 296)

8.3 Discuss brain development in early childhood, including synaptic growth and pruning, lateralization and handedness, and other advances in brain development that help to establish links between parts of the brain. (pp. 296–299)

8.4 Describe the effects of heredity and hormones, emotional well-being, restful sleep, nutrition, infectious disease, and childhood injury on physical growth and health in early childhood. (pp. 300–308)

8.5 Summarize individual, family, community, and societal factors related to childhood injuries, and describe ways to prevent them. (pp. 308–311)

8.6 Cite major milestones of gross and fine motor development in early childhood. (pp. 312–316)

8.7 Discuss individual differences in preschoolers' motor skills, and cite ways to enhance early motor development. (pp. 316–317)

STUDY QUESTIONS

Body Growth

1. True or False: In contrast to the rapid increases in body size seen during infancy, early childhood is marked by a slower pattern of growth. (p. 293)

2. On average, children add ____ to ____ inches in height and about ____ pounds in weight each year. (p. 293)

3. True or False: Growth norms and trends in body size are consistent across cultures. (p. 294)

Skeletal Growth

1. Between ages 2 and 6, approximately 45 new _____, or growth centers in which cartilage hardens into bone, emerge in various parts of the skeleton. (p. 294)

2. Explain how both genetics and environment influence the age at which children lose their primary, or "baby," teeth. (p. 294)

   Genetics: _____

   _____

   Environment: _____

   _____

3. True or False: Care of primary teeth is essential because diseased baby teeth can affect the health of permanent teeth. (p. 294)

Asynchronies in Physical Growth

1. Describe the *general growth curve,* which represents changes in body size from infancy to adolescence. (p. 296)

   _____

   _____

   _____

2. List three exceptions to the trend depicted by the general growth curve. (p. 296)

   A. _____

   B. _____

   C. _____

Brain Development

1. True or False: By 4 years of age, the child's brain has produced an overabundance of synaptic connections, contributing to the plasticity of the young brain. (p. 296)

2. For most children, the (right / left) hemisphere is especially active between 3 and 6 years of age and then levels off. In contrast, activity in the (right / left) hemisphere increases steadily throughout early and middle childhood. This helps to explain the pattern of development for which skills? (p. 297)

   _____

   _____

   _____

Handedness

1. Handedness reflects the greater capacity of one side of the brain, or the _____ *cerebral hemisphere,* to carry out skilled motor action. (p. 297)

2. For left-handed individuals, language is occasionally located in the right hemisphere, or more often, language is shared between the brain hemispheres. This indicates that brains of left-handers tend to be (less / more) strongly lateralized than those of right-handers. (p. 297)

3. List three theories regarding the origins of handedness. (p. 298)

   A. _____

   _____

   B. _____

   _____

   C. _____

   _____

4. True or False: Many left-handers have serious developmental problems. Explain your answer. (p. 298)

   _____

   _____

Other Advances in Brain Development

1. For each of the following brain structures, describe developmental changes in early childhood, and indicate its impact on children's physical and cognitive skills: (pp. 298–299)

   Cerebellum

   Changes: _____

   _____

   Impact: _____

   _____

   Reticular Formation

   Changes: _____

   _____

   Impact: _____

   _____

   Hippocampus

   Changes: _____

   _____

   Impact: _____

   _____

   Corpus Callosum

   Changes: _____

   _____

   Impact: _____

   _____

Influences on Physical Growth and Health

Biology and Environment: Low-Level Lead Exposure and Children's Development

1. What two factors have led to a sharp decline in children's lead levels from 1980 to today? (p. 300)

   A. _____

   B. _____

2. Describe the developmental consequences associated with high levels of lead exposure. (pp. 300–301)

   _____

   _____

   _____

3. Although the overall impact of low-level lead exposure on all developmental outcomes is modest, cognitive consequences were much greater for (low / high)-SES children. Briefly explain why this is the case. (p. 301)

   _____

   _____

   _____

Heredity and Hormones

1. The _____ *gland,* located near the base of the brain, releases hormones affecting physical growth. (p. 301)

2. Describe the impact of growth hormone (GH) and thyroid-stimulating hormone (TSH) on body growth, and indicate what happens when there are deficiencies of these hormones. (pp. 301–302)

   GH: _____

   _____

   _____

   TSH: _____

   _____

   _____

Emotional Well-Being

1. Describe the cause and characteristics of *psychosocial dwarfism.* (p. 302)

   Cause: _____

   _____

   Characteristics: _____

   _____

   _____

2. True or False: Even when children with psychosocial dwarfism are removed from their emotionally inadequate environments at an early age, their growth is permanently stunted. (p. 302)

Sleep Habits and Problems

1. Total sleep time (increases / decreases) in early childhood. (p. 302)

2. Provide three recommendations that parents can follow to help young children get a good night's sleep. (p. 303)

   A. _____

   B. _____

   C. _____

3. Is parent–child cosleeping associated with sleep problems in early childhood? Explain. (p. 303)

   _____

   _____

4. List three sleep problems of early childhood. (p. 303)

   A. _____

   B. _____

   C. _____

Nutrition

1. True or False: It is normal for children's appetite to decline in early childhood. (p. 304)

2. Explain how the social and emotional climates influence young children's food preferences and eating habits. (pp. 304–305)

   Social: _____

   _____

   _____

   Emotional: _____

   _____

   _____

3. Describe three ways to encourage good nutrition in early childhood. (p. 305)

   A. _____

   _____

   B. _____

   _____

   C. _____

   _____

4. List the most common dietary deficiencies during the preschool years. (p. 305)

   A. _____

   B. _____

   C. _____

   D. _____

   E. _____

Infectious Disease

1. Describe the bidirectional relationship between infectious disease and malnutrition. (p. 306)

    _____

    _____

    _____

2. Most developmental impairments and deaths due to diarrhea can be prevented with a nearly cost-free
    _____, a glucose, salt, and water solution that quickly replaces fluids
    the body loses. (p. 306)

3. True or False: Nearly one-quarter of American preschoolers lack essential immunizations. (p. 306)

4. What are some causes of inadequate immunization in the United States? (pp. 306, 308)

    _____

    _____

5. Childhood illness (rises / remains the same) with child-care attendance. (p. 308)

Cultural Influences: Child Health Care in the United States and Other Western Nations

1. Describe the relationship between socioeconomic status and health care coverage in the United States, noting its
    impact on child development. (p. 307)

    Relationship: _____

    _____

    _____

    Impact: _____

    _____

    _____

2. Describe child health care initiatives in the Netherlands and Norway, two countries whose services stand in sharp
    contrast to those available in the United States. (p. 307)

    Netherlands: _____

    _____

    _____

    Norway: _____

    _____

    _____

3. Describe the State Children's Health Insurance Program (SCHIP), and note some of the problems with this
    health initiative. (p. 307)

    Program: _____

    _____

    _____

    Problems: _____

    _____

    _____

Social Issues: Health: Otitis Media and Development

1. Explain how otitis media affects language development and academic progress. (p. 309)

_____

_____

_____

_____

2. List three factors linked to increased rates of otitis media. (p. 309)

A. _____

B. _____

C. _____

3. Describe four ways of preventing otitis media. (p. 309)

A. _____

_____

B. _____

_____

C. _____

_____

D. _____

_____

Childhood Injuries

1. True or False: Unintentional injuries are the leading cause of childhood mortality in industrialized countries. (p. 308)

2. List three of the most common causes of injury during early childhood. (p. 308)

A. _____

B. _____

C. _____

3. Summarize individual, family, community, and societal factors linked to childhood injury. (pp. 309–310)

Individual: _____

_____

Family: _____

_____

Community: _____

_____

Societal: _____

_____

4. Why are injury rates in the United States and Canada higher than in other developed nations? (p. 310)

    _____

    _____

    _____

5. List four ways to reduce unintentional injuries in early childhood. (pp. 310–311)

    A. _____

    B. _____

    C. _____

    D. _____

6. Programs based on _____ have been used to improve parent and child safety practices. (p. 311)

Motor Development

Gross Motor Development

1. As children's bodies become more streamlined and their center of gravity shifts downward, _____ improves greatly, paving the way for new motor skills involving large muscles of the body. (p. 312)

2. Match the following sets of gross motor developments with the ages at which they are typically acquired. (p. 312)

_____ Walks up stairs with alternating feet; flexes upper body when jumping and hopping; throws with slight involvement of upper body, still catches against chest; pedals and steers tricycle	1. 2 to 3 years 2. 3 to 4 years 3. 4 to 5 years 4. 5 to 6 years
_____ Walks down stairs with alternating feet; gallops; throws ball with transfer of weight on feet; catches with hands; rides tricycle rapidly, steers smoothly	
_____ Hurried walk changes to run; jumps, hops, throws, and catches with rigid upper body; little steering	
_____ Engages in true skipping; displays mature throwing and catching pattern; rides bicycle with training wheels	

Fine Motor Development

1. To parents, fine motor development is most evident in which two areas? (p. 313)

    A. _____   B. _____

2. Match the following sets of fine motor developments with the ages at which they are typically acquired. (pp. 312, 313–315)

_____ Draws first tadpole image of a person; copies vertical line and circle; uses scissors; fastens and unfastens large buttons	1. 2 to 3 years 2. 3 to 4 years 3. 4 to 5 years 4. 5 to 6 years
_____ Draws a person with six parts; copies some numbers and words; ties shoes; uses knife	
_____ Copies triangle, cross, and some letters; cuts along line with scissors; uses fork effectively	
_____ Scribbles gradually become pictures; puts on and removes simple items of clothing; zips large zippers; uses spoon effectively	

3. List and briefly describe the three-stage sequence in which drawing skills develop during early childhood. (pp. 313–315)

   A. _____

   _____

   B. _____

   _____

   C. _____

   _____

4. Describe evidence indicating that culture has a significant impact on the development of drawing skills. (p. 315)

   _____

   _____

   _____

5. At approximately what age do children realize that writing stands for language? (p. 315)

   _____

6. In addition to fine motor control, what other skill contributes to printing ability? (p. 316)

   _____

Individual Differences in Motor Skills

1. Discuss sex differences in motor development during early childhood. (p. 317)

   _____

   _____

   _____

   _____

   _____

2. Provide an example of how social pressures might exaggerate small, genetically based sex differences in motor skills. (p. 317)

   _____

   _____

Enhancing Early Childhood Motor Development

1. True or False: Preschoolers exposed to formal lessons in motor skills are generally more advanced in their motor development than agemates who do not take such lessons. (p. 317)

2. List three ways to foster young children's motor development. (p. 317)

   A. _____

   B. _____

   C. _____

ASK YOURSELF . . .

For *Ask Yourself* questions for this chapter, along with feedback on the accuracy of your answers, please log on to MyDevelopmentLab (for registration and access, please visit mydevelopmentlab.com or follow the directions on p. ix).

1)   Select the Chapter of the *Ask Yourself.*
2)   Open the E-Book and select the Explore icon next to the *Ask Yourself.*
3)   Complete questions and choose "Submit answers for grading" or "Clear Answers" to start over.

SUGGESTED STUDENT READINGS

Golomb, C. (2004). *The child's creation of a pictorial world* (2nd ed.). Mahwah, NJ: Erlbaum. Using a developmental framework, this book examines the emergence of artistic skills in young children. The author combines theoretical perspectives with research on average, emotionally disturbed, and exceptional children.

Kagan, J., & Herschkowitz, N. (2005). *A young mind in a growing brain.* Mahwah, NJ: Erlbaum. Presents up-to-date research on early brain growth and development, emphasizing important milestones through the first eight years of life.

Palfrey, J. S. (2006). *Child health in America: Making a difference through advocacy.* Baltimore, MD: John Hopkins University Press. A compelling look at the state of American health care, this book explains how parents, teachers, and community agencies can enhance the health and well-being of all children.

PUZZLE 8.1 TERM REVIEW

Across

2. The _____ cerebral hemisphere of the brain is responsible for skilled motor action

8. The _____ growth curve represents overall changes in body size: rapid growth rate during infancy, slow gains in early and middle childhood, and rapid growth once again during adolescence

9. _____ dwarfism is a growth disorder caused by extreme emotional deprivation

Down

1. An inner-brain structure that plays a vital role in memory and in spatial images we use to help us find our way

3. A pituitary hormone that stimulates the thyroid gland to release thyroxine, which is necessary for normal brain development and body growth (abbr.)

4. A brain structure that aids in balance and control of body movements

5. Corpus _____: large bundle of fibers that connects the two hemispheres of the brain

6. _____ formation: brain structure that maintains alertness and consciousness

7. The _____ gland, located near the base of the brain, releases hormones affecting physical growth

8. A pituitary hormone that affects the development of all body tissues except the central nervous system and the genitals (abbr.)

PRACTICE TEST #1

1. On average, preschoolers add _____ inches to their height each year. (p. 293)
   a. 1 to 2
   b. 2 to 3
   c. 3 to 4
   d. 4 to 5

2. By age 6½, North American children typically (p. 294)
   a. grow their first epiphyses.
   b. lose their remaining baby fat.
   c. lag behind European children in weight gain.
   d. get their first secondary tooth.

3. The lymph glands grow quickly during infancy and childhood because (p. 296)
   a. all glands grow at a rapid pace during these years.
   b. the lymph system helps with the growth of teeth.
   c. the lymph system helps fight infection and assists with the absorption of nutrients.
   d. their growth is supported by rapid growth of the brain during these years.

4. By age 8 to 10, synaptic density falls to an adult level because (p. 296)
   a. synaptic pruning disposes of many neurons, making room for increasingly elaborate neural structures.
   b. brain plasticity steadily increases.
   c. right-hemispheric activity increases, drawing energy away from other parts of the brain.
   d. lateralization lowers energy metabolism throughout the brain.

5. Handedness reflects (p. 297)
   a. weak brain lateralization in early childhood.
   b. the greater capacity of one side of the brain to carry out skilled motor action.
   c. the fact that nurture has little to do with the development of a dominant cerebral hemisphere.
   d. an inherited gene bias.

6. The growth and myelination of fibers linking the cerebellum and cerebral cortex are responsible for (p. 298)
   a. reticular formation during infancy.
   b. increased brain lateralization between birth and age 3 years.
   c. the development of memory.
   d. gains in motor coordination from birth through the preschool years.

7. An array of research findings have suggested that persistent exposure to lead in early childhood (p. 300)
   a. can be counteracted with drugs that induce excretion of lead.
   b. causes very young children to have a low activity level.
   c. contributes to antisocial behavior in adolescence.
   d. has little effect on children's mental test scores.

8. Growth hormone is responsible for (p. 301)
   a. the development of all body tissues except the genitals and central nervous system.
   b. stimulating the release of thyroxine.
   c. normal growth of the hippocampus.
   d. body growth in infancy and toddlerhood only.

9. Sleep contributes to body growth because (p. 302)
   a. vital synaptic pruning occurs during sleep.
   b. GH is released during the child's sleeping hours.
   c. while the brain rests, metabolic energy flows to the developing bones, muscles, and other organs.
   d. the thyroid gland is largely dormant during waking hours.

10. Preschoolers' appetites typically decline because (p. 304)
    a. their growth has slowed.
    b. they crave a varied diet, so they reject the familiar foods that are offered to them.
    c. they tend to find meals stressful.
    d. their sleeping hours have lengthened.

11. A diet that is deficient in protein and in essential vitamins and minerals (p. 305)
    a. is common in the developing world but is rarely seen in North America and Western Europe.
    b. is not associated with cognitive problems in school-age children because they are past the sensitive period for brain development.
    c. is related to attention difficulties, poorer mental test scores, and behavior problems throughout childhood and adolescence.
    d. is risky for infants and toddlers but less of a problem for older children, who have developed physical resilience.

12. In developing nations, infectious diseases tend to occur (p. 306)
    a. after age 3.
    b. much earlier than in industrialized nations.
    c. in 30 percent of children.
    d. in children with large families.

13. Infants and preschoolers who are in child care are at greater risk of developing _____ as a result of a respiratory infection than agemates who are cared for at home. (p. 308)
    a. diarrhea
    b. rubella
    c. whooping cough
    d. otitis media

14. Many U.S. states face the prospect of reducing enrollment or coverage in their SCHIP programs because of (p. 307)
    a. lack of public interest in these programs.
    b. federal pressure to reduce all public-assistance rolls.
    c. funding shortfalls.
    d. mismanagement.

15. Research findings indicate that frequent otitis media infections are associated with (p. 309)
    a. delayed language progress in early childhood.
    b. later problems with the immune system.
    c. high susceptibility to respiratory infections from early childhood through adolescence.
    d. heightened sensitivity to other bacterial infections in early and middle childhood.

16. In the United States, a leading factor related to the high child injury rate is (p. 310)
    a. the high cost of child car seats and other safety equipment.
    b. a high rate of births to teenagers.
    c. heavy and increasing road traffic.
    d. declining standards of nutrition.

17. About 10 percent of Canadian parents and 40 percent of U.S. parents (p. 310)
    a.   do not install window guards in their homes to prevent falls.
    b.   neglect to teach safety rules to their children.
    c.   fail to place their preschoolers in car safety seats.
    d.   purchase medication in bottles without child-resistant caps.

18. As children's bodies become more streamlined, their balance improves because (p. 312)
    a.   their center of gravity shifts downward.
    b.   they have better hand-eye coordination.
    c.   their muscles grow longer and stronger.
    d.   they perform motions exclusively with their trunk and limbs.

19. Of the following gains in fine motor skills, which do children typically display at 4 to 5 years? (p. 312)
    a.   They have the ability to zip and unzip large zippers.
    b.   They can feed themselves without assistance.
    c.   They can follow a line when cutting with scissors.
    d.   They can copy some numbers and simple words.

20. Western parents and teachers typically spend much time promoting 2- and 3-year-olds' (p. 314)
    a.   drawing abilities.
    b.   running, jumping, and skipping.
    c.   throwing and catching.
    d.   language and make-believe play.

21. When 3- and 4-year-olds learn to use lines to represent the boundaries of objects, they (p. 314)
    a.   are able to draw their first picture of a person.
    b.   can integrate object parts into realistic wholes.
    c.   are ready to write their own names.
    d.   start to recognize shapes and can label them.

22. When asked to write, 4-year-olds typically make a "drawing of print" because they (p. 315)
    a.   are copying what they see in most storybooks.
    b.   are applying their understanding of the symbolic function of drawing.
    c.   have not yet mastered the fine motor skills needed for actual writing.
    d.   are representing the universal beginning of writing.

23. Preschoolers' first attempts to print often involve (p. 315)
    a.   their own names.
    b.   letters with shapes that they find pleasing.
    c.   words for their favorite toys.
    d.   the words "Mommy" and "Daddy."

24. The fact that boys can throw a ball much farther than girls only when using their dominant hand suggests that (p. 317)
    a.   their advantage over girls is primarily genetic, not learned.
    b.   sex differences in motor skills increase as children get older.
    c.   social pressures can exaggerate small, genetically based sex differences.
    d.   handedness is more pronounced in boys than in girls.

25. Daily routines, such as pouring juice and dressing oneself, support (p. 317)
    a.   self-expression.
    b.   fine motor development.
    c.   socialization to important cultural norms.
    d.   play.

PRACTICE TEST #2

1. Children's bodies normally achieve proportions similar to those of adults by age (p. 294)
   a. 3.
   b. 4.
   c. 5.
   d. 6.

2. Young children in homes with regular smokers are three times more likely than their agemates to have (p. 294)
   a. decayed teeth.
   b. healthy immune systems.
   c. malformed epiphyses.
   d. problems with posture and balance.

3. Physical growth is described as *asynchronous,* meaning that (p. 296)
   a. boys and girls grow at different rates.
   b. growth does not follow any regular pattern.
   c. growth patterns vary from culture to culture.
   d. body systems differ in their patterns of growth.

4. fMRI evidence reveals that around age 4, (p. 296)
   a. the child's brain has reached 90 percent of its adult weight.
   b. energy metabolism in the cerebral cortex reaches its peak.
   c. overproduced synapses in the frontal lobes begin to die.
   d. the child's brain loses much of the plasticity it had in infancy.

5. Evidence that left-handers' brains are less strongly lateralized than those of right-handers is seen in the fact that (p. 297)
   a. for left-handers, language is usually shared between the hemispheres.
   b. right-handers' brains are generally more plastic.
   c. right-handers are typically ambidextrous.
   d. as children, left-handers typically need less practice to develop handedness.

6. The rapid development of the hippocampus during the second half of the first year is responsible for (p. 299)
   a. gradual gains in motor coordination.
   b. greater alertness and consciousness.
   c. dramatic gains in recall memory and spatial understanding.
   d. the integration of many aspects of thinking.

7. Rapid development of the hippocampus and surrounding areas of the cerebral cortex (p. 299)
   a. contributes to dramatic gains in motor coordination in the preschool years.
   b. supports smooth coordination of movements on both sides of the body.
   c. does not begin until the second half of the second year.
   d. makes possible the expansion of autobiographical memory.

8. Cognitive consequences of low-level lead exposure (p. 301)
   a. are similar for children at all SES levels.
   b. persist over time and seem to be permanent.
   c. can be reversed by giving drugs that induce excretion of lead.
   d. generally decline by adolescence, whether or not the child receives treatment.

9. Infants born with a deficiency of thyroxine can suffer (p. 302)
   a. malformation of the pituitary gland.
   b. extreme elongation of the limbs.
   c. bone malformations.
   d. mental retardation.

10. When children suffering from psychosocial dwarfism are placed in emotionally adequate environments, (p. 302)
    a. their emotional responses to others rapidly mature.
    b. they lead happier lives but experience no physical changes.
    c. their GH levels quickly return to normal.
    d. extra epiphyses dissolve from their bones, enabling normal skeletal growth.

11. About half of 3- to 6-year-olds experience (p. 303)
    a. nightmares.
    b. sleepwalking.
    c. an aversion to cosleeping.
    d. sleep terrors.

12. Parents can increase children's acceptance of new foods by (p. 304)
    a. adding flavor with salt or sugar.
    b. offering bribes for tasting an unfamiliar food.
    c. exposing them to such foods repeatedly, but without pressure.
    d. making sure that they get adequate sleep.

13. Children's bodies require vitamin A to (p. 305)
    a. support neural communication.
    b. facilitate wound healing
    c. support cell duplication.
    d. help maintain eyes, skin, and a variety of internal organs.

14. Studies have revealed that children who have persistent diarrhea in early childhood (p. 306)
    a. suffer from damage to the immune system as a result of loss of zinc.
    b. are shorter in height and score lower on mental tests.
    c. are likely to have dangerous blood glucose levels.
    d. typically compensate by overeating, leading to obesity and overweight.

15. Overall, _____ percent of American preschoolers lack essential immunizations. (p. 306)
    a. 7
    b. 10
    c. 19
    d. 24

16. Under the 1997 State Children's Health Insurance Program (SCHIP), U.S. states (p. 307)
    a. receive $4 billion a year in federal matching funds for upgrading children's health insurance.
    b. must establish well-baby and child clinics in all communities.
    c. insure only children who live below the official poverty line.
    d. send nurses to children's homes to make sure the children receive immunizations.

17. Boys are 1.5 times more likely to be injured than girls because (p. 309)
    a. they are more likely to be irritable and inattentive, characteristics associated with risk of injury.
    b. girls mature physically and cognitively faster than boys.
    c. boys have a higher activity level and a greater willingness to take risks.
    d. worldwide, girls are more likely to live in industrialized nations, where the risk of injury is lower.

18. Of the following changes in gross motor skills, which do children typically display at 3 to 4 years? (p. 312)
    a. They walk more rhythmically.
    b. They walk up stairs, alternating feet.
    c. They gallop and skip with one foot.
    d. They ride a bicycle with training wheels.

19. Because of the number of skills involved, shoe tying illustrates the close connection between (p. 313)
    a. gross and fine motor development.
    b. genetic and environmental factors that affect development.
    c. fine motor development and self-image.
    d. cognitive and motor development.

20. Around age 3, children (p. 314)
    a. first show interest in drawing.
    b. begin to scribble.
    c. produce their first representational forms when drawing.
    d. are able to create realistic drawings.

21. Children come to desire greater realism in their drawings as (p. 315)
    a. their fine motor and cognitive skills improve.
    b. they learn that adults will praise such realism.
    c. their understanding of what their culture values deepens.
    d. they study drawings by older peers.

22. Until children begin to read, they often have an especially hard time discriminating (p. 316)
    a. letters from pictures.
    b. capital letters from lower-case letters.
    c. individual words.
    d. mirror-image letter pairs.

23. In early childhood, boys are typically ahead of girls in skills that emphasize (p. 317)
    a. lateralization.
    b. force and power.
    c. balance and precision of movement.
    d. language ability.

24. Formal lessons in physical activities during the preschool years (p. 317)
    a. have little impact on motor development.
    b. are especially beneficial for children from low-SES families.
    c. can minimize sex differences in motor skills.
    d. can provide benefits that last into adolescence.

25. The U.S. National Association for Sport and Physical Education recommends that each day, preschoolers engage in unstructured physical activity for (p. 317)
    a. 20 to 30 minutes.
    b. 30 to 45 minutes.
    c. no more than an hour.
    d. at least 60 minutes.

CHAPTER 9
COGNITIVE DEVELOPMENT IN EARLY CHILDHOOD

BRIEF CHAPTER SUMMARY

Early childhood brings dramatic advances in mental representation. Piaget believed that children's cognitive change resulted primarily from sensorimotor activity. But other theorists disagree with Piaget and put more emphasis on the link between language and thought. Make-believe play during the preschool years reflects the child's growing symbolic mastery and eventually includes sociodramatic play—make-believe with others, which begins by age 2½. Play, especially sociodramatic play, not only reflects but also contributes to children's cognitive and social skills.

Before age 3, most children have trouble with dual representation—viewing a symbolic object as both an object in its own right and a symbol. Adults can help promote their gradual understanding of symbol–real world relationships by exposing them to diverse symbols.

Aside from gains in representation, Piaget described preschool children in terms of their cognitive limitations, as his term *pre*operational suggests. He identified egocentrism, animistic thinking, inability to conserve, and irreversibility as illogical features of preoperational thought. But newer research reveals that Piaget overestimated these deficiencies and that, when tasks are simplified and made relevant to their everyday experiences, preschoolers show the beginnings of logical, reflective thought, including reasoning about transformation, understanding of cause-and-effect relationships, and organization of everyday knowledge into nested categories. During the third year, they also show some ability to distinguish appearance from reality. All this evidence suggests that operational thought develops gradually, not abruptly, as Piaget had thought. But despite its limitations, Piaget's theory has had a powerful influence on education, promoting child-oriented approaches to teaching and learning.

Whereas Piaget believed that language is of little importance in cognitive development, Vygotsky, who emphasized the social context of cognitive development, regarded language as the foundation for all higher cognitive processes. Social interaction promotes cognitive development through intersubjectivity and scaffolding or, more broadly, guided participation. As adults and more skilled peers provide children with verbal guidance on challenging tasks, children incorporate these dialogues into their private, or self-directed, speech and use them to regulate their own behavior. A Vygotskian classroom emphasizes not just independent discovery but also assisted discovery, including verbal support from teachers and peer collaboration.

A variety of information-processing skills improve during early childhood, including sustained attention, planning, and memory. Recognition memory becomes highly accurate, while recall develops more slowly because preschoolers are not yet effective users of memory strategies. Like adults, young children remember familiar, repeated events in terms of scripts. Between ages 3 and 6, they develop increasingly well-organized, detailed autobiographical memory, or memory for unique, meaningful events. Adults who use an elaborative, rather than a repetitive, conversational style with children promote the development of the child's autobiographical narratives.

Preschoolers make great strides in problem-solving skills. Overlapping-waves theory describes how young children experiment with diverse problem-solving strategies, eventually selecting the best ones on the basis of two criteria: accuracy and speed. Around the same time, children begin to develop a theory of mind, or metacognition—a coherent set of ideas about mental activities. Language, cognitive abilities, make-believe play, and social experiences promote understanding of the mind. Preschoolers also develop a basic understanding of written symbols and mathematical concepts, which is best promoted through informal literacy and mathematical experiences rather than through formal instruction.

A stimulating home environment, warm parenting, and reasonable demands for mature behavior continue to predict gains in mental development in early childhood. Formal academic training in early childhood undermines motivation and other aspects of emotional well-being. Although test score gains resulting from early intervention such as Head Start eventually decline, at-risk children show broader long-term benefits in school adjustment. High-quality child care can serve as effective intervention, whereas poor-quality child care undermines children's development regardless of SES background.

Educational media, including television, computers, and the Internet, are features of most children's lives in industrialized nations. Educational TV can promote literacy and number concepts, as well as general knowledge and social skills, but heavy viewing of entertainment TV detracts from children's school success and social experiences. While computer programming promotes both problem solving and social interaction, computer game playing often introduces children to content that is full of violence and gender stereotypes.

Language development proceeds rapidly during early childhood. By the end of the preschool years, children have an extensive vocabulary, use most of the grammatical constructions of their language competently, and are effective conversationalists. Opportunities for conversational give-and-take with adults enhance these skills.

LEARNING OBJECTIVES

After reading this chapter, you should be able to:

9.1   Describe advances in mental representation during the preschool years, including changes in make-believe play. (pp. 322–323)

9.2   Describe what Piaget regarded as deficiencies of preoperational thought. (pp. 323–326)

9.3   Discuss recent research on preoperational thought, and note the implications of such findings for the accuracy of Piaget's preoperational stage. (pp. 326–332)

9.4   Describe the educational principles derived from Piaget's theory. (pp. 332–333)

9.5   Describe Vygotsky's perspective on the social origins and significance of children's private speech, and contrast Piaget's view of children's private speech with that of Vygotsky. (pp. 333–336)

9.6   Discuss applications of Vygotsky's theory to education. (p. 336)

9.7   Summarize recent challenges to Vygotsky's theory, and evaluate his major ideas. (pp. 336–337)

9.8   Describe advances in attention, memory, and problem solving during early childhood. (pp. 338–342)

9.9   Discuss preschoolers' understanding of mental activities, noting factors that contribute to early metacognition, as well as limitations of the young child's theory of mind. (pp. 342–344)

9.10 Describe early literacy and mathematical development during the preschool years, and discuss appropriate ways to enhance children's development in these areas. (pp. 344–348)

9.11 Summarize the content of early childhood intelligence tests, and explain the impact of home, preschool and kindergarten programs, child care, and educational media on mental development. (pp. 349–355)

9.12 Trace the development of vocabulary, grammar, and conversational skills in early childhood. (pp. 355–360)

9.13 Cite factors that support language learning in early childhood. (pp. 360–361)

STUDY QUESTIONS

Piaget's Theory: The Preoperational Stage

1.   As children move from the sensorimotor to the *preoperational stage,* the most obvious change is an extraordinary increase in _____. (p. 322)

Advances in Mental Representation

1.   True or False: Piaget believed that language plays a major role in cognitive development. (p. 322)

Make-Believe Play

1. List three important changes in make-believe play during early childhood, and give an example of each. (pp. 322–323)

   A. _____

   _____

   Example: _____

   B. _____

   _____

   Example: _____

   C. _____

   _____

   Example: _____

2. What is *sociodramatic play*? (p. 323)

   _____

   _____

3. Summarize contributions of make-believe play to children's cognitive and social development. (p. 323)

   Cognitive: _____

   _____

   Social: _____

   _____

4. True or False: Recent research indicates that the creation of imaginary companions is a sign of maladjustment. Explain your answer. (p. 323)

   _____

5. Describe three ways to enhance preschoolers' make-believe play. (p. 324)

   A. _____

   _____

   B. _____

   _____

   C. _____

   _____

Symbol–Real World Relations

1. _____ refers to the ability to view a symbolic object as both an object in its own right and a symbol. Provide an example, and note the age at which children typically acquire this understanding. (p. 324)

   Example: _____

   _____

   Age: _____

2.   What factors contribute to children's understanding of *dual representation*? (p. 324)

_____

_____

Limitations of Preoperational Thought

1.   Piaget described preschoolers in terms of what they (can / cannot) understand. (p. 325)

2.   According to Piaget, young children are not capable of _____, or mental actions that obey logical rules. (p. 325)

3.   Piaget believed that _____, the inability to distinguish the symbolic viewpoints of others from one's own, is the most serious deficiency of preoperational thought. (p. 325)

4.   The preoperational belief that inanimate objects have lifelike qualities, such as thoughts, wishes, and intentions, is called _____. (p. 325)

5.   What is *conservation*? (p. 325)

_____

_____

6.   The inability to conserve highlights three aspects of preoperational children's thinking. List and describe them. (p. 325)

   A.   _____

   _____

   B.   _____

   _____

   C.   _____

   _____

7.   The most important illogical feature of preoperational thought is _____, an inability to mentally go through a series of steps in a problem and then reverse direction, returning to the starting point. (p. 325)

8.   Describe *hierarchical classification*. What Piagetian task demonstrates this limitation? (p. 326)

   A.   _____

   _____

   B.   _____

   _____

Follow-Up Research on Preoperational Thought

1.   Current research (challenges / supports) Piaget's account of a cognitively deficient preschooler. (p. 326)

2.   Cite two examples of nonegocentric responses in preschoolers' everyday interactions. (pp. 326–327)

   A.   _____

   B.   _____

3. Piaget (overestimated / underestimated) preschoolers' animistic beliefs. Provide evidence to support your answer. (p. 327)

_____

_____

4. Between 4 and 8 years of age, as familiarity with physical events and principles increases, children's magical beliefs (increase / decline). (p. 327)

5. Expalin how religion and culture affect how quickly children give up certain fantastic ideas. (p. 327)

_____

_____

6. Cite evidence showing how preschoolers are capable of logical thought when given tasks that are simplified and made relevant to their everyday lives. (pp. 327–328)

_____

_____

_____

_____

7. Explain the sequence of children's categorical understanding across the early childhood years. (pp. 328–330)

_____

_____

_____

_____

8. List two factors that support preschoolers' impressive skill at categorizing. (p. 330)

A. _____

B. _____

9. How can adults strengthen children's categorical learning? (p. 330)

_____

_____

_____

10. What factor largely accounts for young children's difficulty on appearance–reality problems? (p. 331)

_____

Social Issues: Education: Young Children's Understanding of Death

1. Name and briefly describe the five concepts that lead to an accurate understanding of death. (p. 328)

A. _____

B. _____

C. _____

D. _____

E. _____

2. Most children grasp the components of the death concept by age _____. (p. 328)

3. Describe two cultural influences on children's understanding of death. (pp. 328–329)

A. _____

_____

B. _____

_____

4. Explain how adults can help children develop an accurate understanding of death. (p. 329)

_____

_____

_____

Evaluation of the Preoperational Stage

1. The finding that logical operations develop gradually across the preschool years (supports / challenges) Piaget's stage concept. (p. 331)

2. Some neo-Piagetian theorists combine Piaget's stage concept with the information-processing emphasis on task-specific change. Briefly describe this viewpoint. (pp. 331–332)

_____

_____

_____

Piaget and Early Childhood Education

1. List and describe three educational principles derived from Piaget's theory. (pp. 332–333)

A. _____

_____

B. _____

_____

C. _____

_____

2. What is perhaps the greatest challenge to educational applications of Piaget's theory? (p. 333)

_____

Vygotsky's Sociocultural Theory

1. True or False: Vygotsky placed a greater emphasis than did Piaget on the role of language in cognitive development. (p. 333)

Children's Private Speech

1. Contrast Piaget's view of children's egocentric speech with Vygotsky's view of *private speech*. (pp. 333–334)

Piaget: _____

_____

Vygotsky: _____

_____

2. Most research findings have supported (Piaget's / Vygotsky's) view of children's private speech. (p. 334)

3. Under what circumstances are children likely to use private speech? (p. 334)

_____

_____

Social Origins of Early Childhood Cognition

1. Vygotsky believed that children's learning takes place within a zone of proximal development. Explain what this means. (pp. 334–335)

_____

_____

2. Explain how two features of social interaction, *intersubjectivity* and *scaffolding,* facilitate children's cognitive development. (p. 335)

Intersubjectivity: _____

_____

Scaffolding: _____

_____

3. Define the term *guided participation*, noting how it differs from scaffolding. (p. 335)

_____

_____

_____

4. Describe features of effective adult scaffolding that foster children's cognitive development. (pp. 335–336)

_____

_____

_____

Vygotsky and Early Childhood Education

1. What features do Piagetian and Vygotskian classrooms have in common? On which features do they differ? (p. 336)

A. _____

_____

B. _____

_____

2. Vygotsky saw _____ as the ideal social context for fostering cognitive development in early childhood. (p. 336)

Evaluation of Vygotsky's Theory

1. Discuss two contributions and two criticisms of Vygotsky's theory of cognitive development. (pp. 336–337)

   Contributions:

   A. _____

   _____

   B. _____

   _____

   Criticisms:

   A. _____

   _____

   B. _____

   _____

Cultural Influences: Children in Village and Tribal Cultures Observe and Participate in Adult Work

1. Summarize cultural differences in children's access to and participation in adult work, providing examples from American, Efe, and Mayan cultures. (p. 337)

   American: _____

   _____

   _____

   Efe: _____

   _____

   _____

   Mayan: _____

   _____

   _____

2. Briefly explain how cultural differences in young children's daily participation in adult work affect their competencies and behavior. (p. 337)

   _____

   _____

   _____

   _____

Information Processing

Attention

1. What factors are responsible for gains in sustained attention during early childhood? (pp. 338–339)

   _____

   _____

2. Describe preschoolers' ability to plan, including what they are likely to plan well, as well as limitations in their *planning*. (p. 339)

   Planning abilities: _____

   _____

   _____

   Limitations: _____

   _____

   _____

3. Explain how cultural tools support planning skills. (p. 339)

   _____

   _____

Memory

1. Preschoolers' recall memory is much (better / worse) than their recognition memory. (p. 339)

2. Explain why preschoolers are ineffective at using *memory strategies*. (pp. 339–340)

   _____

   _____

3. Describe *episodic memory,* and provide an example. (p. 340)

   A. _____

   B. _____

4. Like adults, preschoolers remember familiar experiences in terms of _____,
   general descriptions of what occurs and when it occurs in a particular situation. What are the benefits of using this strategy to aid memory and recall? (p. 340)

   _____

   _____

5. How does autobiographical memory change in early childhood? (pp. 340–341)

   _____

   _____

6. Describe two styles adults use for promoting children's autobiographical narratives, and note which style leads to better memory of events over time. (p. 341)

   Elaborative: _____

   _____

   Repetitive: _____

   _____

Problem Solving

1.   Describe Siegler's *overlapping-waves theory* of problem solving. (pp. 341–342)

_____

_____

_____

2.   List three factors that facilitate children's movement from less to more efficient problem-solving strategies. (p. 342)

A.   _____

B.   _____

C.   _____

The Young Child's Theory of Mind

1.   A theory of mind, also called _____, is a coherent set of ideas about mental activities. (p. 342)

2.   Trace changes in children's awareness of mental life from the toddlerhood through the preschool years. (pp. 342–343)

_____

_____

_____

3.   List three benefits of false-belief understanding. (p. 343)

A.   _____

B.   _____

C.   _____

4.   Briefly describe four factors that contribute to preschoolers' theory of mind. (pp. 343–344)

A.   _____

_____

B.   _____

_____

C.   _____

_____

D.   _____

_____

5.   Provide an example of how social interaction promotes understanding of the mind. (p. 344)

_____

6.   Cite two ways in which preschoolers' awareness of inner cognitive activities is incomplete. (p. 344)

A.   _____

B.   _____

Biology and Environment: "Mindblindness" and Autism

1. Describe three core areas of functioning in which children with autism display deficits. (p. 345)

   A. _____

   _____

   B. _____

   _____

   C. _____

   _____

2. True or False: Researchers agree that autism stems from abnormal brain functioning, usually due to genetic or prenatal environmental causes. (p. 345)

3. Growing evidence reveals that children with autism have a deficient theory of mind. Cite several consequences of this deficit. (p. 345)

   _____

   _____

   _____

4. How might impairments in executive processing affect the thinking and behavior of children with autism? (p. 345)

   _____

   _____

   _____

Early Literacy and Mathematical Development

1. True or False: Preschoolers cannot understand written language until they learn to read and write. (p. 346)

2. A young child's active effort to construct literacy knowledge through informal experiences is called _____ literacy. (p. 346)

3. _____ refers to the ability to reflect on and manipulate the sound structure of spoken language. (p. 346)

4. List four ways in which adults can foster literacy development in young children. (p. 347)

   A. _____

   B. _____

   C. _____

   D. _____

5. Discuss SES differences in language and literacy learning opportunities. (p. 347)

   _____

   _____

   _____

6. List four steps in the development of preschoolers' mathematical reasoning that correspond with the following general age ranges: (p. 348)

14 to 16 months:

_____

_____

2 to 3 years:

_____

_____

3 1/2 to 4 years:

_____

_____

4 to 5 years:

_____

_____

7. True or False: Basic arithmetic knowledge emerges in a universal sequence around the world. (p. 348)

Individual Differences in Mental Development

Early Childhood Intelligence Tests

1. What types of tasks are commonly included on early childhood intelligence tests? (p. 349)

_____

2. Why do minorities and children from low-SES homes sometimes do poorly on intelligence tests? What steps can be taken to help improve their performance? (p. 349)

A. _____

_____

B. _____

_____

3. Intelligence tests (do / do not) sample all human abilities, and performance (is / is not) affected by cultural and situational factors. (p. 349)

4. True or False: By age 6 or 7, scores on early childhood intelligence tests are good predictors of later IQ and academic achievement. (p. 349)

Home Environment and Mental Development

1. Describe the characteristics of homes that foster young children's intellectual growth. (pp. 349, 350)

_____

_____

_____

2. Research suggests that the home environment (does / does not) play a major role in the generally poorer intellectual performance of low-SES children in comparison to their higher-SES peers. (p. 349)

Preschool, Kindergarten, and Child Care

1. Largely because of maternal employment, the number of young children enrolled in preschool or child care has steadily (decreased / increased), reaching nearly _____ percent in the United States and some Canadian provinces. (p. 350)

2. A _____ is a program with planned educational experiences aimed at enhancing the development of 2- to 5-year-olds. In contrast, _____ includes a variety of arrangements for supervising children of employed parents. (p. 350)

3. Describe the differences between *child-centered preschools* and *academic preschools*. (p. 350)

   Child-centered: _____

   _____

   _____

   Academic: _____

   _____

   _____

4. True or False: Children in academic preschools demonstrate higher levels of achievement than those in child-centered preschools, including greater mastery of motor, academic, language, and social skills. (pp. 350–351)

5. Briefly describe Montessori education, and discuss the benefits associated with this type of education. (p. 351)

   Montessori education: _____

   _____

   Benefits: _____

   _____

6. Summarize the goal and program components of *Project Head Start* and Canada's *Aboriginal Head Start*. (p. 351)

   Goal: _____

   Components of the program: _____

   _____

   _____

   _____

7. Cite two long-term benefits of preschool intervention. (pp. 351–352)

   A. _____

   B. _____

8. Why do Head Start preschoolers demonstrate weaker gains than preschoolers who attend university-based programs? (p. 352)

   _____

   _____

   _____

9. Explain how parent involvement in early intervention contributes to improved school adjustment in children. (p. 352)

_____

_____

_____

10. True or False: Preschoolers exposed to poor-quality child care, regardless of family SES level, score lower on measures of cognitive and social skills and display more behavior problems. (p. 353)

11. List four characteristics of high-quality child care. (pp. 353, 354)

A. _____

B. _____

C. _____

D. _____

Educational Media

1. Describe the benefits of watching educational programs, such as *Sesame Street.* (pp. 353–354)

_____

_____

_____

2. The average 2- to 6-year-old watches TV programs and videos from _____ to _____ hours a day. (p. 354)

3. What does research reveal about the effects of heavy TV viewing on children's cognitive development? (p. 354)

_____

_____

4. Cite several benefits associated with children's use of educational computer programs. (p. 355)

_____

_____

Language Development

Vocabulary

1. True or False: Preschoolers learn an average of 5 new words each day, increasing their vocabulary from 200 words at age two to 10,000 words at age six. (p. 356)

2. Explain how children build their vocabularies so quickly over the preschool years. (p. 356)

_____

_____

_____

3. How does culture contribute to children's *fast mapping*? (p. 356)

_____

_____

4. The principle of _____ refers to an assumption made by children in the early stages of vocabulary growth that words refer to entirely separate (nonoverlapping) categories. (p. 356)

5. When children figure out the meaning of a word by observing how it is used in the structure of a sentence, they are using _____ *bootstrapping*. (p. 357)

6. Discuss two ways adults support children's vocabulary growth during early childhood. (p. 357)

    A. _____

    _____

    B. _____

    _____

7. Provide two explanations for vocabulary development during early childhood. (pp. 357–358)

    A. _____

    _____

    B. _____

    _____

Grammar

1. True or False: English-speaking children show wide variability in the sequence in which they master grammatical markers. (p. 358)

2. When children overextend grammatical rules to words that are exceptions—for example, saying "I runned fast" instead of "I ran fast"—they are making an error called _____. (p. 358)

3. True or False: By the end of the preschool years, children use most of the grammatical constructions of their language competently, with the exception of passive expressions. (pp. 358–359)

4. Describe at least two differing perspectives in the debate over how children acquire grammar. (p. 359)

    A. _____

    _____

    B. _____

    _____

Conversation

1. The practical, social side of language that is concerned with how to engage in effective and appropriate communication with others is known as _____. (p. 359)

2. Preschoolers are skilled conversationalists. Provide an example to support this statement. (p. 359)

    _____

3. True or False: Having an older sibling facilitates the acquisition of pragmatic language. (p. 360)

4. Preschoolers (do / do not) adjust their speech to fit the age, sex, and social status of their listeners. (p. 360)

5. Explain the conditions in which preschoolers are likely to experience a break down of conversational skills. (p. 360)

    _____

    _____

    _____

Supporting Language Learning in Early Childhood

1. Explain how adults can use *expansions* and *recasts* to promote preschoolers' language development. (p. 360)

   Expansions: _____

   _____

   Recasts: _____

   _____

ASK YOURSELF . . .

For *Ask Yourself* questions for this chapter, along with feedback on the accuracy of your answers, please log on to MyDevelopmentLab (for registration and access, please visit mydevelopmentlab.com or follow the directions on p. ix).

   1) Select the Chapter of the *Ask Yourself*.
   2) Open the E-Book and select the Explore icon next to the *Ask Yourself*.
   3) Complete questions and choose "Submit answers for grading" or "Clear Answers" to start over.

SUGGESTED STUDENT READINGS

Lillard, A. (2007). *Montessori: The science behind the genius.* New York: Oxford University Press. Presents an alternative to traditional educational practices by focusing on children's learning and cognition, their natural interest in learning, meaningful learning contexts, the importance of peers, and adult interaction styles and child outcomes.

McGee, L. M., & Richgels, D. J. (2007). *Literacy's beginnings: Supporting young readers and writers.* Boston: Allyn and Bacon. An excellent resource for anyone interested in education, child development, or related professions, this book presents developmentally-appropriate strategies for teaching reading and writing.

Schneider, W., Schumann-Hengsteler, R., & Sodian, B. (2006). *Young children's cognitive development: Interrelationships among executive functioning, working memory, verbal ability, and theory of mind.* Mahwah, NJ: Erlbaum. Using research by leading experts in the field, this book examines how advances in information processing contribute to young children's cognitive development.

Singer, D. Hirsh-Pasek, K., & Golinkoff, R. (Eds.). (2006). *Play=Learning: How play motivates and enhances children's cognitive and social-emotional growth.* New York: Oxford University Press. A collection of chapters highlighting the diverse benefits of play for children's learning. The authors argue that in trying to create a generation of "Einsteins," many parents and educators are overlooking the importance of play in early child development.

PUZZLE 9.1 TERM REVIEW

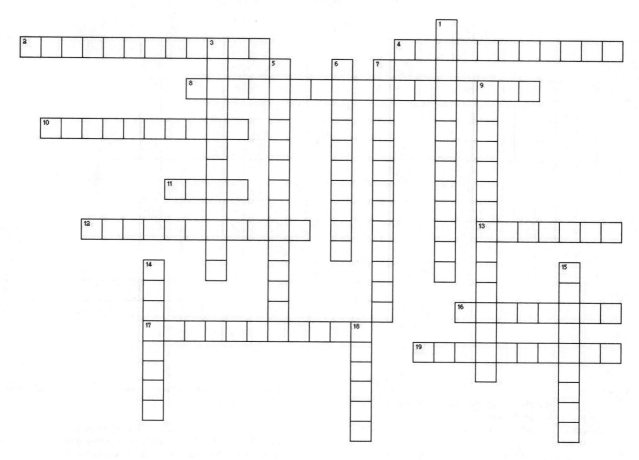

Across

2. _____classification: organization of objects into classes and subclasses based on similarities and differences
4. The inability to distinguish the symbolic viewpoints of others from one's own
8. Process whereby two participants who begin a task with different understandings arrive at a shared understanding
10. Memory _____: deliberate mental activities that improve our chances of remembering
11. _____ representation: representations of a symbolic object as both an object in its own right and a symbol
12. Mutual _____ bias: assumption that words refer to entirely separate categories
13. General descriptions of what occurs and when it occurs in a particular situation
16. Thinking out a sequence of acts ahead of time and allocating attention accordingly to reach a goal
17. A changing quality of support over the course of a teaching session in which the adult adjusts the assistance provided to fit the child's current level of performance
19. Tendency to focus on one aspect of a situation and neglect other important features

Down

1. Make-believe play with others
3. Understanding that certain physical features of an object remain the same, even when their outward appearance changes
5. Piaget's second stage; marked by rapid growth in representation
6. Canada's _____ Head Start provides preschool education and nutritional and health services for children and encourages parent involvement
7. Thinking about thought
9. The inability to mentally go through a series of steps and then reverse direction, returning to the starting point
14. Memory for everyday experiences
15. _____ thinking: the belief that inanimate objects have lifelike qualities
18. _____ participation calls attention to adult and child contributions to cooperative dialogue without specifying the precise features of communication

PUZZLE 9.2 TERM REVIEW

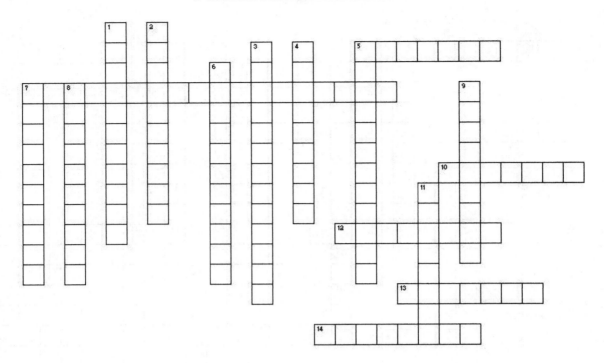

Across

5. _____ speech: self-directed speech that children use to plan and guide their behavior
7. Application of regular grammatical rules to words that are exceptions
10. Fast _____: connecting a new word with an underlying concept after only a brief encounter
12. Preschools in which teachers structure the children's learning and teach through formal lessons
13. Adult responses that restructure children's incorrect speech into a more appropriate form
14. _____ bootstrapping: figuring out grammatical rules by relying on word meanings

Down

1. _____-waves theory: children generate a variety of strategies on challenging problems and gradually select those that result in rapid, accurate solutions
2. The practical, social side of language that is concerned with how to engage in effective and appropriate communication with others
3. Preschools in which teachers provide a variety of activities from which children select; most of the day is devoted to free play (2 words)
4. Project _____ _____ is a federal program that provides low-SES children with a year or two of preschool, along with nutritional and medical services (2 words)
5. _____ awareness: ability to reflect on and manipulate the sound structure of spoken language
6. Principle stating that the last number in a counting sequence indicates the quantity of items in the set
7. Principle specifying order relationships between quantities
8. Adult responses that elaborate on a child's utterance, increasing its complexity
9. _____ bootstrapping: figuring out word meanings by observing how words are used in the structure of sentences
11. _____ literacy refers to young children's active efforts to construct literacy knowledge through informal experiences

PRACTICE TEST #1

1. According to Piaget, the primary ingredient in childhood cognitive change is (p. 322)
   a. children's creation of internal images of experience resulting from sensorimotor activity.
   b. children's make-believe play.
   c. the development of language.
   d. children's preoperational experience.

2. Research into imaginary playmates suggests that children with such companions (p. 323)
   a. are maladjusted.
   b. display less complex and imaginative pretend play than agemates without imaginary companions.
   c. are delayed in emotional understanding.
   d. typically treat them with care and affection and say that the imaginary playmate returns that care.

3. According to Piaget, preoperational children are not capable of (p. 325)
   a. egocentrism.
   b. mental actions that obey logical rules.
   c. self-centered play.
   d. self-conscious emotions.

4. Preoperational children's inability to conserve highlights the fact that (p. 325)
   a. their thought is reversible.
   b. they are adept at hierarchical classification.
   c. their thought is characterized by centration.
   d. they are aware of dynamic transformation.

5. Follow-up research on preoperational children's illogical thought has revealed that (p. 328)
   a. 3- and 4-year-olds can use causal expressions, such as if–then, as accurately as adults do.
   b. most 3- to 5-year-olds, when shown a substance dissolving in water, believe that the substance ceases to exist.
   c. children cannot reason by analogy until around age 6.
   d. most 3- and 4-year-olds think illogically about even simplified tasks.

6. Research suggests that preschoolers have trouble distinguishing between "looks like" and "is really and truly" tasks because of (p. 331)
   a. difficulty in distinguishing appearance from reality.
   b. inability to understand basic-level categories.
   c. difficulty with dual representation.
   d. trouble with the language of the tasks.

7. The major criticism of educational applications of Piaget's theory has to do with (p. 333)
   a. their failure to accept children's varying rates of cognitive development.
   b. Piaget's insistence that young children learn primarily through acting on the environment.
   c. their tendency to impose new skills to speed up development.
   d. Piaget's failure to notice how young children can engage in logical thought.

8. Contrary to Piaget's view, Vygotsky argued that young children speak to themselves (p. 334)
   a. within their zones of proximal development.
   b. because they are egocentric.
   c. to understand others' point of view.
   d. for self-guidance in tasks.

9. Research shows that children's planning and problem solving improve most through (p. 336)
   a. peer disagreement.
   b. working on tasks with same-age peers.
   c. working with a partner who is either an "expert" peer or an adult.
   d. working by themselves.

10. Vygotsky's theory has been criticized for (p. 337)
    a. saying little about how elementary capacities, such as attention, spark changes in children's social experience.
    b. failing to account for the effects of verbal communication.
    c. assuming that all Western parents scaffold their young children's mastery of challenging tasks.
    d. overlooking the role of sociodramatic play in expanding the child's zone of proximal development.

11. Preschoolers sometimes generate and follow a plan (p. 339)
    a. when adults do not give them directions.
    b. for tasks that are familiar and not too complicated.
    c. to play within the rules of a new game.
    d. when asked to compare detailed pictures.

12. Studies have shown that better recall in early childhood is strongly associated with (p. 339)
    a. language development.
    b. improved recognition memory.
    c. the ability to rehearse information.
    d. increasing skill at memory strategies.

13. The elaborative style enables children to reestablish and organize their memories of unique events because it (p. 341)
    a. provides little information, thus guiding the child toward more detailed recall.
    b. stimulates episodic memory.
    c. follows the child's lead, using varied questions and adding information.
    d. relies on recognition more than recall.

14. According to the overlapping-waves theory, as children home in on effective strategies for solving problems, they eventually display the most efficient strategy: (p. 342)
    a. min.
    b. automatic retrieval of the answer.
    c. recognition of two possible answers.
    d. counting on their fingers.

15. Although 3-year-olds realize that thinking takes place inside their heads, both 2- and 3-year-olds think that (p. 342)
    a. both beliefs and desires determine behavior.
    b. memories are objects they carry inside their heads like marbles in a bag.
    c. others' perspectives often differ from their own.
    d. people always behave in ways consistent with their desires.

16. Make-believe play helps children develop a theory of mind because it (p. 344)
    a. enables them to reason about the implications of situations that contradict reality.
    b. helps them identify thoughts and beliefs.
    c. allows them to share beliefs with playmates.
    d. enables them to use complex sentences including mental-state words.

17. Children younger than age 5 typically conclude that mental activity stops when there are no obvious cues to indicate it, a fact that suggests that they (p. 344)
    a. understand only the most obvious mental inferences.
    b. cannot yet reflect on thoughts.
    c. pay little attention to the process of thinking.
    d. have not yet reached the necessary level of frontal-lobe development.

18. Phonological awareness is a strong predictor of emergent literacy and later reading and spelling achievement because it involves (p. 346)
    a. grammatical knowledge.
    b. the ability to reflect on and manipulate the sound structure of spoken language.
    c. sound–letter knowledge.
    d. interactive reading.

19. In the process of developing mathematical reasoning, children around age 4 realize that (p. 348)
    a. min is a more efficient strategy than estimation.
    b. their ability to count is limited by the number of their fingers.
    c. the words for numbers correspond to amounts of objects.
    d. subtraction cancels out addition.

20. Studies reveal that the negative outcomes associated with formal academic training in preschool and kindergarten are strongest for (p. 351)
    a. low-SES children.
    b. children when they reach adolescence.
    c. very high-SES children and very low-SES children.
    d. Canadian-Aboriginal children and Native-American children.

21. The most extensive studies of preschool intervention have found that children who attended such programs (p. 352)
    a. scored higher on IQ tests than those in the High/Scope Perry Preschool Project.
    b. enjoyed the benefits only into adolescence.
    c. remained consistently ahead on real-life measures of school adjustment compared with children who did not.
    d. showed only minor improvements in verbal and math skills.

22. Children tend to learn verbs later than labels for objects because verbs (p. 356)
    a. require more complex understanding of relationships between objects and actions.
    b. cannot be fast-mapped as easily as nouns.
    c. are less available to syntactic bootstrapping.
    d. require mastery of the mutual exclusivity bias, which children do not generally achieve until age 2½ or 3.

23. Children are most likely to make the error of overregularization with (p. 358)
    a. frequently used irregular verbs.
    b. common regular verbs.
    c. adverbs and adjectives.
    d. plural nouns.

24. Many researchers have questioned Chomsky's theory of a language acquisition device because (p. 359)
    a. evidence has shown that grammatical development is an extended process.
    b. Chomsky's related idea of semantic bootstrapping has been proved false.
    c. no recent study supports the notion that children have a special language-making capacity.
    d. children master language at vastly different rates throughout the world.

25. Some researchers question the importance of adults' recasts and expansions of children's speech because (p. 361)
    a. restructuring and elaborating can discourage children from freely using language.
    b. those techniques are not used in all cultures and do not consistently affect children's usage.
    c. Vygotsky's theory, as applied to language acquisition, has been proved wrong.
    d. adults do not always apply grammatical rules consistently.

PRACTICE TEST #2

1. As preschoolers achieves greater symbolic mastery, play (p. 322)
   a. includes fewer combinations of schemes.
   b. becomes less self-centered.
   c. is less likely to be sociodramatic.
   d. adheres more closely to the real-life conditions associated with it.

2. Children grasp dual representation (p. 324)
   a. through exposure to diverse symbols, such as picture books and drawings.
   b. through interaction with an imaginary companion.
   c. largely through self-centered play.
   d. in the first half of the second year.

3. According to Piaget, children's egocentrism is responsible for their (p. 325)
   a. ability to accommodate their reasoning to their physical and social worlds.
   b. grasp of dual representation.
   c. ability to perform operations.
   d. animistic thinking.

4. Follow-up research on preoperational thought has revealed that (p. 327)
   a. Piaget was essentially correct about children's egocentrism.
   b. beginning in infancy, children can distinguish animate from inanimate objects.
   c. preschoolers believe that magic can alter their everyday experiences.
   d. children cannot give psychological explanations for people's actions until around age 4.

5. For young children trying to understand death, the ideas of *applicability* and *causation* are the hardest to master because (p. 328)
   a. young children are likely to blame themselves for the death of a relative or pet.
   b. these ideas are based on the idea of inevitability, which is even more difficult for young children to understand.
   c. these ideas require a firm grasp of some basic notions of biology.
   d. young children have not yet developed religious ideas of an afterlife or purpose on earth.

6. Challenging Piaget's assumptions, research on children's categorization has revealed that (p. 329)
   a. young children's thinking is governed by the way things appear.
   b. 2- to 5-year olds are uncertain in the inferences they draw using nonobservable characteristics shared by category members.
   c. categorization does not begin until children have acquired language.
   d. by the third or fourth year, children move easily between basic-level categories and general categories.

7. Research findings revealing that preschoolers have some logical understanding suggest that (p. 331)
   a. they attain logical operations gradually, rather than suddenly at particular stages.
   b. Piaget's stage definition has been entirely discredited by later research.
   c. these children build sophisticated category systems.
   d. operational thought appears around age 3.

8. Research shows that children use more private speech when they (p. 334)
   a. adapt what they say to listeners.
   b. work through tasks that are challenging but within their zone of proximal development.
   c. cease to use self-directed speech.
   d. confront problems that they find especially easy to solve.

9. Between ages 3 and 5, children strive for intersubjectivity
   a. as they scaffold tasks within groups of playmates.
   b. by sharing private speech with one another.
   c. in dialogues with peers.
   d. only when working with more expert partners.

10. According to Vygotsky, the ideal social context for fostering cognitive development is (p. 336)
    a. make-believe play.
    b. assisted discovery.
    c. independent discovery.
    d. intersubjectivity.

11. Unlike most Western preschoolers, Yucatec Mayan preschoolers (p. 337)
    a. do not spontaneously take responsibility for tasks.
    b. are highly competent at self-care.
    c. engage in rich and varied make-believe play.
    d. cannot sit quietly for long periods.

12. Scripts help children remember familiar events by enabling them to (p. 340)
    a. ignore stimuli that otherwise would interfere with memory.
    b. move beyond episodic memory to more sequential memory.
    c. recall the sequences of digit-span tasks.
    d. organize, interpret, and predict everyday experiences.

13. According to the overlapping-waves theory, children gradually come to use _____ as their criteria in choosing problem-solving strategies.
    a. min and recall
    b. organization and rehearsal
    c. accuracy and speed
    d. recall and recognition

14. From early to middle childhood, children's increasing efforts to alter others' beliefs suggest that they (p. 343)
    a. more firmly realize the power of belief to influence action.
    b. are convinced that their own perspectives are identical to those of others.
    c. recognize that believing, like thinking, takes place inside their heads.
    d. have no awareness of false belief.

15. Language helps preschoolers develop a theory of mind because it (p. 343)
    a. enables them to inhibit inappropriate responses.
    b. gives them the ability to reflect on thoughts.
    c. allows them to view people as intentional beings.
    d. enables them to move beyond the stage of false belief.

16. The belief that children with autism have a deficient theory of mind comes from research revealing that they (p. 345)
    a. attribute mental states to inanimate objects rather than people.
    b. establish overly intense joint attention with one person.
    c. use words such as think and know in the wrong contexts.
    d. have great difficulty with false belief.

17. Early in the period of emergent literacy, preschoolers are likely to (p. 346)
    a. understand the symbolic function of elements of print.
    b. distinguish between drawing and writing.
    c. think that a single letter stands for a whole word.
    d. grasp that individual letters are linked to sounds.

18. In the early preschool years, children's grasp of ordinality advances to the point that they (p. 348)
    a. begin to add and subtract.
    b. attach verbal labels to amounts and sizes.
    c. grasp that the last number in a counting sequence indicates quantity.
    d. understand the meaning of numbers up to 15.

19. Low-SES preschoolers often score lower on mental tests than their abilities should allow because they (p. 349)
    a. may look to the adult for attention and approval, rather than defining the testing situation in terms of achievement.
    b. are more interested in playing than in taking the test.
    c. tend to do well on nonverbal tasks and to lag on verbal tasks.
    d. are often sensitive to the tester's ethnicity.

20. In the United States, the children especially likely to be in preschools and child-care centers, rather than cared for by relatives or at home, are those of (p. 350)
    a. Asian-American parents.
    b. middle-SES and single parents.
    c. parents who wish to enhance their children's development.
    d. higher-income parents and very low-income parents.

21. A distinctive feature of the Montessori approach to education is the emphasis on (p. 351)
    a. giving children intensive academic training in math.
    b. providing long periods for individual and small-group learning in child-chosen activities.
    c. hiring only teachers who have advanced academic degrees.
    d. involving children in teacher-directed tasks of increasing difficulty.

22. Large-scale studies of child care reveal that the developmentally appropriate group size in early childhood programs is (p. 354)
    a. 5 children to 1 teacher.
    b. 1 teacher and 1 assistant for every 12 children.
    c. 18 to 20 children with 2 teachers.
    d. 20 to 25 children with 3 teachers or 2 teachers and an assistant.

23. *Sesame Street* has reduced its rapid-paced format in favor of more leisurely episodes because (p. 354)
    a. research has shown that slower-paced programs with easy-to-follow narratives can lead to more elaborate make-believe play than those that offer quick, disconnected bits of information.
    b. its producers are trying to emulate educational computer games.
    c. girls, who generally can focus more easily than boys on slow narratives, are the program's primary audience.
    d. much of the program's audience consists of children who are nonnative speakers of English.

24. Children use most of the grammatical constructions of their language competently by (p. 359)
    a. age 2.
    b. 3 to 3½ years.
    c. late middle childhood.
    d. the end of the preschool years.

25. Children acquire the pragmatics of language as they (p. 359)
    a. learn basic rules of grammar.
    b. engage in social interaction that promotes effective and appropriate communication.
    c. expand their vocabulary.
    d. learn which situations require more verbal description and which less.

CHAPTER 10
EMOTIONAL AND SOCIAL DEVELOPMENT
IN EARLY CHILDHOOD

BRIEF CHAPTER SUMMARY

Erikson's stage of initiative versus guilt offers an overview of the personality changes of early childhood. During the preschool years, children's self-concepts begin to take shape. Their self-esteem is high, supporting their enthusiasm for mastering new skills. Preschoolers' growing self-understanding includes awareness of the I-self and me-self, which forms the basis of self-concept. Self-esteem emerges and differentiates, and children gain in understanding of emotion, emotional self-regulation, capacity to experience self-conscious emotions, and capacity for empathy and sympathy. Cognition, language, and warm, sensitive parenting support these developments.

During the preschool years, peers provide an important context for the development of a wide range of social skills. Peer interaction increases, cooperative play becomes common, and children form first friendships. Preschoolers learn to use their new social problem-solving skills to resolve conflicts. Peer relations are influenced by parental encouragement and the quality of sibling ties.

Three approaches to understanding early childhood morality—psychoanalytic, social learning, and cognitive-developmental—emphasize different aspects of moral functioning. Although most researchers reject Freud's account of conscience development, the power of inductive discipline is recognized. Social learning theorists believe that children learn to act morally through modeling, while the cognitive-developmental perspective regards children as active thinkers about social rules. A hostile family atmosphere, poor parenting practices, and heavy viewing of violent television and other media promote childhood aggression, which can develop into serious antisocial activity.

Gender typing develops rapidly over the preschool years. Heredity contributes to gender-typed behavior, but environmental forces—parents, siblings, teachers, peers, media, and the broader social environment—also play powerful roles. Neither cognitive-developmental theory nor social learning theory provide a complete account of the development of gender identity. Gender schema theory is an information-processing approach that shows how environmental pressures and children's cognition combine to affect gender-role development.

Compared to children of authoritarian and permissive parents, children whose parents use an authoritative style are most likely to be well-adjusted and socially mature. Warmth, explanations, and reasonable demands for mature behavior account for the effectiveness of the authoritative style. Child-rearing beliefs and practices vary in different ethnic groups, so child-rearing styles should always be viewed in light of cultural values and the circumstances in which parents and children live.

Child maltreatment, including both abuse and neglect, is the combined result of factors within the family, the community, and the broader culture. Interventions at all of these levels are essential for preventing it.

LEARNING OBJECTIVES

After reading this chapter, you should be able to:

10.1   Describe Erikson's initiative versus guilt stage, noting the personality changes that take place during this stage. (p. 366)

10.2   Discuss preschoolers' self-concepts and the development of autobiographical memory and self-esteem. (pp. 366–369)

10.3   Identify changes in understanding and expressing emotion during early childhood, citing factors that influence those changes. (pp. 369–372)

10.4   Discuss the development of self-conscious emotions, empathy, and sympathy during early childhood, noting how parenting and temperament affect emotional development in these areas. (pp. 372–373)

10.5   Describe advances in peer sociability over the preschool years, with particular attention to Parten's play types, and discuss cultural variations in peer sociability. (pp. 374–376)

10.6   Describe the quality of preschoolers' first friendships, noting how parents and siblings influence early peer relations, and discuss the emergence of social problem solving during early childhood. (pp. 376–379)

10.7   Compare the central features of psychoanalytic, social learning, and cognitive-developmental approaches to moral development. (pp. 380–386)

10.8   Trace milestones in preschoolers' moral understanding, highlighting the importance of social experience. (p. 386)

10.9   Describe the development of aggression in early childhood, including family and media influences, and cite ways to control aggressive behavior. (pp. 386–391)

10.10   Describe preschoolers' gender-stereotyped beliefs and behaviors, and discuss genetic and environmental influences on gender-role development. (pp. 391–395)

10.11   Describe and evaluate the major theories of gender identity development, and cite ways to reduce gender stereotyping in young children. (pp. 395–398)

10.12   Describe the three features that distinguish major styles of child rearing. Compare each style, indicating which is most effective, and discuss cultural variations in child-rearing beliefs and practices. (pp. 398–401)

10.13   Describe the multiple origins of child maltreatment, its consequences for development, and prevention strategies. (pp. 401–405)

STUDY QUESTIONS

Erikson's Theory: Initiative versus Guilt

1.   Define *initiative versus guilt,* and describe how it is exhibited in preschoolers. (p. 366)

   A. _____

   _____

   B. _____

   _____

2.   Was Erikson's belief that play is the central means through which children find out about themselves and their social world accurate? Explain. (p. 366)

   _____

   _____

   _____

   _____

3.   Compare Erikson's theory of development during the preschool years with that of Freud. (p. 366)

   _____

   _____

   _____

   _____

4. According to Erikson, what leads to a negative outcome of the initiative versus guilt stage? (p. 366)

_____

_____

_____

_____

Self-Understanding

1. Describe the two distinct aspects of self identified by William James. (p. 366)

A. _____

_____

B. _____

_____

2. How does language contribute to self-understanding? (p. 366)

_____

_____

3. Define *self-concept.* (p. 366)

_____

_____

_____

Foundations of Self-Concept

1. Describe the quality of preschoolers' self-descriptions. (p. 367)

_____

_____

_____

2. Explain the link between preschoolers' self-development and their possessiveness of objects. Given this relationship, how can adults promote friendly peer interaction? (p. 367)

A. _____

_____

B. _____

_____

Cultural Influences: Cultural Variations in Personal Storytelling: Implications for Early Self-Concept

1. Discuss differences in storytelling practices between Chinese and Irish-American parents, and explain the influence on children's self-image. (p. 368)

   A. _____

   _____

   B. _____

   _____

2. Whereas most North Americans believe that favorable self-esteem is (crucial / unimportant) for healthy development, Chinese adults generally regard self-esteem as (crucial / unimportant). (p. 368)

Emergence of Self-Esteem

1. Define *self-esteem.* (p. 368)

   _____

   _____

2. Why do preschoolers often rate their own ability as extremely high and underestimate task difficulty? (p. 368)

   _____

   _____

3. List several ways adults can promote children's self-esteem. (p. 369)

   _____

   _____

   _____

   _____

Emotional Development

1. Between ages 2 and 6, children make strides in the emotional abilities that researchers refer to as _____ competence. (p. 369)

Understanding Emotion

1. By age _____ to _____, children can correctly judge the causes of many basic emotions. (p. 370)

2. Preschoolers (do / do not) realize that thoughts and feelings are interconnected. (p. 370)

3. Provide an example illustrating how preschoolers can predict what a playmate expressing a certain emotion might do next. (p. 370)

   _____

   _____

4. True or False: In situations with conflicting cues about how a person is feeling, preschoolers can easily reconcile this differing information. (p. 370)

5. Explain how parent-child discussions can facilitate children's understanding of emotions. (pp. 370–371)

_____

_____

_____

_____

6. Discuss how make-believe play contributes to emotional understanding. (p. 371)

_____

_____

_____

Emotional Self-Regulation

1. Summarize the relationship between language and emotional self-regulation. (pp. 371–372)

_____

_____

2. Explain how effortful control helps young children manage emotion. (p. 371)

_____

_____

_____

3. Cite two characterisitcs of emotionally reactive children. (p. 371)

A. _____

B. _____

4. How can parents foster preschoolers' emotional self-regulation? (p. 371)

_____

_____

_____

5. List two factors that make fears common in early childhood. (p. 371)

A. _____

B. _____

Self-Conscious Emotions

1. Preschoolers experience self-conscious emotions (more / less) often than do toddlers. (p. 372)

2. Beginning in early childhood, (guilt / shame) is associated with feelings of personal inadequacy and is linked with maladjustment. In contrast, (guilt / shame), as long as it occurs in appropriate circumstances, is related to positive adjustment, perhaps because it helps children resist harmful impulses. (p. 372)

Empathy and Sympathy

1. Empathy serves as an important motivator of _____, or _____ behavior—actions that benefit another person without any expected reward for the self. (p. 373)

2. Distinguish between *empathy* and *sympathy*. (p. 373)

   Empathy: _____

   _____

   _____

   Sympathy: _____

   _____

   _____

3. True or False: In some children, empathizing with an upset peer or adult escalates into personal distress. (p. 373)

4. Discuss the impact of parenting on children's development of empathy and sympathy. (p. 373)

   _____

   _____

   _____

   _____

Peer Relations

Advances in Peer Sociability

1. Describe Parten's three-step sequence of social development. (p. 374)

   A. _____

   _____

   B. _____

   _____

   C. 1. _____

   _____

   C. 2. _____

   _____

2. True or False: Longitudinal research shows that play types emerge in the order Parten suggested, with later-appearing ones replacing earlier ones in a developmental sequence. (p. 374)

3. True or False: It is the *type*, rather than the *amount*, of solitary and parallel play that changes during early childhood. (p. 374)

4. What types of nonsocial activity in the preschool years are cause for concern? (p. 375)

   _____

   _____

5. Most preschoolers with low rates of peer interaction are not socially anxious. Cite research that supports this statement. (p. 375)

_____

_____

_____

6. How does sociodramatic play support emotional and social development during early childhood? (p. 375)

_____

_____

_____

7. True or False: Peer sociability takes essentially the same form in collectivist and individualistic cultures. (p. 375)

8. Provide an example of how cultural beliefs about the importance of play affect early peer associations. (p. 376)

_____

_____

_____

_____

First Friendships

1. Summarize children's understanding of friendship in early childhood. (p. 376)

_____

_____

_____

2. Describe the unique quality of preschoolers' interactions with friends. (p. 376)

_____

_____

_____

3. Cite several benefits of kindergarten friendships. (pp. 376–377)

_____

_____

_____

Social Problem Solving

1. Explain the importance of peer conflicts during early childhood. (p. 377)

_____

_____

_____

2. List the six steps in Crick and Dodge's *social problem-solving* model. (pp. 377–378)

A. _____

B. _____

C. _____

D. _____

E. _____

F. _____

3. Discuss how social problem solving affects peer relations. (p. 378)

_____

_____

_____

_____

4. Summarize improvements in social problem solving during the preschool and early school years. (p. 378)

_____

_____

_____

5. Cite several ways that intervening with children who have weak social problem-solving skills can enhance development. (p. 378)

_____

_____

_____

Parental Influences on Early Peer Relations

1. List two ways that parents directly influence their children's social relationships. (p. 378)

A. _____

B. _____

2. Explain how parent–child attachment and parent–child play can promote children's peer interaction skills. (p. 379)

Attachment:

_____

_____

Play:

_____

_____

Foundations of Morality

1. List two points on which most theories of moral development are in agreement. (p. 380)

   A. _____

   B. _____

2. Match each of the following major theories of moral development with the aspect of moral functioning that it emphasizes: (p. 380)

   ____ Emotional side of conscience
   ____ Ability to reason about justice and fairness
   ____ Moral behavior

   1. Psychoanalytic theory
   2. Social learning theory
   3. Cognitive-developmental theory

The Psychoanalytic Perspective

1. Briefly summarize Freud's psychoanalytic theory of morality development. (p. 380)

   _____

   _____

   _____

2. True or False: Most researchers agree with Freud's assertion that fear of punishment and loss of parental love motivates children to behave morally. (p. 380)

3. A special type of discipline called _____ supports conscience development by pointing out the effects of the child's misbehavior on others. Cite three ways in which it does so. (pp. 380–381)

   A. _____

   _____

   B. _____

   _____

   C. _____

   _____

4. What type of parenting interferes with the development of empathy and prosocial responding? (p. 381)

   _____

   _____

5. Discuss ways children's characteristics affect the success of parenting techniques. (p. 381)

   _____

   _____

   _____

   _____

6. Recent research shows that Freud was (correct / incorrect) in his assertion that guilt is an important motivator of moral action. Explain your answer. (pp. 381–382)

   _____

   _____

   _____

Social Learning Theory

1.   Explain why operant conditioning is insufficient for children to acquire moral responses. (p. 382)

_____

_____

_____

2.   Social learning theorists believe that children learn to behave morally largely through
     _____—observing and imitating adults who demonstrate appropriate behavior.
     (p. 382)

3.   List three characteristics of models that affect children's willingness to imitate them. (p. 382)

     A.   _____

     B.   _____

     C.   _____

4.   True or False: Punishment promotes immediate compliance but does not produce long-lasting changes in
     children's behavior. (p. 382)

5.   List four undesirable side effects of harsh punishment. (p. 383)

     A.   _____

     B.   _____

     C.   _____

     D.   _____

6.   Describe two alternatives to harsh punishment. (pp. 383–384)

     A.   _____

     _____

     B.   _____

     _____

7.   Describe three ways that parents can increase the effectiveness of punishment when they do decide to use it.
     (pp. 384–385)

     A.   _____

     _____

     B.   _____

     _____

     C.   _____

     _____

8.   Explain positive discipline, noting how it reduces the need for punishment. (p. 385)

     _____

     _____

     _____

     _____

9. Provide three examples of positive discipline. (p. 385)

A. _____

B. _____

C. _____

Cultural Influences: Ethnic Differences in the Consequences of Physical Punishment

1. Use of physical punishment is highest among (low-SES minority parents / middle-SES white parents). (p. 384)

2. Although corporal punishment is linked with a wide variety of negative child outcomes, exceptions do exist. Describe these exceptions. (p. 384)

_____

_____

_____

3. Discuss differences in African-American and Caucasian-American parental attitudes toward physical punishment. (p. 384)

African-American: _____

_____

_____

Caucasian-American: _____

_____

_____

The Cognitive-Developmental Perspective

1. In what major way does the cognitive-developmental perspective of morality differ from the psychoanalytic and social learning approaches? (pp. 385–386)

_____

_____

2. Preschoolers are able to distinguish _____ *imperatives,* which protect people's rights and welfare, from two other forms of action: _____ *conventions,* or customs determined solely by consensus, such as table manners and dress style, and *matters of* _____, which do not violate rights or harm others, are not socially regulated, and therefore are up to the individual. (p. 386)

3. Explain how young children learn to make distinctions between moral and social-conventional transgressions. (p. 386)

_____

_____

_____

_____

4. List three features of parent communication that help children reason about morality. (p. 386)

A. _____

B. _____

C. _____

The Other Side of Morality: Development of Aggression

1. By the end of the preschool years, two general types of aggression emerge. The most common is
   _____ *aggression*, aimed at obtaining an object, privilege, or space with no deliberate intent to
   harm. The other type is _____ *aggression*, which is intended to hurt another person.
   (pp. 386–387)

2. Match the following types of hostile aggression with the appropriate descriptions. (p. 387)

   _____ Physical aggression
   _____ Verbal aggression
   _____ Relational aggression

   A. Harms others through threats of physical aggression, name-
      calling, or hostile teasing
   B. Social exclusion, malicious gossip, or friendship manipulation
   C. Pushing, hitting, kicking, or punching others; destroying other's
      property

3. In early childhood, (physical / verbal) aggression gradually replaces (physical / verbal) aggression. What
   accounts for this change? (p. 387)

4. Discuss sex differences in aggression throughout the preschool years. (pp. 387–388)

5. Explain how a hostile family atmosphere promotes and sustains high rates of childhood aggression. (p. 388)

6. True or False: Girls are more likely than boys to be targets of harsh physical discipline and parental
   inconsistency. (p. 387)

7. Cite three negative outcomes for highly aggressive children. (pp. 387–388)

   A. _____
   B. _____
   C. _____

8. True or False: Violent content in children's programming occurs at above average rates, and cartoons are the most
   violent. (p. 388)

9. Explain why young children are especially likely to be influenced by television. (pp. 388–389)

10. Briefly summarize the long-term effects of TV violence on children's behavior. (p. 389)

_____

_____

_____

_____

11. True or False: Media violence hardens children to aggression, making them more willing to tolerate it in others. Briefly explain your response. (p. 389)

_____

_____

_____

_____

12. What is the V-Chip, and why is it an incomplete solution for regulating children's TV? (pp. 389–390)

_____

_____

_____

_____

13. List three strategies parents can use to regulate children's TV viewing and computer use. (p. 390)

A. _____

_____

B. _____

_____

C. _____

_____

14. List several ways to help parents and children break the cycle of hostilities between family members. (pp. 390–391)

Parents:

A. _____

_____

B. _____

_____

Children:

A. _____

_____

B. _____

_____

Gender Typing

1. What is *gender typing?* (p. 391)

_____

_____

_____

Gender-Stereotyped Beliefs and Behaviors

1. Preschoolers' gender stereotypes are (flexible / rigid). Explain your answer. (pp. 391–392)

_____

_____

_____

2. Most preschoolers (do / do not) realize that characteristics associated with each sex (for example, activities, clothes, hairstyles, and occupation) do not determine whether a person is male or female. (p. 392)

Biological Influences on Gender Typing

1. Discuss Eleanor Maccoby's argument that hormonal differences between males and females have important consequences for gender typing, including play styles evidenced in early childhood. (p. 392)

_____

_____

_____

_____

_____

2. Girls exposed to high levels of androgens prenatally display (more / less) "masculine" behavior. (p. 392)

Biology and Environment: David: A Boy Who Was Reared as a Girl

1. Explain how David Reimer's personal experience confirms the impact of genetic sex and prenatal hormones on a person's sense of self as male or female, as well as highlighting the importance of social experience. (p. 393)

Genetic sex and prenatal hormones: _____

_____

_____

_____

Social experience: _____

_____

_____

_____

Environmental Influences on Gender Typing

1. Describe ways in which parents encourage gender-stereotyped beliefs and behavior in their children. (pp. 393–394)

_____

_____

_____

_____

2. Of the two sexes, (girls / boys) are clearly more gender-stereotyped. Why might this be the case? (p. 394)

_____

_____

_____

3. Discuss gender typing in the classroom setting, noting its impact on social behaviors. (p. 394)

_____

_____

_____

4. Peer rejection is greater for (girls / boys) who frequently engage in "cross-gender" behavior. (p. 395)

5. Discuss the different styles of social influence promoted within gender-segregated peer groups. (p. 395)

Boys: _____

_____

Girls: _____

_____

6. Cite three factors that work together to sustain gender segregation and the gender typing that occurs within it. (p. 395)

A. _____

B. _____

C. _____

7. How do TV and media influence children's endorsement of gender stereotypes? (p. 395)

_____

_____

_____

_____

Gender Identity

1. Define _gender identity,_ and indicate how it is measured. (p. 395)

_____

_____

_____

2. _____ refers to a type of gender identity in which the person scores highly on both masculine and feminine personality characteristics. (p. 395)

3. How is gender identity related to psychological adjustment? (p. 395)

_____

_____

_____

4. Contrast social learning and cognitive-developmental accounts of the emergence of gender identity. (p. 396)

   Social Learning: _____

_____

_____

_____

   Cognitive-Developmental: _____

_____

_____

_____

5. *Gender* _____ refers to the understanding that sex is biologically based and remains the same even if clothing, hairstyles, and play activities change. (p. 396)

6. Name and briefly describe the three-step sequence in which preschoolers master gender constancy. (p. 396)

   A. _____

   B. _____

   C. _____

7. Is gender constancy responsible for children's gender-typed behavior? Why or why not? (p. 396)

_____

_____

_____

8. Explain *gender schema theory.* (p. 396)

_____

_____

_____

9. Define *gender schemas,* and explain how they influence gender-typed preferences and behavior. (pp. 396–397)

   A. _____

_____

   B. _____

_____

10. How does gender-schematic thinking affect children's behavior? (p. 397)

_____

_____

_____

Reducing Gender Stereotyping in Young Children

1. Cite several ways that parents and teachers can reduce gender stereotyping in young children. (pp. 397–398)

_____

_____

_____

_____

Child Rearing and Emotional and Social Development

Styles of Child Rearing

1. Based on the research findings of Baumrind and others, cite three features that consistently differentiate between more and less effective parenting styles. (p. 398)

A. _____

B. _____

C. _____

2. Describe the four *child-rearing styles,* noting where each stands in relation to the characteristics listed above. (pp. 399–400)

Authoritative: _____

_____

Authoritarian: _____

_____

Permissive: _____

_____

Uninvolved: _____

_____

3. Match each of the following child-rearing styles with the correct outcomes. (pp. 399–400)

_____ Authoritative
_____ Authoritarian
_____ Permissive
_____ Uninvolved

1. Children are anxious, unhappy, low in self-esteem and self-reliance; when frustrated, they react with hostility
2. Disrupts virtually all aspects of development—children have poor emotional self-regulation, school achievement difficulties, and antisocial behavior
3. Linked to many aspects of competence—upbeat mood, self-control, task persistence, high self-esteem, social and moral maturity, and favorable academic performance
4. Children are impulsive, disobedient, rebellious, overly demanding, dependent on adults, and have poor social achievement

4.   Which child-rearing approach is the most successful, and why? (p. 399)

A. _____

B. _____

5.   (Authoritarian / Authoritative) parents engage in a subtle type of control called _____ control, in which they intrude on and manipulate children's verbal expression, individuality, and attachments to parents. (p. 399)

6.   At its extreme, uninvolved parenting is a form of child maltreatment called _____. (p. 400)

What Makes Authoritative Child Rearing Effective?

1.   Cite four reasons that authoritative parenting is especially effective. (p. 400)

A. _____

_____

B. _____

_____

C. _____

_____

D. _____

_____

Cultural Variations

1.   Describe how the parenting practices of the following cultural groups often differ from those of Caucasian Americans: (p. 401)

Chinese: _____

_____

Hispanic, Asian Pacific Island, and Caribbean (of African and East Indian origin): _____

_____

_____

African-American: _____

_____

2.   What do the cultural variations in question 1 remind us about child-rearing styles? (p. 401)

_____

_____

Child Maltreatment

1. List and describe four forms of child maltreatment. (p. 402)

   A. _____

   _____

   B. _____

   _____

   C. _____

   _____

   D. _____

   _____

2. (Parents / Strangers) commit more than 80 percent of abusive incidents. (p. 402)

3. True or False: Researchers have identified a single "abusive" personality type. (p. 402)

4. List parent, child, and family environment characteristics associated with an increased likelihood of abuse. (pp. 402–403)

   Parent: _____

   _____

   Child: _____

   _____

   Family Environment: _____

   _____

5. Cite two reasons that most abusive parents are isolated from supportive ties to their communities. (p. 403)

   A. _____

   _____

   B. _____

   _____

6. Societies that view violence as an appropriate way to solve problems set the stage for child abuse. These conditions (do / do not) exist in the United States and Canada. Explain your answer. (pp. 403–404)

   _____

   _____

   _____

   _____

7. Summarize the consequences of child maltreatment for abused children. (p. 404)

_____

_____

_____

_____

8. Describe the pathways through which the damaging consequences of child maltreatment occur. (p. 404)

_____

_____

_____

_____

9. Discuss strategies for preventing child maltreatment in the family. (p. 404)

_____

_____

_____

10. Explain how Hawaii's Healthy Families America program identifies families at risk for child maltreatment, and describe the services offered through this program. (p. 404)

    Identification: _____

    _____

    Services: _____

    _____

    _____

11. How does adding a cognitive component to home visitation increase the effectiveness of abuse prevention programs? (pp. 404–405)

    _____

    _____

    _____

12. Child maltreatment is a crime that is (difficult / easy) to prove. (p. 405)

13. In child maltreatment cases, judges are often hesitant to remove the child from the family. List three reasons for their reluctance. (p. 405)

    A. _____

    B. _____

    C. _____

ASK YOURSELF . . .

For *Ask Yourself* questions for this chapter, along with feedback on the accuracy of your answers, please log on to MyDevelopmentLab (for registration and access, please visit mydevelopmentlab.com or follow the directions on p. ix).

1) Select the Chapter of the *Ask Yourself.*
2) Open the E-Book and select the Explore icon next to the *Ask Yourself.*
3) Complete questions and choose "Submit answers for grading" or "Clear Answers" to start over.

SUGGESTED STUDENT READINGS

Donnelly, M., & Straus, M. A. (Eds.). (2005). *Corporal punishment of children in theoretical perspective.* New Haven, CT: Yale University Press. A theoretical approach to understanding the uses causes, and consequences of corporal punishment. Topics include: historical perspectives, the effects of punishment on attachment, and the relationship between punishment and stress responses in children.

Hartup, W. W., & Tremblay, R. E. (2005). *Developmental origins of aggression.* New York: Guilford. Examines the biological and environmental correlates of childhood aggression, including longitudinal research on the developmental trajectories of children who display aggression early in life. The authors also describe sex differences in adaptive and maladaptive aggression.

Hines, M. (2005). *Brain gender.* New York: Oxford University Press. Examines both biological and environmental factors that contribute to sex differences in human behavior. Topics include sex differences in play, mathematical and verbal ability, aggression, and the development of gender identity.

Olfman, S. (Ed.). (2005). *Childhood lost: How American culture is failing our kids.* New York: Guildford. Using contributions from various disciplines, this book examines the negative impact of American culture on child development. Chapters address such topics as why parenting matters, lack of societal supports for child rearing, the consequences of children developing sexual awareness at younger and younger ages, and what can happen when television and computers replace family time.

PUZZLE 10.1 TERM REVIEW

Across

4. Set of attributes, abilities, attitudes, and values that individuals believe define who they are (2 words, hyph.)
6. Play with others that is directed toward a common goal
8. Erikson regarded _____ versus guilt as the critical psychological conflict of the preschool years.
9. Activity involving unoccupied, onlooker behavior and solitary play
11. Play that involves separate activities but exchange of toys and comments
14. A form of hostile aggression that does damage to another's peer relationships

Down

1. _____ problem solving: resolving conflicts in ways that are both acceptable to others and beneficial to the self
2. Aggression aimed at obtaining an object, privilege, or space with no intent to harm
3. Actions that benefit another person without any expected reward for the self are known as _____, or altruistic, behaviors
5. Play that occurs near other children, with similar materials, but involves no interaction
7. Judgments we make about our own self-worth and the feelings associated with those judgments (2 words, hyph.)
10. Aggression intended to harm another person
12. Feelings of concern or sorrow for another's plight
13. Gender identity in which the person scores high on both masculine and feminine personality traits

PUZZLE 10.2 TERM REVIEW

Across

1. Gender _____: the process of developing gender roles
6. Style of child rearing that combines low acceptance and involvement, little control, and indifference to autonomy granting
7. _____ aggression: a form of hostile aggression that harms others through physical injury to individuals or their property
11. Matters of _____ _____: concerns that do not violate rights and are up to each individual, such as choice of friends or color of clothing
13. _____ imperatives: standards that protect people's rights and welfare
14. _____ conventions: customs determined solely by consensus, such as table manners
15. Gender _____: image of oneself as relatively masculine or feminine in characteristics
16. Mild punishment involving removal of the child from the immediate setting until he/she is ready to behave appropriately (2 words)
17. Gender _____ theory: approach to gender typing that combines social learning and cognitive-developmental features
18. The self as knower and actor, which is separate from the surrounding world, remains the same person over time, has a private inner life not accessible to others, and can control its own thoughts and actions
19. The self as an object of knowledge, consisting of all physical, psychological, and social characteristics that make the self unique

Down

2. Type of discipline that involves communicating the effects of the child's misbehavior on others
3. Gender _____: understanding that sex remains the same even if outward appearance changes
4. _____-_____ styles: combinations of parenting behaviors that occur over a wide range of situations (2 words, hyph.)
5. Style of child rearing that is low in acceptance and involvement, high in coercive control, and low in autonomy granting
8. _____ aggression: a form of hostile aggression that harms others through threats of physical aggression, name-calling, or hostile teasing
9. _____ control: parental behaviors that intrude on and manipulate children's verbal expression, individuality, and attachment to parents
10. Child-rearing style that is high in acceptance but overindulging and inattentive, low in control, and lax rather than appropriate in autonomy granting
12. Style of child rearing the involves high acceptance and involvement, adaptive control techniques, and appropriate autonomy granting

225

PRACTICE TEST #1

1. According to Erikson, play helps children learn about themselves and their social world by (p. 366)
   a. permitting them to try new skills with little risk of criticism and failure.
   b. allowing them to identify with same-sex agemates.
   c. advancing the development of the superego.
   d. enabling children to establish a dominance hierarchy.

2. According to William James, the I-self (p. 366)
   a. consists of all the distinctive qualities that make the self unique.
   b. changes over time.
   c. has a private inner life that is not accessible to others.
   d. includes social characteristics, such as roles and relationships with others.

3. A study of Chinese and Irish-American families revealed that by the end of the preschool years, the Chinese children's self-image (p. 368)
   a. was highly self-critical.
   b. emphasized membership in the collective and obligations to others.
   c. had a stronger me-self than I-self.
   d. was autonomous, consisting largely of personal descriptions.

4. Preschoolers usually rate their own ability to complete tasks as extremely high because (p. 368)
   a. they have difficulty distinguishing between their desired and their actual competence.
   b. they do not yet have a fully developed superego.
   c. their capacity for initiative has outstripped their capacity for guilt.
   d. they have excessively high self-esteem.

5. A good predictor of 2-year-olds' emotion language is (p. 370)
   a. the frequency with which they use self-directed speech.
   b. intense conflict among family members.
   c. friendly, considerate behavior toward agemates.
   d. maternal prompting of emotional thoughts.

6. To promote good social relations, most cultures teach children to (p. 371)
   a. mimic mothers' emotion words.
   b. communicate positive feelings and inhibit unpleasant ones.
   c. externalize negative emotion.
   d. react critically to others' emotional outbursts.

7. Among Western children, beginning in early childhood, intense shame is associated with (p. 372)
   a. good adjustment.
   b. culturally inappropriate self-assertion.
   c. favorable adjustment for boys but not girls.
   d. feelings of personal inadequacy.

8. Children most likely to display sympathy and prosocial behavior are those who (p. 373)
   a. are sociable, assertive, and good at regulating emotion.
   b. feel empathic personal distress at others' sadness.
   c. show high EEG brain-wave activity when faced with someone in need.
   d. are adept at scaffolding their emotional responses.

9. Follow-up research in peer sociability has revealed that nonsocial activity persists (p. 374)
   a. only until the end of the second year.
   b. in conjunction with parallel play until around age 3½.
   c. into kindergarten, where it continues to occupy about one-third of children's free-time play.
   d. until preschoolers learn to engage in parallel play.

10. One study showed that compared with North American preschoolers, Chinese preschoolers (p. 375)
    a. tend to be outgoing in large groups.
    b. are more willing to include a quiet, reserved child in play.
    c. spend a great deal of time unoccupied or in parallel play.
    d. engage in more imitative behavior involving close physical contact.

11. Many experts believe that when assessing preschoolers for kindergarten readiness, the most important skills to evaluate are (p. 377)
    a. social, because learning to interact prosocially with peers is the primary purpose of kindergarten attendance.
    b. academic, because today's kindergartners are expected to master academic skills, such as reading, that formerly were not taught until first grade.
    c. both academic and social skills, because children who are too friendly and outgoing have trouble settling down and focusing on academic skills.
    d. both academic and social skills, because preschoolers' social maturity contributes to later school performance.

12. The information-processing model of social problem solving accounts for children's mental states by factoring in their (p. 377)
    a. ability to notice social cues.
    b. formulations of social goals.
    c. representations of past social experiences.
    d. evaluations of the probable effectiveness of problem-solving strategies.

13. Discipline that relies heavily on threats of punishment can (p. 381)
    a. make children more aware of the impact of their actions on others.
    b. make children so anxious and frightened that they cannot think clearly enough to figure out what they should do.
    c. give children useful scripts that help them determine how to act in the future so as to avoid punishment.
    d. provide children with clear reasons for changing their behavior.

14. When parents discipline by inducing empathy-based guilt, the child's guilt reactions are associated with (p. 381)
    a. withdrawal of love.
    b. feelings of failure and worthlessness.
    c. stopping harmful actions and repairing damage caused by misdeeds.
    d. rejection of prosocial behavior.

15. Explanations can increase the effectiveness of punishment because they (p. 381)
    a. help children recall their misdeed and relate it to expectations of future behavior.
    b. warn children of impending punishment.
    c. function as a verbal time out.
    d. enable children to visualize spanking and other physical punishments.

16. Studies of ethnically and culturally diverse families and children revealed that spanking was associated with a rise in behavior problems when parents (p. 384)
    a. were still in their teens.
    b. used it when they were very angry.
    c. were cold and rejecting.
    d. tended to use it in public.

17. Preschoolers' instrumental aggression declines as (p. 387)
    a. their language skills improve.
    b. they begin to learn indirect forms of relational aggression.
    c. their capacity to delay gratification improves.
    d. their play becomes more gender-stereotyped.

18. Canada's regulation of children's television differs from that of the United States in that Canada (p. 389)
    a. requires TV sets to contain the V-chip.
    b. bans from children's shows realistic scenes of violence that minimize consequences.
    c. mandates violence ratings for children's programs.
    d. does not regulate the sexual content of children's shows.

19. According to evolutionary theorists, environmental experiences (p. 392)
    a. can significantly alter the intensity of biologically based sex differences.
    b. affect the gender typing of girls more than boys.
    c. have only slight effects on gender typing.
    d. cannot eradicate aspects of gender typing that served adaptive functions in human history.

20. Boys are generally more gender typed than girls because (p. 394)
    a. mothers of boys tend to use more generic utterances with them.
    b. boys' gender-associated characteristics are stronger than those of girls.
    c. fathers tend to apply more pressure for gender-role conformity to sons than to daughters.
    d. parents of boys are more likely to hold stereotyped gender values.

21. Unlike social learning theory, cognitive-developmental theory maintains that gender identity begins with (p. 396)
    a. an acquired appreciation of gender constancy.
    b. modeling and reinforcement.
    c. androgyny that usually later shifts to a masculine or feminine identity.
    d. gender stability.

22. The authoritative child-rearing style is successful in autonomy granting because parents who use this style (p. 399)
    a. often make demands by using psychological control.
    b. are warm but overindulgent or inattentive.
    c. permit the child to make many decisions before he or she is ready.
    d. encourage the child to express thoughts, feelings, and desires.

23. Research finding suggest that when African-American families live in crime-ridden neighborhoods, strict parental control (p. 401)
    a. exacerbates negative environmental effects, creating aggressive, defiant children.
    b. may have a positive effect, preventing antisocial involvements.
    c. benefits girls more than boys.
    d. encourages children to become overdependent on parents.

24. More than 80 percent of incidents of child maltreatment are committed by (p. 402)
    a. relatives.
    b. school officials.
    c. parents.
    d. other children.

25. A family characteristic strongly associated with child abuse is (p. 404)
    a. spouse abuse.
    b. excessive exposure to violent television programming.
    c. parental history of being abused as a child.
    d. a permissive child-rearing style.

PRACTICE TEST #2

1. According to Erikson, the negative outcome of early childhood is (p. 366)
   a. failure to identify with either parent.
   b. too much initiative resulting from too little discipline.
   c. an overly strict superego, causing children to feel too much guilt.
   d. not enough play.

2. As the child's I-self becomes more firmly established, (p. 366)
   a. it takes on many attributes of the me-self.
   b. the child focuses more intently on the me-self.
   c. the child begins to identify the I-self with the surrounding world.
   d. the child's me-self gradually diminishes.

3. Parents and teachers can most successfully promote children's friendly interaction with peers by (p. 367)
   a. allowing them to be possessive so that they can learn to settle disputes over possessions with peers.
   b. drawing their attention to others' me-self.
   c. insisting that they share.
   d. accepting their possessiveness as a sign of self-assertion and encouraging compromise.

4. Because preschoolers have difficulty interpreting situations that offer conflicting emotional cues, they tend to (p. 370)
   a. focus on the most obvious aspect of the situation, neglecting other relevant information.
   b. turn away from the situation in confusion.
   c. emphasize the most positive aspect of the situation.
   d. reconcile the conflicting cues.

5. By age 3 to 4, children's emotional self-regulation has developed to the point that they can (p. 371)
   a. scaffold their emotional interactions with peers.
   b. reliably distinguish clearly between appearance and reality in most situations.
   c. verbalize a variety of strategies for adjusting their emotional arousal to a more comfortable level.
   d. move from rudimentary effortful control to more complex emotional dialogues.

6. Preschoolers generally depend on adults to know when to feel self-conscious emotion because they are (p. 372)
   a. sensitive to praise but unaware of criticism.
   b. still developing standards of excellence and conduct.
   c. still developing effortful control.
   d. not yet capable of complex feelings of self-esteem.

7. Unlike shame, guilt may cause children to (p. 372)
   a. adapt to collectivist social values.
   b. feel personally inadequate.
   c. be less receptive to parental feedback about conduct or performance.
   d. resist harmful impulses and behave more considerately.

8. In some children, empathy does not lead to sympathy because (p. 373)
   a. their feelings of empathy escalate into personal distress.
   b. they do not have the words to communicate empathic feelings.
   c. sympathy requires that they feel altruism.
   d. they are not yet capable of self-evaluation.

9. According to Mildred Parten, children engage in *associative play* when they (p. 374)
   a. are unoccupied onlookers who simply observe other children's play.
   b. play near one another with similar materials but do not try to influence one another's behavior.
   c. engage in separate activities but exchange toys and comment on one another's behavior.
   d. orient themselves toward a common goal.

10. Especially common during the first two years, functional play involves activities like (p. 375)
    a.   running around a room or rolling a toy car back and forth.
    b.   drawing a picture or putting together a puzzle.
    c.   looking on while others run, draw, or build.
    d.   acting out storybook or television characters.

11. Because children with peer difficulties often hold biased social expectations, they (p. 378)
    a.   avoid play with other children.
    b.   notice too many social cues, becoming confused as a result.
    c.   generate problem-solving strategies with no more than one other child.
    d.   attend selectively to social cues and misinterpret others' behavior.

12. Most developmental theories agree that children's morality is initially controlled by (p. 380)
    a.   adults.
    b.   peer-generated standards of justice.
    c.   inner standards.
    d.   emotional reactions.

13. One reason that induction so successfully promotes conscience formation in children is that it encourages them to (p. 381)
    a.   feel guilt in response to their misbehavior.
    b.   adopt moral standards because those standards make sense.
    c.   criticize other children for misbehavior.
    d.   develop a strong superego.

14. Social learning theorists believe that children learn to behave morally largely through modeling because (p. 382)
    a.   models reinforce prosocial acts.
    b.   children respond positively to consistency between assertions and behavior.
    c.   conscience is a learned, rather than innate, capacity.
    d.   the initial infrequency with which many prosocial acts occur suggests that reinforcement alone cannot explain their rapid development in early childhood.

15. When used frequently, punishment promotes (p. 382)
    a.   lasting changes in children's behavior.
    b.   positive responses to parents' competence and power.
    c.   only immediate compliance.
    d.   a reduction in children's aggression.

16. According to the cognitive-developmental view, preschoolers can distinguish moral imperatives from social conventions because they (p. 386)
    a.   actively make sense of their experiences.
    b.   understand the potential consequences of personal choice.
    c.   grasp that social conventions are arbitrary while moral imperatives are absolute.
    d.   observe adults modeling that distinction.

17. Troubled families often instill aggressive behavior in children through a pattern that typically begins with (p. 388)
    a.   willful disobedience in the children.
    b.   forceful and often inconsistent discipline.
    c.   aggression between siblings.
    d.   impulsiveness in boys.

18. One cognitive explanation for preschoolers' typically one-sided judgments about gender is their (p. 392)
    a. association of certain toys and articles of clothing with one sex or the other.
    b. inability to formulate a gender schema.
    c. difficulty interpreting gender-related social cues.
    d. difficulty understanding that the characteristics associated with one's sex do not determine whether one is male or female.

19. The case of David Reimer confirms the (p. 393)
    a. predominant influence of social experience on gender.
    b. close emotional connection of siblings.
    c. impact of genetic sex and prenatal hormones on a person's sense of sex and gender.
    d. fact that males are especially uncomfortable with gender stereotypes.

20. By age 3, when preschoolers engage in cross-gender activities, (p. 395)
    a. peers criticize them.
    b. they easily form mixed-gender peer groups.
    c. teachers tend to guide them toward gender-typed activities.
    d. boys tend to become less aggressive and girls more so.

21. According to gender schema theory, children use gender schemas to (p. 396)
    a. build gender-salience filters.
    b. acquire gender-stereotyped preferences and behaviors from others.
    c. achieve gender consistency.
    d. organize experiences into masculine and feminine categories that help them interpret their world.

22. The permissive child-rearing style tends to yield children who are (p. 400)
    a. anxious, unhappy, and low in self-esteem.
    b. upbeat, self-controlled, and cooperative.
    c. impulsive, disobedient, and rebellious.
    d. withdrawn, depressed, and aggressive.

23. Hispanic and Asian Pacific Island families typically combine firm insistence on respect for parental authority with (p. 401)
    a. permissiveness in all other areas.
    b. high parental warmth.
    c. psychological coercion.
    d. a tendency to withhold praise.

24. The majority of abusive parents (p. 403)
    a. are members of ethnic minority groups.
    b. were raised permissively.
    c. are middle-SES people whose jobs are unstable.
    d. are isolated from both formal and informal social supports.

25. Research indicates that the most important factor in preventing mothers who were abused as children from repeating the cycle is (p. 404)
    a. a trusting relationship with another person.
    b. intensive individual counseling.
    c. intervention by child-protection officials.
    d. improved economic conditions.

CHAPTER 11
PHYSICAL DEVELOPMENT IN MIDDLE CHILDHOOD

BRIEF CHAPTER SUMMARY

As in the preschool years, gains in body growth are slow in middle childhood. Large individual differences in body size, resulting from a combination of heredity and environment, remain apparent. Because of improved health and nutrition, children in industrialized nations are growing larger and reaching physical maturity earlier than they did in previous generations.

In middle childhood, the bones of the body lengthen and broaden. The primary teeth are all lost and replaced with permanent ones. In the brain, white matter increases, especially in the frontal lobes of the cerebral cortex. Gray matter declines as a result of synaptic pruning and neuron death. Much brain development in middle childhood may take place at the level of neurotransmitters, which permit neurons to communicate across synapses. Hormones also affect brain functioning.

Although children from economically advantaged homes are at their healthiest in middle childhood, health problems do occur. Vision and hearing difficulties, malnutrition, obesity, bedwetting, asthma, and unintentional injuries are the most frequent health concerns of the school years. Although school-age children are capable of learning a wide range of health information, it has little impact on their everyday behavior. Interventions must also reduce health hazards, coach children in good health practices, and model and reinforce these behaviors.

Growth in body size and muscle strength supports improved motor coordination in middle childhood. Gains in flexibility, balance, agility, force, and reaction time underlie improvements in children's gross motor skills. Fine motor coordination also increases. Children's writing becomes more legible, and their drawings show greater organization, more detail, and the addition of the depth dimension. As in younger children, marked individual differences in motor capacities are evident in middle childhood.

The physical activities of school-age children reflect advances in the quality of their play. Child-organized games with rules become common and support emotional and social development. Increasingly, children participate in adult-organized youth sports. Some researchers are concerned that this trend may have an adverse effect on development. Rough-and-tumble play and the establishment of dominance hierarchies are aspects of children's interaction that reflect our evolutionary past. Wide individual differences in athletic performance exist, influenced by both genetic and environmental factors. Physical education classes help ensure that all children have access to the benefits of regular exercise and play. Many experts believe that schools should offer more frequent physical education classes and should shift their focus to enjoyable, informal games and individual exercise. In recent years, school recess has diminished to allow more time for academics, but research findings indicate that recess provides practice in vital social skills, as well as a valuable opportunity for regular physical activity.

LEARNING OBJECTIVES

After reading this chapter, you should be able to:

11.1   Describe changes in body size, body proportions, and skeletal maturity during middle childhood, noting secular trends in physical growth. (pp. 412–414)

11.2   Describe brain development in middle childhood, including the influence of neurotransmitters and hormones. (pp. 414–415)

11.3   Describe the overall status of children's health during middle childhood. (p. 415)

11.4   Explain the causes and consequences of serious nutritional problems in middle childhood, giving special attention to obesity. (pp. 416–422)

11.5   Discuss factors that contribute to nocturnal enuresis and to asthma, noting how these health problems can be reduced. (pp. 422–423)

11.6   Describe changes in the occurrence of unintentional injuries during middle childhood, and cite effective interventions. (pp. 423–424)

11.7   Summarize ways parents and teachers can encourage good health practices in school-age children. (pp. 424–426)

11.8   Cite major changes in gross and fine motor development during middle childhood. (pp. 427–428)

11.9   Describe individual differences in motor performance during middle childhood. (pp. 428–430)

11.10   Discuss the quality of children's play during middle childhood, and identify features of children's physical activity that reflect our evolutionary past. (pp. 430–432)

11.11   Cite steps that schools can take to promote physical fitness in middle childhood. (pp. 432–433)

STUDY QUESTIONS

Body Growth

1.   During middle childhood, children continue to add _____ inches in height and _____ pounds in weight each year. (p. 412)

2.   Describe sex differences in body growth and proportions during middle childhood. (p. 412)

_____

_____

_____

_____

Worldwide Variations in Body Size

1.   True or False: Growth norms in countries throughout the world reveal few individual differences in body growth. (p. 413)

2.   Discuss both hereditary and environmental factors that account for differences in physical size among children around the world. (p. 413)

Hereditary: _____

_____

Environmental: _____

_____

Secular Trends in Physical Growth

1.   What are *secular trends in physical growth*? (p. 413)

_____

2.   Summarize the factors responsible for current secular growth patterns. (p. 413)

_____

_____

_____

Skeletal Growth

1. Describe advances in bone, muscle, and ligament growth during middle childhood. What unusual ability is evident during this time? (p. 413)

    Bone: _____

    Muscle: _____

    Ligament: _____

    Ability: _____

2. Between ages ___ and ___, all primary teeth are lost and replaced by permanent ones, with (boys / girls) losing their teeth slightly earlier than (boys / girls). (p. 414)

3. True or False: Over 50 percent of North American children have some tooth decay. (p. 414)

4. One-third of school-age children suffer from _____, a condition in which the upper and lower teeth do not meet properly. (p. 414)

5. List two causes of *malocclusion*. (p. 414)

    A. _____

    B. _____

Brain Development

1. True or False: The weight of the brain increases only 10 percent during middle childhood and adolescence. (p. 414)

2. Describe changes in white and gray matter during middle childhood. (p. 414)

    White matter: _____

    _____

    Gray matter: _____

    _____

3. Briefly summarize changes in neurotransmitters and hormones during middle childhood, noting their effects on brain functioning. (pp. 414–415)

    Neurotransmitters: _____

    _____

    _____

    Hormones: _____

    _____

    _____

Common Health Problems

Vision and Hearing

1. The most common vision problem of middle childhood is _____, or nearsightedness. (p. 415)

2. Cite evidence indicating that both heredity and environment contribute to *myopia*. (pp. 415–416)

   Heredity: _____

   _____

   _____

   Environment: _____

   _____

   _____

3. True or False: Repeated ear infections put children at risk for hearing loss. (p. 416)

Malnutrition

1. The percentage of children who eat dinner with their families (drops / rises) sharply between ages 9 and 14. Cite the benefits of family dinnertimes. (p. 416)

   _____

   _____

2. What do school-age children say is a major barrier to healthy eating? (p. 416)

   _____

3. Summarize the effects of prolonged malnutrition that become apparent by middle childhood. (p. 416)

   _____

   _____

   _____

4. Malnutrition that persists from infancy or early childhood into the school years usually leads to (permanent / temporary) physical and mental deficits. (p. 416)

Obesity

1. About _____ percent of Canadian children and _____ percent of American children are obese. (p. 417)

2. *Obesity* is a greater-than-_____-percent increase over healthy weight, based on body mass index—a ratio of weight to height associated with body fat. (p. 417)

3. Obesity rates are increasing (slowly / rapidly) in developing countries. What factors are responsible for this trend? (p. 417)

   _____

   _____

   _____

4. Over _____ percent of obese children retain their overweight status into adulthood. (p. 417)

5. Summarize the lifelong health problems associated with obesity. (p. 417)

_____

_____

_____

_____

6. True or False: Heredity is the single most important contributing factor to childhood obesity. (pp. 417–418)

7. (Low-SES / Middle-SES) children are more likely to be overweight. Cite three factors that contribute to this trend. (p. 418)

A. _____

B. _____

C. _____

8. Describe the relationship between sleep and weight during middle childhood. (p. 418)

_____

_____

_____

9. True or False: Children who were undernourished in their early years are at risk for later excessive weight gain. (p. 418)

10. Describe parenting practices that contribute to obesity, along with their consequences for children's eating habits. (p. 418)

A. _____

_____

B. _____

_____

11. Describe the relationship between TV viewing and obesity. (p. 419)

_____

_____

_____

12. Provide an example illustrating how the broader food environment affects the incidence of obesity. (p. 419)

_____

_____

13. Summarize several emotional and social consequences of childhood obesity. (p. 419)

_____

_____

_____

14. List characteristics of effective interventions for treating obesity. (pp. 420–421)

_____

_____

_____

15. What can schools do to help reduce childhood obesity? (p. 422)

_____

_____

_____

**Social Issues: Health: The Obesity Epidemic:
How Americans Became the Heaviest People in the World**

1. What percent of American and Canadian children and adults are overweight or obese? (p. 420)

   American: Children and adolescents: _____   Adults: _____

   Canadian: Children and adolescents: _____   Adults:_____

2. Summarize four societal factors that have contributed to the widespread rapid weight gain in Western nations. (p. 420)

   A. _____

   _____

   B. _____

   _____

   C. _____

   _____

   D. _____

   _____

3. Cite five suggestions for combating obesity at the societal level. (p. 421)

   A. _____

   B. _____

   C. _____

   D. _____

   E. _____

Bedwetting

1. Ten percent of American school-age children suffer from _____, or bedwetting during the night. (p. 422)

2. In the majority of cases, *nocturnal enuresis* is caused by (biological / environmental) factors. (p. 422)

3. Describe the most effective treatment for enuresis. (p. 422)

_____

_____

Illnesses

1. What accounts for the somewhat higher rate of illness during the first two years of elementary school? (p. 422)

_____

2. The most common chronic illness, representing the most frequent cause of school absence and childhood hospitalization, is _____. (p. 422)

3. Describe the characteristics of children who are at greatest risk for asthma. (p. 423)

_____

_____

_____

4. Besides physical discomfort, what other negative consequences are associated with chronic childhood illness? (p. 423)

_____

_____

_____

5. List six interventions for chronically ill children and their families that foster improvements in family interactions and child adjustment. (p. 423)

A. _____
B. _____
C. _____
D. _____
E. _____
F. _____

Unintentional Injuries

1. List two environmental factors linked to high injury rates in childhood and adolescense. (p. 423)

A. _____
B. _____

2. What is the leading cause of injury during the school years? (p. 423)

_____

3. Cite three characteristics of effective safety education programs. (p. 423)

A. _____
B. _____
C. _____

4. What simple safety precaution leads to an 85 percent reduction in risk of head injury? (p. 423)

_____

5. Describe characteristics of children who are most at risk for injury in middle childhood. (p. 424)

_____

_____

_____

Health Education

1. Why is the school-age period especially important for fostering healthy lifestyles? (p. 424)

_____

_____

_____

2. List three reasons why efforts to impart health concepts to school-age children often have little impact on their behavior. (p. 426)

    A. _____

    B. _____

    C. _____

3. Discuss four strategies for fostering healthy lifestyles in school-age children. (p. 426)

    A. _____

    _____

    B. _____

    _____

    C. _____

    _____

    D. _____

    _____

Social Issues: Education: Children's Understanding of Health and Illness

1. Trace changes in children's understanding of health and illness from preschool into adolescence. (p. 425)

    Preschool and early school age (3- to 8-year-olds): _____

    _____

    Older school age (9- to 10-year-olds): _____

    _____

    Early adolescence (11- to 14-year-olds): _____

    _____

2. Describe factors that affect children's understanding of health and illness. (p. 425)

_____

_____

_____

3. Provide an example of how education can help children develop an accurate appreciation of disease transmission and prevention. (p. 425)

_____

_____

Motor Development and Play

Gross Motor Development

1. Describe gains in four basic motor capacities that support improvements in gross motor skills during middle childhood. (pp. 427–428)

   A. _____

   _____

   B. _____

   _____

   C. _____

   _____

   D. _____

   _____

2. Explain how more efficient information processing contributes to the improved motor performance of school-age children. (p. 428)

   _____

   _____

Fine Motor Development

1. Describe typical gains in writing and drawing during middle childhood. (p. 428)

   Writing: _____

   _____

   Drawing: _____

   _____

Individual Differences in Motor Skills

1. Discuss the influence of socioeconomic status on children's motor development. (pp. 428–429)

   _____

   _____

   _____

2. Summarize sex differences in motor skills, and explain how environmental factors contribute to these differences. (p. 429)

   A. _____

   _____

   B. _____

   _____

3. List two strategies that can help raise girls' participation, self-confidence, and sense of fair treatment in athletics. (pp. 429–430)

    A. _____

    B. _____

Child-Organized Games

1. What cognitive capacity permits the transition to rule-oriented games during middle childhood? (p. 430)

    _____

2. Explain how child-invented games contribute to emotional and social development. (p. 430)

    _____

    _____

    _____

Adult-Organized Youth Sports

1. Compared with past generations, school-age children today spend less time gathering informally on sidewalks and in playgrounds. Explain why. (p. 430)

    _____

    _____

2. Participation on community athletic teams (is / is not) associated with increased self-esteem and social competence. (p. 430)

3. Summarize four criticisms of adult-organized youth sports. (p. 430)

    A. _____

    _____

    B. _____

    _____

    C. _____

    _____

    D. _____

    _____

4. Explain four ways to ensure that organized sports provide positive, developmentally appropriate experiences for children. (p. 430)

    A. _____

    _____

    B. _____

    _____

    C. _____

    _____

    D. _____

    _____

Shadows of Our Evolutionary Past

1. _____ *play* is a form of peer interaction involving friendly chasing and play-fighting. (p. 430)

2. Describe sex differences in rough-and-tumble play. (p. 431)

   _____

   _____

3. Explain how rough-and-tumble play assists children in establishing a *dominance hierarchy,* and note how this is adaptive for peer relations. (pp. 431–432)

   A. _____

   _____

   B. _____

   _____

Physical Education

1. True or False: Nearly 90 percent of U.S. elementary schools have daily physical education. (p. 432)

2. What kinds of activities should physical education classes emphasize to help the largest number of children develop active and healthy lifestyles? (p. 432)

   _____

   _____

3. List three benefits of being physically fit in childhood. (p. 432)

   A. _____

   B. _____

   C. _____

Social Issues: Education: School Recess—A Time to Play, A Time to Learn

1. True or False: Seven percent of U.S. schools no longer provide recess to students as young as second grade. (p. 433)

2. Discuss the physical, academic, and social benefits of recess periods for school-age children. (p. 433)

   Physical: _____

   _____

   Academic: _____

   _____

   Social: _____

   _____

ASK YOURSELF . . .

For *Ask Yourself* questions for this chapter, along with feedback on the accuracy of your answers, please log on to MyDevelopmentLab (for registration and access, please visit mydevelopmentlab.com or follow the directions on p. ix).

1) Select the Chapter of the *Ask Yourself.*
2) Open the E-Book and select the Explore icon next to the *Ask Yourself.*
3) Complete questions and choose "Submit answers for grading" or "Clear Answers" to start over.

SUGGESTED STUDENT READINGS

Critser, G. (2004). *Fat land: How Americans became the fattest people in the world.* Boston: Houghton Mifflin. Explores how multiple aspects of American life—class, politics, culture, and economics—have contributed to the obesity epidemic. Also presents up-to-date research on childhood obesity, marketing tactics of fast-food chains, and adult-onset diabetes resulting from poor eating habits and includes suggestions for how American society should go about tackling this growing epidemic.

De Lench, B. (2006). *The critical role of mothers in youth sports.* New York: HarperCollins. A comprehensive look at youth sports, including injury rates, relationships between parents, coaches, and players, the importance and dangers of competition, and the benefits of participation.

Pellegrini, A. (2005). *Recess and its role in education and development.* Hillsdale, NJ: Erlbaum. Examines the diverse benefits of recess in elementary school education, including its contribution to physical, cognitive, and social-emotional development. An excellent resource for parents, educators, and anyone interested in working with school-age children.

PUZZLE 11.1 TERM REVIEW

Across

2. Nocturnal _____: repeated bedwetting during the night
4. An illness in which highly sensitive bronchial tubes fill with mucus, leading to episodes of coughing, wheezing, and breathing
5. Condition in which the upper and lower teeth do not meet properly
6. _____ hierarchy: stable ordering of group members that predicts who will win when conflict arises

7. A greater-than-20-percent increase over healthy weight, based on sex, age, and physical build
8. _____ trends in physical growth refer to changes in body size from one generation to the next

Down

1. Nearsightedness
3. _____-_____-_____ play: a form of peer interaction involving friendly chasing and play-fighting (3 words, hyph.)

PRACTICE TEST #1

1. At age 6, the average North American child weighs about (p. 412)
   a.   37 pounds.
   b.   45 pounds.
   c.   52 pounds.
   d.   60 pounds.

2. When families move from poor to wealthy nations, their children (p. 413)
   a.   grow to the top of the average range for their ethnic group.
   b.   tend to grow heavier rather than taller.
   c.   grow just about as tall as the parents.
   d.   not only grow taller but also change to a longer-legged body shape.

3. Secular gains in physical growth generally increase most noticeably during (p. 413)
   a.   infancy.
   b.   childhood and early adolescence.
   c.   late adolescence.
   d.   early adulthood.

4. During middle childhood, children typically have unusual flexibility of movement because (p. 413)
   a.   their bones are lengthening and broadening.
   b.   they have not yet undergone malocclusion.
   c.   their muscles are strengthening, but their ligaments are not yet firmly attached to bones.
   d.   they spend more hours exercising than adolescents or adults.

5. As children acquire more complex abilities, their brain's neural fibers become more elaborate and myelinated, a process that causes (p. 414)
   a.   the adrenal glands to secrete androgens.
   b.   a loss of white matter due to synaptic pruning.
   c.   neurons to become more selective.
   d.   a steady increase in the amount of white matter.

6. Kinship studies reveal that compared to children with no myopic parents, those with one myopic parent have (p. 415)
   a.   twice the risk of becoming myopic.
   b.   three times the risk of becoming myopic.
   c.   five times the risk of becoming myopic.
   d.   eight times the risk of becoming myopic.

7. During middle childhood, otitis media becomes less frequent than in infancy and early childhood because (p. 416)
   a.   children develop a greater tendency to sleep on their sides rather than on their back.
   b.   skull growth reduces the number of spaces in which bacteria can collect.
   c.   the eustachian tube becomes longer, narrower, and more slanted, preventing fluid and bacteria from traveling so easily from the mouth to the ear.
   d.   children's increasing rate of activity prevents bacteria from settling in the ears.

8. In research focusing on school-aged children from middle- to high-SES families, insufficient dietary iron and folate predicted (p. 416)
   a.   greater nervous activity in boys.
   b.   slightly lower mental test performance.
   c.   poorer athletic achievement.
   d.   moderate increases in behavior problems in boys and girls.

9. During the past several decades, the rise in obesity in Western nations has been most dramatic in (p. 417)
   a. the United States.
   b. Canada.
   c. Great Britain.
   d. New Zealand.

10. Reduced sleep can promote weight gain by (p. 418)
    a. leading parents to interpret the child's sleep problems as a desire for food.
    b. making children more responsive to taste, sight, time of day, and other stimuli.
    c. prompting children to eat faster and chew their food less thoroughly.
    d. disrupting the brain's regulation of hunger and metabolism.

11. The rising obesity rates seen in the United States have spread to other Western nations, including Canada, where the percentage of adults who are overweight or obese is (p. 420)
    a. 47.
    b. 59.
    c. 68.
    d. 74.

12. Less than 20 percent of obese children get any treatment for their weight problem because (pp. 419–420)
    a. most don't want treatment.
    b. they tend to be from low-SES families, so their parents are wary of institutional interventions.
    c. only one-fourth of overweight parents judge their overweight children to have a weight problem.
    d. both the children and their parents prefer to be sedentary.

13. The most effective treatment for nocturnal enuresis is (p. 422)
    a. consistent punishment for bedwetting.
    b. antidepressant drugs that reduce the amount of urine produced.
    c. gradual training of the muscles that govern urination.
    d. a urine alarm that wakes the child at the first sign of dampness.

14. The group of children at greatest risk of developing asthma are (p. 423)
    a. children who live in poverty.
    b. girls.
    c. Asian-American children.
    d. children who are overweight at birth.

15. In North America, the leading cause of injury from middle childhood to adolescence is (p. 423)
    a. bicycle accidents.
    b. aggressive contact sports.
    c. motor vehicle accidents.
    d. physical abuse.

16. By middle childhood, the children who take the greatest risks and are, therefore, most prone to injury tend to be those (p. 424)
    a. whose older siblings are especially impulsive and reckless.
    b. whose parents do not act as safety-conscious models.
    c. who range farthest from home.
    d. who watch many hours of violent television programming.

17. Health is seldom an important goal for children because they (p. 425)
    a. tend to be impulsive.
    b. are not capable of absorbing health information until adolescence.
    c. typically reject information from adults.
    d. feel good most of the time and are more concerned with schoolwork, play, and friends.

18. Children almost always develop the ability to explain health and illness biologically by age (p. 425)
    a. 7 or 8.
    b. 8 or 9.
    c. 9 or 10.
    d. 10 or 11.

19. After age 9, children's performance at precision jumping and hopping (p. 427)
    a. levels off.
    b. continues to improve dramatically through adolescence.
    c. declines slightly, reflecting reduced flexibility as ligaments bind more tightly to bones.
    d. stays at a consistent level until a new burst of improvement begins in earl adolescence.

20. Around age 6, children's handwriting tends to be large because they (p. 428)
    a. find the oversized letter forms pleasing.
    b. make strokes with the entire arms rather than just the wrist and fingers.
    c. are often too impatient to make small, careful strokes.
    d. do not yet distinguish between uppercase and lowercase letters.

21. During middle childhood, as throwing speed, accuracy, and distance increase, (p. 429)
    a. girls and boys perform equally well until around age 8, when girls begin accumulating body fat, which interferes with their performance.
    b. boys' performance improves faster than girls' until around age 12, when girls begin to catch up.
    c. boys and girls generally perform at the same level.
    d. boys' performance develops much faster than girls'.

22. Weak athletic performance generally leads to social ostracism, especially among (p. 430)
    a. girls.
    b. adolescents.
    c. boys.
    d. children with older siblings.

23. Rough-and-tumble play is more common among boys than among girls, probably because (p. 431)
    a. boys are typically more aggressive than girls.
    b. parents tend to encourage boys to engage in such play but express disapproval of rough play among girls.
    c. boys use rough-and-tumble to break down dominance hierarchies.
    d. prenatal exposure to androgens predisposes boys toward active play.

24. Among North American 5- to 17-year-old girls, approximately _____ percent are active enough for good health. (p. 432)
    a. 20
    b. 35
    c. 40
    d. 50

25. The importance of recess breaks during the school day has been demonstrated by studies showing that (p. 433)
    a. school-age children are more attentive in the classroom after recess than before it.
    b. boys are less disruptive after recess than before it.
    c. recess breaks reinforce the lessons learned in gym classes.
    d. recess periods enable children to apply skills, such as following rules, that they have learned in the classroom.

PRACTICE TEST #2

1. After age 8, girls begin accumulating fat at (p. 412)
   a. a rate directly proportional to the rate of growth of their lower bodies.
   b. the same rate as boys accumulate muscle.
   c. a rate of about 4 pounds per year until they reach adulthood.
   d. a faster rate than they did previously.

2. Worldwide, the difference in height between the shortest and tallest 8-year-olds is (p. 413)
   a. 3 inches.
   b. 7 inches.
   c. 9 inches.
   d. 13 inches.

3. Secular gains in physical growth are smaller for low-income children because (p. 413)
   a. they tend to have poorer diets and are more likely to suffer from growth-stunting illnesses.
   b. their parents often score low on intelligence tests.
   c. they often come from shorter ethnic groups.
   d. their parents frequently do not encourage them to exercise.

4. About 14 percent of children who have malocclusion (p. 414)
   a. sucked their thumbs or fingers until middle childhood.
   b. have crowded permanent teeth.
   c. were born with malformed lower jaws.
   d. have serious difficulties in biting and chewing.

5. As synaptic pruning reduces the amount of gray matter in the brain, (p. 414)
   a. the number of myelinated nerve fibers also decreases.
   b. lateralization of the cerebral hemispheres increases.
   c. the corpus callosum shrinks to the typical adult size.
   d. white matter takes its place.

6. By the end of the school years, myopia affects nearly (p. 415)
   a. 8 percent of children.
   b. 17 percent of children.
   c. 25 percent of children.
   d. 33 percent of children.

7. Myopia progresses more rapidly during the school year because children (p. 415)
   a. are often in a hurry and eat poorly, leading to deficiencies that negatively affect vision.
   b. spend more time reading and doing other close work than in the summer months.
   c. often work while they are tired, thus straining their eyes.
   d. frequently forget to wear corrective lenses while working.

8. Animal evidence reveals that a deficient diet (p. 416)
   a. alters the production of neurotransmitters in the brain.
   b. causes the body to produce more stress hormones in stressful situations.
   c. causes the brain's white matter to break down.
   d. leads to premature elongation of the bones.

9. In developing countries, urbanization has led to increasing obesity rates because it (p. 417)
   a. creates pollution that, in turn, alters human metabolism.
   b. encourages consumption of diets high in starch.
   c. induces parents to give children large portions of dairy products.
   d. shifts populations toward sedentary activities and diets high in meat and refined foods.

10. Overweight children tend to (p. 417)
    a. be abnormally tall.
    b. have been overfed during infancy.
    c. have overweight parents.
    d. come from middle- and high-SES home where all types of foods, including fattening foods, are abundant.

11. High-fructose corn syrup and palm oil, two food additives that have become common since the 1970s, contribute to obesity by (p. 420)
    a. lowering the body's metabolism.
    b. increasing the amount of sweetener and saturated fat in foods.
    c. stimulating the hunger mechanism in the brain.
    d. increasing the carbohydrate content of foods.

12. Family-based weight-loss programs are most effective when they focus on (p. 420)
    a. punishment for failing to adhere to the program.
    b. depriving the child of food except for three nutritionally balanced meals a day.
    c. the amount of food consumed at school.
    d. changing behaviors and reinforcing those changes.

13. Most children who suffer from nocturnal enuresis are likely to (p. 422)
    a. have a parent who also suffered from it in childhood.
    b. be experiencing emotional stress at home.
    c. be taking antidepressant drugs, which tend to increase urine production.
    d. have a fraternal twin who also wets the bed.

14. Of the following chronic childhood illnesses, which is the most frequent cause of school absence and childhood hospitalization? (p. 422)
    a. Diabetes
    b. Influenza
    c. Asthma
    d. Cancer

15. In adolescence, chronically ill children are more likely than their agemates to (p. 423)
    a. develop additional diseases.
    b. suffer from low self-esteem and depression.
    c. become obese.
    d. have well-functioning families.

16. From middle childhood to adolescence, the rate of injury fatalities for girls (p. 423)
    a. remains about the same as the rate for boys.
    b. drops behind the rate for boys.
    c. rises more rapidly than the rate for boys, so that by late adolescence, the rates are about the same for both sexes.
    d. surpasses that for boys.

17. As studies have revealed, 3- to 8-year-olds generally account for the occurrence of illness by using (p. 425)
    a. their deepening understanding of how their internal organs work.
    b. the information given to them by parents and doctors.
    c. information they gain through conversation with peers.
    d. their rich knowledge of people's behavior.

18. In surveys of school-age children, about half incorrectly believed that (p. 425)
    a. everyone is equally at risk for AIDS.
    b. disease occurs as a result of moral failing.
    c. germs affect only those people who allow them to do so.
    d. they can catch a cold by playing outdoors in freezing temperatures.

19. Between ages 6 and 12, children's flexibility (p. 427)
    a. declines compared with that of preschoolers because their ligaments attach to the bones.
    b. declines because the last of their epiphyses have closed.
    c. increases compared with that of preschoolers, a difference that is seen in their skill at batting, jumping, and tumbling.
    d. increases as a result of more efficient information processing.

20. Around age 9 to 10 years, children's drawings typically begin to display a grasp of (p. 428)
    a. human body structure.
    b. the third dimension.
    c. how to copy and integrate two-dimensional shapes.
    d. color contrast.

21. The major factor determining boys' superiority in gross motor skills is (p. 429)
    a. boys' genetic advantage in muscle mass.
    b. girls' typical unwillingness to engage in vigorous physical activity.
    c. parental expectations for boys' athletic performance.
    d. boys' tendency toward greater impulsiveness.

22. Child-invented games usually (p. 430)
    a. permit children to try out various styles of cooperating, competing, winning, and losing.
    b. involve complex rules and physical skills that are more advanced when the participants are older.
    c. become contests of individual ability, especially among boys.
    d. involve minimal planning of how the games should proceed.

23. Girls' rough-and-tumble play tends to consist of (p. 431)
    a. wrestling and restraining.
    b. constantly shifting dominance hierarchies.
    c. light hitting.
    d. running and chasing.

24. In adolescence, boys' rough-and-tumble play becomes linked to (p. 432)
    a. the desire to impress girls.
    b. aggression.
    c. excellence at demanding organized sports.
    d. maladaptive behaviors, often caused by family stresses.

25. Many experts believe that school physical education programs should emphasize (p. 432)
    a. more training in competitive sports.
    b. gender-segregated activities.
    c. enjoyable, informal games and individual exercise.
    d. short periods of exercise so that children have more time to devote to academics.

CHAPTER 12
COGNITIVE DEVELOPMENT
IN MIDDLE CHILDHOOD

BRIEF CHAPTER SUMMARY

During Piaget's concrete operational stage, from about age 7 to 11, thought becomes more logical, flexible, and organized than in early childhood. This is seen in children's grasp of concepts like conservation, classification, and seriation, as well as improvements in spatial reasoning. However, children cannot yet think abstractly: Their organized, logical thinking is limited to concrete, directly perceived information. Cross-cultural findings indicate that mastery of Piagetian tasks does not emerge spontaneously but, rather, is dependent on specific cultural and school practices. Information-processing research helps explain the gradual mastery of logical concepts, challenging Piaget's assumption of an abrupt, stagewise transition to logical thought.

Brain development leads to gains in information-processing speed and capacity, as well as in inhibition, which facilitate diverse aspects of thinking. Information-processing research reveals that attention becomes more selective, adaptable, and planful, and use of memory strategies, such as rehearsal and organization, becomes more effective. Children learn much about planning by collaborating with more expert planners. By the end of the school years, children start to use elaboration, which contributes to improvements in memory. However, the value of memory strategies depends on cultural circumstances: It is limited to societies in which children learn through formal schooling.

Children's theory of mind, or metacognition, becomes much more elaborate and refined in middle childhood, increasing children's ability to reflect on their own mental life. School-age children, unlike preschoolers, regard the mind as an active, constructive agent and are conscious of mental inferences and mental strategies. Still, school-age children have difficulty with cognitive self-regulation—monitoring their progress toward a goal and redirecting unsuccessful efforts. In both reading and mathematics, academic instruction that combines an emphasis on meaning and understanding with training in basic skills may be most effective.

Intelligence tests for children measure overall IQ as well as separate intellectual factors. Sternberg's triarchic theory of intelligence defines three broad, interacting intelligences (analytical, creative, and practical); intelligent behavior involves balancing all three. Gardner's theory of multiple intelligences highlights at least eight independent intelligences, including several not measured by IQ scores. And Goleman's concept of emotional intelligence refers to emotional abilities that enable individuals to process and adapt to emotional information, so that they can act wisely in social situations.

Heritability estimates and adoption research shows that both genetic and environmental factors contribute to individual differences in intelligence. Because of different communication styles and lack of familiarity with test content, IQ scores of low-SES ethnic minority children often do not reflect their true abilities. Stereotype threat also has a negative effect. Supplementing IQ tests with measures of adaptive behavior and adjusting testing procedures to account for cultural differences—for example, through dynamic assessment—can reduce test bias.

Language development continues during the school years, although changes are less dramatic than in early childhood. At this age, children develop metalinguistic awareness—the ability to think about language as a system. Vocabulary increases rapidly, and pragmatic skills are refined. Bilingual children are advanced in cognitive development and, specifically, in metalinguistic awareness.

Schools are powerful forces in children's development. Class size, the school's educational philosophy, teacher–pupil interaction, grouping practices, and the way computers are used in classrooms all affect motivation and achievement in middle childhood. Teachers face special challenges in meeting the needs of children who have learning difficulties as well as those with special intellectual strengths. North American students have fared unevenly in recent international comparisons of academic achievement. Efforts are currently underway to upgrade the quality of North American education.

LEARNING OBJECTIVES

After reading this chapter, you should be able to:

12.3   Cite basic changes in information processing during middle childhood. (pp. 442–443)

12.4   Describe changes in attention and memory during middle childhood. (pp. 443–447)

12.5   Describe the school-age child's theory of mind and capacity to engage in cognitive self-regulation. (pp. 447–449)

12.6   Discuss applications of information processing to acedemic learning, noting current controversies over teaching reading and mathematics to elementary school children. (pp. 449–452)

12.7   Describe the Stanford-Binet Intelligence Scale and the Wechsler Intelligence Scale for Children-IV, the two scales most commonly used to assess intelligence in school-age children. (pp. 452–454)

12.8   Discuss recent developments in defining intelligence, including Sternberg's triarchic theory of successful intelligence and Gardner's theory of multiple intelligences. (pp. 454–456)

12.9   Cite evidence indicating that both heredity and environment contribute to intelligence. (pp. 456–458)

12.10   Describe cultural influences on intelligence test performance, and discuss efforts to overcome cultural bias in intelligence testing. (pp. 458–461)

12.11   Summarize changes in metalinguistic awareness, vocabulary, grammar, and pragmatics during middle childhood. (pp. 462–464)

12.12   Discuss the major issues surrounding bilingual development and bilingual education, noting the advantages of bilingualism in childhood. (pp. 464–465)

12.13   Discuss the impact of class size, educational philosophies, teacher–student interaction, and grouping practices on student motivation and academic achievement. (pp. 466–470)

12.14   Describe educational benefits of computer use as well as concerns about computers. (p. 471)

12.15   Summarize the conditions under which placement of mildly mentally retarded and learning disabled children in regular classrooms is successful. (p. 472)

12.16   Describe the characteristics of gifted children, and discuss current efforts to meet their educational needs. (pp. 472–474)

12.17   Compare the North American cultural climate for academic achievement with that of other industrialized nations. (pp. 474–476)

STUDY QUESTIONS

Piaget's Theory: The Concrete Operational Stage

Achievements of the Concrete Operational Stage

1. How does thought change as children enter the *concrete operational stage*? (p. 438)

   _____

2. Match the following terms with the appropriate descriptions and examples. (p. 438)

   _____ The ability to order items along a quantitative dimension, such as length or weight

   _____ The ability to focus on relations between a general category and two specific categories

   _____ The ability to seriate mentally

   _____ The ability to focus on several aspects of a problem and relate them rather than centering on just one aspect

   1. Decentration
   2. Reversibility
   3. Classification
   4. Seriation
   5. Transitive inference

3. Advances in spatial reasoning are evidenced by children's understanding of directions and maps. Summarize changes in these two areas as children move from preoperational thought to concrete operational thought. (pp. 438–439)

   Directions: _____

   _____

   _____

   Maps: _____

   _____

   _____

4. Explain how cultural frameworks influence children's map making. (p. 439)

   _____

   _____

Limitations of Concrete Operational Thought

1. Describe the major limitation of concrete operational thought. (pp. 439–440)

   _____

   _____

Follow-Up Research on Concrete Operational Thought

1. Cite two examples that illustrate how culture and schooling contribute to children's mastery of conservation and other Piagetian tasks. (p. 440)

   A. _____

   _____

   B. _____

   _____

2. True or False: The forms of logic required by Piagetian tasks emerge spontaneously during childhood and are not heavily influenced by training, context, or cultural conditions. (p. 440)

3. Briefly summarize Case's information-processing view of cognitive development. (pp. 440–441)

_____

_____

_____

_____

4. What are *central conceptual structures*? (p. 441)

_____

_____

5. Based on Case's theory, cite two reasons why children's understandings appear in specific situations at different times rather than being mastered all at once. (p. 441)

A. _____

_____

B. _____

_____

Evaluation of the Concrete Operational Stage

1. Many researchers believe that two types of change may be involved in the school-age child's approach to Piagetian problems. List these two changes. (p. 442)

A. _____

B. _____

Information Processing

1. List two categories that underlie every act of cognition. (p. 442)

A. _____   B. _____

2. Discuss two ways in which brain development contributes to changes in information processing. (pp. 442–443)

A. _____

_____

B. _____

_____

Attention

1. Cite three ways in which attention changes during middle childhood. (pp. 443–444)

A. _____

B. _____

C. _____

2. List and describe the four-step sequence of attentional strategy development. (p. 443)

   A. _____

   _____

   B. _____

   _____

   C. _____

   _____

   D. _____

   _____

3. Cite two ways in which school-age children's attentional strategies become more planful. (pp. 443–444)

   A. _____

   _____

   B. _____

   _____

4. Explain how children typically learn planning skills, and discuss what adults can do to foster the development of planning in school-age children. (p. 444)

   A. _____

   _____

   B. _____

   _____

Biology and Environment: Children with Attention-Deficit Hyperactivity Disorder

1. Describe typical characteristics of children with attention-deficit hyperactivity disorder (ADHD). (p. 444)

   A. _____

   _____

   B. _____

   _____

2. True or False: Children with ADHD perform as well as other children on tests of intelligence. (p. 444)

3. Researchers agree that deficient executive processing underlies ADHD symptoms. Briefly describe the two views that contribute to this theory. (p. 444)

   A. _____

   _____

   B. _____

   _____

4. Cite evidence that ADHD is influenced by both heredity and environment. (pp. 444–445)

Heredity: _____

_____

_____

Environment: _____

_____

_____

5. Discuss three ways to treat ADHD, noting which method is the most *common* and which method is the most *effective*. (p. 445)

A. _____

_____

B. _____

_____

C. _____

_____

6. True or False: ADHD is a lifelong disorder, with problems usually persisting into adulthood. (p. 445)

Memory Strategies

1. List and describe three memory strategies that emerge during middle childhood, noting the order in which they typically appear. (pp. 445–446)

A. _____

_____

B. _____

_____

C. _____

_____

2. Cite two factors required for perfecting memory strategies. (p. 446)

A. _____   B. _____

3. How is young children's use of memory strategies adaptive? (p. 446)

_____

_____

The Knowledge Base and Memory Performance

1. Explain how extensive knowledge and use of memory strategies are closely related to and support one another. (p. 446)

_____

_____

_____

2. Explain why knowledge is not the only important factor in children's memory processing. (p. 446)

_____

_____

Culture, Schooling, and Memory Strategies

1. True or False: People in non-Western cultures who have no formal schooling are likely to use and benefit from instruction in memory strategies. (p. 447)

2. Discuss how culture and schooling are related to the development of memory strategies. (p. 447)

_____

_____

_____

The School-Age Child's Theory of Mind

1. Describe how a school-age child's theory of mind differs from that of a preschooler. (p. 447)

_____

_____

_____

2. How does the ability to make mental inferences assist children in understanding others' perspectives? (p. 447)

_____

_____

_____

3. What are second-order false beliefs, and how do they contribute to perspective taking? (p. 447)

A. _____

_____

B. _____

_____

4. How does schooling contribute to the school-age child's theory of mind? (pp. 447–448)

_____

_____

Cognitive Self-Regulation

1. What is *cognitive self-regulation,* and how do researchers study it? (p. 448)

A. _____

_____

B. _____

_____

2. School-age children (are / are not) good at cognitive self-regulation. Cite evidence to support your response. (p. 448)

_____

_____

_____

3. Why does cognitive self-regulation develop gradually during middle childhood? (pp. 448–449)

_____

_____

_____

4. Discuss ways that parents and teachers can foster self-regulation. (p. 449)

_____

_____

_____

5. Children who acquire effective self-regulatory skills develop a sense of _____, confidence in their own ability, which supports future self-regulation. (p. 449)

Applications of Information Processing to Academic Learning

1. List the diverse information-processing skills that contribute to the process of reading. (p. 449)

_____

_____

2. Summarize the two sides of the debate over how to teach beginning reading. (p. 449)

    A. _____

    _____

    B. _____

    _____

3. Explain why combining *phonics* with *whole language* is often the best strategy for teaching children to read. (p. 450)

_____

_____

_____

4. Trace the general sequence of reading development, noting reading abilities at the following grade levels: (p. 450)

    Preschool and kindergarten (2–6 years): _____

    _____

    Grades 1 and 2 (6–7 years): _____

    _____

Grades 2 and 3 (7–8 years): _____

_____

Grades 4 to 9 (9–14 years): _____

_____

Grades 10 to 12 (15–17 years): _____

_____

College (18 years and older): _____

_____

5. Arguments about how to teach mathematics closely resemble those in reading. Summarize these arguments. (p. 451)

A. _____

_____

B. _____

_____

6. Briefly explain why students in Asian countries often excel at both math reasoning and computation. (p. 452)

_____

_____

_____

Individual Differences in Mental Development

Defining and Measuring Intelligence

1. Describe the types of items commonly included on intelligence tests for children. (p. 452)

_____

_____

_____

2. Distinguish between group- and individually administered intelligence tests, and cite the advantages of each. (p. 453)

Group administered: _____

_____

_____

Individually administered: _____

_____

_____

3. Match each of the following intelligence tests with the appropriate descriptions. (pp. 453–454)

_____ Appropriate for individuals age 6–16	1. Stanford-Binet
_____ Appropriate for individuals between 2 years of age and adulthood	Intelligence Scales
_____ Assesses four broad intellectual factors: verbal reasoning, perceptual reasoning, working memory, and processing speed	2. Wechsler Intelligence Scale for Children-IV
_____ Assesses five broad intellectual factors: general knowledge, quantitative reasoning, visual-spatial processing, working memory, and basic information processing	3. Wechsler Preschool and Primary Scale of Intelligence—Revised
_____ First test to be standardized on samples representing the total population of the United States, including ethnic minorities	
_____ Appropriate for children 2 years 6 months through 7 years 3 months	

Recent Efforts to Define Intelligence

1. What is a *componential analysis,* and why is it used? (p. 454)

    A. _____

    _____

    B. _____

    _____

2. What other factors are as important as efficient thinking in predicting IQ? (p. 454)

    _____

    _____

3. What is the major shortcoming of the componential approach? (p. 454)

    _____

    _____

4. List and briefly describe the three broad intelligences outlined in Sternberg's *triarchic theory of successful intelligence.* (pp. 454–455)

    A. _____

    _____

    B. _____

    _____

    C. _____

    _____

5. Explain how Sternberg's theory emphasizes the complexity of intelligent behavior and the limitations of current intelligence tests in assessing that complexity. (p. 455)

    _____

    _____

    _____

6. Define Gardner's *theory of multiple intelligences,* and list his eight independent intelligences. (pp. 455–456)

_____

_____

A. _____   B. _____

C. _____   D. _____

E. _____   F. _____

G. _____   H. _____

7. True or False: In Gardner's theory, intelligence has a purely biological basis and is not affected by cultural values or learning opportunities. (p. 455)

8. Gardner's theory (is / is not) firmly grounded in research. (p. 455)

9. Cite one contribution of Gardner's theory. (p. 456)

_____

_____

Social Issues: Education: Emotional Intelligence

1. Define *emotional intelligence*, and explain how researchers measure it. (p. 457)

   A. _____

   _____

   B. _____

   _____

2. True or False: Emotional intelligence is modestly related to IQ, and it is positively associated with self-esteem, empathy, prosocial behavior, and life satisfaction. (p. 457)

3. How can teachers help foster social and emotional intelligence in school-age children? (p. 457)

   _____

   _____

Explaining Individual and Group Differences in IQ

1. Summarize evidence related to ethnic and SES differences in IQ. (pp. 456–458)

   Ethnic differences: _____

   _____

   _____

   SES differences: _____

   _____

   _____

2. What do kinship studies reveal about the role of heredity in IQ? (p. 458)

   _____

   _____

   _____

3. What do adoption studies suggest about the contribution of environmental factors in IQ? (p. 458)

_____

_____

_____

4. Research shows a dramatic secular trend in mental test performance. Explain what this means. (p. 458)

_____

_____

5. What is test bias in IQ measurement? Briefly discuss the controversy surrounding test bias and ethnic differences in IQ. (pp. 458–459)

A. _____

_____

B. _____

_____

6. Explain how ethnic minority families foster unique communication skills that do not fit with the expectations of most classrooms and testing situations. (p. 459)

_____

_____

_____

_____

7. Describe the difference between collaborative and hierarchical styles of communication, noting how each is likely to affect performance in school and on IQ tests. (p. 459)

Collaborative: _____

_____

_____

Hierarchical: _____

_____

_____

8. True or False: Using nonverbal intelligence tests that tap spatial reasoning and performance skills considerably raises the scores of ethnic minority children. Explain your answer. (p. 459)

_____

_____

9. Define *stereotype threat,* and explain how it is likely to influence low-SES minority children's performance on intelligence tests. (pp. 459–460)

Definition: _____

_____

Influence: _____

_____

10. Cite two components of self-discipline that predict school performance at least as well as, and sometimes better than, IQ does. (p. 460)

A. _____   B. _____

Reducing Cultural Bias in Testing

1. Why is assessment of adaptive behavior especially important for minority children? (p. 460)

_____

_____

2. Describe *dynamic assessment,* and discuss its effectiveness for reducing cultural bias in testing. (pp. 460–461)

_____

_____

_____

_____

3. True or False: Dynamic assessment is more effective than traditional tests in predicting academic achievement. Explain your answer. (p. 461)

_____

_____

Language Development

1. School-age children develop _____ *awareness,* the ability to think about language as a system. (p. 462)

Vocabulary

1. True or False: The rate of vocabulary growth during the school years exceeds that of early childhood. (p. 462)

2. Cite four strategies that assist school-age children in building their vocabularies. (p. 462)

A. _____

_____

B. _____

_____

C. _____

_____

D. _____

_____

3. Provide an example illustrating the school-age child's more reflective and analytic approach to language. (p. 462)

_____

_____

_____

Grammar

1.   Cite two grammatical achievements of middle childhood. (pp. 462–463)

   A. _____

   _____

   B. _____

   _____

Pragmatics

1.   Describe three advances in pragmatic speech that take place during middle childhood. (p. 463)

   A. _____

   _____

   B. _____

   _____

   C. _____

   _____

2.   Summarize cultural differences in children's narrative styles of communication. (pp. 463–464)

   _____

   _____

   _____

Learning Two Languages at a Time

1.   Cite two ways in which children can become bilingual, and discuss children's development in each instance. (p. 464)

   A. _____

   _____

   B. _____

   _____

2.   True or False: When bilingual children engage in code switching, they do not violate the grammar of either language. Briefly explain your response. (p. 464)

   _____

   _____

3.   True or False: There is a sensitive period for second-language development. (p. 464)

4.   List the cognitive benefits of bilingualism. (p. 464)

   _____

   _____

   _____

5.   Briefly describe Canada's language immersion programs. (pp. 464–465)

_____

_____

6.   Summarize the current debate regarding how American ethnic minority children with limited English proficiency should be educated. (p. 465)

_____

_____

_____

_____

7.   Discuss the benefits of combining children's native language with English in the classroom. (p. 465)

_____

_____

_____

Children's Learning in School

1.   Describe four characteristics of high-quality education in elementary school. (pp. 466–470)

A.   _____

_____

B.   _____

_____

C.   _____

_____

D.   _____

_____

Class Size

1.   Describe evidence that class size is influential in children's learning. (p. 466)

_____

_____

_____

2.   List two reasons why small class size is beneficial. (p. 466)

A.   _____

B.   _____

Educational Philosophies

1. Describe *traditional classrooms* and *constructivist classrooms,* and cite educational outcomes associated with each. (p. 467)

   Traditional: _____

   _____

   Outcomes: _____

   _____

   Constructivist: _____

   _____

   Outcomes: _____

   _____

2. Describe the nature of *social-constructivist* classrooms. (p. 467)

   _____

   _____

3. List and describe three Vygotskian-inspired teaching methods. (p. 467)

   A. _____

   _____

   B. _____

   _____

   C. _____

   _____

4. _____ refers to a method of learning in which a teacher and 2 to 4 students form a cooperative group and take turns leading dialogues on the content of a text passage. Describe four cognitive strategies that group members apply during these dialogues. (p. 468)

   A. _____

   B. _____

   C. _____

   D. _____

5. What are *communities of learners,* and what is the philosophy behind this educational approach? (p. 469)

   Description: _____

   _____

   Philosophy: _____

   _____

Social Issues: Education: School Readiness and Grade Retention

1. Delaying kindergarten entry (is / is not) beneficial for children whose birth dates are close to the cutoff for enrollment. Explain your answer. (p. 468)

_____

_____

_____

_____

2. True or False: Children retained in kindergarten or one of the primary grades show many learning benefits, as well as other positive consequences in motivation, self-esteem, and attitudes toward school. Explain your response. (p. 468)

_____

_____

_____

3. _____ classes, or waystations between kindergarten and first grade, are a form of homogeneous grouping and have the same implications for teacher–student interactions as other "low-ability" groups. (p. 468)

4. What position does the U.S. National Association for the Education of Young Children hold on school readiness? (p. 468)

_____

_____

Teacher–Student Interaction

1. Describe how teachers interact differently with high-achieving, well-behaved students versus low-achieving, disruptive students. (p. 469)

High-achieving, well-behaved students: _____

_____

_____

Low-achieving, disruptive students: _____

_____

_____

2. What are _educational self-fulfilling prophecies,_ and how do they affect students' motivation and performance? (p. 470)

Definition: _____

_____

Affect: _____

_____

_____

3. Why do teacher expectations have a greater impact on low-achieving than high-achieving students? (p. 470)

_____

_____

Grouping Practices

1. What are homogeneous groups, and how can they be a potential source of self-fulfilling prophecies? (p. 470)

_____

_____

_____

2. Discuss the benefits of multigrade classrooms, noting how student training in *cooperative learning* contributes to the success of such classrooms. (p. 470)

Benefits: _____

_____

_____

Training in cooperative learning: _____

_____

_____

Computers and Academic Learning

1. Explain how the use of word processing programs can be beneficial to children as they learn to read and write. (p. 471)

_____

_____

_____

2. On average, children and adolescents use the computer a ____ hour a day for schoolwork and ____ hour a day for pleasure. (p. 471)

3. Summarize sex differences in computer use and choice of activities. (p. 471)

_____

_____

_____

Teaching Children with Special Needs

1. What is an *inclusive classroom*? (p. 472)

_____

_____

_____

2. Describe characteristics of children with mild mental retardation and *learning disabilities*. (p. 472)

A. _____

_____

B. _____

_____

3. Discuss findings on the effectiveness of placement in regular classrooms for children with disabilities. (p. 472)

_____

_____

_____

_____

4. Special-needs children placed in regular classrooms often do best when they receive instruction in a resource room for part of the day and in the regular classroom for the remainder of the day. Describe this approach to instruction. (p. 472)

_____

_____

_____

5. Cite three ways in which teachers can promote peer acceptance in inclusive classrooms. (p. 472)

A. _____

B. _____

C. _____

6. Describe the characteristics of *gifted* children. (pp. 472–473)

_____

_____

7. _____ refers to the ability to produce work that is original yet appropriate. (p. 473)

8. Distinguish between *convergent* and *divergent thinking*. (p. 473)

Convergent: _____

_____

Divergent: _____

_____

9. _____ refers to outstanding performance in a particular field. (p. 473)

10. Describe family characteristics that foster talent. (pp. 473–474)

_____

_____

_____

11. Summarize risk factors associated with extreme giftedness, noting sex differences. (p. 474)

_____

_____

_____

12. List three models for educating gifted children. (p. 474)

A. _____

_____

B. _____

_____

C. _____

_____

How Well-Educated Are North American Children?

1. Explain how instructional practices and student study habits contribute to American children's lagging academic accomplishments. (p. 475)

Instructional practices: _____

_____

Student study habits: _____

_____

2. Describe four social forces that foster a stronger commitment to learning in Asian families and schools than in their North American counterparts. (pp. 475–476)

A. _____

_____

B. _____

_____

C. _____

_____

D. _____

_____

3. Why are many U.S. schools taking steps to increase parent involvement? (p. 476)

_____

_____

ASK YOURSELF . . .

For *Ask Yourself* questions for this chapter, along with feedback on the accuracy of your answers, please log on to MyDevelopmentLab (for registration and access, please visit mydevelopmentlab.com or follow the directions on p. ix).

1) Select the Chapter of the *Ask Yourself*.
2) Open the E-Book and select the Explore icon next to the *Ask Yourself*.
3) Complete questions and choose "Submit answers for grading" or "Clear Answers" to start over.

SUGGESTED STUDENT READINGS

Boothe, D., & Stanley, J. C. (Eds.). (2005). *In the eyes of the beholder: Critical issues for diversity in gifted education.* Waco, TX: Prufrock Press. An insightful look at key issues in gifted education, this book examines the unique needs of gifted students, particularly those from diverse racial and ethnic backgrounds. Also includes chapters from leading experts in intelligence testing and gifted education, such as Howard Gardner and Robert Sternberg.

Brown, T. E. (2006). *Attention deficit disorder: The unfocused mind in children and adults.* New Haven, CT: Yale University Press. Presents a thorough overview of Attention Deficit/Hyperactivity Disorder, including identification, treatment, common myths, and challenges of living and dealing with this disorder.

Sternberg, R. J., & Pretz, J. E. (Eds.). (2005). *Cognition and intelligence: Identifying the mechanisms of the mind.* New York: Cambridge University Press. Written by leading experts, this book presents an extensive overview of research on cognition and intelligence, including current theories, recent studies, and future directions.

Sullivan, S., & Glanz, J. (2006). *Building effective learning communities: Strategies for leadership, learning, and collaboration.* Thousand Oaks, CA: Corwin Press. Examines the use and importance of collaborative learning in the classroom, including strategies for improving standardized test scores for children of all ages.

PUZZLE 12.1 TERM REVIEW

Across

3. Transitive _____: ability to mentally order items along a quantitative dimension
4. _____ strategy use: consistent use of a mental strategy that leads to improved performance
5. Memory strategy of repeating information
10. _____ maps: children's mental representations of familiar, large-scale spaces, such as their school or neighborhood
12. Disorder involving inattentiveness, impulsivity, and excessive motor activity that results in academic and social problems (abbr.)
14. Cognitive _____-_____: process of continually monitoring progress toward a goal, checking outcomes, and redirecting unsuccessful efforts (2 words, hyph.)
15. The ability to order items along a quantitative dimension
16. Piaget's _____ operational stage is marked by logical, flexible, and organized thought

Down

1. Memory strategy of grouping together related items
2. The ability to think about language as a system is known as _____ awareness
6. Ability to mentally go through a series of steps in a problem and then reverse direction, returning to the starting point
7. _____ deficiency: inability to consistently execute a mental strategy
8. The ability to focus on and relate several aspects of a problem at the same time
9. Memory strategy of creating a relation between two or more items that are not members of the same category
11. _____ deficiency: failure to produce a mental strategy when it could be helpful
13. _____ deficiency: inability to improve performance even with consistent use of a mental strategy

PUZZLE 12.2 TERM REVIEW

Across

3. Vygotsky-inspired method of teaching in which a teacher and 2 to 4 students form a cooperative learning group

4. _____ assessment: individualized teaching is introduced into the testing situation to see what the child can attain with social support

6. Stereotype _____: fear of being judged on the basis of a negative stereotype

8. Outstanding performance in a particular field

10. In _____ classrooms, children construct their own knowledge and are viewed as active agents who reflect on and coordinate their own thoughts rather than absorbing those of others

13. A set of emotional abilities that enable individuals to process and adapt to emotional information is called _____ intelligence

14. Displaying exceptional intellectual strengths, including high IQ, creativity, and talent

15. _____ thinking: generation of multiple and unusual possibilities when faced with a problem

16. Sternberg's _____ theory of intelligence states that information processing skills, ability to learn efficiently in novel situations, and contextual factors interact to determine intelligent behavior

17. An approach to beginning reading instruction that emphasizes coaching children on the basic rules for translating written symbols into sounds is called the _____ approach

18. Gardner's theory of _____ intelligences proposes at least eight independent intelligences

19. Classrooms in which students with learning disabilities learn alongside typical students in a regular education setting is called _____ classroom

Down

1. Approach to beginning reading that parallels children's natural language learning (2 words, hyph.)

2. _____ thinking: generation of a single correct answer to a problem

5. The ability to produce work that is original yet appropriate

7. Learning _____: specific learning disorders leading to poor academic achievement despite average or above-average IQ

9. _____ of learners: teachers guide the overall learning process, but otherwise, no distinction is made between adult and child contributors

11. In _____ classrooms, children are passive learners who acquire information presented by teachers

12. Educational _____-_____ prophecy: children may adopt teachers' positive or negative attitudes toward them and start to live up to these expectations

PRACTICE TEST #1

1. Between ages 7 and 10, children can pass Piaget's class inclusion problem because they (p. 437)
    a. are no longer inhibited by decentration.
    b. can focus on relations between a general category and two specific categories at the same time.
    c. have acquired the capacity for reversibility.
    d. have moved beyond the concrete operational stage.

2. In a study comparing school-age children in India and in the United States, when the U.S. children were asked to draw maps of their neighborhoods, they represented (p. 439)
    a. a rich array of landmarks and aspects of social life.
    b. landmarks distributed haphazardly with no relation to an organized route of travel.
    c. a better grasp of proportional relations than their Indian agemates.
    d. a more formal, extended space, highlighting main streets and key directions but including few landmarks.

3. Research into the impact of culture and schooling suggests that the forms of logic required by Piagetian tasks emerge (p. 440)
    a. largely as a result of specific cultural and school practices.
    b. more or less spontaneously.
    c. earliest in tribal and village societies that emphasize various kinds of conservation tasks in daily life.
    d. only after children have acquired basic skills of seriation.

4. In elementary school, children move from a control deficiency to a utilization deficiency when they (p. 443)
    a. begin to engage in attentional strategies.
    b. are able to produce strategies, but not consistently.
    c. can execute strategies consistently, but without improved performance.
    d. use strategies consistently, with improved performance as a result.

5. Researchers agree that symptoms of attention-deficit hyperactivity disorder result from (p. 444)
    a. social rejection by peers.
    b. deficient executive processing.
    c. lack of opportunity for fast-paced play.
    d. enlarged frontal lobes of the cerebral cortex.

6. Children who are highly knowledgeable about a particular topic can organize information in their area of expertise with little or no effort because (p. 446)
    a. they use elaboration to create shared meanings.
    b. the memory centers of their brains are unusually large and active.
    c. their memories no longer suffer from a control deficiency.
    d. they can devote more working memory to using recalled information to reason and solve problems.

7. Unlike preschoolers, older children view the mind as (p. 447)
    a. a passive container of information.
    b. a product of social influences.
    c. an active, constructive agent that selects and transforms information.
    d. the agent that keeps their impulses under control.

8. As cognitive self-regulation develops, children can (p. 448)
    a. apply useful memory strategies more effectively because they understand why a particular strategy works.
    b. block out distractions so they can remember teachers' instructions and complete tasks.
    c. identify and explain second-order false beliefs.
    d. engage in metacognition.

9. Research has revealed that children who are taught complex math skills, such as carrying in addition and borrowing in subtraction, by rote (p. 451)
   a. learn those skills more effectively than those who spend time learning why certain strategies work.
   b. cannot apply the procedure to new problems and, therefore, persistently make mistakes.
   c. perform well on problems involving the metric system because of its consistent pattern of grouping by ones, tens, hundreds, and thousands.
   d. retrieve answers more rapidly than children who have been taught to think about the concepts behind strategies.

10. The *Wechsler Intelligence Scale for Children–IV* differs from the *Stanford-Binet Intelligence Scales, Fifth Edition,* in that (p. 453)
    a. it includes a factor devoted entirely to quantitative reasoning.
    b. it is useful for testing individuals with hearing impairments.
    c. it is designed to test 2- through 16-year-olds.
    d. only its verbal reasoning factor emphasizes culture-dependent information.

11. According to Sternberg's triarchic theory, children high in analytical intelligence are advanced in (p. 454)
    a. using information-processing skills.
    b. solving novel problems.
    c. applying intellectual skills in everyday situations.
    d. balancing a variety of skills in all aspects of life.

12. Unlike Sternberg's triarchic theory, Gardner's theory of multiple intelligences (p. 456)
    a. accepts the idea of general intelligence.
    b. argues that cultural values are the primary factor determining intelligence.
    c. proposes that each intelligence has a unique biological basis.
    d. proposes that each intelligence follows the same basic course of development.

13. Some researchers worry that assessments of emotional intelligence will lead teachers and psychologists to (p. 457)
    a. emphasize emotional intelligence over other kinds of intelligence.
    b. lose sight of the fact that the adaptiveness of emotional and social behavior often varies across situations.
    c. intervene inappropriately to correct emotional competencies they perceive as weak.
    d. neglect children's emotional self-regulation in favor of expressiveness.

14. Use of a collaborative communication style at home may contribute to low-SES minority students' lower IQ and school performance because this style (p. 459)
    a. overemphasizes knowledge of facts about the world.
    b. directs children to carry out an aspect of a task.
    c. does not sufficiently emphasize emotional intelligence.
    d. emphasizes close adult–child engagement rather than independent work.

15. During the "intervene" phase of dynamic assessment, the adult (p. 460)
    a. evaluates the results of the pretest phase.
    b. uses a static assessment to determine what strategies to present to the child.
    c. seeks the teaching style best suited to the child and communicates strategies the child can apply in new situations.
    d. retests the child in a less stimulating environment.

16. Eight- to 10-year-olds' comprehension of subtle metaphors, such as "sharp as a tack," demonstrates their ability to (p. 462)
    a. grasp double meanings of words.
    b. offer concrete descriptions based on appearance.
    c. analyze the structure of words.
    d. provide synonyms and explanations of categorical relationships.

17. Peer interaction probably contributes greatly to school-age children's development of clear communication because peers (p. 463)
    a. understand one another's vague descriptions because they share a context for understanding what the speaker means.
    b. challenge unclear messages that adults accept.
    c. model and reinforce one another's grammatical achievements.
    d. are less able than adults to distinguish between what people say and what they mean.

18. Bilingual children who code-switch the most are those (p. 464)
    a. who have a poor vocabulary in one language or the other.
    b. whose communities emphasize one language more than another.
    c. who are in the sensitive period for language development.
    d. whose parents often do so.

19. Small class size is beneficial because (p. 466)
    a. smaller classes tend to include children from similar SES and cultural backgrounds.
    b. teachers can discipline smaller groups more thoroughly than large groups.
    c. children who learn in smaller groups show better concentration, higher-quality class participation, and more favorable attitudes toward school.
    d. smaller classes tend to include a teacher's aide, which allows for more attention to individual students.

20. Research indicates that constructivist educational settings are associated with (p. 467)
    a. gains in critical thinking and greater social and moral maturity.
    b. poor discipline among younger school-age children.
    c. improved achievement test scores.
    d. less positive attitudes toward school.

21. In the Vygotsky-inspired reciprocal teaching approach, (p. 469)
    a. no distinction is made between teachers and students.
    b. a dialogue leader (at first a teacher) asks questions about the content of a text passage.
    c. teachers emphasize the form of symbolic communication best suited to the students.
    d. the teacher does not participate but simply observes the students, allowing them to scaffold one another's learning.

22. One drawback of heterogeneous grouping is that (p. 470)
    a. it can create educational self-fulfilling prophecies.
    b. teachers tend to focus more attention on the older students in a class.
    c. younger students tend to disrupt the class by competing with older students.
    d. students often engage in poorer quality interaction than is typically seen in homogeneous groups of above-average students.

23. A variety of tests of divergent thinking are available because (p. 473)
    a. any single test would pull the child toward convergent thinking, thus failing to measure his or her true ability.
    b. highly creative children are often better at some types of tasks than others.
    c. many tests are needed to determine the number of solutions to a problem a creative child can generate.
    d. a single test would be a poor predictor of a child's creative accomplishment.

24. Gifted children thrive in learning environments that (p. 474)
    a. focus on their particular talents.
    b. involve close parental and teacher supervision.
    c. place them among similarly talented peers so that they are only average.
    d. permit them to choose topics for extended projects and to take intellectual risks.

25. International studies reveal that compared with students in top-achieving nations, U.S. students (p. 475)
    a. are about equal with Canadian students.
    b. study by memorizing rather than relating information to previously acquired knowledge.
    c. are less likely to believe that their native ability is the key to academic success.
    d. perform largely above the international average.

PRACTICE TEST #2

1. As one study has revealed, around age 8 to 10 years, children can use a "mental walk" strategy to (p. 438)
   a. perform transitive inferences.
   b. arrange classification hierarchies.
   c. seriate items distributed across a broad area.
   d. give clear directions by imagining another person's movements along a route.

2. The major limitation of concrete operational thought is that school-age children (p. 440)
   a. cannot understand concrete information that is taught in school unless they have also encountered the same information in day-to-day life.
   b. cannot combine landmarks and routes into an overall view of space.
   c. do not come up with general logical principles and then apply them to all relevant situations.
   d. cannot perform mental rotations in order to take the viewpoint of a person in a different orientation.

3. According to Robbie Case, as cognitive schemes demand less attention and become more automatic, children (p. 441)
   a. can focus more on combining old schemes and generating new ones.
   b. need more working memory to access and apply them.
   c. require fewer central conceptual structures to perform tasks.
   d. can acquire and master many new understandings at once.

4. The development of planning illustrates how attention becomes coordinated with other cognitive processes because to solve complex problems, children must (p. 444)
   a. overcome utilization deficiency.
   b. postpone action in favor of weighing alternatives, organizing task materials, and remembering the steps of their plan.
   c. see the problem as a whole and not get distracted by considering each individual step.
   d. be able to limit the amount of time they spend monitoring and revising the plan.

5. The most effective treatment for attention-deficit hyperactivity disorder is (p. 445)
   a. stimulant medication.
   b. family intervention that focuses on appropriate child-rearing styles.
   c. special classes that isolate diagnosed children from their non-ADHD peers.
   d. a combination of medication and interventions that model and reinforce appropriate academic and social behavior.

6. The memory strategy of elaboration becomes increasingly common in adolescence and adulthood because it (p. 446)
   a. involves the sophisticated repetition of important pieces of information.
   b. emerges along with the ability to experiment adaptively.
   c. requires considerable effort and space in working memory.
   d. enables adolescents and adults to group together many seemingly unrelated items of information.

7. Research has revealed that Western school-age children get so much practice with classroom learning through memory strategies that they (p. 447)
   a. do not refine techniques that rely on spatial location and arrangement of objects.
   b. often have difficulty with recall while participating in daily activities.
   c. tend to favor one strategy over the others.
   d. are often more competent at information processing than children in non-Western cultures.

8. The ability of school-age children to grasp mental inference enables them to (p. 447)
   a. hear themselves think through private speech.
   b. conceive of the mind as an agent that actively transforms information.
   c. expand their knowledge of false belief.
   d. understand the relationship between remembering and understanding.

9. Reading instruction that combines phonics and whole language works best because it (p. 449)
    a. exposes children to whole texts so that they can appreciate the communicative function of language.
    b. teaches children relationships between letters and sounds, enabling them to decode unfamiliar words.
    c. requires children to read aloud fluently, so that they register meaning.
    d. teaches children to use reading as a way of learning new knowledge.

10. The *Stanford-Binet Intelligence Scales, Fifth Edition,* is useful for assessing individuals with limited English because it includes (p. 453)
    a. nonverbal subtests that do not require spoken language.
    b. group-administered tasks that allow testers to separate native speakers of English from non-native speakers.
    c. culturally neutral knowledge and quantitative reasoning factors.
    d. measures of general intelligence and reasoning ability.

11. The major shortcoming of componential analysis is that it (p. 454)
    a. tries to measure IQ through so many factors that it is cumbersome to use.
    b. regards intelligence as entirely due to causes within the child.
    c. does not take the functioning of the nervous system into sufficient account.
    d. relies too heavily on tests involving culture-dependent information.

12. Sternberg's triarchic theory improves upon current approaches to measuring intelligence by accounting for (p. 455)
    a. information-processing capacities.
    b. differences between boys and girls.
    c. various kinds of analytic intelligence.
    d. the range and complexity of intelligent behavior.

13. According to Gardner's theory of multiple intelligences, a child high in intrapersonal intelligence would be especially skilled at (p. 456)
    a. re-creating aspects of visual experience in the absence of relevant stimuli.
    b. working with the sounds, rhythms, and meaning of words and the functions of language.
    c. discriminating complex inner feelings and to use them to guide his or her own behavior.
    d. detecting and responding appropriately to the moods and intentions of others.

14. In explaining individual and group differences in IQ, adoption studies improve upon heritability estimates by (p. 458)
    a. providing clearer evidence that genes are the primary factor contributing to intelligence.
    b. taking greater account of the environmental influences on intelligence.
    c. factoring out the perceived black–white gap.
    d. using theories of multiple intelligences to control for cultural biases.

15. Research indicates that exposure to the factual knowledge and ways of thinking valued in classrooms (p. 459)
    a. has a sizable impact on children's intelligence test performance.
    b. no longer varies according to SES and ethnic background, because of children's near-universal exposure to such knowledge through the mass media.
    c. reduces children's reactions to stereotype threat.
    d. benefits African-American children more than Hispanic children.

16. During the elementary school years, children's vocabularies grow on average at a rate of about _____ new words each day. (p. 462)
    a. 10
    b. 15
    c. 20
    d. 25

17. During the school years, children's mastery of grammatical constructions typically improves to the point that they can (pp. 462–463)
    a. compress passive statements into abbreviated structures.
    b. extend the passive voice to inanimate objects and include passive forms of experiential verbs.
    c. comprehend the passive voice if the subject of the sentence is a person and the verb an action word.
    d. learn to construct full passive statements by listening to adults.

18. During the school years, children's narratives gradually lengthen and take on a classic form in which they (p. 463)
    a. become less topic-associating and more topic-focused.
    b. include more evaluative comments.
    c. add orienting information.
    d. build to a high point and then resolve.

19. The high rates of school failure and dropout among low-SES Hispanic youngsters is thought to result partly from (p. 465)
    a. semilingualism.
    b. Spanish-only instruction.
    c. parents' lack of English skills.
    d. Canadian-style language immersion in English.

20. According to Vygotsky's sociocultural theory, school-age children who appear to lack the necessary knowledge, skills, and attitudes for school success should (p. 468)
    a. start kindergarten a year later.
    b. be placed in transition classes between kindergarten and first grade.
    c. be given classroom experiences that foster their individual progress.
    d. repeat kindergarten or first grade.

21. When teachers emphasize competition and publicly compare children, they are likely to (p. 470)
    a. impose educational self-fulfilling prophecies on students.
    b. undermine the progress of high-achieving students more than that of low-achieving students.
    c. create lively, stimulating communities of learners.
    d. combat stereotype threats effectively by giving children a chance to excel in a competitive environment.

22. By the end of elementary school, girls are more likely than boys to use computers for (p. 471)
    a. downloading games and music.
    b. writing programs and analyzing data.
    c. creating personal websites.
    d. information gathering and communicating by e-mail.

23. Children with special learning needs often do best when they (p. 472)
    a. are placed in inclusive classrooms that include gifted children as well as more typical children.
    b. receive instruction in a resource room for part of the day and in the regular classroom for the remainder.
    c. receive one-on-one instruction from a specially trained teacher.
    d. are excused from regular classroom instruction.

24. Few talented youths become highly creative because (p. 474)
    a. they often try to hide their abilities in order to be better liked.
    b. most parents do not know how to nurture their children's abilities.
    c. rapidly mastering an existing field requires different skills than innovating in that field.
    d. talented individuals tend to produce work that is original but not appropriate.

25. Unlike elementary schools in the United States, Japanese, Korean, and Taiwanese elementary schools (p. 475)
    a. do not organize students into ability groups.
    b. view academic success as a matter of personal choice and achievement.
    c. teach mathematics through rigorous repetition.
    d. typically have a highly-structured eight-hour day that is focused exclusively on academics.

CHAPTER 13
EMOTIONAL AND SOCIAL DEVELOPMENT
IN MIDDLE CHILDHOOD

BRIEF CHAPTER SUMMARY

According to Erikson, the combination of adult expectations and children's drive toward mastery sets the stage for the psychosocial conflict of middle childhood, industry versus inferiority. It is resolved positively when experiences lead children to develop a sense of competence at useful skills and tasks. During middle childhood, psychological traits and social comparisons appear in children's self-concepts, and a hierarchically organized self-esteem emerges. Attribution research has identified adult communication styles that affect children's explanations for success and failure and, in turn, their academic self-esteem, motivation, and task performance. Gains occur in self-conscious emotions, understanding of emotional states, and emotional self-regulation. Cognitive maturity and social experiences support gains in perspective-taking skill. An expanding social world, the capacity to consider more information when reasoning, and perspective taking all promote great improvements in moral understanding during middle childhood.

By the end of middle childhood, children form peer groups, which give them insight into larger social structures. Friendships become more complex and psychologically based, with a growing emphasis on mutual trust and assistance. Researchers have identified four categories of peer acceptance: popular, rejected, controversial, and neglected children. Peer acceptance is a powerful predictor of current and future psychological adjustment. Rejected children tend to engage in antisocial behavior that leads agemates to dislike them. During the school years, boys' masculine gender identities strengthen, whereas girls' identities become more flexible and androgynous. Cultural values and parental attitudes influence these trends.

In middle childhood, the amount of time children spend with parents declines dramatically. Child rearing shifts toward coregulation as parents grant children more decision-making power while still retaining general oversight. Sibling rivalry tends to increase in middle childhood, and siblings often attempt to reduce it by striving to be different from one another. Only children are no less well–adjusted than children with siblings and are advantaged in self-esteem and achievement motivation. Children of gay and lesbian parents are well-adjusted, and the large majority are heterosexual. The situations of children in never-married, single-parent families can be improved by strengthening social support, education, and employment opportunities for parents.

When children experience divorce—often followed by entry into blended families as a result of remarriage—child, parent, and family characteristics all influence how well they fare. Growing up in a dual-earner family can have many benefits for school-age children, particularly when mothers enjoy their work, when work settings and communities support parents in their child-rearing responsibilities, and when high-quality child care is available, including appropriate after-school programs as an alternative to self-care.

As children experience new demands in school and begin to understand the realities of the wider world, their fears and anxieties are directed toward new concerns, including physical safety, media events, academic performance, parents' health, and peer relations. Child sexual abuse has devastating consequences for children and is especially difficult to treat. Personal characteristics of children, a warm, well-organized home life, and the presence of social supports outside the immediate family are related to the development of resilience—the ability to cope with stressful life conditions.

LEARNING OBJECTIVES

After reading this chapter, you should be able to:

13.1   Explain Erikson's stage of industry versus inferiority, noting major personality changes. (pp. 481–482)

13.2   Describe school-age children's self-concept and self-esteem, and discuss factors that affect their achievement-related attributions. (pp. 482–488)

13.3   Cite changes in the expression and understanding of emotion in middle childhood. (pp. 489–491)

13.4   Trace the development of perspective taking in middle childhood, and discuss the relationship between perspective taking and social skills. (pp. 491–492)

13.5   Describe changes in moral understanding during middle childhood, including children's understanding of diversity and inequality. (pp. 492–497)

13.6   Describe changes in peer sociability during middle childhood, including characteristics of peer groups and friendships and the contributions of each to social development. (pp. 497–499)

13.7   Describe the four categories of peer acceptance, noting how each is related to social behavior, and discuss ways to help rejected children. (pp. 500–503)

13.8   Summarize changes in gender-stereotyped beliefs and gender identity during middle childhood, noting sex differences and cultural influences. (pp. 503–505)

13.9   Discuss changes in parent–child communication during middle childhood. (pp. 506–507)

13.10   Describe changes in sibling relationships during middle childhood, and compare the experiences and developmental outcomes of only children with those of children with siblings. (pp. 507–508)

13.11   Describe gay and lesbian families, and discuss the developmental outcomes of children raised in such families. (p. 508)

13.12   Describe the characteristics of never-married, single-parent families, and explain how living in a single-parent household affects children. (p. 512)

13.13   Explain children's adjustment to divorce and blended families, noting the influence of parent and child characteristics and social supports within the family and surrounding community. (pp. 509–514)

13.14   Discuss the impact of maternal employment and dual-earner families on school-age children's development, noting the influence of environmental supports, and summarize research on child care for school-age children. (pp. 514–516)

13.15   Discuss common fears and anxieties in middle childhood. (pp. 516–517)

13.16   Discuss factors related to child sexual abuse, its consequences for children's development, and its prevention and treatment. (pp. 517–519)

13.17   Cite factors that foster resilience in middle childhood. (pp. 519–522)

STUDY QUESTIONS

Erikson's Theory: Industry versus Inferiority

1.   According to Erikson, what two factors set the stage for the psychological conflict of middle childhood, *industry versus inferiority*? (pp. 481–482)

   A. _____

   B. _____

2.   Describe the positive resolution of the industry versus inferiority stage. (p. 482)

   _____

   _____

3.   Explain how the beginning of formal schooling puts some children at risk for developing a sense of inferiority during middle childhood. (p. 482)

   _____

   _____

   _____

Self-Understanding

Self-Concept

1. List three ways in which self-concept changes during middle childhood. (pp. 482–483)

    A. _____

    B. _____

    C. _____

Cognitive, Social, and Cultural Influences on Self-Concept

1. Describe changes in the structure of the self during middle childhood. (p. 483)

    _____

    _____

2. Discuss the relationship between perspective-taking skills and self-concept development. (p. 483)

    _____

    _____

    _____

    _____

3. Explain the importance of parental support for self-development in middle childhood. (p. 483)

    _____

    _____

4. True or False: The content of children's self-concept varies little from culture to culture. (p. 483)

Self-Esteem

1. List four self-esteems that children form by the age of 6 or 7. (p. 484)

    A. _____

    B. _____

    C. _____

    D _____

2. True or False: Once children's self-esteem takes on a hierarchical structure, separate self-esteems contribute equally to general self-esteem. (p. 484)

3. During childhood and adolescence, perceived (academic competence / physical appearance) correlates more strongly with overall self-worth than does any other self-esteem factor. (p. 485)

4. Self-esteem (rises / drops) during the early elementary school years. Explain your answer. (p. 485)

    _____

    _____

    _____

Influences on Self-Esteem

1. Summarize ethnic and sex differences in children's self-esteem. (pp. 485–486)

    Ethnic: _____

    _____

    _____

    Sex: _____

    _____

    _____

2. Differentiate child-rearing practices associated with high versus low self-esteem in middle childhood. (p. 486)

    High: _____

    _____

    Low: _____

    _____

3. What is the best way to foster a positive, secure self-image in school-age children? (p. 486)

    _____

4. _____ are our common, everyday explanations for the causes of behavior. (p. 486)

5. Distinguish between *mastery-oriented attributions* and *learned helplessness*. (pp. 486–487)

    Mastery-oriented attributions: _____

    _____

    _____

    Learned helplessness: _____

    _____

    _____

6. Briefly explain how children's attributions affect their goals. (p. 487)

    _____

    _____

    _____

7. Summarize how communication from parents and teachers influences children's attributional style. (p. 487)

    Parents: _____

    _____

    Teachers: _____

    _____

8. True or False: Girls and low-income ethnic minority children are especially vulnerable to learned helplessness. (p. 488)

9. Explain how cultural values affect the likelihood that children will develop learned helplessness. (p. 488)

_____

_____

_____

10. _____ is an intervention that encourages learned-helpless children to believe that they can overcome failure by exerting more effort. Briefly describe this technique. (p. 488)

_____

_____

_____

11. Discuss four ways to foster a mastery-oriented approach to learning in middle childhood. (p. 489)

A. _____

_____

B. _____

_____

C. _____

_____

D. _____

_____

Emotional Development

Self-Conscious Emotions

1. Discuss changes in how children experience the self-conscious emotions of pride and guilt during middle childhood. (p. 489)

Pride: _____

_____

Guilt: _____

_____

2. Under what circumstances are pride and guilt beneficial? What are the consequences of profound feelings of shame? (pp. 489–490)

A. _____

_____

B. _____

_____

Emotional Understanding

1. List three advances in school-age children's understanding of emotions. (p. 490)

    A. _____

    B. _____

    C. _____

2. How do cognitive development and social experiences contribute to gains in emotional understanding? (p. 490)

    _____

    _____

Emotional Self-Regulation

1. Differentiate between *problem-centered* and *emotion-centered* coping strategies, noting the circumstances in which children are likely to use one strategy versus the other. (p. 490)

    Problem-centered: _____

    _____

    _____

    Emotion-centered: _____

    _____

    _____

2. When the development of emotional self-regulation has gone well, young people acquire a sense of emotional _____—a feeling of being in control of their emotional experience. (p. 491)

3. Distinguish characteristics of emotionally well-regulated children versus children with poor emotional regulation. (p. 491)

    Well-regulated: _____

    _____

    Poorly-regulated: _____

    _____

4. Briefly explain the role of culture in the development of self-regulation. (p. 491)

    _____

    _____

Understanding Others: Perspective Taking

1. Define *perspective taking*. (p. 491)

    _____

    _____

2. Match each of Selman's stages of perspective taking with the appropriate descriptions. (p. 492)

_____ Recognize that self and others can have different perspectives, but confuse the two
_____ Understand that different perspectives may be due to access to different information
_____ Can imagine how the self and others are viewed from the perspective of an impartial third person
_____ Can view own thoughts, feelings, and behavior from others' perspectives
_____ Understanding that third-party perspective taking can be influenced by larger societal values

1. Undifferentiated
2. Social-informational
3. Self-reflective
4. Third-party
5. Societal

3. Cite factors that contribute to individual differences in perspective-taking skill. (p. 492)

_____

_____

_____

Moral Development

Learning about Justice Through Sharing

1. Define *distributive justice.* (p. 493)

_____

_____

2. List and briefly describe Damon's three-step sequence of distributive justice reasoning. (p. 493)

A. _____

_____

B. _____

_____

C. _____

_____

3. True or False: Peer interaction is particularly important in the development of standards of justice. (p. 493)

Moral and Social-Conventional Understanding

1. Provide an example illustrating cultural differences in children's appreciation of moral rules. (p. 493)

_____

_____

2. Describe two changes in moral and social-conventional understanding that take place during middle childhood. (p. 493)

A. _____

_____

B. _____

_____

Understanding Individual Rights

1. How do notions of personal choice enhance children's moral understandings? (p. 494)

    _____

    _____

2. Older school-age children place limits on individual choice. Provide an example that supports this statement.
    (p. 494)

    _____

    _____

Culture and Moral Understanding

1. True or False: Children in Western and non-Western cultures use the same criteria to distinguish moral and
    social-conventional concerns. Explain your answer. (p. 494)

    _____

    _____

Cultural Influences: Children's Understanding of God

1. Trace children's understanding of God from preschool through adolescence. (p. 495)

    Preschool and school-age children: _____

    _____

    _____

    Adolescents: _____

    _____

    _____

2. Explain how the research strategies used to study children's understanding of God influence their responses.
    (p. 495)

    _____

    _____

    _____

3. Children's understanding of God (is / is not) limited to an anthropomorphic, "big person" image. (p. 495)

Understanding Diversity and Inequality

1. Discuss the development of prejudice, including the terms in-group favoritism and out-group prejudice in your
    response. (pp. 494–496)

    _____

    _____

    _____

2. Many ethnic-minority children show a pattern of _____ favoritism, in which they assign positive
    characteristics to the privileged white majority and negative characteristics to their own group. (p. 496)

3. True or False: After age 7 or 8, both majority and minority groups express in-group favoritism. (p. 496)

4. List three personal and situational factors that influence the extent to which children hold racial and ethnic biases. (pp. 496–497)

   A. _____

   B. _____

   C. _____

5. Describe two ways to reduce prejudice in school-age children. (p. 497)

   A. _____

   _____

   B. _____

   _____

Peer Relations

Peer Groups

1. Describe the characteristics of *peer groups*. (p. 498)

   _____

   _____

   _____

2. Summarize the functions of children's peer groups. (p. 498)

   _____

   _____

   _____

   _____

3. Explain how school-age children view peer exclusion, noting gender differences. (p. 498)

   _____

   _____

   _____

4. Describe the social and emotional consequences of being excluded from a peer group. (p. 498)

   Social: _____

   _____

   Emotional: _____

   _____

Friendships

1. Briefly describe changes in children's conception of friendship during middle childhood. (p. 499)

   _____

   _____

   _____

   _____

2. Cite the defining feature of friendship in middle childhood. (p. 499)

_____

3. True or False: New ideas about the meaning of friendship lead school-age children to be less selective in their choice of friends than they were at younger ages. (p. 499)

4. High-quality friendships (do / do not) tend to remain stable over middle childhood. (p. 499)

5. Discuss the qualities of aggressive children's friendships. (p. 499)

   Aggressive girls: _____

   _____

   Aggressive boys: _____

   _____

Peer Acceptance

1. Define *peer acceptance*, noting how it is different than friendship. (p. 500)

   _____

   _____

   _____

2. Explain how researchers commonly assess peer acceptance. (p. 500)

   _____

   _____

3. Name and describe four categories of peer acceptance. (p. 500)

   A. _____

   B. _____

   C. _____

   D. _____

4. True or False: All school-age children fit into one of the four categories of peer acceptance described above in Question 3. (p. 500)

5. Identify and describe two subtypes of popular children. (pp. 500–501)

   A. _____

   _____

   B. _____

   _____

6. Describe the social behavior of *rejected-aggressive* and *rejected-withdrawn* children. (p. 501)

   Aggressive: _____

   _____

   Withdrawn: _____

   _____

7. Cite four consequences of peer rejection. (p. 501)

A. _____

B. _____

C. _____

D. _____

8. True or False: Controversial children are hostile and disruptive but also engage in high rates of positive, prosocial acts. (p. 501)

9. True or False: Controversial children have as many friends as popular children. (p. 501)

10. True or False: Neglected children are more poorly adjusted and display less socially competent behavior than do their "average" counterparts. Explain your answer. (p. 501)

_____

_____

11. Describe three interventions designed to help rejected children. (pp. 501, 503)

A. _____

_____

B. _____

_____

C. _____

_____

Biology and Environment: Bullies and Their Victims

1. What is *peer victimization*? (p. 502)

_____

_____

2. Describe typical characteristics of bullies. (p. 502)

_____

_____

_____

3. Describe characteristics of victimized children. (p. 502)

_____

_____

_____

4. True or False: One of out four middle-school students report they have experienced "cyberbullying"—bullying through e-mail or other electronic media. (p. 502)

5. True or False: Victims of peer victimization are rarely, if ever, aggressive. Explain your answer. (p. 502)

_____

_____

_____

6. Discuss individual and school-based interventions for peer victimization. (p. 502)

Individual: _____

_____

School-based: _____

_____

Gender Typing

Gender-Stereotyped Beliefs

1. Gender-stereotyping of personality traits (decreases / increases) steadily during middle childhood. (p. 503)

2. Provide an example illustrating how parents contribute to children's stereotyping of personality traits. (p. 503)

_____

_____

3. Differentiate academic subjects and skills that children regard as either masculine or feminine. (p. 503)

Masculine: _____

_____

Feminine: _____

_____

4. True or False: As school-age children extend their knowledge of gender stereotypes, they become more closed-minded about what males and females can do. (p. 504)

Gender Identity and Behavior

1. Contrast the gender identity development of girls and boys during middle childhood, and note implications for behavior. (p. 504)

Girls: _____

_____

Boys: _____

_____

2. List and briefly describe three self-evaluations that influence gender identity and adjustment in middle childhood. (pp. 504–505)

A. _____

_____

B. _____

_____

C. _____

_____

Peers, Gender Typing, and Culture

1. True or False: Between fourth and seventh grade, more young people say it is OK to exclude a peer on the basis of gender than on ethnicity. (p. 505)

2. Provide an example of cultural variations in peer interaction and gender typing. (p. 505)

   _____

   _____

   _____

Family Influences

Parent–Child Relationships

1. In middle childhood, the amount of time that children spend with their parents (declines / increases) dramatically. (p. 506)

2. During the school years, child rearing becomes easier for those parents who established a(n) _____ style during the early years. (p. 506)

3. What is *coregulation,* and how does it foster a cooperative relationship between parent and child? (p. 506)

   _____

   _____

   _____

4. How do mothers and fathers differ in their interactions with same-sex and other-sex children? (p. 507)

   Mothers: _____

   _____

   Fathers: _____

   _____

Siblings

1. During middle childhood, sibling rivalry tends to (increase / decrease). Explain your answer. (p. 507)

   _____

   _____

2. School-age siblings (do / do not) rely on each other for companionship and assistance. Explain your answer. (p. 507)

   _____

   _____

Only Children

1. True or False: Research indicates that sibling relationships are essential for normal development. (p. 507)

2. True or False: Research supports the commonly held belief that only children are spoiled and selfish. (p. 508)

3. Discuss the adjustment of children in one-child families. (p. 508)

   _____

   _____

   _____

Gay and Lesbian Families

1. True or False: Research shows that gay and lesbian parents are as committed to and effective at child-rearing as are heterosexual parents. Provide evidence to support your response. (p. 508)

_____

_____

_____

2. True or False: Children from gay and lesbian families do not differ from other children in sexual orientation—the large majority are heterosexual. (p. 508)

3. Are most children of gay and lesbian parents stigmatized by their parents' sexual orientation? Explain. (p. 508)

_____

_____

Never-Married Single-Parent Families

1. What group constitutes the largest proportion of never-married parents, and what factors may contribute to this trend? (p. 509)

    A. _____

    B. _____

2. Cite outcomes associated with children raised in never-married single-parent families. (p. 509)

_____

_____

_____

Divorce

1. True or False: The United States has the highest divorce rate in the world. (p. 509)

2. Of the 45 percent of American and 30 percent of Canadian marriages that end in divorce, _____ percent involve children. (pp. 509–510)

3. Divorce is not a single event in the lives of parents and children. Explain what this means. (p. 510)

_____

_____

_____

4. Summarize ways in which divorce has an immediate impact on the home environment. (p. 510)

_____

_____

_____

_____

5. Discuss how children's ages affect their reactions to divorce, noting differences between younger and older children. (pp. 510–511)

_____

_____

_____

_____

6. Summarize sex differences in children's reactions to divorce. (p. 511)

Boys: _____

_____

_____

Girls: _____

_____

_____

7. (Boys / Girls) of divorcing parents receive less emotional support from mothers, teachers, and peers. (p. 511)

8. Most children show improved adjustment by _____ years after divorce. (p. 511)

9. Summarize the potential long-term negative consequences of parental divorce, noting who is most at risk for such adjustment difficulties. (p. 511)

_____

_____

_____

_____

10. What is the overriding factor in positive adjustment following divorce? (p. 511)

_____

11. Explain why a good father–child relationship is important for both boys and girls following divorce. (pp. 511–512)

Girls: _____

_____

Boys: _____

_____

12. True or False: Making the transition to a low-conflict, single-parent household is better for children than staying in a high-conflict intact family. (p. 512)

13. Describe _divorce mediation_, and explain why it is likely to have benefits for children. (p. 512)

_____

_____

_____

_____

14. In _____, the court grants the mother and father equal say in important decisions regarding the child's upbringing. Describe common living arrangements associated with this option, noting their impact on children's adjustment. (p. 512)

Living arrangements: _____

_____

Impact: _____

_____

15. List four ways to help children adjust to divorce. (p. 512)

A. _____

_____

B. _____

_____

C. _____

_____

D. _____

_____

Blended Families

1. What is a *blended*, or *reconstituted, family?* (p. 513)

_____

_____

2. List two reasons why blended families present adjustment difficulties for many children. (p. 513)

A. _____

_____

B. _____

_____

3. The most frequent form of blended family is a _____ arrangement. Contrast boys' and girls' adjustment in this family arrangement. (p. 513)

Boys: _____

_____

Girls: _____

_____

4. Explain why older children and adolescents of both sexes living in mother-stepfather families display more irresponsible, acting out, and antisocial behavior than do their agemates in nonstepfamilies. (pp. 513–514)

_____

_____

_____

5. Remarriage of noncustodial fathers often leads to (reduced / increased) contact with children. (p. 514)

6. Cite two reasons why children tend to react negatively to the remarriage of custodial fathers. (p. 514)

    A. _____

    B. _____

7. (Girls / Boys) have an especially hard time getting along with stepmothers. Briefly explain your response. (p. 514)

    _____

    _____

    _____

8. Explain how family life education and counseling can help parents and children in blended families adapt to the complexities of their new circumstances. (p. 514)

    _____

    _____

    _____

    _____

9. The divorce rate for second marriages is (higher / lower) than for first marriages. (p. 514)

Maternal Employment and Dual-Earner Families

1. In North America today, more than _____ of mothers with school-age children are employed. (p. 514)

2. Describe potential benefits of maternal employment for school-age children, and note the circumstances under which such outcomes are achieved. (p. 514)

    _____

    _____

    _____

3. True or False: Maternal employment results in more time with fathers, who take greater responsibility for child care. (p. 515)

4. List four supports that help parents juggle the demands of work and child rearing. (p. 515)

    A. _____

    B. _____

    C. _____

    D. _____

5. Differentiate *self-care children* who fare well from those who fare poorly. (p. 515)

    Children who fare well: _____

    _____

    _____

    Children who fare poorly: _____

    _____

    _____

6. Before age _____ or _____, children should not be left unsupervised because most are not yet competent to handle emergencies. (p. 515)

7. True or False: After-school enrichment programs are especially common in inner-city neighborhoods. (p. 516)

Some Common Problems of Development

Fears and Anxieties

1. Summarize new fears and anxieties that emerge in middle childhood. (p. 516)

    _____

    _____

    _____

2. What do children in Western nations mention as the most common source of their fears? (p. 516)

    _____

3. An intense, unmanageable fear that leads to persistent avoidance of the feared situation is called a(n) _____. (p. 517)

4. Describe the symptoms associated with school phobia. (p. 517)

    _____

    _____

5. Distinguish common causes of school phobia in early childhood from those in later childhood and adolescence, noting implications for treatment. (p. 517)

    Early childhood: _____

    _____

    _____

    Later childhood and adolescence: _____

    _____

    _____

Cultural Influences: The Impact of Ethnic and Political Violence on Children

1. Discuss children's adjustment to war and social crises, noting differences between situations involving temporary crises and those involving chronic danger. (p. 518)

    _____

    _____

    _____

    _____

2. What is the best safeguard against lasting problems for children exposed to ethnic and political violence? (p. 518)

    _____

3. Discuss some interventions used to help children from Public School 31 in Brooklyn, New York, in the wake of the September 11 attack on the World Trade Center. (p. 518)

_____

_____

_____

Child Sexual Abuse

1. Sexual abuse is committed against children of both sexes, but more often against (girls / boys). (p. 517)

2. Describe typical characteristics of sexual abusers. (p. 517)

_____

_____

_____

_____

3. Describe the characteristics of children who are especially vulnerable to abuse. (p. 519)

_____

_____

_____

4. Discuss the adjustment problems of sexually abused children, noting differences between younger children and adolescents. (p. 519)

Younger children: _____

_____

Adolescents: _____

_____

5. Describe common behavioral characteristics of sexually abused children as they move into young adulthood. (p. 519)

_____

_____

_____

6. Why is it difficult to treat victims of child sexual abuse? (p. 519)

_____

_____

_____

7. Discuss the role of educational programs in preventing child sexual abuse. (p. 519)

_____

_____

_____

Social Issues: Health: Children's Eyewitness Testimony

1. True or False: Children as young as age 3 are frequently asked to provide testimony in court cases involving child abuse and neglect. (p. 520)

2. Summarize age differences in children's ability to provide accurate testimony. (p. 520)

_____

_____

_____

_____

3. Identify several reasons why young children are more prone to memory problems than older children. (p. 520)

_____

_____

_____

4. True or False: When adults lead children by suggesting incorrect information, they increase the likelihood of incorrect reporting among preschool and school-age children alike. (p. 520)

5. True or False: Special interviewing methods involving the use of anatomically correct dolls have been successful in prompting more accurate recall of sexual abuse experiences, particularly among preschoolers. (p. 520)

6. Summarize interventions that can be used to assist child witnesses. (p. 520)

_____

_____

_____

_____

Fostering Resilience in Middle Childhood

1. Cite personal, family, school, and community resources that foster resilience in middle childhood. (p. 521)

Personal: _____

_____

Family: _____

_____

School: _____

_____

Community: _____

_____

2. Summarize components of the *Resolving Conflicts Creatively Program,* and note program outcomes for child behavior. (p. 522)

Components: _____

_____

_____

Outcomes: _____

_____

_____

ASK YOURSELF . . .

For *Ask Yourself* questions for this chapter, along with feedback on the accuracy of your answers, please log on to MyDevelopmentLab (for registration and access, please visit mydevelopmentlab.com or follow the directions on p. ix).

1) Select the Chapter of the *Ask Yourself.*
2) Open the E-Book and select the Explore icon next to the *Ask Yourself.*
3) Complete questions and choose "Submit answers for grading" or "Clear Answers" to start over.

SUGGESTED STUDENT READINGS

Feerick, M. M., & Silverman, G. B. (Eds.). (2006). *Children exposed to violence.* Baltimore, MD: Paul H. Brookes. With an emphasis on domestic violence, community violence, and war and terrorism, this book explores the effects of violence on all aspects of child development, including physical health, psychological well-being, academic achievement, and social competence.

Jacobs, J. A., & Gerson, K. (2005). *The time divide: Work, family, and gender inequality.* Cambridge, MA: Harvard University Press. Examines the multitude of benefits and challenges facing dual-earner families. The authors also explore how public policies in the United States and other industrialized nations affect family and work, including gender inequalities in the workplace.

Ladd, G. W. (2005). *Children's peer relations and social competence: A century of progress.* New Haven: Yale University Press. Using over a century's worth of research, this book examines the importance of peer relations for healthy child and adolescent development. Topics include early research on peer relations, friendship, the origins of social competence, and the role of gender, emotion, and culture in peer relationships.

Marquardt, E. (2006). *Between two worlds: The inner lives of children of divorce.* New York: Crown Publishing. Based on extensive longitudinal research, this book examines the effects of divorce on children, including emotional reactions, resilience, and adjusting to blended families.

PUZZLE 13.1 TERM REVIEW

Across

8. _____-_____ attributions credit success to high ability and failure to insufficient effort

10. _____-centered coping: appraising a situation as changeable, identifying the difficulty, and deciding what to do about it

Down

1. Social _____: judgments of appearance, abilities, behavior, and other characteristics in relation to those of others

2. _____ versus inferiority: Erikson's psychological conflict of middle childhood

3. Common, everyday explanations for the causes of behavior

4. Attribution _____ is an intervention aimed at modifying the attributions of learned-helpless children

5. _____-centered coping: internal, private, and aimed at controlling distress when little can be done about an outcome

6. Learned _____: attributions that credit success to luck and failure to low ability

7. _____ taking: the capacity to imagine what others may be thinking and feeling

9. Beliefs about how to divide up material goods fairly is known as _____ justice

PUZZLE 13.2 TERM REVIEW

Across

3. Children who are actively disliked and get many negative votes on sociometric measures of peer acceptance
6. Divorce _____ attempts to settle disputes of divorcing adults while avoiding legal battles that intensify family conflict
11. Children who get a large number of positive and negative votes on sociometric measures of peer acceptance
14. Children who are seldom chosen, either positively or negatively, on sociometric measures of peer acceptance
17. Popular-_____ children: good students who communicate with peers in sensitive, friendly, and cooperative ways

Down

1. An intense, unmanageable fear that leads to persistent avoidance of a feared situation
2. Family structure resulting from cohabitation or remarriage that includes parent, child, and steprelatives
4. Supervision in which parents exercise general oversight but permit children to manage moment-to-moment decisions
5. Peer _____: certain children become frequent targets of verbal and physical attacks or other forms of abuse

7. Popular-_____ children: highly aggressive, yet viewed by peers as "cool"
8. Rejected-_____ children are a subgroup of rejected children who engage in high rates of conflict, hostility, hyperactivity, inattention, and impulsivity
9. Peer _____: the extent to which a child is viewed by a group of agemates as a worthy social partner
10. Social units of peers who generate unique values and standards for behavior and a social structure of leaders and followers (2 words)
12. _____-_____ children look after themselves while their parents are at work (2 words, hyph.)
13. Rejected-_____ children are a subgroup of rejected children who are passive and socially awkward
15. Children who get many positive votes on sociometric measures of peer acceptance
16. _____ custody: arrangement following divorce in which both parents are granted equal say in important decisions regarding the child's upbringing

305

PRACTICE TEST #1

1. According to Erikson, children resolve the industry-versus-inferiority conflict positively when (p. 482)
   a. they realize their inadequacy in the face of new tasks.
   b. they compare themselves favorably to peers.
   c. experiences lead them to develop a sense of competence at useful skills and tasks.
   d. they reach a new level of sophistication in make-believe play.

2. In a comparative study of U.S. and Chinese children, when asked to recall personally significant past experiences, the Chinese children tended to (p. 483)
   a. refer to social interactions and to others rather than themselves.
   b. describe their personal preferences, interests, and skills.
   c. describe themselves as polite and obedient.
   d. refer to others' positive reaction to their social traits.

3. In childhood and adolescence, the self-esteem factor that correlates most strongly with overall self-worth is (p. 485)
   a. academic competence.
   b. physical appearance.
   c. social competence.
   d. physical/athletic competence.

4. As research shows, gender-stereotyped beliefs contribute to girls' advantage in (p. 485)
   a. self-esteem related to their abilities in math and science.
   b. self-esteem related to their willingness to help others.
   c. physical/athletic self-esteem.
   d. language-arts self-esteem.

5. Mastery-oriented children typically focus on learning goals because they (p. 487)
   a. hold a fixed view of their ability.
   b. seek positive evaluations of their sense of ability and avoid negative ones.
   c. understand that they can obtain information on how to increase their ability.
   d. attribute their successes to external factors.

6. Attributing poor performance to lack of ability is common among (p. 488)
   a. girls.
   b. children of mastery-oriented parents.
   c. boys.
   d. middle-SES immigrant children.

7. During the school years, children typically report guilt (p. 489)
   a. only when adults are present.
   b. for any mishap in which they were involved.
   c. only for intentional wrongdoing.
   d. only to peers but not to adults.

8. Children shift from problem-centered coping to emotion-centered coping when (p. 490)
   a. their sense of emotional self-efficacy is low.
   b. they appraise a situation as not changeable.
   c. they believe they can change a situation if they can gain control of their emotional response.
   d. adults do not encourage their efforts to deal with the situation.

9. According to Selman, children who have reached the level of social-informational perspective taking can (p. 492)
   a. recognize that self and other can have different thoughts and feelings, but they frequently confuse the two.
   b. understand that different perspectives may result because people have access to different information.
   c. view their own thoughts, feelings, and behavior from the other person's perspective.
   d. understand that third-party perspective taking can be influenced by one or more systems of larger societal values.

10. School-age children distinguish between social conventions that have a clear purpose and those that have no obvious justification, and they tend to regard violations of purposeful conventions as (p. 493)
    a. closer to moral transgressions.
    b. acceptable if the intention is modesty.
    c. more or less severe according to context.
    d. going against the principle of strict equality.

11. Research shows that, contrary to previous assumptions, children conceive of God much as adults do in that they (p. 495)
    a. view God as an abstract, formless, and omniscient being.
    b. draw little influence from religious education.
    c. have a view of God that blends both tangible and intangible features.
    d. assign anthropomorphic characteristics to God.

12. Research indicates that many ethnic-minority children respond to racial bias by developing (p. 496)
    a. in-group favoritism.
    b. overly high self-esteem.
    c. attitudes similar to those of their parents.
    d. out-group favoritism.

13. One of the more promising approaches to reducing children's racial bias involves inducing them to (p. 497)
    a. divide the social world into groups on the basis of positive distinctions.
    b. view others' traits as changeable.
    c. role-play as people who experience out-group prejudice.
    d. tell stories involving ethnic minorities and then identify the stereotyped traits they included.

14. Compared with friendships among preschoolers, school-age children's friendships are likely to (p. 499)
    a. be more selective, because they are based on trust.
    b. be more unstable, usually lasting a few months at most.
    c. involve criticism.
    d. be defined by conflict.

15. Rejected-withdrawn children are especially likely to be targeted by bullies because they (p. 501)
    a. mistrust peers.
    b. typically display a strange blend of positive and negative social behaviors.
    c. tend to have an inept and submissive style of interacting with others.
    d. are more likely than other children to choose opposite-sex friends.

16. Research indicates that most bullies are (p. 502)
    a. low-SES children eager to increase their status among peers.
    b. boys who use both physical and verbal attacks.
    c. children who were initially admired for some special ability but later rejected.
    d. girls who bombard a vulnerable classmate with verbal hostility.

17. According to one study of sixth graders from diverse cultures, although girls consistently had higher grades than boys, they (p. 504)
    a. continued to believe that they were truly skilled only in art and music.
    b. reported the belief that they surpassed boys only in obedience.
    c. tended to echo their parents' evaluations of their skills.
    d. believed they were less talented than boys.

18. Research indicates that girls are more likely than boys to consider future work roles (p. 504)
    a. that are stereotyped for the other gender.
    b. according to their sense of gender contentedness.
    c. based on their mother's evaluations of their skills.
    d. typically defined as masculine.

19. Between fourth and seventh grade, boys especially say it is more acceptable to exclude on the basis of gender than on ethnicity because (p. 505)
    a. during those years, boys tend to be highly gender-typical.
    b. boys are more susceptible than girls to gender-typed messages from adults.
    c. they are concerned about group functioning related to sex differences in interests and communication styles.
    d. boys tend to be more individualistic than girls.

20. Virtually all studies of children of gay and lesbian parents have concluded that (p. 508)
    a. the parents' lifestyle emotionally damages the children.
    b. the children do not differ from other children in sexual orientation.
    c. siblings experience less rivalry than those in families with heterosexual parents.
    d. the children are almost universally stigmatized by the parents' sexual orientation.

21. Research indicates that about 20 to 25 percent of children in divorced families display severe behavioral problems because (p. 510)
    a. they blame themselves for their parents' marital problems.
    b. that percentage also come from economically disadvantaged homes.
    c. parents tend to become permissive and indulgent.
    d. the more parents argue and fail to provided warmth and guidance, the poorer the children's adjustment.

22. In mother-stepfather blended families, girls tend to (p. 513)
    a. welcome a stepfather who is warm and refrains from exerting authority too quickly.
    b. notice and challenge unfair treatment of biological children more quickly than boys.
    c. have difficulty with their custodial mother's remarriage and resist the stepfather.
    d. have less contact with the noncustodial parent.

23. Research has revealed that regardless of SES, daughters of employed mothers (p. 514)
    a. still choose careers based on gender-stereotyped evaluations of their skills.
    b. perceive women's roles as involving more freedom of choice and satisfaction.
    c. tend to become self-care children.
    d. benefit less than sons from paternal involvement in child-rearing.

24. Outcomes for children of ethnic and political violence, such as anxiety, depression, aggression, and antisocial behavior, appear to be (p. 518)
    a. culturally universal.
    b. more pronounced in impoverished countries, where children already feel the effects of poverty.
    c. less severe for girls than for boys.
    d. worse in collectivist societies, where violence destroys community ties.

25. Programs like Resolving Conflict Creatively are successful because they (p. 522)
    a. focus on social and emotional attributes.
    b. target low-SES children who have experienced an especially traumatic divorce.
    c. reduce parental stress.
    d. recognize that resilience is a capacity that develops, not a preexisting attribute.

PRACTICE TEST #2

1. Between ages 8 and 11, children's self-concept develops to include (p. 483)
    a. social comparisons of multiple individuals, including themselves.
    b. unqualified self-descriptions.
    c. comparisons with a single close friend.
    d. descriptions that emphasize specific behaviors.

2. According to George Herbert Mead, perspective-taking skills are crucial to the development of a self-concept because they enable children to (p. 483)
    a. replace the ideal self with the real self.
    b. become more thoroughly vested in their parents' feedback.
    c. build a secure I-self that can filter out other's attitudes toward them.
    d. infer what others are thinking and incorporate these messages into their self-definitions.

3. Self-esteem typically declines during the first few years of elementary school because (p. 485)
    a. peer relationships become more complicated, often involving exclusion and rejection.
    b. children receive more competence-related feedback and judgments of their performances in relation to those of others.
    c. parents' expectations increase and become more rigid.
    d. children have less opportunity for physical activity and make-believe play.

4. The controlling style of authoritarian parents tends to communicate to children (p. 486)
    a. a sense of inadequacy that is linked to low self-esteem.
    b. a reasonable sense of their limitations that ultimately strengthens their self-esteem.
    c. a sense of self-worth that is absolutely fixed, regardless of the evaluations of others.
    d. confidence in their ability to make sensible choices.

5. Children's self-evaluations and school grades conform relatively closely to parental judgments when parents (p. 487)
    a. hold an incremental view of ability.
    b. are intensely mastery-oriented.
    c. communicate a fixed view of ability.
    d. have a learned-helpless approach to their own learning.

6. One common form of attribution retraining intervention encourages learned-helpless children to (p. 488)
    a. emphasize mastery rather than ability.
    b. work at difficult tasks in which they will experience some failure but also receive feedback that focuses on their effort.
    c. work to improve their grades in small, specified increments over a long period of time.
    d. set their own standards of achievement and work to meet them.

7. Research indicates that as school-age children learn to appreciate mixed emotions, they (p. 490)
    a. realize that people's expressions may not reflect their true feelings.
    b. become less self-conscious about their own emotions.
    c. grow increasingly confused by contradictory facial and situational cues.
    d. expect others to clarify their emotions and display empathy.

8. Between ages 7 and 12, children's perspective-taking skills develop to the point that they first (p. 492)
    a. recognize that self and other can have different thoughts and feelings, but frequently confuse the two.
    b. understand that people may have different perspectives because they have access to different information.
    c. view their own thoughts, feelings, and behavior from another person's perspective.
    d. are able to step outside a two-person situation and imagine how the self and the other are viewed from a third point of view.

9. By age 6 to 7, children's sense of distributive justice becomes more mature and is based on the idea of (p. 493)
    a. strict equality.
    b. merit.
    c. equality and benevolence.
    d. social justice.

10. In middle childhood, children realize that responsibility for moral transgressions may vary according to a person's (p. 493)
    a. sense of purposeful social convention.
    b. gender.
    c. sense of equity and benevolence.
    d. knowledge.

11. Research suggests that one reason for the general decline of prejudice in middle childhood is that children at that stage typically (p. 494)
    a. resolve conflicting moral and personal concerns in favor of fairness, even in cases of ethnic and/or gender difference.
    b. make few distinctions based on ethnic and gender difference.
    c. apply the principle of strict equality to matters of ethnic and gender difference.
    d. view the treatment of someone of a different gender or ethnicity as a matter for democratic decision making.

12. Research suggests that children with very high self-esteem are more likely to hold racial or ethnic prejudices because they (p. 497)
    a. believe that people's personality traits are fixed and unchanging.
    b. tend to view people in terms of group distinctions.
    c. seem to belittle disadvantaged individuals or groups to justify their own favorable self-evaluations.
    d. are less aware than their peers of the immorality of discrimination.

13. Most school-age children view the exclusion of a peer from a group as justified when (p. 498)
    a. the peer has an unconventional appearance or behavior.
    b. they have experienced exclusion themselves.
    c. they perceive themselves as different from the excluded peer.
    d. the peer threatens group functioning by acting disruptively or lacking skills to participate in a valued group activity.

14. Unlike rejected-aggressive children, popular-antisocial children (p. 500)
    a. frequently experience moments of passivity and social awkwardness.
    b. are deficient in perspective taking but good at emotional regulation.
    c. enhance their own status by ignoring, excluding, and spreading rumors about other children.
    d. have few or no friends.

15. According to research on cyberbullying, (p. 502)
    a. most victims and bystanders did not report the incidents to adults.
    b. girls were more likely than boys to engage in this type of bullying.
    c. almost none of the perpetrators engaged in this type of harassment more than once.
    d. the bullies tended to be middle-SES children.

16. According to one study, girls' self-perceptions, as well as their career choices in their mid-twenties, are predicted by (pp. 503–504)
    a. the extent to which fathers emphasize a mastery-oriented attributional style.
    b. mothers' early perceptions of their daughters' competence at math.
    c. peers' reinforcement of success in particular academic subjects and skill areas.
    d. how much praise girls receive from parents and teachers for obedience.

17. School-age children realize that sex is not a certain predictor of a person's personality traits or activities, an awareness that increases as they (p. 504)
    a. develop the capacity to integrate conflicting social cues.
    b. absorb messages about gender from teachers and parents.
    c. grasp the difference between social and biological influences.
    d. form mixed-gender peer groups.

18. According to a longitudinal study of third through seventh graders, children who were gender-atypical (p. 505)
    a. experienced a gradual increase in self-esteem from year to year as pressure toward gender typicality declined.
    b. felt more or less pressure to conform to gender roles, depending on their peer group.
    c. declined in feelings of self-worth over the following year.
    d. were highly gender-discontented by the time they reached seventh grade.

19. Research indicates that both mothers and fathers tend to devote more time to (p. 507)
    a. only children of the opposite sex.
    b. achievement-related recreational pursuits with sons.
    c. ensuring that children meet responsibilities for homework, after-school lessons, and chores.
    d. children of their own sex.

20. Most studies indicate that children of gay and lesbian parents rarely suffer teasing or bullying because (p. 508)
    a. the children tend to be popular-prosocial.
    b. both parents and children carefully manage the information they reveal to others.
    c. these children seek out friends tolerant of nonconformity.
    d. these children gain the trust and friendship of their peers by being unusually open about their family life.

21. Many children in single-mother homes display adjustment problems because (p. 509)
    a. they tend to live under conditions of economic hardship.
    b. their mothers generally do not look to their extended families for help.
    c. such homes are bad environments for children regardless of the mother's SES or education.
    d. the father typically refuses to provide any financial support.

22. Children of divorced parents who share joint custody tend to (p. 512)
    a. experience less sibling rivalry than children with single-parent custody.
    b. have more behavior problems than those with single-parent custody.
    c. be better adjusted than children in sole maternal-custody homes.
    d. resent having to see one parent on a fixed schedule.

23. Nighttime fears often increase between ages 7 and 9 because (p. 516)
    a. such fears often grow from the school phobias common during those years.
    b. at that point, children are especially susceptible to the effects of negative information on television.
    c. during those years, children tend to be especially afraid of the dark.
    d. children often mull over frightening thoughts at bedtime.

24. In about 25 percent of cases of sexual abuse, the offender is a (p. 517)
    a. stepfather, usually with a girl in middle childhood.
    b. mother, more often with a son.
    c. homosexual relative with a child of the same sex.
    d. male relative or acquaintance who exposed the child to pornography.

25. To increase the accuracy of children's courtroom testimony, legal professionals may (p. 520)
    a. use unbiased, open-ended questions that prompt children to disclose details.
    b. have children write their version of the event in question before giving testimony in court.
    c. isolate child witnesses from all adults and other sources of potentially biased information before taking their testimony.
    d. request testimony only from children over the age of 10.

CHAPTER 14
PHYSICAL DEVELOPMENT IN ADOLESCENCE

BRIEF CHAPTER SUMMARY

Adolescence is a time of dramatic physical change leading to an adult-sized body and sexual maturity. Although early biologically based theories viewed puberty as a period of emotional turmoil, recent research shows that serious psychological disturbance is not common during the teenage years. A balanced point of view identifies adolescent development and adjustment as products of a combination of biological, psychological, and social forces.

The dramatic physical changes of puberty are regulated by genetically influenced hormonal processes. On average, girls reach puberty two years earlier than boys, but wide individual differences exist. The first outward sign of puberty is the growth spurt, accompanied by changes in physical features related to sexual functioning. Heredity contributes substantially to the timing of pubertal changes, and variations also exist between world regions and between SES and ethnic groups. A secular trend toward earlier maturation has occurred in industrialized nations, with rising rates of overweight and obesity possibly playing a role.

Most adolescents greet the beginning of menstruation and the first ejaculation of seminal fluid with mixed feelings, depending on prior knowledge and support from family members. Puberty is related to increased moodiness and a mild rise in conflict between parents and children. The effects of maturational timing involve a complex blend of biological, social, and cultural factors.

The arrival of puberty brings new health concerns. For some teenagers, the cultural ideal of thinness combines with family and psychological problems, as well as cultural admiration of thinness, to produce two serious eating disorders: anorexia nervosa and bulimia nervosa. The rate of unintentional injuries rises in adolescence as a result of risk taking, with automobile accidents as the leading killer of American teenagers. In the United States, firearms cause the majority of other fatal injuries. Sports-related injuries are also common.

Sexual attitudes in North America are relatively restrictive, despite prevailing images of sexually free adolescents. Most adolescents learn about sex from friends and from the media, which tend to glorify sexual excitement and experimentation, in contrast to the more restrictive views of adults. Rates of extramarital sex among American and Canadian young people rose for several decades but have declined in recent years. Early, frequent teenage sexual activity is linked to personal, family, peer, and educational characteristics. Adolescent contraceptive use has risen in recent years, but many teenagers fail to take precautions, putting them at risk for unintended pregnancy. Sexual orientation is affected strongly by heredity, as well as by a variety of prenatal biological influences. Adolescents have the highest rate of sexually transmitted diseases of all age groups. Although AIDS education has provided teenagers with basic information about AIDS, many hold false beliefs that put them at risk. Adolescent sexual activity is accompanied by high rates of pregnancy and parenthood, which is especially challenging and stressful for teenagers, who have not yet established a clear direction in their own lives. Although most teenagers engage in some experimentation with alcohol and drugs, a worrisome minority make the transition from use to abuse.

LEARNING OBJECTIVES

After reading this chapter, you should be able to:

14.1 Discuss changing conceptions of adolescence over the twentieth century, and identify the three phases of adolescence recognized in modern industrialized nations. (pp. 530–531)

14.2 Describe physical changes associated with puberty, including hormonal changes, body growth, and sexual maturation. (pp. 531–536)

14.3 Cite factors that influence the timing of puberty. (pp. 536–537)

14.4 Describe brain development and changes in the organization of sleep and wakefulness during adolescence. (pp. 537–538)

14.5 Cite factors that influence adolescents' reactions to the physical changes of puberty. (p. 539)

14.6   Discuss the impact of maturational timing on adolescent adjustment, noting sex differences, as well as immediate and long-term consequences. (pp. 540–543)

14.7   Summarize the nutritional needs of adolescents. (pp. 543–544)

14.8   Describe the symptoms of anorexia nervosa and bulimia nervosa, and cite personal and environmental factors that contribute to these disorders. (pp. 544–546)

14.9   Cite common unintentional injuries in adolescence. (p. 546)

14.10   Discuss social and cultural influences on adolescent sexual attitudes and behavior. (p. 547)

14.11   Discuss biological and environmental contributions to homosexuality. (pp. 551–552)

14.12   Discuss factors related to sexually transmitted diseases in adolescence, particularly AIDS, and cite strategies for STD prevention. (pp. 552–555)

14.13   Summarize factors related to adolescent pregnancy, consequences of early childbearing for adolescent parents and their children, and strategies for preventing adolescent pregnancy. (pp. 555–559)

14.14   Distinguish between substance use and abuse, including personal and social factors related to each, discuss the consequences of substance abuse, and cite strategies for prevention and treatment. (pp. 559–561)

STUDY QUESTIONS

Conceptions of Adolescence

The Biological Perspective

1.   Describe G. Stanley Hall and Anna Freud's biological perspective of adolescence. (p. 530)

G. Stanley Hall: _____

_____

Anna Freud: _____

_____

The Social Perspective

1.   True or False: Rates of psychological disturbance increase dramatically during adolescence, supporting the conclusion that it is a period of storm and stress. (p. 530)

2.   Describe Margaret Mead's perspective of adolescence. (p. 530)

_____

_____

A Balanced Point of View

1.   True or False: The length of adolescence is the same in all cultures. Briefly explain your response. (p. 531)

_____

_____

2.   List and describe the three phases of adolescence. (p. 531)

A.   _____

B.   _____

C.   _____

Puberty: The Physical Transition to Adulthood

Hormonal Changes

1. During sexual maturation, the boy's testes release large quantities of the androgen
   _____, which leads to muscle growth, body and facial hair, and other male sex
   characteristics, as well as contributing to gains in body size. (p. 531)

2. The release of _____ from the girl's ovaries causes the breasts, uterus, and vagina to
   mature, the body to take on feminine proportions, and fat to accumulate. (p. 531)

Body Growth

1. The first outward sign of puberty is the rapid gain in height and weight known as the
   _____. (p. 532)

2. On average, the adolescent growth spurt is underway for North American girls shortly after age _____ and for
   boys around age _____. (p. 532)

3. True or False: During puberty, the cephalocaudal trend reverses, with hands, legs, and feet growing first,
   followed by growth of the torso. (pp. 532–533)

4. Describe sex differences in body proportions and muscle–fat makeup during adolescence. (p. 533)

   Boys: _____

   _____

   Girls: _____

   _____

Motor Development and Physical Activity

1. Briefly summarize sex differences in gross motor development during adolescence. (pp. 533–534)

   Boys: _____

   _____

   Girls: _____

   _____

2. True or False: Use of creatine and anabolic steroids improves teenagers' athletic performance while having no
   adverse side effects. (p. 534)

3. Among American and Canadian youths, rates of physical activity (rise / decline) during adolescence. (p. 534)

4. Cite the benefits of sports participation and exercise during adolescence. (pp. 534–535)

   _____

   _____

   _____

5. What is one of the best predictors of adult physical exercise, and why? (p. 535)

   A. _____

   B. _____

Sexual Maturation

1.   Distinguish between *primary* and *secondary sexual characteristics*. (p. 535)

Primary: _____

_____

Secondary: _____

_____

2.   _____ is the scientific name for first menstruation. It typically happens around _____
years of age for North American girls. (p. 535)

3.   List early signs of puberty in boys. (p. 536)

_____

_____

4.   The growth spurt occurs much (earlier / later) in the sequence of pubertal events for boys than for girls. (p. 536)

5.   Around age 13½, _____, or first ejaculation, occurs in boys. (p. 536)

Individual Differences in Pubertal Growth

1.   Explain how heredity, nutrition, and exercise contribute to the timing of puberty. (p. 536)

Heredity: _____

_____

Nutrition: _____

_____

Exercise: _____

_____

2.   Describe how SES and ethnicity influence pubertal growth. (p. 536)

_____

_____

_____

3.   How do early family experiences contribute to the timing of puberty? (pp. 536–537)

_____

_____

_____

The Secular Trend

1.   Describe the secular trend in pubertal timing in industrialized nations, noting factors believed to be responsible
for it. (p. 537)

_____

_____

_____

Brain Development

1. Briefly summarize changes in synaptic pruning, myelination, and connections between cerebral hemispheres during adolescence, noting the impact of such changes on adolescent cognitive functioning. (p. 537)

_____

_____

_____

_____

Impact: _____

_____

2. Describe changes in neurotransmitter activity during adolescence, and explain how this impacts behavior. (pp. 537–538)

Changes: _____

_____

Impact: _____

_____

Changing States of Arousal

1. Describe the sleep "phase delay," noting factors that contribute to it. (p. 538)

A. _____

_____

B. _____

_____

2. List the negative consequences of sleep deprivation in adolescence. (p. 538)

_____

_____

The Psychological Impact of Pubertal Events

Reactions to Pubertal Changes

1. Discuss two factors that affect girls' reactions to menarche. (p. 539)

A. _____

B. _____

2. Overall, boys seem to get (more / less) social support for the physical changes of puberty than girls. (p. 539)

3. Many tribal and village societies celebrate puberty with a(n) _____—a community-wide event that marks an important change in privilege and responsibility. Contrast this experience with that of adolescents in Western societies. (p. 539)

_____

_____

_____

_____

Pubertal Change, Emotion, and Social Behavior

1. Research shows that adolescents report (more / less) favorable moods than school-age children and adults. (p. 540)

2. Cite factors associated with high and low points in mood during adolescence. (p. 540)

    High points: _____

    _____

    Low points: _____

    _____

3. When do teenagers' frequent reports of negative mood level off, and what accounts for this change? (p. 540)

    A. _____

    B. _____

4. How might parent–child conflict during adolescence serve an adaptive function? (p. 541)

    _____

    _____

5. True or False: During adolescence, parent-daughter conflict tends to be more intense than parent-son conflict. (p. 541)

6. Most disputes between parents and adolescents are (mild / severe). (p. 541)

Pubertal Timing

1. Discuss research findings on the effects of maturational timing for the following groups of adolescents: (p. 541)

    Early-maturing boys: _____

    _____

    Early-maturing girls: _____

    _____

    Late-maturing boys: _____

    _____

    Late-maturing girls: _____

    _____

2. List two factors that largely account for trends in the effects of maturational timing. (p. 542)

    A. _____

    B. _____

3. Discuss the impact of maturational timing on adolescents' body images, noting ethnic differences. (p. 542)

    _____

    _____

    _____

    _____

4. Early-maturing adolescents of both sexes tend to seek (younger / older) companions. Describe the consequences of this trend in peer relations. (p. 542)

_____

_____

5. The young person's environmental context greatly (decreases / increases) the likelihood that early pubertal timing will lead to (negative / positive) outcomes. Provide an example to support your response. (p. 542)

_____

_____

_____

6. Describe the long-term effects of maturational timing for early- and late-maturing individuals. (p. 543)

Early-maturing: _____

_____

Late-maturing: _____

_____

_____

Health Issues

Nutritional Needs

1. Of all age groups, the eating habits of adolescents are the (best / poorest). What factors contribute to this trend? (p. 544)

_____

_____

2. What is the most common nutritional problem of adolescence? (p. 544)

_____

3. Frequency of family meals is (strongly / weakly) associated with healthy eating in teenagers. (p. 544)

Serious Eating Disturbances

1. What is the strongest predictor of the onset of an eating disorder in adolescence? (p. 544)

_____

2. Describe the physical and behavioral symptoms of _anorexia nervosa_. (pp. 544–545)

_____

_____

_____

3. Explain how forces within the person, family, and larger culture contribute to anorexia nervosa. (p. 545)

Person: _____

_____

Family: _____

_____

Culture: _____

_____

4. Describe three approaches to treating anorexia nervosa, and note which is the most successful. (p. 545)

A. _____

B. _____

C. _____

5. True or False: Over 90 percent of anorexics make a full recovery. (p. 545)

6. Describe characteristics of *bulimia nervosa*. (p. 545)

_____

_____

_____

7. Bulimia is (more / less) common than anorexia. (p. 545)

8. Identify similarities and differences between persons with anorexia and bulimia. (pp. 545–546)

Similarities: _____

_____

Differences: _____

_____

Injuries

1. The total rate of unintentional injuries (increases / decreases) during adolescence. Cite research to support your answer. (p. 546)

_____

_____

_____

2. Outside of automobile accidents, the majority of adolescent deaths are caused by
_____. (p. 546)

3. How do coaches often contribute to sports injuries in adolescents? (p. 546)

_____

_____

_____

Sexual Activity

1. True or False: Exposure to sex, education about it, and efforts to limit the sexual curiosity of children and adolescents are very similar in nations around the world. (p. 547)

2. Contrast the messages that adolescents receive from parents and the media regarding sexual activity, and note the impact of such contradictory messages on adolescents' understanding of sex. (pp. 547–548)

   Parents: _____

   _____

   Media: _____

   _____

   Impact: _____

   _____

3. The sexual attitudes and behavior of American adolescents have become (more / less) liberal over the past 40 years. (p. 548)

4. (Males / Females) tend to have their first sexual experience earlier than members of the opposite sex. (p. 548)

5. Cite personal, familial, peer, and educational variables linked to early and frequent teenage sexual activity. (p. 549)

   Personal: _____

   Family: _____

   Peer: _____

   Educational: _____

6. Early sexual activity is (more / less) common among low-SES adolescents. Explain why. (pp. 549–550)

   _____

   _____

7. Early and prolonged father absence predicts (higher / lower) rates of intercourse and pregnancy among adolescent girls. Explain why. (p. 550)

   _____

   _____

   _____

8. Discuss cognitive and social factors that may contribute to adolescents' reluctance to use contraception. (p. 550–551)

   Cognitive: _____

   _____

   _____

   Social: _____

   _____

   _____

9. Cite characteristics of adolescents who are more likely to use contraception. (p. 551)

_____

_____

10. About _____ percent of young people identify as lesbian, gay, or bisexual. (p. 551)

11. Describe evidence suggesting that both heredity and prenatal biological influences contribute to homosexuality. (p. 551)

    Heredity: _____

    _____

    Prenatal biological influences: _____

    _____

12. List several stereotypes and misconceptions about homosexuality. (p. 551)

    _____

    _____

Social Issues: Education: Parents and Teenagers (Don't) Talk About Sex

1. What percentage of parents report talking with their children about sex and contraception? (p. 548)

    _____

2. Explain why many parents avoid discussing sexual issues with their teenage children. (p. 548)

    _____

    _____

    _____

3. Why are adolescents reluctant to discuss sex with their parents? (p. 548)

    _____

    _____

    _____

4. Describe qualities of successful parent–child communication about sex. (p. 549)

    _____

    _____

    _____

Biology and Environment: Gay, Lesbian, and Bisexual Youths: Coming Out to Oneself and Others

1. Describe the three-phase sequence that homosexual adolescents and adults move through in coming out to themselves and others. (pp. 552–553)

   A. _____

   _____

   _____

   B. _____

   _____

   _____

   C. _____

   _____

   _____

2. For homosexual individuals, a first sense of their sexual orientation typically appears between the ages of _____ and _____. In what context does this typically occur? (p. 552)

   _____

3. True or False: Most adolescents resolve their feelings of confusion and discomfort at being attracted to same-sex individuals by crystallizing a gay, lesbian, or bisexual identity quickly—with a flash of insight into their sense of being different. (p. 552)

4. True or False: Most parents respond to their adolescent child's disclosure of homosexuality with severe rejection. (p. 553)

5. Explain how coming out has the potential to foster psychological growth in homosexual adolescents. (p. 553)

   _____

   _____

   _____

Sexually Transmitted Disease

1. True or False: Adolescents have the highest incidence of sexually transmitted disease (STD) of any age group. (p. 552)

2. Which teenagers are at greatest risk of contracting STDs? (p. 552)

   _____

3. True or False: Nearly all cases of AIDS that appear in young adulthood originate in adolescence. (p. 552)

4. True or False: 90 percent of high school students are aware of the basic facts about AIDS. (p. 553)

5. Discuss four ways of preventing STDs. (p. 553)

A. _____

_____

B. _____

_____

C. _____

_____

D. _____

_____

Adolescent Pregnancy and Parenthood

1. An estimated _____ to _____ teenage girls in the United States become pregnant anually. (p. 555)

2   List three factors that heighten the incidence of adolescent pregnancy. (p. 555)

A. _____

B. _____

C. _____

3. Summarize personal characteristics and life conditions that contribute to adolescent childbearing. (p. 556)

Personal characteristics: _____

_____

Life conditions: _____

_____

4. Discuss the consequences of adolescent parenthood in relation to the following areas: (p. 556)

Educational attainment: _____

_____

Marital patterns: _____

_____

Economic circumstances: _____

_____

5. Why are teenage girls especially likely to experience prenatal and birth complications? (p. 556)

_____

_____

6. True or False: Adolescent mothers are as knowledgeable about child development as are adult mothers, and they are just as effective at interacting with their children. (p. 556)

7. Cite three factors that protect teenage mothers and their children from long-term difficulties. (p. 557)

A. _____

B. _____

C. _____

8. List four components of effective sex education programs. (p. 558)

   A. _____

   B. _____

   C. _____

   D. _____

9. What is the most controversial aspect of adolescent pregnancy prevention programs, and why? (p. 558)

   A. _____

   B. _____

10. True or False: In European countries where contraception is readily available to teenagers, sexual activity is *not* more common than in the United States but pregnancy, childbirth, and abortion rates are much lower. (p. 558)

11. In addition to sex education and access to contraceptives, what other strategies are essential for preventing adolescent pregnancy and parenthood? (p. 558)

   _____

   _____

12. List characteristics of school programs that increase adolescent mothers' educational success and prevent additional childbearing. (p. 558)

   _____

   _____

   _____

13. Older adolescent mothers display (more / less) effective parenting when they establish their own residence with the assistance of relatives. (p. 558)

14. True or False: Fewer than one-fourth of adolescent fathers maintain regular contact into the child's school-age years. (p. 559)

15. Under what circumstances are fatherhood interventions especially effective? (p. 559)

   _____

   _____

Social Issues: Health: Like Parent, Like Child: Intergenerational Continuity in Adolescent Parenthood

1. Research indicates that first-generation mothers' age at first childbirth (strongly / weakly) predicts the age at which second-generation young people became parents. (p. 557)

2. Describe three family conditions and personal characteristics that are associated with second-generation adolescent parenthood. (p. 557)

   A. _____

   _____

   B. _____

   _____

   C. _____

   _____

Substance Use and Abuse

1. Explain why adolescent drug use in the U.S. has declined since the mid-1990s. (p. 559)

    _____

    _____

2. Why do so many young people subject themselves to the health risks of alcohol and drugs? (p. 559)

    _____

    _____

3. Describe characteristics of minimal experimenters. How do experimenters differ from drug abusers? (p. 559)

    A. _____

    _____

    B. _____

    _____

4. Explain how culture affects adolescent substance use. (p. 559)

    _____

    _____

    _____

5. List environmental factors that promote adolescent substance abuse. (p. 559)

    _____

    _____

    _____

6. Cite three life-long consequences of adolescent substance abuse. (p. 560)

    A. _____

    B. _____

    C. _____

7. List four features of school and community programs that reduce drug experimentation. (p. 561)

    A. _____

    _____

    B. _____

    _____

    C. _____

    _____

    D. _____

    _____

8. Discuss prevention and treatment strategies for drug abuse. (p. 561)

    Prevention: _____

    _____

    _____

    Treatment: _____

    _____

    _____

ASK YOURSELF . . .

For *Ask Yourself* questions for this chapter, along with feedback on the accuracy of your answers, please log on to MyDevelopmentLab (for registration and access, please visit mydevelopmentlab.com or follow the directions on p. ix).

1) Select the Chapter of the *Ask Yourself*.
2) Open the E-Book and select the Explore icon next to the *Ask Yourself*.
3) Complete questions and choose "Submit answers for grading" or "Clear Answers" to start over.

SUGGESTED STUDENT READINGS

Dahl, R. E., & Spear, L. P. (Eds.). (2004). *Adolescent brain development: Vulnerabilities and opportunities.* New York: New York Academy of Sciences. Presents leading research on adolescent brain development, including risk taking and novelty seeking, the effects of hormones on behavior, sleep and arousal, and nicotine and alcohol use.

Hayward, C. (Ed.). (2003). *Gender differences at puberty.* New York: Cambridge University Press. An ecological examination of the effects of puberty, this book focuses on the impact of puberty on physical, social, and psychological development. Other topics include changes in body image, aggression, sexual abuse, and romantic relationships.

Kirke, D. M. (2006). *Teenagers and substance use: Social networks and peer influence.* New York: Palgrave Macmillan. An insightful look at teenagers who abuse alcohol and drugs, this book explores how adolescents' peer groups and social networks contribute to or buffer against substance abuse.

PUZZLE 14.1 TERM REVIEW

Across

5. Biological changes at adolescence leading to an adult-size body and sexual maturity

6. Transition between childhood and emerging adulthood

7. Body _____: conception of and attitude toward one's physical appearance

8. _____ sexual characteristics are those that directly involve the reproductive organs

9. _____ nervosa: eating disorder in which individuals engage in strict dieting and excessive exercise accompanied by binge eating, often followed by deliberate vomiting or purging with laxatives

Down

1. Growth _____: rapid gains in height and weight during adolescence

2. _____ sexual characteristics are features visible on the outside of the body that do not involve the reproductive organs

3. First ejaculation of seminal fluid

4. First menstruation

6. _____ nervosa: eating disorder in which individuals starve themselves due to a compulsive fear of becoming fat and a distorted body image

PRACTICE TEST #1

1. Based on her research in Samoa, Margaret Mead concluded that (p. 530)
   a. the social environment is entirely responsible for the range of teenage experiences.
   b. the overall rate of serious psychological disturbance rises only slightly from childhood to adolescence.
   c. during adolescence, young people learn to fulfill their biological destiny: sexual reproduction and survival of the species.
   d. adolescence is tumultuous and difficult, regardless of cultural factors.

2. Fifty percent of boys experience temporary breast enlargement because (p. 531)
   a. initial testosterone secretions cause body parts to grow at different rates.
   b. androgens have a GH-enhancing effect.
   c. adrenal androgens influence their growth until their testosterone levels increase.
   d. the testes secrete small amounts of estrogen.

3. Around age 8, girls start to (p. 533)
   a. develop larger skeletal muscles, hearts, and lung capacity.
   b. add more fat than boys on their arms, legs, and trunk.
   c. grow larger hands and feet than boys.
   d. gain more muscle strength than boys, a trend that reverses around age 11.

4. According to recent surveys, about _____ percent of North American high school seniors have used performance-enhancing drugs. (p. 534)
   a. 4
   b. 6
   c. 8
   d. 10

5. According to a recent study, one of best predictors of adult physical exercise is (p. 535)
   a. adolescent exertion during exercise, defined as sweating and breathing heavily.
   b. parental encouragement of adolescent exercise.
   c. adolescent participation in team sports.
   d. adolescent participation in individual sports at least three times a week.

6. The first sign of puberty in boys is (p. 536)
   a. a height spurt.
   b. the appearance of pubic hair.
   c. enlargement of the testes.
   d. spermarche.

7. Recent studies suggest that a modest, continuing trend toward earlier menarche in North America and some European countries may be caused by (p. 537)
   a. declining poverty rates.
   b. a slight increase in rates of marital conflict and separation.
   c. a small decrease in the quality of sanitation and control of infectious disease.
   d. soaring rates of overweight and obesity.

8. During adolescence, the brain changes by (p. 537)
   a. losing white matter.
   b. developing additional linkages between the two hemispheres through the corpus callosum.
   c. growing new gray matter.
   d. losing unused connections between the frontal lobes of the cerebral cortex.

9. Studies suggest that today's teenagers get much less sleep than previous generations because they (p. 538)
    a. experience increased neural sensitivity to evening light.
    b. are more likely to abuse drugs and alcohol.
    c. frequently suffer from depressed moods.
    d. often have evening social activities and part-time jobs, as well as TVs, computers, and phones in their rooms.

10. Research has revealed that teenagers' frequent reports of negative mood (p. 540)
    a. level off around the tenth grade.
    b. continue to fluctuate significantly into the early twenties.
    c. decline after age 15 for boys but increase for girls until they level off around age 18.
    d. tend to coincide with Friday and Saturday evenings, when they felt the most pressure to fit in with agemates.

11. In recent studies, early-maturing boys reported (p. 541)
    a. a great deal of pressure to maintain their body image.
    b. anxiety, talkativeness, and attention-seeking behaviors.
    c. more psychological stress and problem behaviors than their later-maturing agemates.
    d. a lack of self-confidence despite pride in their physical attractiveness.

12. Studies suggest that the long-term negative consequences of early maturation tend to be the most pronounced for (p. 543)
    a. boys.
    b. low-SES African-American children.
    c. high-SES Caucasian boys.
    d. girls.

13. African-American girls are less at risk for anorexia nervosa than Asian-American, Caucasian-American, and Hispanic girls because (p. 544)
    a. African-American girls tend to be more satisfied with their size and shape.
    b. genetic factors make Asian-American, Caucasian-American, and Hispanic girls more likely to mature early.
    c. African-American girls are more likely to suffer from bulimia nervosa.
    d. Asian-American, Caucasian-American, and Hispanic girls are more likely to be perfectionists.

14. Unlike anorexics, bulimics (p. 546)
    a. tend to have controlling parents.
    b. usually feel guilty about their abnormal easting habits and are desperate to get help.
    c. are more likely to be gay and bisexual boys.
    d. often lose 25 to 50 percent of their body weight.

15. U.S. and Canadian studies reveal that in nations with strict handgun registration, safety, and control policies, the firearm death rate among 15- to 19-year-olds is, on average, (p. 546)
    a. two to three times the U.S. rate.
    b. about the same as the U.S. and Canadian rates.
    c. half the U.S. rate.
    d. one-fourth the U.S. rate.

16. According to a recent study, youths who had more encounters with Internet pornography were those who (p. 547)
    a. suffered from eating disorders.
    b. felt depressed, had been victimized by peers, or were involved in delinquent activities.
    c. encountered pornographic sites while casually surfing the Internet.
    d. were already sexually active.

17. According to one study, in Spanish-speaking families in the United States, parents' messages to children about sex usually took the form of (p. 549)
    a. cautions to use a condom while having intercourse.
    b. threats of punishment for touching a member of the opposite sex.
    c. warm, frank, and supportive discussion of physical changes, intercourse, and pregnancy.
    d. strict limits on dating age, behavior, and place.

18. Compared with their Canadian and Western European counterparts, American youths (p. 549)
    a. have had fewer sexual partners in the past year.
    b. begin sexual activity at younger ages.
    c. are more likely to have encountered Internet pornography multiple times in the past year.
    d. delay sexual activity until late adolescence or even later.

19. According to 2006 U.S. Department of Health and Human Services statistics, the fraction of girls who voluntarily had sex but later indicated that they really did not want to was (p. 551)
    a. one-fourth.
    b. one-third.
    c. one-half.
    d. two-thirds.

20. Evidence that homosexuality may be X-linked comes from the fact that (p. 551)
    a. identical twins of both sexes are more likely to share a homosexual orientation.
    b. homosexuality seems to be linked to prenatal antibodies to androgens.
    c. boys who experience same-sex attraction also tend to prefer "feminine" kinds of play.
    d. homosexuality tends to be more common on the maternal than the paternal side of families.

21. Research indicates that Canada exceeds many other Western nations in (p. 552)
    a. new HIV/AIDS cases.
    b. incidence of unprotected oral sex.
    c. incidence of common STDs, such as chlamydia and herpes.
    d. effective STD education.

22. According to U.S. government findings, only about 70 percent of adolescent mothers (p. 556)
    a. go on to have a second or third child.
    b. graduate from high school.
    c. marry the father of their first child.
    d. earn enough money to support their child or children.

23. Studies indicate that intergenerational continuity in adolescent parenthood, especially for daughters, was far greater (p. 557)
    a. the higher the HOME scores of the mother's family.
    b. when the first-generation mother was 14 or younger at first childbirth.
    c. when the mother went on to use birth control responsibly.
    d. when the teenage mother remained unmarried.

24. According to the most recent nationally representative survey of U.S. high school students, about _____ percent have tried at least one highly addictive toxic substance. (p. 559)
    a. 10
    b. 20
    c. 35
    d. 50

25. Longitudinal evidence reveals that the cognitive, emotional, and social deficiencies characteristic of drug abusers are (p. 560)
    a. difficult to detect before early adolescence.
    b. almost always linked to environmental factors.
    c. in many cases present in experimenters as well.
    d. often evident in the preschool years.

PRACTICE TEST #2

1. The early-twentieth-century theorist G. Stanley Hall viewed adolescence as (p. 530)
   a. the genital stage, when sexual impulses awaken, triggering psychological conflict and volatile behavior.
   b. a phase of growth so turbulent that it resembles the era in which humans evolved from savages into civilized beings.
   c. the period in which young people find intimate partners and, consequently, their inner forces achieve a new harmony.
   d. a relatively calm phase of life.

2. Adolescence is greatly extended in industrialized nations because (p. 531)
   a. environmental factors tend to slow the biological changes of the period.
   b. parents tend to shield children from the burdens of adult life for as long as possible.
   c. successful participation in economic life requires many years of education.
   d. their cultures place a high value on youth.

3. The typical girl is taller and heavier than the typical boy during early adolescence because (p. 532)
   a. adrenal androgens cause girls to gain height and weight quickly.
   b. girls' epiphyses close more rapidly than boys'.
   c. of secular changes in adult body size for males and females.
   d. estrogens trigger and then restrain GH secretion more readily than androgens.

4. Taking anabolic steroids to boost muscle mass is dangerous because these steroids are associated with (p. 534)
   a. muscle cramping.
   b. damage to reproductive organs.
   c. brain seizures.
   d. a dangerously slow heart rate.

5. Studies indicate that over the teenage years, activity rates of U.S. and Canadian youths (p. 534)
   a. decline overall.
   b. increase for girls and drop for boys.
   c. increase overall.
   d. decline for U.S. youths but increase for Canadian youths.

6. Female puberty begins with (p. 535)
   a. menarche.
   b. the appearance of underarm hair.
   c. the budding of breasts, the growth spurt, and the appearance of pubic hair.
   d. the deepening of the voice.

7. In developing countries, girls from higher-income families typically reach menarche (p. 536)
   a. later because they often begin rigorous athletic training at young ages.
   b. 6 to 18 months earlier than those living in economically disadvantaged homes.
   c. 12 to 18 months later than those living in economically disadvantaged homes, because the latter tend to be overweight, even obese.
   d. within only 2 to 3 months of those living in economically disadvantaged homes because leptin levels do not vary significantly between these groups.

8. Adolescents react more intensely to both stressful events and pleasurable stimuli because (p. 537)
   a. of the increase in white matter in their brains.
   b. connections through the corpus callosum strengthen during puberty.
   c. communication among parts of their brains becomes more rapid.
   d. neurons become more responsive to excitatory neurotransmitters during puberty.

9. In contrast to may tribal and village societies, Western societies (p. 539)
    a. grant little formal recognition to movement from childhood to adolescence or from adolescence to adulthood.
    b. encourage parents to talk openly with children about the physical changes of puberty.
    c. have developed more elaborate initiation rights over the past few decades.
    d. encourage children to share information about their experience of puberty with one another.

10. In North America, the frequency of parent–child arguing during puberty (p. 541)
    a. is especially high between parents and sons.
    b. has steadily declined since the 1950s.
    c. continues to be intense into late adolescence.
    d. is quite similar across North American subcultures.

11. In a study of several hundred ethnically diverse urban teenage girls, early maturers engaged in more antisocial acts only if (p. 542)
    a. their older sisters were late maturers.
    b. they had internalized the cultural ideal of female attractiveness.
    c. they lived in neighborhoods with high concentrations of poverty, inadequate housing, and poor schools.
    d. their parents disciplined them coercively and inconsistently.

12. The most common nutritional problem of adolescence is (p. 544)
    a. obesity.
    b. iron deficiency.
    c. overconsumption of carbohydrates.
    d. riboflavin deficiency.

13. The most successful treatment for anorexia nervosa is (p. 545)
    a. family therapy and medication to reduce anxiety and neurotransmitter imbalances.
    b. hospitalization.
    c. behavior modification that reinforces good eating habits.
    d. close parental supervision of the anorexic child's behaviors and social contacts.

14. Teenagers who are especially likely to suffer injury during sports are those who (p. 546)
    a. mature late.
    b. overestimate their sports ability.
    c. are perfectionists.
    d. have a poor body image.

15. The majority of North American children learn about sex from (p. 547)
    a. their parents or other close relatives.
    b. school counselors.
    c. health and sex education classes.
    d. friends and the popular media.

16. The high rate of sexual activity among African-American teenagers is largely accounted for by (p. 550)
    a. widespread poverty in the black population.
    b. greater openness about sexuality within the black community, compared with other groups.
    c. the fact that black youths tend to mature early.
    d. the low quality of sex education in schools and the difficulty in obtaining contraception.

17. Research indicated that teenagers most likely to use birth control are those who (p. 551)
    a. were forced to have sex.
    b. know where to get birth control counseling and devices.
    c. report good relationships with parents and talk openly with them about sex and contraception.
    d. have advanced perspective-taking skills.

18. Compared with children who are confident of their homosexuality, sexual-questioning children report (p. 552)
    a. greater dissatisfaction with their biological gender and greater gender nonconformity.
    b. increased pressure to begin sexual activity early.
    c. greater comfort with being perceived as different.
    d. greater desires to escape into drugs, alcohol, and suicidal thinking.

19. Currently, 37 percent of new U.S. AIDS cases among adolescents and young adults are seen in (p. 553)
    a. males.
    b. Asian Americans.
    c. females.
    d. low-SES individuals.

20. The number of North American teenage births is lower than it was 35 years ago because (p. 555)
    a. young people in the United States and Canada are delaying sexual activity.
    b. both Canada and the United States have introduced effective sex education programs.
    c. in both Canada and the United States, contraception has become inexpensive and widely available.
    d. 40 percent of U.S. and 50 percent of Canadian teenage pregnancies end in abortion.

21. Evaluations reveal that sex education programs focusing on abstinence have (p. 558)
    a. little or no impact on delaying teenage sexual activity or on preventing pregnancy.
    b. led to reduced sexual activity among older adolescents.
    c. resulted in higher pregnancy rates among teenagers who have participated in such programs.
    d. led to lower pregnancy rates in the United States, comparable to levels in Canada and Western Europe.

22. Teenage fathers are more likely to stay involved with their children when they (p. 559)
    a. are forced by law to provide financial and child-care assistance.
    b. receive support from family members.
    c. have more than one child with the same mother.
    d. are from high-SES families.

23. One factor behind trends in adolescent drug use is that compared to a decade or two ago, (p. 559)
    a. the use of sedatives, inhalants, and OxyContin has declined.
    b. doctors more often prescribe, and parents are more likely to seek, medication to treat children's problems.
    c. cigarette and alcohol advertising is less often designed to appeal to teenagers.
    d. adolescents are more knowledgeable about the risks associated with many drugs.

24. Among North American youths, the group who rank highest in drug taking are (p. 560)
    a. African Americans.
    b. Hispanics.
    c. Caucasians.
    d. Native Americans and Canadian Aboriginals.

25. Research indicates that relapse rates for participants in comprehensive drug treatment programs are (p. 561)
    a. 10 to 15 percent.
    b. 25 to 50 percent.
    c. 35 to 85 percent.
    d. 40 to 90 percent.

CHAPTER 15
COGNITIVE DEVELOPMENT IN ADOLESCENCE

BRIEF CHAPTER SUMMARY

During Piaget's formal operational stage, young people develop the capacity for abstract, systematic, scientific thinking. They become capable of hypothetico-deductive reasoning, in which they begin with a *hypothesis,* or prediction, from which they *deduce* logical inferences. Piaget used the term *propositional thought* to describe adolescents' ability to evaluate the logic of verbal statements without referring to real-world circumstances. However, follow-up research reveals that school-age children already have some capacity for hypothetico-deductive reasoning, although they are less competent at it than adolescents. And many adults do not fully achieve formal operational thinking. Cross-cultural research challenges Piaget's view of formal operations as a universal change in cognition that results from adolescents' independent efforts to make sense of their world. Rather, it may be a culturally transmitted way of reasoning specific to literate societies and fostered by school experiences.

According to the information-processing perspective, cognitive change in adolescence is based on specific mechanisms supported by brain development and experience, including selective attention, improved inhibition, more effective strategies, increased knowledge, expanded metacognition, improved cognitive self-regulation, and increased thinking and processing speed. Metacognition, in particular, is central to adolescent cognitive development.

Adolescent cognitive changes lead to dramatic revisions in the ways adolescents see themselves, others, and the larger world. They develop distorted images of the relationship between self and other and are able to construct visions of ideal worlds. The dramatic cognitive changes of adolescence are reflected in many aspects of everyday behavior, including self-consciousness and self-focusing, idealism and criticism, and difficulties with planning and decision making.

Although boys and girls do not differ in general intelligence, they do vary in specific mental abilities. Throughout adolescence, girls continue to score higher than boys on tests of verbal ability, while boys continue to have an advantage in mathematical performance. These differences are related to heredity but also reflect cultural factors, including social pressures.

Language development continues during adolescence, in subtle but important ways that are influenced by improvements in metalinguistic awareness—the ability to think about language as a system. Vocabulary expands as adolescents add many abstract words. They also master irony and sarcasm, figurative language, and more complex grammatical constructions. As a result, communication skills improve.

School transitions create adjustment problems for adolescents, especially girls. Teenagers who must cope with added stresses are at greatest risk for adjustment problems following school change. Enhanced support from parents, teachers, and peers eases the strain of school transition. Academic achievement reflects both personal traits and environmental factors, including child-rearing styles, parent–school partnerships, peer influences, and the responsiveness of school environments. A significant number of young people, more often boys than girls, drop out of school, often with dire consequences. School dropout is related to a variety of student, family, school, and community characteristics that undermine chances for success.

During late adolescence, young people face a major life decision: the choice of a suitable work role. Young people move through several periods of vocational development: a fantasy period in early and middle childhood, a tentative period in early adolescence, and finally a realistic period in which they narrow their options and take steps to enter a career. Factors influencing adolescents' vocational choices include personality, family, teachers, and gender stereotypes in the larger social environment, as well as access to vocational information. High-quality vocational preparation for non-college-bound adolescents is scarce in North America compared with some European nations. A national apprenticeship system would improve the transition to work for those who terminate their education with a high school diploma.

LEARNING OBJECTIVES

After reading this chapter, you should be able to:

15.1 Describe the major characteristics of formal operational thought. (pp. 566–567)

15.2 Discuss recent research on formal operational thought and its implications for the accuracy of Piaget's formal operational stage. (pp. 567–569)

15.3 Explain how information-processing researchers account for the development of abstract thought during adolescence. (p. 569)

15.4 Summarize the development of scientific reasoning during adolescence. (pp. 569–571)

15.5 Describe typical reactions of adolescents that result from their advancing cognition. (pp. 571–574)

15.6 Describe sex differences in mental abilities at adolescence, along with factors that influence them. (pp. 574–577)

15.7 Describe changes in vocabulary, grammar, and pragmatics during adolescence. (pp. 577–578)

15.8 Discuss the impact of school transitions on adolescent adjustment, and cite ways to ease the strain of these changes. (pp. 578–580)

15.9 Discuss family, peer, and school influences on academic achievement during adolescence. (pp. 580–585)

15.10 Describe personal, family, and school factors related to dropping out, and cite ways to prevent early school leaving. (pp. 585–588)

15.11 Trace the development of vocational choice, and describe the factors that influence adolescents' vocational decisions. (pp. 589–591)

15.12 Discuss the problems faced by non-college bound North American youths in making the transition from school to work, along with ways to help them. (pp. 591–593)

STUDY QUESTIONS

Piaget's Theory: The Formal Operational Stage

1. Summarize the basic difference between concrete and formal operational reasoning. (p. 566)

_____

_____

_____

Hypothetico-Deductive Reasoning

1. Piaget believed that at adolescence, young people first become capable of _____.
Briefly describe this type of reasoning. (p. 566)

_____

_____

_____

2. Describe changes in performance on Piaget's pendulum problem during adolescence. (p. 566)

_____

_____

_____

Propositional Thought

1. Describe features of *propositional thought.* (p. 567)

_____

_____

_____

2. True or False: While Piaget did not view language as playing a central role in young children's cognitive development, he acknowledged its importance in adolescence. (p. 567)

Follow-Up Research on Formal Operational Thought

1. Cite examples illustrating that school-age children show signs of hypothetico-deductive reasoning and propositional thought but are not yet as competent at it as adolescents. (pp. 567–568)

Hypothetico-deductive reasoning: _____

_____

_____

Propositional thought: _____

_____

_____

2. Children fail to grasp the _____ of propositional reasoning—that the accuracy of conclusions drawn from premises rests of the rules of logic, not real-world confirmation. (p. 568)

3. List three advances in reasoning during adolescence that illustrate their ability to apply logic. (p. 568)

A. _____

B. _____

C. _____

4. Explain why so many adults are not fully formal operational. (p. 568)

_____

_____

_____

5. True or False: Despite few opportunities to solve hypothetical problems, most people in tribal and village societies still master formal operational tasks. (pp. 568–569)

An Information-Processing View of Adolescent Cognitive Development

1. Information-processing theorists refer to a variety of specific mechanisms that underlie cognitive change in adolescence. Briefly describe them. (p. 569)

Attention: _____

_____

Inhibition: _____

_____

Strategies: _____

_____

Knowledge: _____

_____

Metacognition: _____

_____

Cognitive self-regulation: _____

_____

Speed of thinking and processing capacity: _____

_____

2. Which of the mechanisms of change do researchers regard as central to adolescent cognitive development? (p. 569)

_____

Scientific Reasoning: Coordinating Theory with Evidence

1. Cite major changes in scientific reasoning from childhood into adolescence and adulthood. (p. 570)

_____

_____

_____

2. Identify two factors that support adolescents' skill at coordinating theory with evidence. (p. 570)

A. _____

B. _____

How Scientific Reasoning Develops

1. How does schooling influence scientific reasoning? (p. 570)

_____

_____

2. Briefly explain how advances in metacognitive understanding promote adolescents' cognitive development. (pp. 570–571)

_____

_____

_____

3. True or False: Like Piaget, information-processing theorists maintain that scientific reasoning develops from an abrupt, stagewise change. (p. 571)

Consequences of Adolescent Cognitive Changes

1. List four ways to handle teenagers' new cognitive capacities. (p. 572)

   A. _____

   B. _____

   C. _____

   D. _____

Self-Consciousness and Self-Focusing

1. Describe two distorted images of the relation between self and others that appear at adolescence. (pp. 571–572)

   Imaginary audience: _____

   _____

   _____

   Personal fable: _____

   _____

   _____

2. The _imaginary audience_ and _personal fable_ (do / do not) result from egocentrism, as Piaget suggested. Explain your response. (p. 572)

   _____

   _____

Idealism and Criticism

1. Explain how the emergence of formal operations leads to idealism and criticism in adolescence. (p. 573)

   _____

   _____

   _____

2. How are idealism and criticism advantageous to teenagers? (p. 573)

   _____

   _____

Planning and Decision Making

1. Briefly summarize changes in *cognitive self-regulation* and *comprehension monitoring* during adolescence. (p. 573)

   Cognitive self-regulation: _____

   _____

   Comprehension monitoring: _____

   _____

2. True or False: Like adults, adolescents use a rational process for planning and decision making in everyday life. (p. 573)

3. Describe two reasons why teenagers have difficulty with decision making. (pp. 573–574)

   A. _____

   _____

   B. _____

   _____

4. Why is adult spervision important as adolescents refine their decision-making skills? (p. 574)

   _____

   _____

Sex Differences in Mental Abilities

Verbal Abilities

1. Describe sex differences in verbal abilities. (pp. 574–575)

   _____

   _____

   _____

2. (Boys / Girls) continue to score higher on tests of verbal ability than (boys / girls) during adolescence. What accounts for this trend? (pp. 574–575)

   _____

   _____

3. What types of parent involvement foster good work habits and skill at reading and writing? (p. 575)

   _____

   _____

Mathematical Abilities

1. Describe sex differences in mathematic abilities. (pp. 575–576)

   _____

   _____

   _____

2. Summarize how heredity and social pressures contribute to the gender gap in mathematics. (pp. 575–576)

Heredity: _____

_____

Social pressures: _____

_____

3. Cite three strategies used to promote girls' interest in and confidence at math and science. (p. 576)

A. _____

B. _____

C. _____

Biology and Environment: Sex Differences in Spatial Abilities

1. Describe two spatial tasks on which individuals evidence a notable sex difference in performance. (p. 576)

A. _____

_____

B. _____

_____

2. True or False: Sex differences in spatial abilities persist throughout the lifespan. (p. 576)

3. Summarize biological and environmental factors that may contribute to sex differences in spatial abilities. (pp. 576–577)

Biological: _____

_____

_____

Environmental: _____

_____

_____

Language Development

Vocabulary and Grammar

1. Describe three changes in adolescents' vocabularies. (pp. 577–578)

A. _____

_____

B. _____

_____

C. _____

_____

2. Discuss two gains in grammatical development during the teenage years. (p. 578)

A. _____

_____

B. _____

_____

3. Explain why overt grammar instruction in U.S. schools is making a comeback. (p. 578)

_____

_____

Pragmatics

1. Summarize gains in adolescents' communication skills. (p. 578)

_____

_____

_____

2. Explain the social function of teenage slang. (p. 578)

_____

_____

Learning in School

School Transitions

1. List several reasons why adolescents' grades decline at the transition to secondary school. (p. 579)

A. _____

B. _____

C. _____

2. The (earlier / later) the school transition occurs, the more dramatic and long-lasting its impact on adolescents' psychological well-being. Why is this the case, especially for girls? (p. 579)

_____

_____

3. List three ways that parents, teachers, and peers can ease the strain of school transitions. (p. 580)

A. _____

B. _____

C. _____

4. Describe small changes that promote favorable adjustment after a school transition. (p. 580)

_____

_____

_____

Academic Achievement

1. List four environmental factors that support high academic achievement in adolescence. (p. 581)

   A. _____

   B. _____

   C. _____

   D. _____

2. How do each of the four child-rearing styles contribute to adolescents' academic achievement? Which is the most effective, and why? (pp. 580–581)

   Authoritative: _____

   Authoritarian: _____

   Permissive: _____

   Uninvolved: _____

   Most effective: _____

3. How does combining parental warmth with moderate to high control promote school success? (p. 581)

   _____

   _____

4. How do parent-school partnerships foster academic achievement? (pp. 581–582)

   _____

   _____

5. List five ways schools can strengthen parent-school partnerships. (pp. 581–582)

   A. _____

   B. _____

   C. _____

   D. _____

   E. _____

6. Summarize peer influences on achievement during adolescence. (p. 582)

   _____

   _____

   _____

7. Discuss ethnic variations in the strength of peer support for academic achievement and valuing of school success. (p. 582)

   _____

   _____

   _____

8. Compare the classroom experiences of adolescents who make gains in academic motivation and cognitive self-regulation versus students who show a decline in these areas. (p. 583)

   Increase in motivation and cognitive self-regulation: _____

   _____

   Decrease in motivation and cognitive self-regulation: _____

   _____

9. A (large / small) number of low-SES minority students are assigned to noncollege tracks in high school. What effect does this have on student achievement? (pp. 583–585)

   _____

   _____

   _____

10. Explain how tracking in the United States differs from that in Japan, China, and many Western European nations, and note the impact of these differences on student outcomes. (p. 585)

   _____

   _____

   _____

   _____

   _____

Social Issues: Education: High-Stakes Testing

1. Explain how the U.S. No Child Left Behind Act broadens high-stakes testing. (p. 584)

   _____

   _____

   _____

2. Summarize potential benefits of high-stakes testing. (p. 584)

   _____

   _____

   _____

3. Evidence indicates that high-stakes testing (undermines / upgrades) the quality of education. (p. 584)

4. Discuss concerns about high-stakes testing. (p. 584)

   _____

   _____

5. True or False: High-stakes testing has led to an increased emphasis on teaching for deeper understanding. (p. 584)

Dropping Out

1. About _____ percent of U.S. and Canadian young people leave high school without a diploma. (p. 585)

2. Cite two consequences of dropping out of high school. (p. 585)

   A. _____

   B. _____

3. Summarize personal, familial, and school characteristics related to dropping out. (p. 586)

   Personal: _____

   _____

   Familial: _____

   _____

   School: _____

   _____

4. Describe the school experiences of academically marginal students who dropout. (p. 586)

   _____

   _____

5. Discuss four strategies to prevent school dropout. (p. 587)

   A. _____

   _____

   B. _____

   _____

   C. _____

   _____

   D. _____

   _____

6. Over the second half of the twentieth century, the percentage of American and Canadian adolescents completing high school has (increased / decreased) steadily. (p. 587)

7. True or False: About one-third of high school dropouts return to finish their secondary education within a few years. (p. 587)

Social Issues: Education—Extracurricular Activities: Contexts for Positive Youth Development

1. What types of extracurricular activities promote diverse academic and social skills and have a lasting positive impact on adjustment? (p. 588)

   _____

   _____

2. Cite immediate and long-term benefits of involvement in extracurricular activities. (p. 588)

   Immediate: _____

   _____

   Long-term: _____

   _____

3. True or False: Adolescents who spend many afternoons and evenings engaged in unstructured activities show similar adjustment outcomes relative to adolescents who engage in structured, goal-oriented activities. (p. 588)

4. Who is especially likely to benefit from extracurricular activities, and what accounts for this effect? (p. 588)

   A. _____

   B. _____

Vocational Development

Selecting a Vocation

1. Describe the three phases of vocational development, noting the developmental period at which each occurs. (p. 589)

   Fantasy period: _____

   _____

   Tentative period: _____

   _____

   Realistic period: _____

   _____

Factors Influencing Vocational Choice

1. Match each of the following personality types that affect vocational development with the appropriate description. (pp. 589–590)

   _____ Likes well-structured tasks and values social status; tends to choose business occupations

   _____ Prefers real-world problems and work with objects; tends toward mechanical occupations

   _____ Adventurous, persuasive, and a strong leader; drawn toward sales and supervisory positions

   _____ Enjoys working with ideas; likely to select scientific occupations

   _____ Has high need for emotional and individual expression; drawn toward fields like writing, music, and the visual arts

   1. Investigative
   2. Social
   3. Realistic
   4. Artistic
   5. Conventional
   6. Enterprising

2. The relationship between personality and vocational choice is (weak / moderate / strong). (p. 590)

3. Identify three reasons why young people's vocational aspirations correlate strongly with their parents' jobs. (p. 590)

   A. _____

   B. _____

   C. _____

4. Explain how teachers influence adolescents' career decisions. (pp. 590–591)

   _____

   _____

5. True or False: Over the past 30 years, young women's career preferences have remained strongly gender stereotyped. (p. 591)

6. Women's progress in entering and excelling at male-dominated professions has been (slow / rapid). (p. 591)

7. True or False: Sex differences in vocational achievement can be directly attributed to differences in ability. Explain your answer. (p. 591)

   _____

   _____

8. Cite two ways in which girls can be encouraged to maintain high career aspirations. (p. 591)

   A. _____

   _____

   B. _____

   _____

Vocational Preparation of Non-College-Bound Adolescents

1. Non-college-bound high school graduates have (more / fewer) work opportunities than they did several decades ago. (p. 592)

2. Summarize the challenges faced by non-college-bound young adults in trying to gain employment, and describe the type of jobs they are likely to find. (p. 592)

   Challenges: _____

   _____

   Type of jobs: _____

   _____

3. Describe the nature of most jobs held by adolescents, and discuss the impact of heavy job commitment on adolescents' attitudes and behaviors. (p. 592)

   A. _____

   _____

   B. _____

   _____

4. True or False: Like some European nations, the United States and Canada has a widespread training system designed to prepare youth for skilled business and industrial occupations and manual trades. (p. 592)

5. Summarize the features of Germany's work–study apprenticeship system, and explain how it creates a smooth transition from school to work. (pp. 592–593)

_____

_____

_____

_____

_____

6. Identify three major challenges to the implementation a national apprenticeship program in the United States. (p. 593)

A. _____

B. _____

C. _____

ASK YOURSELF . . .

For *Ask Yourself* questions for this chapter, along with feedback on the accuracy of your answers, please log on to MyDevelopmentLab (for registration and access, please visit mydevelopmentlab.com or follow the directions on p. ix).

1) Select the Chapter of the *Ask Yourself.*
2) Open the E-Book and select the Explore icon next to the *Ask Yourself.*
3) Complete questions and choose "Submit answers for grading" or "Clear Answers" to start over.

SUGGESTED STUDENT READINGS

Conchas, G. Q. (2006). *The color of success: Race and high-achieving urban youth.* New York: Teachers College Press. Examines academic achievement in minority youth, including personal success stories, learning environments that foster high achievement, and strategies for overcoming inequality in public schools.

Gallagher, A. M., & Kaufman, J. C. (Eds.). (2005). *Gender differences in mathematics: An integrative psychological approach.* New York: Cambridge University Press. Provides a comprehensive overview of gender differences in mathematics achievement, including both biological and environmental factors that contribute to these differences.

Petersen, A. C., & Mortimer, J. T. (Eds.). (2006). *Youth unemployment and society.* New York: Cambridge University Press. An interdisciplinary look at the importance of meaningful work experiences in adolescence, this book explores societal and developmental consequences of youth unemployment in the United States and Europe.

PUZZLE 15.1 TERM REVIEW

Across

4. Adolescents' belief that they are the focus of everyone's attention and concern is referred to as the _____ audience
5. Period of vocational development in which adolescents focus on a general career category and eventually settle on a single occupation
6. _____-deductive reasoning begins with a hypothesis, from which logical inferences can be deduced and then tested in a systematic fashion
8. Period of vocational development in which children explore career options through make-believe play
9. The personal _____ refers to adolescents' belief that they are special and unique

Down

1. _____ operational stage: Piaget's final stage, in which adolescents develop the capacity for abstract, scientific thinking
2. _____ necessity: specifies that the accuracy of conclusions drawn from premises rests on the rules of logic, not on real-world confirmation
3. _____ thought: evaluating the logic of verbal statements without referring to real-world circumstances
7. Period of vocational development in which adolescents weigh vocational options against their interests, abilities, and values

PRACTICE TEST #1

1. According to Piaget, when adolescents engage in hypothetico-deductive reasoning, they (p. 566)
    a. form a prediction about variables that might affect an outcome.
    b. operate on reality.
    c. move randomly through testable inferences.
    d. typically fail to notice variables that are not immediately suggested by the concrete materials of the task.

2. Research indicates that when given a situation involving no more than two causal variables, 6-year-olds (p. 567)
    a. are not able to deduce logical, testable inferences.
    b. understand that hypotheses must be confirmed by appropriate evidence.
    c. do not separate the effects of the individual variables.
    d. use a symbolic system to solve the operation.

3. The fact that college coursework leads to improvements in formal reasoning related to course content suggests that, contrary to Piaget's conclusions, (p. 568)
    a. formal operational tasks often are not mastered at all.
    b. the basic rules of formal logic are innate concepts.
    c. operational thought involves verbal reasoning about abstract concepts.
    d. formal operational reasoning does not emerge all at once, but is specific to situation and task.

4. Of the mechanisms underlying cognitive change in adolescence, the one researchers regard as central to adolescent cognitive development is (p. 569)
    a. attention.
    b. inhibition.
    c. metacognition.
    d. knowledge.

5. According to Deanna Kuhn's findings, the capacity to reason like a scientist (p. 570)
    a. levels off in the late teens and early twenties.
    b. improves faster for boys than girls.
    c. improves with age.
    d. slows in middle childhood, then speeds up again in adolescence.

6. The cognitive distortions that Piaget's followers call the *imaginary audience* and the *personal fable* are (p. 572)
    a. an outgrowth of gains in perspective taking, which causes adolescents to be more concerned with what others think.
    b. strongest during middle and late adolescence.
    c. a result of egocentrism.
    d. evidence of adolescents' generally low self-esteem.

7. Research evidence shows that adolescents are less likely than adults to (p. 573)
    a. fall back on well-learned intuitive judgments.
    b. learn from feedback by revising their decision-making strategies.
    c. make impulsive decisions in areas where they have little experience.
    d. make decisions based on the personal opinions of a few close friends.

8. The fact that girls' advantage in reading and writing achievement increases over adolescence is a special concern because (p. 575)
    a. it is a trend evident primarily in the developing world.
    b. language arts have traditionally been viewed as "masculine."
    c. differences in literacy skills are believed to be major contributors to a widening gender gap in college enrollments.
    d. researchers fear that boys in general may be showing delayed development of the left hemisphere of the cerebral cortex.

9. When all adolescents are considered, the male advantage in math is (p. 575)
   a. small but has been widening over the past thirty years.
   b. least significant among the most capable students.
   c. due more to genetic than to social factors.
   d. evident in virtually every country where males and females have equal access to secondary education.

10. Research indicates that women whose prenatal androgen levels were abnormally high (p. 577)
    a. showed superior performance on mental rotation tasks.
    b. needed low daily variations in androgen levels to perform well on spatial tasks.
    c. were especially susceptible to maternal stimulation in spatial tasks during the preschool years.
    d. did not achieve as well in reading and writing in high school as women whose prenatal androgen levels were normal.

11. Research suggests that reading proficiency fosters adolescents' understanding of (p. 578)
    a. sarcasm.
    b. discrepancies between statement and context.
    c. metalinguistic awareness.
    d. proverbs.

12. Research on adolescents shows that both authoritarian and permissive parenting styles are linked to (p. 580)
    a. high academic achievement but low self-esteem.
    b. lower grades.
    c. higher dropout rates.
    d. the poorest grades and worsening school performance over time.

13. In a nationally representative sample of more than 15,000 American adolescents, students' grade point average in tenth grade was strongly predicted by (p. 581)
    a. SES and previous academic achievement.
    b. an authoritarian parenting style.
    c. their parents' school involvement in eighth grade.
    d. their parents' willingness to allow children full autonomy.

14. According to one study, integration into the school peer network predicted higher grades among (p. 582)
    a. Asians and African Americans.
    b. Caucasians and Hispanics.
    c. Native Americans and Canadian Aboriginals.
    d. children of Asian and European immigrants.

15. Many high school seniors graduate deficient in basic academic skills because (p. 584)
    a. they were given too much autonomy and too little direction in their choice of learning activities.
    b. they scored poorly on high-stakes tests.
    c. many secondary schools do not consistently provide interesting, challenging teaching.
    d. their schools emphasized separate classes in each subject.

16. Because the main goal of high-stakes testing is to upgrade the test performance of poorly performing students, (p. 584)
    a. the educational needs of gifted and talented students are neglected.
    b. eighth and tenth graders do more advanced work than twelfth graders.
    c. all students benefit from greater academic rigor.
    d. such testing is a good motivator for upgrading teaching and learning.

17. Longitudinal research following thousands of U.S. students from eighth to twelfth grade revealed that assignment to a vocational or general education track (p. 583)
    a. speeds up academic progress.
    b. encourages students to develop the self-motivation they need to change tracks.
    c. helps students who perform poorly in a particular subject to focus on improvement in that subject.
    d. decelerates academic progress.

18. Research suggests that risk factors that predict later dropout can appear as early as (p. 586)
    a. preschool.
    b. first grade.
    c. middle school.
    d. the first year of high school.

19. Recent studies indicate that urban minority teenagers, even those within a year or two of graduating, will (p. 587)
    a. blame discrimination rather than effort for their poor performance.
    b. initially drop out but return to school within a year.
    c. opt out of school as soon as work requiring only on-the-job training becomes available in their communities.
    d. remain in school rather than take on family responsibilities.

20. The most powerful way to prevent school dropout is to (p. 587)
    a. address the academic and social problems of at-risk students in elementary school, and to involve their parents.
    b. place at-risk students in a college preparatory track, regardless of their prior achievement, so that their higher-achieving peers can help them.
    c. permit at-risk students to fail courses as many times as necessary so that they eventually develop the skills necessary to pass.
    d. limit at-risk students' participation in extracurricular activities so that they have more time to focus on academic work.

21. During the fantasy period of vocational development, children (p. 589)
    a. gather information about possibilities that blend with their personal characteristics.
    b. focus on a general vocational category.
    c. have career preferences based largely on familiarity, glamour, and excitement.
    d. become aware of the personal and educational requirements for different vocations.

22. Research indicates that parent-child vocational similarity is a function especially of (p. 590)
    a. similarity in personality.
    b. SES.
    c. similarity in intellectual abilities.
    d. similarity in educational attainment.

23. Students with academic and behavior problems generally have (p. 591)
    a. neither family nor teacher supports.
    b. closer relationships with family members than with teachers.
    c. relationships with peers that are strong, though not necessarily positive.
    d. strong support from teachers in vocational subjects but weak support from those in academic subjects.

24. Research indicates that the more hours students work at part-time jobs, the (p. 592)
    a. more likely they are to meet their educational and vocational goals.
    b. less likely they are to participate in extracurricular activities and the more likely they are to drop out.
    c. less likely they are to report distance from their parents.
    d. more likely they are to be considered responsible by their peers.

25. One of the major challenges to implementing an apprenticeship system in the United States is (p. 593)
    a. overcoming employers' reluctance to assume part of the responsibility for vocational training.
    b. preventing qualifying examinations from becoming just another form of high-stakes testing.
    c. overcoming the widespread perception of such systems as low-status.
    d. gaining parental support for students' enrollment in apprenticeship programs.

PRACTICE TEST #2

1. Piaget understood that for adolescents to engage in formal operations, they need (p. 567)
    a. logical propositions.
    b. to focus on variables that are suggested by the concrete materials of a task.
    c. to use language-based and other symbolic systems that do not stand for real things.
    d. to begin solving a problem with the most obvious predictions about the situation.

2. In early adolescence, young people become better at (p. 568)
    a. analyzing the logic of a series of propositions, regardless of their content.
    b. formulating second premises.
    c. freeing their thought from logical necessity.
    d. using well-learned knowledge that casts doubt on the truthfulness of a premise.

3. Research indicates that early adolescent gains in propositional thought are fully accounted for by (p. 569)
    a. training in formal logic.
    b. years of schooling.
    c. selectivity of attention.
    d. the ability to apply verbal-hypothetical reasoning to the real world.

4. Many adolescents and adults continue to show a self-serving bias in scientific reasoning by (p. 570)
    a. blending evidence and theory into a single representation.
    b. applying logic more effectively to ideas they doubt than to ideas they favor.
    c. showing a flexible, open-minded approach to the process of evaluation.
    d. thinking about theories and isolating variables.

5. According to research on the imaginary audience, adolescents (p. 572)
    a. spend a great deal of time talking to themselves.
    b. develop an inflated opinion of their own importance.
    c. become extremely self-conscious and often go to great lengths to avoid embarrassment.
    d. believe that others could not possibly understand their experiences.

6. In the heat of the moment, when making good decisions requires them to inhibit "feel-good" behavior, adolescents are far more likely than adults to (p. 574)
    a. rate the risks of that behavior higher than peers who have not tried it.
    b. assess the likelihood of various possible outcomes.
    c. use feedback to revise their decision-making strategies.
    d. emphasize short-term over long-term goals.

7. Some research suggests that high-achieving African-American boys are particularly likely to have (p. 575)
    a. mothers who provide verbal stimulation starting in the preschool years.
    b. access to computers equipped with educational software.
    c. fathers who are warm, verbally communicative, and demanding of achievement.
    d. a parent or parents who discipline them severely for poor school performance.

8. Of the following factors, the one that reduces girls' willingness to consider math- or science-related careers in college is (p. 575)
    a. girls' advantage over boys in reading and writing achievement.
    b. the level of maternal stimulation they receive from the preschool years through adolescence.
    c. the belief of many parents that boys are better than girls at math.
    d. the tendency of girls to blame their errors on lack of ability.

9. Research shows that grammatically accurate written expression is best learned (p. 578)
    a. in the context of writing.
    b. through practice in persuasive speaking.
    c. though traditional grammar instruction.
    d. by listening to the figurative language of proverbs.

10. Teenagers are far more likely than school-age children to (p. 578)
    a.   respond to strangers cheerfully and courteously.
    b.   become so self-conscious that they stutter and mumble.
    c.   define themselves by narrowing the range of language they use, regardless of the situation.
    d.   practice what they want to say in an expected situation, review what they did say, and figure out how they could say it better.

11. Studies show that as a result of the transition from elementary school to middle or junior high school, (p. 579)
    a.   girls' self-esteem rises slightly.
    b.   students tend to rate their middle or junior high school experiences more favorably than their elementary school experiences.
    c.   many young people feel less academically competent, and their liking for school and motivation decline.
    d.   boys, but not girls, tend to report that teachers care less about them and stress competition more.

12. Research indicates that students in middle or junior high school are less likely to feel angry and depressed, to be truant, or to show declines in self-esteem, when (p. 580)
    a.   schools minimize competition and differential treatment based on ability.
    b.   parents grant them full autonomy immediately.
    c.   they are assigned to classes with one or two familiar peers.
    d.   they have to make few important decisions about where to go and what classes to take.

13. Adolescents who achieve especially well tend to have parents who (p. 581)
    a.   are warm and permissive.
    b.   encourage self-regulation but discourage reflective thought.
    c.   engage in joint decision making, gradually permitting more autonomy with age.
    d.   maintain very high expectations for children's capacity to take responsibility for their own behavior.

14. In a study that followed seventh graders during their first year after school transition, students in peer groups whose members disliked school (p. 582)
    a.   tended to dislike school themselves even after they moved to a group with more positive attitudes toward school.
    b.   reported higher school enjoyment during the second year.
    c.   performed about as well as they had in their previous school, regardless of their new peers' attitudes.
    d.   showed an especially large drop in school enjoyment.

15. An important benefit of separate classrooms in each subject is that adolescents (p. 583)
    a.   have greater opportunities to exercise autonomy though choice of learning activities.
    b.   can engage in focused, competitive work in that subject.
    c.   can be taught by experts, who are more likely to encourage high-level thinking.
    d.   can develop cognitive self-regulation more effectively than in a single classroom devoted to several subjects.

16. Research indicates that at least into middle or junior high school, mixed-ability classes (p. 583)
    a.   contribute to poorly performing students' declines in self-esteem.
    b.   can mitigate some of the negative effects of high-stakes testing.
    c.   can reinforce African-American students' self-doubts about their academic success.
    d.   effectively support the motivation and achievement of students who vary widely in academic progress.

17. Compared to students in higher tracks, those in lower tracks exert substantially less effort, a difference due partly to the fact that (p. 585)
    a.   tracking often goes hand-in-hand with high-stakes testing.
    b.   when capable students end up in low tracks, they sink to the performance level of their trackmates.
    c.   students in lower tracks are inclined to link their performance to ability rather than to effort.
    d.   SES differences in quality of education are higher in North America than in most other industrialized regions.

18. In contrast to North American students, those in China, Japan, and most Western European countries (p. 585)
   a. take a national examination to determine their track placement in high school.
   b. can make a wide range of decisions about their own education.
   c. typically drop out of school after failing to gain admission to the track they wanted.
   d. nearly always get a college education, regardless of their educational track in secondary school.

19. Among U.S. and Canadian young people, about _____ percent leave high school without a diploma. (p. 585)
   a. 4
   b. 6
   c. 10
   d. 17

20. Students in general education and vocational tracks are three times more likely to drop out than those in a college preparatory track because (p. 586)
   a. the former students typically attend large, impersonal schools.
   b. teaching in the former tracks tends to be less stimulating.
   c. the former students tend to have after-school jobs with long hours.
   d. parents of the former students tend to push them too hard to move into a college preparatory track.

21. The extracurricular activities most likely to produce positive, lasting benefits are (p. 588)
   a. unstructured, relaxing pastimes like pool, video games, and TV.
   b. those in which adolescents create the rules without adult involvement.
   c. highly structured, goal-oriented activities that require teenagers to take on challenging roles and responsibilities.
   d. activities that reinforce academic skills.

22. In their late teens and early twenties, young people typically crystallize their vocations when they (p. 589)
   a. focus on a general vocational category, within which they experiment for a time before settling on a specific occupation.
   b. first begin to gather information about career possibilities that blend with their personal characteristics.
   c. gain insight into a variety of career options by fantasizing about them.
   d. begin to think about possible careers in terms of their abilities and values.

23. According to John Holland, the *realistic* person (p. 590)
   a. enjoys working with ideas and is likely to select a scientific occupation.
   b. likes interacting with people and gravitates toward human services.
   c. prefers working with objects rather than people and tends to choose a mechanical occupation.
   d. is adventurous and persuasive and is drawn to supervisory positions.

24. According to recent U.S. Census Bureau findings, women (p. 591)
   a. made significant gains between 1983 and 2006 in engineering and other traditionally masculine professions.
   b. have higher career aspirations during their college years than their male classmates.
   c. are more likely today to ignore gender stereotypes than they were in 1983.
   d. remain concentrated in less-well-paid, traditionally feminine occupations, such as writing and nursing.

25. North American employers regard recent high school graduates as poorly prepared for skilled business and industrial occupations and manual trades because most graduates (p. 592)
   a. concentrated on academic work rather than vocational work in school.
   b. have work experience that is limited to low-level repetitive tasks, providing little contact with adult supervisors and therefore little opportunity for serious vocational exploration.
   c. had family responsibilities that prevented them from gaining useful vocational training.
   d. did not go into state apprenticeship programs.

CHAPTER 16
EMOTIONAL AND SOCIAL DEVELOPMENT
IN ADOLESCENCE

BRIEF CHAPTER SUMMARY

Erikson defined the psychological conflict of adolescence as identity versus role confusion. Current theorists, unlike Erikson, do not view the typical process of developing a mature identity as a "crisis," but rather as a process of exploration followed by commitment. Self-concept changes as adolescents unify separate traits into more abstract generalizations about themselves, with more emphasis on social virtues and inclusion of enduring beliefs and plans. Self-esteem further differentiates in adolescence and tends to rise, while individual differences in self-esteem become increasingly stable. These advances in self-concept and self-esteem provide the cognitive foundation for forming an identity.

Researchers identify four identity statuses typical of adolescents: identity achievement, moratorium, foreclosure, and diffusion. Identity achievement and moratorium are both adaptive statuses, while teenagers who remain in a state of identity foreclosure or diffusion are likely to have adjustment difficulties. Positive identity development is promoted by the adolescent's own personality characteristics and influenced by parents, peers, school and community opportunities, and adolescent's culture.

Kohlberg's theory of moral development, inspired by Piaget's earlier work on the moral judgment of the child, describes the development of morality from late childhood into adulthood in terms of the way individuals at different stages reason about hypothetical moral dilemmas. Kohlberg identified three moral levels (preconventional, conventional, and postconventional, each including two stages, for a total of six moral stages, beginning with a reliance on external authority and advancing to an orientation based on universal ethical principles. Although Kohlberg's theory emphasizes a "masculine" morality based on rights and justice rather than a "feminine" morality based on care, it does not underestimate the moral maturity of females. Influences on moral development include personality, family, school, peer, and cultural factors. As individuals advance through Kohlberg's stages, moral reasoning becomes more closely related to behavior, though this depends on moral self-relevance—the degree to which morality is central to self-concept. Religious involvement can also play a positive role.

Biological, social, and cognitive forces combine to make early adolescence a period of gender intensification. Over the adolescent years, relationships with parents and siblings change as teenagers strive to establish a healthy balance between family connection and separation. As adolescents spend more time with peers, intimacy and loyalty become central features of friendship. The Internet has expanded teenagers' opportunities for friendships beyond their schools and communities, but also poses dangers, especially for youths with adjustment problems. Adolescent peer groups are typically organized into *cliques,* tightly knit groups of close friends, who may come together with other cliques sharing similar values and interests to form a *crowd,* which gives the adolescent an identity within the larger social structure of the school. Early adolescent dating relationships tend to be shallow and stereotyped, but dating that does not begin too soon provides valuable lessons in cooperation, etiquette, and other aspects of relationships. Peer pressure rises in early adolescence, but most teenagers do not blindly conform to the dictates of agemates.

The most common psychological problem of adolescence is depression, which results from a combination of diverse biological and environmental factors. Severe depression can lead to suicidal thoughts, and the suicide rate increases dramatically at adolescence. Although many teenagers become involved in some delinquent activity, only a few become serious, repeat offenders. Personal, family, school, peer, and neighborhood factors are related to delinquency.

LEARNING OBJECTIVES

After reading this chapter, you should be able to:

16.1   Discuss Erikson's theory of identity development, noting the major personality achievement of adolescence. (p. 598)

16.2   Describe changes in self-concept and self-esteem during adolescence. (pp. 598–601)

16.3   Describe the four identity statuses, noting how each is related to psychological adjustment, and summarize the factors that promote identity development. (pp. 601–605)

16.4   Describe Kohlberg's theory of moral development, and evaluate its accuracy. (pp. 606–609)

16.5   Evaluate claims that Kohlberg's theory does not adequately represent the morality of females, with particular attention to Gilligan's argument. (pp. 609–611)

16.6   Describe influences on moral reasoning, and discuss the relationship between moral reasoning and behavior. (pp. 611–615)

16.7   Explain why early adolescence is a period of gender intensification. (p. 615)

16.8   Discuss familial influences on adolescent development, including changes in the parent–child and sibling relationships. (pp. 616–619)

16.9.   Summarize the characteristics of adolescent friendships and peer groups, and discuss the contribution of each to emotional and social development. (pp. 619–623)

16.10   Describe adolescent dating relationships. (pp. 624–625)

16.11   Discuss conformity to peer pressure in adolescence, noting how parental behavior is related to adolescent conformity. (pp. 625–626)

16.12   Cite factors related to adolescent depression and suicide, along with approaches for prevention and treatment. (pp. 626–630)

16.13   Discuss factors related to delinquency, and cite strategies for prevention and treatment. (pp. 631–634)

16.14   Review factors that foster resilience in adolescence. (pp. 634–635)

STUDY QUESTIONS

Erikson's Theory: Identity versus Role Confusion

1.   Explain how young people construct an *identity*. (p. 598)

_____

_____

2.   Discuss Erikson's notion of an *identity crisis*. (p. 598)

_____

_____

3.   Current theorists (do / do not) agree with Erikson that the process of identity development constitutes a "crisis." (p. 598)

4.   Describe the negative outcome of Erikson's psychological conflict of adolescence—role confusion. (p. 598)

_____

_____

_____

Self-Understanding

Changes in Self-Concept

1. Provide an example illustrating how early adolescents unify separate traits into more abstract descriptors. (p. 599)

_____

2. Compared to school-age children, teenagers place (more / less) emphasis on social virtues, such as being friendly, considerate, kind, and cooperative. Explain why. (p. 599)

_____

_____

Changes in Self-Esteem

1. Cite three new dimensions of self-esteem that emerge during adolescence. (p. 600)

   A. _____   B. _____

   C. _____

2. True or False: Except for temporary declines associated with school transitions, self-esteem rises in most adolescents. (p. 600)

3. Certain self-esteem factors are more strongly related to adjustment. Provide an example to support this statement. (p. 600)

_____

_____

Influences on Self-Esteem

1. Of those young people whose self-esteem declines in adolescence, most are girls. Explain why. (p. 600)

_____

_____

2. Explain how both parents and the larger social environment influence adolescents' self-esteem. (pp. 600–601)

   Parents: _____

_____

   Social environment: _____

_____

Paths to Identity

1. Which two key criteria from Erikson's theory do researchers use to evaluate progress in identity development? (p. 601)

   A _____   B. _____

2. Match each of the following identity statuses with the appropriate description. (p. 601)

   _____ Commitment in the absence of exploration
   _____ Exploration without having reached commitment
   _____ Commitment to values, beliefs, and goals following
   a period of exploration
   _____ An apathetic state characterized by lack of both
   exploration and commitment

   1. Identity achievement
   2. Identity moratorium
   3. Identity foreclosure
   4. Identity diffusion

3. Most adolescents start out at "lower" statuses, such as _____ and _____, but by late adolescence, they have moved toward "higher" statuses, including _____ and _____. (p. 602)

4. True or False: Most adolescent girls follow a different path to identity formation than do boys. They postpone the task of establishing an identity, focusing instead on intimacy development. (p. 602)

Identity Status and Psychological Well-Being

1. True or False: Research supports the conclusion that identity achievement and moratorium are psychologically healthy routes to a mature self-definition, whereas long-term identity foreclosure and identity diffusion are maladaptive. (p. 602)

2. Briefly summarize personality characteristics associated with each identity status. (pp. 602–603)

    Identity achievement and moratorium: _____

    _____

    Identity foreclosure: _____

    _____

    Identity diffusion: _____

    _____

Influences on Identity Development

1. Match the following identity statuses with the appropriate description of associated personality, family, school, community, and larger cultural factors. Descriptions may apply to more than one identity status. (pp. 603–604)

    _____ Assume that absolute truth is always attainable
    _____ Lack confidence in the prospect of ever knowing anything with certainty
    _____ Appreciate that they can use rational criteria to choose among alternatives
    _____ Feel attached to parents but are also free to voice their own opinions
    _____ Have close bonds with parents but lack healthy separation
    _____ Report the lowest levels of warm, open communication at home

    1. Identity achievement
    2. Identity moratorium
    3. Identity foreclosure
    4. Identity diffusion

2. Explain how peers contribute to adolescent identity development. (p. 603)

    _____

    _____

    _____

3. Describe ways schools can foster identity development during adolescence. (pp. 603–604)

    _____

    _____

    _____

4. Which aspect of mature identity is not captured by the identity-status approach? (p. 604)

    _____

5. List five ways that adults can support healthy identity development in adolescents. (p. 604)

    A. _____

    B. _____

    C. _____

    D. _____

    E. _____

Cultural Influences: Identity Development among Ethnic Minority Adolescents

1. What is an *ethnic identity*? (p. 605)

    _____

    _____

2. Psychological distress resulting from conflict between the minority and the host culture is called
    _____. (p. 605)

3. Explain why ethnic minority adolescents often experience unique problems in developing a sense of identity.
    (p. 605)

    _____

    _____

    _____

4. List three ways that society can help minority adolescents resolve identity conflicts constructively. (p. 605)

    A. _____

    B. _____

    C. _____

5. Cite several benefits of a strong, secure ethnic identity. (p. 605)

    _____

    _____

6. What is a *bicultural identity*, and how does it benefit minority adolescents? (p. 605)

    _____

    _____

    _____

Moral Development

Kohlberg's Theory of Moral Development

1. Explain Kohlberg's approach to the study of moral development. (pp. 606–607)

    _____

    _____

2. True or False: Kohlberg emphasized that it is the *way an individual reasons* about a dilemma, not the *content of the response,* that determines moral maturity. (p. 607)

3. List two factors that Kohlberg believed to promote moral understanding. (p. 607)

   A. _____

   B. _____

4. Explain the basic characteristics of moral reasoning at each of Kohlberg's three levels: (pp. 607–608)

   Preconventional: _____

   _____

   Conventional: _____

   _____

   Postconventional: _____

   _____

5. Match each of the following moral orientations with the appropriate description. (pp. 607–608)

   _____ Laws must be obeyed under all circumstances; rules must be enforced in the same even-handed manner for everyone, and each member of society has a personal duty to uphold them

   _____ Right action is defined by self-chosen ethical principles of conscience that are valid for all humanity, regardless of law and social agreement

   _____ Ignore people's intentions and focus on fear of authority and avoidance of punishment as reasons for behaving morally

   _____ Desire to obey rules because they promote social harmony

   _____ Regard laws and rules as flexible and emphasize fair procedures for interpreting and changing the law in order to protect individual rights and the interests of the majority

   _____ View right action as flowing from self-interest; reciprocity is understood as equal exchange of favors

   1. Punishment and obedience orientation
   2. Instrumental purpose orientation
   3. "Good boy–good girl" orientation
   4. Social-order-maintaining orientation
   5. Social contract orientation
   6. Universal ethical principle orientation

6. True or False: Longitudinal research suggests that individuals do not move through the stages of moral development in the order in which Kohlberg suggested. (p. 609)

7. True or False: The development of moral understanding is very slow and gradual. (p. 609)

8. (Few / Many) people reach Kohlberg's postconventional stage. What are the implications of this for Kohlberg's theory? (p. 609)

   _____

   _____

9. How do Kohlberg's moral stages compare to Piaget's stages? (p. 609)

   _____

   _____

Are There Sex Differences in Moral Reasoning?

1. Carol Gilligan believes that feminine morality emphasizes an "ethic of care" that is devalued in Kohlberg's model. Explain what she meant by this. (pp. 609–610)

   _____

   _____

   _____

2.   True or False: Research supports Gilligan's claim that Kohlberg's approach underestimates females' moral maturity. (p. 609)

3.   Summarize research findings on sex differences in moral development. (pp. 609–610)

_____

_____

_____

Coordinating Moral, Social-Conventional, and Personal Concerns

1.   Provide an example of a matter of personal choice. Does concern with matters of personal choice differ across cultures? Explain. (p. 610)

A. _____

B. _____

_____

2.   Describe advances in moral reasoning about matters of personal choice during adolescence. (pp. 610–611)

_____

_____

_____

3.   Adolescents think (less / more) intently about conflicts between personal choice and community obligations. Briefly explain your response. (p. 611)

_____

_____

_____

Influences on Moral Reasoning

1.   Explain how having a flexible, open-minded approach to new information and experiences fosters gains in moral reasoning. (p. 611)

_____

_____

_____

2.   Describe child-rearing practices that promote gains in moral development. (p. 611)

_____

_____

_____

3.   True or False: Years of schooling is one of the most powerful predictors of moral maturity. (p. 611)

4.   Cite characteristics of peer interaction that promote moral understanding and movement to higher moral stages. (p. 612)

_____

_____

_____

5. True or False: Cross-cultural research shows that individuals in industrialized nations move through Kohlberg's stages more quickly and advance to higher levels of moral reasoning than do individuals in village societies. Based on your response, provide some possible explanations. (p. 612)

_____

_____

_____

Moral Reasoning and Behavior

1. There is a (weak / moderate / strong) relationship between moral thought and action. Describe research that supports your answer. (p. 613)

_____

_____

_____

2. Define *moral self-relevance*, and cite factors that may contribute to a sense of moral self-relevance. (p. 613)

A. _____

B. _____

Social Issues: Education: Development of Civic Responsibility

1. What is civic responsibility? List its three components. (p. 614)

A. _____

B. _____

C. _____

2. Summarize family, school, and community influences on adolescents' civic responsibility. (p. 614)

Family: _____

_____

School: _____

_____

Community: _____

_____

3. Cite two aspects of involvement in extracurricular activities and youth organizations that account for their lasting impact. (p. 614)

A. _____

B. _____

4. What are service-learning programs? (p. 614)

_____

_____

Religious Involvement and Moral Development

1. During adolescence, formal religious involvement (increases / declines). (p. 613)

2. Summarize the benefits associated with involvement in a religious community. (pp. 613, 615)

_____

_____

_____

3. How might religious institutions be uniquely suited to foster moral and prosocial commitments? (p. 615)

_____

_____

Gender Typing

1. What is *gender intensification,* and when is it strongest? (p. 615)

A. _____

_____

B. _____

2. Although it occurs in both sexes, gender intensification is stronger for (boys / girls). (p. 615)

3. Discuss biological, social, and cognitive factors associated with gender intensification. (p. 615)

Biological: _____

_____

Social: _____

_____

Cognitive: _____

_____

4. (Androgynous / Gender-typed) adolescents tend to be psychologically healthier. (p. 615)

The Family

1. During adolescence, _____—establishing oneself as a separate, self-governing individual—becomes a salient task. (p. 616)

Parent–Child Relationships

1. Describe changes in the parent-child relationship during adolescence. (p. 616)

_____

_____

_____

2. Describe parenting practices that foster adolescent competence. (p. 617)

_____

_____

_____

3.   Explain how parents' own development can lead to friction with teenagers. (pp. 617–618)

_____

_____

_____

_____

4.   True or False: The quality of the parent–child relationship is the most consistent predictor of mental health throughout adolescence. (p. 618)

5.   Explain how mild parent–child conflict is beneficial during adolescence. (p. 618)

_____

_____

_____

6.   True or False: The drop in time spent with the family during adolescence is universal. Briefly explain your response. (p. 618)

_____

_____

Family Circumstances

1.   Describe circumstances in which maternal employment is beneficial to adolescent development. Under what circumstances can it be harmful? (pp. 618–619)

Beneficial: _____

_____

Harmful: _____

_____

Siblings

1.   During adolescence, teenagers invest (more / less) time and energy in siblings. Explain your answer. (p. 619)

_____

_____

2.   Sibling relationships become (more / less) intense during adolescence, in both positive and negative feelings. (p. 619)

3.   True or False: Mild sibling differences in perceived parental affection do not trigger jealousy but, rather, predict an increase in sibling warmth. (p. 619)

Peer Relations

Friendships

1.   Cite the two characteristics of friendship emphasized by teenagers. (p. 620)

A. _____   B. _____

2.   List three changes that result from adolescents' revised view of friendship. (p. 620)

A. _____

B. _____

C. _____

3. Briefly discuss how friendships change during the transition to middle or junior high school. (p. 621)

_____

_____

_____

4. Summarize sex differences in the nature of adolescents' close friendships. (pp. 621–622)

_____

_____

_____

5. True or False: Androgynous boys are just as likely as girls to form intimate same-sex ties, whereas boys who identify strongly with the traditional masculine role are less likely to do so. (p. 621)

6. Describe the potential benefits and costs of closeness in adolescent friendship. (p. 621)

Benefits: _____

_____

Costs: _____

_____

7. Discuss both the benefits and dangers of adolescent friendships on the Internet. (p. 622)

Benefits: _____

_____

Dangers: _____

_____

8. Cite four reasons why gratifying childhood and adolescent friendships are related to psychological health and competence in emerging adulthood. (p. 622)

A. _____

_____

B. _____

_____

C. _____

_____

D. _____

_____

Cliques and Crowds

1. Differentiate between *cliques* and *crowds*, noting the characteristics of each. (p. 623)

Cliques: _____

_____

Crowds: _____

_____

2.   Provide some examples of typical high school crowds. (p. 623)

_____

_____

3.   True or False: Peer group values are often an extension of values learned in the home. (p. 623)

4.   Describe the function of mixed-sex cliques in early adolescence. (p. 623)

_____

_____

_____

5.   True or False: Crowds increase in importance from early to late adolescence. (p. 623)

Dating

1.   Describe younger and older adolescents' different reasons for dating. (p. 624)

Younger: _____

_____

Older: _____

_____

2.   True or False: Early dating is positively associated with social maturity. Explain your answer. (p. 624)

_____

_____

3.   Cite factors associated with dating violence. (p. 624)

_____

_____

4.   Describe the unique challenges faced by homosexual adolescents in initiating and maintaining romances. (p. 625)

_____

_____

_____

5.   Summarize the benefits of adolescent dating. (p. 625)

_____

_____

Peer Pressure and Conformity

1.   True or False: Conformity to peer pressure is greater during adolescence than during childhood or early adulthood. (p. 625)

2.   Cite circumstances in which adolescents are likely to bend to peer pressure. (p. 625)

_____

_____

_____

3. Summarize the link between parenting behavior and adolescents' conformity to peer pressure. (pp. 625–626)

_____

_____

_____

Problems of Development

Depression

1. About _____ to _____ percent of North American teenagers experience mild to moderate feelings of depression, _____ to _____ percent have experienced one or more depressive episodes, and _____ to _____ percent are chronically depressed. (p. 626)

2. Adolescent (boys / girls) are twice as likely as adolescent (boys / girls) to experience persistent depressed mood, a trend that continues from adolescence throughout the lifespan. (p. 626)

3. Summarize consequences of adolescent depression. (pp. 626–627)

_____

_____

4. Explain why adolescents' depressive symptoms tend to be overlooked by parents and teachers. (p. 627)

_____

_____

5. Kinship studies of identical and fraternal twins reveal that heredity (does / does not) play an important role in depression. (p. 627)

6. Explain how experience combines with biology to activate depression in youths. (p. 627)

_____

_____

_____

7. Biological changes associated with puberty (can / cannot) account for sex differences in depression. Explain your answer. (p. 627)

_____

_____

_____

8. Describe how stressful life events and gender-typed coping styles account for girls' higher rates of depression. (p. 627)

_____

_____

_____

Suicide

1. True or False: Suicide is currently the leading cause of death among young people in the United States and Canada. (p. 628)

2. True or False: Adolescent suicide rates are roughly equivalent in all industrialized countries. (p. 628)

3. Discuss sex differences in suicidal behavior, noting whether boys or girls are more likely to kill themselves. (p. 628)

   _____

   _____

   _____

4. Describe ethnic differences in adolescent suicide rates. What accounts for these differences? (pp. 628–629)

   A. _____

   _____

   _____

   B. _____

   _____

   _____

5. True or False: Gay, lesbian, and bisexual youth are three times more likely to attempt suicide than heterosexual youth. (p. 629)

6. Describe two types of young people who tend to commit suicide. (p. 629)

   A. _____

   _____

   B. _____

   _____

7. Explain how biology and environment jointly contribute to adolescent suicidal behavior. (p. 629)

   _____

   _____

   _____

8. Cite cognitive changes that contribute to the rise in suicide among adolescents. (p. 629)

   _____

   _____

9. List five warning signs of suicide. (p. 630)

   A. _____

   B. _____

   C. _____

   D. _____

   E. _____

10. Discuss four ways of responding to an adolescent who might be suicidal. (pp. 629–630)

    A. _____

    _____

    B. _____

    _____

    C. _____

    _____

    D. _____

    _____

11. What types of treatments are available for depressed and suicidal adolescents? (p. 630)

    _____

    _____

    _____

12. True or False: Teenage suicides often take place in clusters. Explain your answer. (p. 630)

    _____

    _____

Delinquency

1. Explain why delinquency rises during early adolescence and then declines into young adulthood. (p. 631)

    _____

    _____

2. Describe sex differences in adolescent delinquency. (p. 631)

    _____

    _____

    _____

3. Do low-SES ethnic minority youths engage in more antisocial acts than their higher-SES white and Asian counterparts? Explain. (p. 631)

    _____

    _____

    _____

4. List personal factors associated with chronic delinquency. (p. 631)

    _____

    _____

5. Explain how ineffective parenting contributes to adolescent aggression and delinquency. (pp. 631–632)

    _____

    _____

6.   How do antisocial friends contribute to adolescent delinquency? (p. 632)

_____

_____

7.   What are zero tolerance policies? Are they effective? Explain. (pp. 632–633)

A. _____

B. _____

8.   Describe characteristics of the most effective treatment programs for adolescent delinquency. (pp. 633–634)

_____

_____

_____

9.   Briefly describe the EQUIP program, and discuss its effectiveness. (p. 634)

A. _____

_____

B. _____

_____

Biology and Environment: Two Routes to Adolescent Delinquency

1.   Identify two paths to adolescent delinquency. (p. 632)

A. _____

B. _____

2.   Longitudinal research reveals that the (early / late) onset type is far more likely to lead to a life-course pattern of aggression and criminality. (p. 632)

3.   Differentiate between early-onset delinquent children who go on to follow the life-course path of delinquency versus those who show a decline in aggression and violence. (p. 632)

_____

_____

_____

4.   Describe characteristics that distinguish early-onset from late-onset delinquent youth. (pp. 632–633)

Early-onset: _____

_____

Late-onset: _____

_____

_____

At The Threshold

1. List five factors that foster resilience in adolescence. (p. 635)

    A. _____

    B. _____

    C. _____

    D. _____

    E. _____

ASK YOURSELF . . .

For *Ask Yourself* questions for this chapter, along with feedback on the accuracy of your answers, please log on to MyDevelopmentLab (for registration and access, please visit mydevelopmentlab.com or follow the directions on p. ix).

1) Select the Chapter of the *Ask Yourself.*
2) Open the E-Book and select the Explore icon next to the *Ask Yourself.*
3) Complete questions and choose "Submit answers for grading" or "Clear Answers" to start over.

SUGGESTED STUDENT READINGS

Heilbrun, K., Goldstein, N., & Redding, R. E. (Eds.). (2005). *Juvenile delinquency: Prevention, assessment, and intervention.* New York: Oxford University Press. An interdisciplinary look at juvenile delinquency, this book examines current research on delinquent youth, including causes, consequences, and treatment of antisocial behavior, resilience, school violence, and the importance of research and public policy.

Kruger, J. (2005). *Identity in adolescence: The balance between self and other.* New York: Routledge. Presents a thorough overview of identity development in adolescence, including theories of identity development, the process of forming an identity, and up-to-date research.

Marcovitz, H. (2004). *Teens and family issues.* Folcroft, PA: Mason Crest Publishers. Based on results from the Gallup Youth Study, which surveys U.S. teenagers' perspectives on family, peers, school, social issues, and other relevant topics, this book examines the importance of family relationships for healthy development.

PUZZLE 16.1 TERM REVIEW

Across

3. Moral _____-_____: the degree to which morality is central to an individual's self concept (2 words, hyph.)
6. Identity _____: identity status of individuals who have explored and committed themselves to self-chosen values and goals
7. Identity versus role _____: Erikson's psychological conflict of adolescence
8. Kohlberg's first level of moral development; moral understanding is based on rewards, punishments, and the power of authority figures
10. Gender _____: increased gender stereotyping of attitudes and behavior
12. Kohlberg's second level of moral development; moral understanding is based on conforming to social rules to ensure positive relationships and social order
14. Identity _____: identity status of individuals who have accepted ready-made values and goals that authority figures have chosen for them
17. A large, loosely organized group consisting of several cliques; membership is based on reputation and stereotype

Down

1. Kohlberg's highest level of moral development; morality is defined in terms of abstract principles and values that apply to all situations and societies
2. Identity constructed by adolescents who explore and adopt values from both their subculture and the dominant culture
4. Sense of self as a separate, self-governing individual
5. Small group of 5 to 7 members who are good friends
9. Identity status of individuals who are exploring alternatives in an effort to find values and goals to guide their life
11. Identity _____: identity status of individuals who have no commitments to values and goals and are not actively trying to reach them
13. A well-organized conception of the self made up of values, beliefs, and goals to which the individual is solidly committed
15. _____ identity: aspect of the self that includes sense of ethnic group membership and attitudes associated with that membership
16. Acculturative _____: psychological distress resulting from conflilct between the minority culture and the host culture

PRACTICE TEST #1

1. According to Erikson's theory of identity versus role confusion, adolescents with little autonomy or initiative (p. 598)
   a. develop an identity when they find an ideal that they can embrace fully.
   b. do not engage in the active exploration required to choose among alternatives.
   c. resolve their search for identity by choosing a vocation that matches their interests and skills.
   d. experience an identity crisis.

2. Compared with school-age children, teenagers place more emphasis on (p. 599)
   a. social virtues, such as being friendly and considerate.
   b. concrete descriptors of their self-concept.
   c. listlike self-descriptions.
   d. rejecting beliefs and plans that had once seemed enduring.

3. Research indicates that a powerful predictor of teenagers' judgments of the importance and usefulness of school subjects, their willingness to exert effort, and their eventual career choice is (p. 600)
   a. social self-esteem.
   b. physical/athletic competence.
   c. academic self-esteem.
   d. job competence.

4. Research shows that before experiencing genuine intimacy in relationships, (p. 602)
   a. boys make more rapid progress than girls in the domain of family versus career priorities.
   b. late adolescents of both sexes typically make progress on identity concerns.
   c. girls show more sophisticated reasoning than boys in most identity domains.
   d. boys are at greater risk than girls for long-term identity foreclosure or diffusion.

5. Young people who are identity-achieved or exploring are more likely than others to (p. 602)
   a. feel in control of their own lives and be more advanced in moral reasoning.
   b. accept a ready-made identity chosen for them by authority figures.
   c. reject the idea that a significant turning point played a major role in their lives.
   d. view school and work as uncertain avenues for realizing their aspirations.

6. In a study comparing Canadian-Aboriginal and cultural-majority 12- to 20-year-olds, the Aboriginal youths tended to describe themselves in terms of (p. 604)
   a. personal crises and disappointments.
   b. individualistic narratives.
   c. an enduring personal essence.
   d. a coherent narrative in which they explained how they changed in meaningful ways.

7. According to Kohlberg's theory, individuals move from Stage 3 to Stage 4 when they resolve moral dilemmas based on (p. 608)
   a. the desire to maintain the affection and approval of friends by being a good person.
   b. taking the larger perspective of societal laws into account.
   c. the realization that people can have different perspectives in moral dilemmas.
   d. a view of laws and rules as flexible instruments for furthering human purposes.

8. In a recent Australian study that presented 18- to 38-year-old university students with a grade-related moral dilemma, the participants of both genders gave the most caring responses when considering a (p. 610)
   a. close friend in class.
   b. classmate whose gender was the opposite of the participant's.
   c. socially distant classmate.
   d. classmate whose relationship to the participant was unspecified.

9. Adolescents who are less likely to be interested in others' moral ideas and justifications tend to be those (p. 611)
   a. who encounter many new social issues in school.
   b. whose friendships foster consensual decision making.
   c. who have difficulty adapting to new experiences.
   d. whose parents ask clarifying questions.

10. Research suggests that a just educational environment may help young people develop moral self-relevance by guiding them (p. 613)
    a. from the punishment and obedience orientation to the instrumental purpose orientation.
    b. toward identity foreclosure.
    c. in democratic decision making and rule setting and in taking responsibility for others' welfare.
    d. toward a deeper appreciation of the role of larger social structures in moral decision making.

11. Compared with youths who are unaffiliated with a religious community, those who have a religious affiliation (p. 613)
    a. tend to be more sexually responsible.
    b. are more involved in community service activities aimed at helping the less fortunate.
    c. are more inclined to rebel against their parents' values.
    d. tend to translate their moral thinking into action only in situations involving people who hold similar worldviews.

12. According to research findings, minority teenagers' experience of acculturative stress is associated with (p. 605)
    a. a rise in deviant behavior.
    b. increased stress as parents confront the fact that their own possibilities are narrowing.
    c. increasing assimilation into the majority culture.
    d. decreasing family closeness and parental demands for obedience.

13. Research indicates that maternal employment or a dual-earner family (p. 618)
    a. does not by itself reduce parental time with teenagers.
    b. can cause temporary acculturative stress.
    c. is harmful to adolescent development.
    d. benefits adolescent sons but not daughters.

14. Siblings who established a positive bond in early childhood continue to display greater affection and caring during the teenage years, an outcome linked to (p. 619)
    a. moderate sibling rivalry in middle childhood.
    b. mild differences in perceived parental affection.
    c. more favorable emotional and social adjustment.
    d. gratifying friendships during early and middle childhood.

15. The strategy of resolving conflicts by minimizing their importance often leads to (p. 621)
    a. increased conflict between boys.
    b. corumination among both boys and girls.
    c. friendships of more variable quality.
    d. friendship break-up among girls.

16. As interest in dating increases, boys' and girls' cliques come together, providing them with (p. 623)
    a. models for how to interact with the other sex and opportunities to do so without having to be intimate.
    b. membership in a crowd based on reputation and stereotype.
    c. rich opportunities for sexual experimentation.
    d. the security of a temporary identity as they construct a coherent sense of self.

17. By late adolescence, teenagers (p. 624)
    a. tend to date for recreation, peer status, and other superficial reasons.
    b. look for a romantic partner who offers personal compatibility, companionship, and social support.
    c. have romantic relationships that are typically brief.
    d. develop greater intimacy with dating partners than with friends.

18. Perhaps because of greater concern with what their friends think of them, early adolescents are more likely than older or young individuals to (p. 625)
    a. give in to peer pressure to engage in drug-taking and delinquent acts.
    b. engage in proadult behavior.
    c. respond to authoritative parenting.
    d. score low in sensation-seeking.

19. Incidence of depressive symptoms increases sharply between ages 13 and 15, when (p. 626)
    a. a genetic disposition toward depression tends to be activated.
    b. teenagers become especially susceptible to maladaptive child rearing.
    c. adolescent identity is most vulnerable to disruption.
    d. the sex difference reverses, with more girls than boys in industrialized nations reporting depression.

20. When attempting suicide, girls tend to (p. 628)
    a. conceal themselves thoroughly so they will not be discovered.
    b. use methods from which they are more likely to be revived.
    c. be depressed for shorter periods of time than boys before making an attempt.
    d. choose techniques that lead to instant death.

21. One likely reason for the increase in suicide during adolescence is (p. 629)
    a. teenagers' improved ability to plan ahead.
    b. the increase in learned helplessness during the teenage years.
    c. high introversion among teenagers as a group.
    d. teenagers' tendency to turn anger and disappointment inward.

22. Research shows that serious violent crime is generally committed by (p. 631)
    a. minority youths, both male and female.
    b. youths who were arrested for the first time before age 16.
    c. boys.
    d. older adolescents.

23. Research indicates that teenagers commit more crimes in neighborhoods with (p. 632)
    a. many affluent but poorly protected homes.
    b. mixed ethnic populations.
    c. limited recreational and employment opportunities and high adult criminality.
    d. many aggressive youths.

24. Of the following factors, the one that best predicts an end to criminal offending among late-onset youths by age 20 to 25 is (p. 633)
    a. punishment through zero-tolerance policies.
    b. being employed or in school and forming positive, close relationships.
    c. first arrest before age 14.
    d. moderate relational aggression in preschool.

25. Research indicates that the most effective approaches to treating serious adolescent offenders (p. 634)
    a. focus on the individual's moral reasoning.
    b. are those that involve zero-tolerance policies.
    c. isolate the teenagers from troubled families.
    d. are lengthy, intensive processes that encompass parent training, social understanding, and instruction in social and cognitive skills.

PRACTICE TEST #2

1. Follow-up research on Erikson's concept of an identity crisis shows that adolescent identity development usually involves (p. 598)
   a. selecting a vocation that matches interests and skills.
   b. arriving at a mature identity through a prolonged and frequently traumatic process of soul-searching.
   c. exploration followed by commitment.
   d. exercising increasing levels of autonomy and initiative.

2. During adolescence, the self-concept continues to differentiate, with self-evaluations broadening to include (p. 600)
   a. physical appearance and academic competence.
   b. social and academic competence.
   c. physical appearance and athletic competence.
   d. close friendship and romantic appeal.

3. A factor that is linked to a positive self-image during adolescence is (p. 600)
   a. encouragement from teachers.
   b. parental feedback that is inconsistent and not contingent on performance.
   c. collectivist social values emphasizing modesty and self-effacement.
   d. reliance on peers to affirm self-esteem.

4. Unlike identity-achieved individuals, those who are in a state of identity moratorium (p. 601)
   a. are in the process of exploring, gathering information, and trying out activities.
   b. are neither committed to values and goals nor actively trying to reach them.
   c. have committed themselves to values and goals without exploring alternatives.
   d. have explored various alternatives and are committed to a clearly formulated set of self-chosen values and goals.

5. According to research findings, long-term identity-diffused teenagers allow situational pressures to dictate their personal decisions by using (p. 602)
   a. an inflexible cognitive style.
   b. an information-gathering cognitive style.
   c. a diffuse-avoidant cognitive style.
   d. a dogmatic cognitive style.

6. Identity-foreclosed adolescents tend to be those who (p. 603)
   a. receive little parental support.
   b. assume that absolute truth is always attainable.
   c. feel securely attached to their parents but also free to voice their own opinions.
   d. have friends who serve as role models for identity development.

7. Research indicates that adolescents who are likely to forge a positive ethnic identity are those (p. 605)
   a. who frequently interact with peers of diverse ethnicities.
   b. whose parents discourage them from developing a bicultural identity.
   c. who initially undergo a long and productive period of ethnic-identity diffusion.
   d. whose families taught them the history, traditions, values, and language of their ethnic group.

8. The influence of situational factors on moral judgments suggests that Kohlberg's moral stages (p. 609)
   a. effectively explain moral reasoning in both hypothetical and real-life situations.
   b. are loosely organized and overlapping, rather than neat and stepwise.
   c. are not a useful tool for understanding the development of moral reasoning.
   d. reveal that people generally draw on the same array of moral responses regardless of context.

9. Research indicates that teenagers in both collectivist and individualist cultures believe that parents have the right to tell them what to do in (p. 611)
   a. matters of personal choice.
   b. all aspects of family functioning.
   c. moral and social-conventional situations.
   d. situations involving ideal reciprocity.

10. One possible reason that individuals in industrialized nations move through Kohlberg's stages more quickly than those in village societies is that in the latter, (p. 612)
   a. responses to moral dilemmas are often less other-directed than in Western Europe and North America.
   b. young people participate in the institutions of their society at early ages.
   c. individuals are encouraged to integrate care- and justice-based reasoning.
   d. moral cooperation is based on direct relations between people, rather than on an appreciation of the role of larger societal structures.

11. Recent research shows that young people who engage in community service that exposes them to people in need or to public issues are especially likely to report (p. 614)
   a. reexamining their beliefs and attitudes and to express a commitment to future service.
   b. a belief that their skills for achieving civic goals were inadequate to the issues they confronted.
   c. a need for schools and districts to adopt policies that encourage or require service-learning.
   d. feelings of disengagement from their communities.

12. Research suggests that androgynous adolescents, especially girls, (p. 615)
   a. are likely to be rejected by their peers.
   b. generally experience less intense hormonal changes in puberty.
   c. tend to be more self-confident, willing to speak their minds, and identity-achieved.
   d. typically have parents who encourage "gender-appropriate" activities.

13. Research findings indicate that high self-reliance, dating competence, advanced identity development, and other positive outcomes are predicted by (p. 616)
   a. the young person's SES and nationality.
   b. parental coercion and control.
   c. parent–adolescent ties that involve appropriate demands for maturity.
   d. how early the teenager deidealizes his or her parents.

14. Research indicates that in well-functioning families, young people remain attached to parents and seek their advice in a context of (p. 618)
   a. tight parental supervision of all aspects of teenagers' lives.
   b. obedience to parental authority.
   c. only a slight drop in the amount of time teenagers spend with their families.
   d. greater freedom.

15. Unlike younger children, teenagers tend to (p. 620)
   a. place less emphasis on loyalty in friendships.
   b. be less possessive of their friends.
   c. value shared interests over intimacy in friendships.
   d. seek friends who are as different from themselves as possible.

16. According to research findings, boys' conversations with male friends usually focus on (p. 621)
   a. self-disclosure.
   b. accomplishments and mastery issues.
   c. mutually supportive statements about attainments.
   d. less competition and conflict than was previously believed.

17. In one recent study, young people's perception of intimacy in a friendship increased as (p. 622)
   a. they shifted from electronic to face-to-face communication.
   b. cell-phone conversations lengthened.
   c. parents' supervision of Internet communication increased.
   d. the amount of instant messaging increased.

18. Research indicates that about 10 to 20 percent of adolescents are physically or sexually abused by dating partners, with boys (p. 624)
    a.   the perpetrators of the violence in more than half of reported cases.
    b.   more likely than girls to report returning violence done to them.
    c.   and girls equally likely to report being victims.
    d.   more likely than girls to report histories of abusive family relationships.

19. According to research findings, adolescents who, regardless of sex, are more depressed are often those who (p. 627)
    a.   experienced especially intense biological changes during puberty.
    b.   identify strongly with "feminine traits."
    c.   experienced too little gender intensification in early adolescence.
    d.   have developed an overly reactive physiological stress response.

20. Among Canadian youths, suicide is the _____-leading cause of death. (p. 628)
    a.   second
    b.   third
    c.   fourth
    d.   fifth

21. The typical warning signs of suicide include (p. 630)
    a.   unusually high desire to socialize.
    b.   sexual promiscuity.
    c.   extreme fatigue, lack of energy, boredom.
    d.   an unusual degree of emotional self-control.

22. Essential ingredients of resilience that prevent repeated suicide attempts include (p. 630)
    a.   solitude, which promotes the suicidal youth's self-reliance.
    b.   reprimands from parents to remind the suicidal youth of the effect his or her suicide would have on others.
    c.   antidepressant medication.
    d.   strengthening social supports and providing training in coping strategies.

23. According to research, among youths who follow the life-course path of aggression and criminality, a strong predictor of their violent delinquency in adolescence is (p. 631)
    a.   a history of ADHD.
    b.   rejection by other deviant youths.
    c.   inept parenting.
    d.   first arrest after age 18.

24. Research on the effects of zero-tolerance policies reveals that (p. 632)
    a.   no evidence exists that such policies reduce youth aggression and other forms of misconduct.
    b.   such policies reduce dropout and delinquency rates.
    c.   such policies are effective tools for combating disruptive and threatening behaviors.
    d.   contrary to previous findings, middle-SES students are more likely to be punished than their low- or high-SES peers.

25. In the multisystemic therapy program, therapists (p. 634)
    a.   made sure that violent youths were punished for any threatening behavior.
    b.   trained parents in communication and other skills and integrated violent youths into positive school, work, and leisure activities.
    c.   removed violent youths from the community and placed them in correctional facilities.
    d.   placed violent youths in peer-culture groups and supplemented these with training in social skills, anger management, and moral reasoning.

CHAPTER 17
EMERGING ADULTHOOD

BRIEF CHAPTER SUMMARY

Emerging adulthood is a recently identified period of development that is marked by great challenge and uncertainty. Young people between the ages of 18 and 25 in industrialized nations are making decisions about education, romantic commitments, and careers later than young people of past generations. Released from the oversight of parents but not yet immersed in adult roles, emerging adults are free to explore many different life paths. Changes in reasoning capacity permit emerging adults to revise their political and religious perspectives.

Cultural changes have contributed to the appearance of this new period of development. As the economies of industrialized nations have become more technologically advanced and information-based, higher levels of education are needed to enter highly-skilled, well-paid careers. Prosperous nations continue to experience gains in life expectancy and, as one result, less reliance on young people's labor. Together, these changes delay the need for young adults to establish financial independence or career commitment, allowing them more time for exploring multiple options. These benefits, however, are not always available to those living in impoverished areas.

To make a successful transition to adulthood, emerging adults must acquire new knowledge and skills. Researchers who study postformal thought have shown that college students make substantial strides in cognition. Older students make more effective use of relativistic thinking than younger students, as they are more aware of the existence of multiple truths. Exposure to a variety of viewpoints encourages young people to look at themselves. As self-understanding increases, emerging adults experience advances in identity in the areas of love, work, and worldview.

Taking a more active role in their own development and participating in vigorous explorations, emerging adults face increased risks. Feelings of loneliness peak during the late teens and early twenties as young people begin to live on their own, often making frequent moves. Certain personal attributes and social supports increase resilience and foster successful passage through this period.

LEARNING OBJECTIVES

After reading this chapter, you should be able to:

17.1   Describe emerging adulthood, noting characteristics of this new transitional period of development. (pp. 642–643)

17.2   Describe the cultural changes that contributed to emerging adulthood, and explain why this period is only available to certain groups of young people. (pp. 643–644)

17.3   Discuss cognitive, emotional, and social changes that take place during emerging adulthood. (pp. 645–652)

17.4   Discuss the risks faced by emerging adults, and summarize factors that foster resilience and a successful transition to adulthood. (pp. 652–654)

STUDY QUESTIONS

1.   Describe the new phase of development known as *emerging adulthood.* (pp. 641–642)

_____

_____

_____

A Period of Unprecedented Exploration

1.   True or False: About 85 percent of American and Canadian young people who enroll in higher education earn their bachelor's degree by age 25. (p. 642)

2.   The average age of first marriage is (increasing / declining) in industrialized nations. (p. 642)

3.   Explain how extended education and delayed career entry and marriage create residential instability for emerging adults. (pp. 642–643)

_____

_____

_____

4.   True or False: Emerging adulthood greatly prolongs identity development. (p. 643)

Cultural Change and Emerging Adulthood

1.   Describe two cultural factors that have contributed to emerging adulthood. (pp. 643–644)

     A. _____

     _____

     B. _____

     _____

2.   True or False: Emerging adulthood is largely limited to industrialized nations. Briefly explain your response. (p. 644)

_____

_____

_____

3.   Emerging adulthood (is / is not) common in low-SES and ethnic minority youths. Explain your answer. (p. 644)

_____

_____

_____

4.   Explain how globalization is expected to impact emerging adulthood. (p. 644)

_____

_____

Development in Emerging Adulthood

Cognitive Changes

1. What is *postformal thought*, and how does college contribute to it? (p. 645)

   A. _____

   B. _____

2. Briefly describe *epistemic cognition.* (p. 645)

   _____

   _____

   _____

3. Trace changes in thought that occur across the college years. Be sure to discuss *dualistic thinking* and *relativistic thinking* in your response. (p. 645)

   Younger students: _____

   _____

   Older students: _____

   _____

4. What is *commitment within realitivistic thinking,* and what factors support its development? (pp. 645–646)

   A. _____

   _____

   B. _____

   _____

5. How do gains in metacognition support epistemic cogntion? (p. 646)

   _____

   _____

6. Explain why peer interaction and reflection are especially important for cognitive development in emerging adulthood. (p. 646)

   _____

   _____

Emotional and Social Changes

1. Discuss changes in identity development during emerging adulthood. (pp. 646–647)

   _____

   _____

   _____

2. What is personal agency, and how does it contribute to emerging adults' emotional and social development? (p. 647)

   A. _____

   B. _____

   _____

3. According to Erikson, _____ is a major task of the early adulthood years. (p. 647)

4. Explain how dating relationships change from adolescence into emerging adulthood. (pp. 647–648)

   _____

   _____

5. Describe how partner similarity and communication affect the likelihood of forming an intimate romantic bond during emerging adulthood. (pp. 648–649)

   Partner similarity: _____

   _____

   _____

   Communication: _____

   _____

   _____

6. True or False: Emerging adults' attachment relationships to their parents have little influence on their romantic partnerships. (p. 648)

7. Although half of American and Canadian young couples cohabit, their relationships are more likely to break up within two years than those of Western European cohabitors. Explain why. (p. 648)

   _____

   _____

   _____

8. Summarize how work-related goals and pursuits differ for young men and women. (p. 649)

   _____

   _____

   _____

9. Describe four experiences common to women who continue to achieve at a high level during the college years. (pp. 649–650)

   A. _____

   _____

   B. _____

   _____

   C. _____

   _____

   D. _____

   _____

10. Describe the experience of emerging adulthood for ethnic minority young people. (pp. 650–651)

_____

_____

_____

11. Discuss ways to improve college success for low-income, ethnic minorities. (p. 650)

_____

_____

_____

12. True or False: Racial bias and discrimination in career opportunities has lessened, especially for college graduates. (p. 650)

13. Why do ethnic minority women have an especially difficult time realizing their career potential? (p. 651)

_____

14. True or False: Emerging adults report that constructing a worldview, or set of beliefs and values to live by, is more important than finishing their education and settling into a career or marriage. (p. 651)

15. True or False: The overwhelming majority of emerging adults develop worldviews that focus on concern for the self. (pp. 651–652)

16. Compared to older people, emerging adults are (more / less) likely to be involved in organizations devoted to specific issues of concern to them. (p. 651)

17. Compared to previous generations, far fewer American, Canadian, and Western European young people vote and engage in political party activities. Explain why. (p. 651)

_____

_____

18. Summarize the development of religious beliefs during emerging adulthood, including the relationship between parenting practices and religious development. (pp. 651–652)

_____

_____

_____

_____

Risk and Resilience in Emerging Adulthood

1. Cite several risks associated with emerging adults' vigorous explorations. (p. 652)

_____

_____

2. True or False: Feelings of loneliness peak during the late teens and early twenties. Explain your answer. (pp. 652–653)

_____

_____

_____

3. Summarize personal attributes and social supports that foster development during emerging adulthood. (p. 653)

Cognitive attributes: _____

_____

_____

Emotional and social attributes: _____

_____

_____

Social supports: _____

_____

_____

ASK YOURSELF . . .

For *Ask Yourself* questions for this chapter, along with feedback on the accuracy of your answers, please log on to MyDevelopmentLab (for registration and access, please visit mydevelopmentlab.com or follow the directions on p. ix).

1) Select the Chapter of the *Ask Yourself*.
2) Open the E-Book and select the Explore icon next to the *Ask Yourself*.
3) Complete questions and choose "Submit answers for grading" or "Clear Answers" to start over.

SUGGESTED STUDENT READINGS

Arnett, J. J. (2006). *Emerging adulthood: The winding road from the late teens through the twenties.* New York: Oxford University Press. Provides a thorough and compelling look at the experiences, challenges, and unique opportunities associated with emerging adulthood.

Massey, D. S., Lundy, G., Charles, C. Z., & Fischer, M. J. (2006). *The source of the river: The social origins of freshmen at America's selective colleges and universities.* New Jersey: Princeton University Press. Using findings from the National Longitudinal Survey of Freshmen, this book examines racial and ethnic differences in academic success, how experiences within the family, peer group, and community contribute to college performance, and how racial stereotypes of intellectual inferiority influence the life chances of many ethnic minority college students.

PUZZLE 17.1 TERM REVIEW

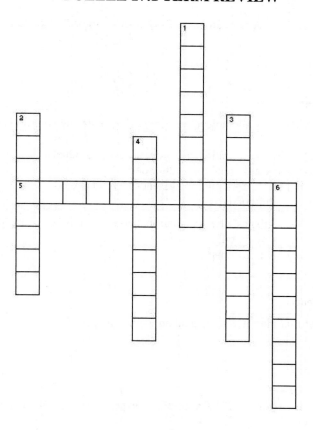

Across

5. _____ thinking: the view that knowledge is embedded in a framework of thought and that multiple truths can exist, each relative to its context

Down

1. The view that knowledge is made up of separate beliefs and propositions, whose truth can be determined by comparing them with objective standards is called _____ thinking

2. A new period of development, extending from the late teens to the twenties, during which young people have left adolescence but have not yet assumed full adult responsibilites is called _____ adulthood

3. Development beyond Piaget's formal operational stage is called _____ thought

4. _____ cognition: reflections on how one arrived at facts, beliefs, and ideas

6. _____ within relativistic thinking: the mature individual's formulation of a perspective that synthesizes contradictions between opposing views, rather than choosing between them

PRACTICE TEST #1

1. According to a recent study of North American 18- to 25-year-olds, most did not feel that they were truly adult until they reached their (p. 641)
   a. early to mid-twenties.
   b. late twenties and early thirties.
   c. mid-thirties.
   d. late thirties and early forties.

2. It is harder to make general statements about development during emerging adulthood than for any other period because (p. 642)
   a. adult milestones are highly diverse in timing and order across individuals.
   b. Western cultures tend to value youth more than adulthood.
   c. few researchers believe that emerging adulthood extends beyond age 20.
   d. little research into emerging adulthood exists.

3. According to U.S. and Canadian statistics, after graduation, about one-third of young people take more years to settle into their desired career track by (p. 642)
   a. volunteering with advocacy organizations.
   b. traveling.
   c. entering graduate school.
   d. taking care of their parents.

4. Currently, the average age of first marriage for Canadian women is (p. 642)
   a. 22.
   b. 28.
   c. 32.
   d. 35.

5. For more than half of North American 18- to 25-year-olds, the preferred way of entering into a committed intimate partnership is (p. 642)
   a. cohabitation.
   b. marriage.
   c. sexual experimentation.
   d. extended friendship before romance.

6. Among African-American, Hispanic, Native American, and Canadian Aboriginal groups, rates of leaving home are lower because (p. 643)
   a. young people in these groups nearly always attend colleges close to home.
   b. of these groups' collectivist values.
   c. young people in these groups are generally less inclined to question their parents' social values and religious perspectives.
   d. of poverty and a cultural tradition of extended family.

7. For many low-SES young people in Western nations, emerging adulthood is limited or nonexistent because (p. 644)
   a. they have not experienced the effects of globalization.
   b. the exciting and productive "floundering period" requires financial independence, which they have not yet attained.
   c. they are burdened by early parenthood, do not finish high school, or do not have access to vocational training.
   d. they belong to cultural minority groups that do not recognize emerging adulthood as a period of exploration.

8. Relativistic thinking leads one to realize that one's own beliefs are often subjective, since (p. 645)
   a. several frameworks may satisfy the criterion of internal logical consistency.
   b. information, values, and authority are divided into absolute frameworks—right and wrong, good and bad, and we and they.
   c. truth can be determined be comparing propositions to standards that exist apart from the thinking person and his or her situation.
   d. the relativistic thinker is acutely aware that he or she has not yet located the source of truth.

9. In a recent study of college learning experiences, seniors who scored high in epistemic cognition typically reported activities that (p. 646)
   a. relived them of the work of choosing between opposing views.
   b. encouraged them to struggle with realistic but ambiguous problems in a supportive environment.
   c. encouraged them to develop intellectual self-reliance by working alone on difficult logic problems.
   d. compelled them to work through the difficult process of developing objective standards of truth.

10. As a result of the self-examination encouraged by exposure to multiple viewpoints, young people often develop (p. 646)
   a. an understanding of standards that exist apart from themselves.
   b. the capacity to engage in collective rationality.
   c. the ability to work alone effectively.
   d. an awareness of their own changing traits and values over time.

11. Research indicates that emerging adults who spend much time exploring in depth without making commitments tend to be (p. 647)
   a. sophisticated relativistic thinkers.
   b. poorly adjusted—depressed and more likely to use drugs.
   c. higher in self-esteem and in academic and social adjustment.
   d. high in personal agency as they become skillful at keeping their options open.

12. By age 25, nearly all North American young people have (p. 647)
   a. become sexually active.
   b. committed to a life partner.
   c. been divorced.
   d. reported feeling unready to choose a committed relationship.

13. Research shows that compared to single people, married couples, on average, (p. 647)
   a. are more stressed.
   b. experience greater financial insecurity.
   c. are physically and mentally healthier and have more frequent and satisfying sex.
   d. less happy than emerging adults.

14. According to research findings, young people who describe both their friendship and romantic partnerships as trusting and happy are those who (p. 648)
   a. have found both friends and romantic partners who are the opposite of themselves in personal characteristics and interests.
   b. recall their attachment experiences with parents as warm and supportive.
   c. were sexually active by the end of high school.
   d. had one or more friendships and/or romantic partnerships that lasted more than a year.

15. North American emerging adults who cohabit prior to engagement tend to (p. 648)
   a. be nearly as committed to each other as married people.
   b. have parents who remained married and provided models of warm intimacy, trust, and support.
   c. marry within three to five years.
   d. be less religious, more androgynous, and more politically liberal.

16. As Daniel Levinson's research revealed, between ages 18 and 22, women constructed "dreams" or images of themselves in the adult world that tended to emphasize (p. 649)
   a. being an independent achiever in a career role.
   b. involvement in warm, supportive relationships.
   c. both marriage and career.
   d. cohabitation before marriage.

17. Research indicates that women with high self-efficacy who pursue male-dominated careers are (p. 649)
   a. less certain than their male counterparts that they can overcome barriers to career success.
   b. more likely than their male counterparts to experience marital difficulties.
   c. more likely than their male counterparts to be recognized as leaders in their fields.
   d. less inclined than their male counterparts to accept guidance from mentors.

18. Most ethnic minority young people from low-SES families who drop out of college do so (p. 650)
    a. after two to three semesters.
    b. by the end of the second year.
    c. during the first year, often within the first six weeks.
    d. after the third year.

19. Based on a study of nearly 700 young people, the factor that best predicted college attendance at age 20 was (p. 650)
    a. stability of romantic relationships.
    b. gender.
    c. employment experiences.
    d. persistence in the face of challenge.

20. In one study, African-American women who had become leaders in diverse fields reported intense persistence fueled by (p. 651)
    a. conflict with mothers who had not achieved as much.
    b. supportive relationships with other women, including teachers and peers.
    c. stable marriages with supportive husbands.
    d. affirmative action.

21. Compared to older people, emerging adults are more likely to (p. 651)
    a. be involved in organizations devoted to specific issues of concern to them.
    b. rate living life to the fullest higher than communal values.
    c. emphasize the importance of positive self-esteem.
    d. desire independence above all else.

22. During the late teens and early twenties, attendance at religious services drops to its lowest level throughout the lifespan because (p. 651)
    a. North American colleges generally offer few opportunities for organized worship.
    b. young people are more concerned with socializing away from adults.
    c. young people continue to question the beliefs they acquired in their families.
    d. during those years, parents often attend services less frequently.

23. As with adolescents, emerging adults who view religion as important in their lives (p. 652)
    a. engage in more community service.
    b. tend not to question their parents' values.
    c. cope less well with stressful, confusing events.
    d. often have low self-efficacy.

24. Young people between ages 19 and 22 are more likely than younger or older individuals to (p. 652)
    a. attend religious services.
    b. cohabit with a romantic partner.
    c. have protected sex.
    d. experiment with prescription and illegal drugs.

25. Of the following resources, the one that has been found to foster resilience in emerging adulthood is (p. 653)
    a. awareness that adulthood is a cultural construction.
    b. an information-gathering cognitive style.
    c. development of strong dualistic thinking skills.
    d. an identity based on exploration in breadth.

PRACTICE TEST #2

1. Research shows that young people who have the economic resources to do so (p. 642)
   a. tend to delay college.
   b. explore alternatives in education, work, personal values, and love more intensely than they did as teenagers.
   c. marry earlier than peers with fewer resources.
   d. pursue experiences that do not relate to a specific career path.

2. According to U.S. and Canadian statistics, only about half of U.S. and one-third of Canadian young people who enroll in higher education (p. 642)
   a. have earned their bachelor's degree by age 25.
   b. graduate.
   c. choose a career that directly relates to their undergraduate field of study.
   d. go on to earn an advanced degree after receiving their bachelor's degree.

3. Today, the majority of North Americans view marriage and parenthood as (p. 642)
   a. crucial markers of adult status.
   b. a means of attaining financial security.
   c. obstacles to career and self-exploration.
   d. personal choices among a range of possible lifestyles.

4. Nearly half of North American 18- to 25-year-olds (p. 642)
   a. move in and out of residence halls, fraternity and sorority houses, and apartments during college.
   b. return to their parents' home for brief periods after first leaving.
   c. marry before they begin their chosen careers.
   d. live abroad for extended periods of time.

5. Which of the following do African-American and Hispanic young people identify as a major marker of adulthood? (p. 644)
   a. Becoming less self-oriented and conducting oneself responsibly
   b. Gaining good control over emotions
   c. Supporting and caring for a family
   d. Avoiding drunk driving

6. As William Perry's research suggests, college students move from dualistic to relativistic thinking when they (p. 645)
   a. regard knowledge as made up of separate units.
   b. view knowledge as embedded in a framework of thought.
   c. cease to reflect on how they arrive at facts, beliefs, and ideas.
   d. become less flexible in their beliefs.

7. Especially mature individuals achieve commitment within relativistic thinking when they (p. 646)
   a. gradually reject differing perspectives to form their own coherent ideas.
   b. consider the justifiability of conclusions that differ from those of others.
   c. arrive at their own objective standards of truth.
   d. work to formulate satisfying perspectives that synthesize contradictions.

8. In emerging adulthood, as young people refine their approach to constructing an identity, they typically explore in depth by (p. 647)
   a. weighing multiple possibilities.
   b. practicing the techniques of epistemic cognition.
   c. evaluating existing commitments.
   d. broadening their interest in literature, the arts, and philosophy.

9. Among emerging adults of diverse ethnicities and SES levels, personal agency is positively related to (p. 647)
    a.   fluctuations in certainty about commitments.
    b.   identity diffusion.
    c.   an information-gathering cognitive style and identity exploration.
    d.   an awareness that all aspects of the life course are socially constructed.

10. With age, emerging adults' romantic ties frequently (p. 647)
    a.   lead to cohabitation.
    b.   require them to individualize their identities.
    c.   involve fewer partners than in adolescence.
    d.   cause them to question trust.

11. Research reveals that about 60 percent of emerging adults have (p. 647)
    a.   become sexually active.
    b.   had only one sexual partner in the previous year.
    c.   seriously considered marriage.
    d.   reevaluated a major commitment.

12. Research shows that the more alike two people are, the (p. 648)
    a.   less frequent and satisfying their sexual relations tend to be.
    b.   more likely they are to separate.
    c.   less likely it is that they met through an Internet dating service.
    d.   more satisfied they tend to be with their relationship.

13. Research indicates that young people with a secure internal working model of attachment relationships (p. 648)
    a.   tend to delay commitment to a life partner until age 25.
    b.   are more at ease in turning to their partner for comfort and assistance than young people with an insecure working model.
    c.   often criticize partners who compromise or accept responsibility too easily.
    d.   tend to have few but stable friendships.

14. Compared with Western European couples who cohabit, North American couples who do so are more likely to (p. 648)
    a.   report unsatisfying sexual activity.
    b.   get married within three years of beginning to live together.
    c.   break up within two years.
    d.   resemble each other in attitudes, personality, and educational plans.

15. In emerging adulthood, work experiences (p. 649)
    a.   increasingly emphasize preparation for adult work roles.
    b.   tend to focus on obtaining spending money.
    c.   often involve split dreams.
    d.   are less likely to involve a mentor than work experiences in adolescence.

16. Research indicates that many mathematically talented college women who remain in the sciences are more likely than their male counterparts to choose careers in (p. 649)
    a.   engineering.
    b.   medicine or other health professions.
    c.   the physical sciences.
    d.   mathematics.

17. Of the following experiences, the one that women who continue to achieve usually have in common is (p. 650)
    a.   parental divorce.
    b.   a stable romantic relationship that began in college and led to marriage.
    c.   mentoring other young women about family—career conflict.
    d.   the opportunity to test their abilities in supportive extracurricular, internship, and work environments.

18. According to U.S. Department of Education statistics, compared to a graduation rate of 63 percent for white students, the rate for African-American students is _____ percent (p. 650)
    a. 20
    b. 36
    c. 43
    d. 57

19. Colleges that have a higher percentage of dropouts are those that (p. 650)
    a. do little to help high-risk students through developmental courses and other support services.
    b. erode students' autonomy by encouraging too much parental involvement in their academic choices.
    c. enroll many low-SES students.
    d. reach out to high-risk students only during the first year.

20. Of the following options, emerging adults say that the most important for attaining adult status is (p. 651)
    a. finishing their education.
    b. settling into a career.
    c. constructing a set of beliefs and values to live by.
    d. getting married.

21. Compared with previous generations, fewer American, Canadian, and Western European young people (p. 651)
    a. join social-justice organizations.
    b. vote or engage in political party activities.
    c. emphasize responsibility to others.
    d. do some form of volunteer work.

22. Emerging adults who hold religious or spiritual beliefs similar to those of their parents tend to be those who (p. 652)
    a. feel securely attached to their parents and view them as having used an authoritative child-rearing style.
    b. attended religious services with their parents regularly through high school.
    c. were taught not to question their parents' beliefs.
    d. feel no need to reconcile religious or spiritual beliefs with scientific principles.

23. According to research findings, contrary to what some young people think, most emerging adults who are religious are (p. 652)
    a. less likely to integrate their parents' perspectives into their own worldview.
    b. compliant and narrow-minded.
    c. likely to become authoritative parents.
    d. energetic, self-reliant individuals for whom religion is part of a broader approach to life.

24. Research indicates that self-defeating attitudes and behavior among emerging adults is associated with (p. 653)
    a. the prospect of settling down to the responsibilities of adulthood.
    b. extreme loneliness.
    c. lack of religious or spiritual commitment.
    d. the need to coordinate demanding life roles.

25. Research shows that the overwhelming majority of young people with access to supportive family, school, and community environments (p. 654)
    a. are highly optimistic about their future.
    b. have had few experiences that foster resilience.
    c. tend not to experiment with illegal drugs between ages 19 and 22.
    d. are nevertheless at risk for overwhelming loneliness.

CROSSWORD PUZZLE SOLUTIONS

PUZZLE 1.1

PUZZLE 1.2

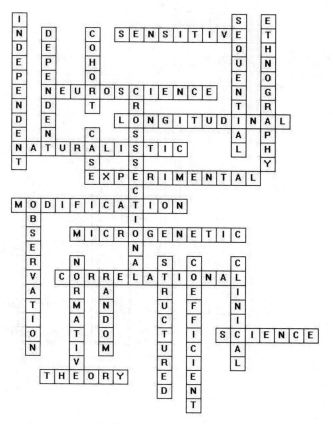

PUZZLE 2.1

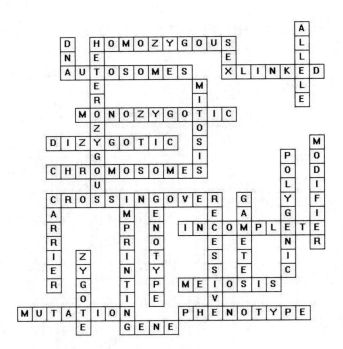

PUZZLE 2.2

PUZZLE 3.1

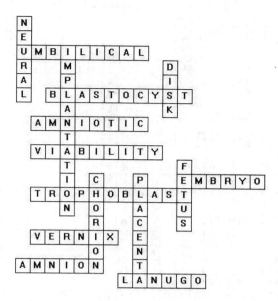

PUZZLE 3.2

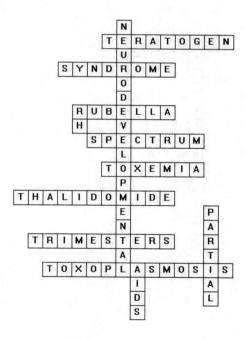

PUZZLE 4.1

PUZZLE 4.2

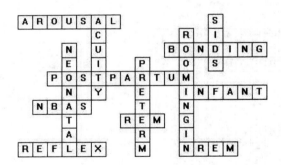

PUZZLE 5.1

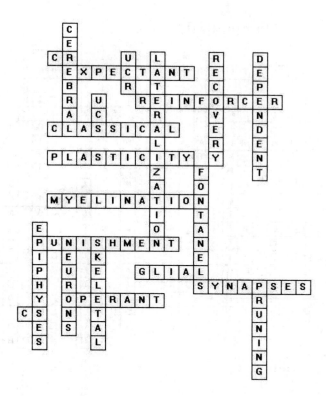

PUZZLE 5.2

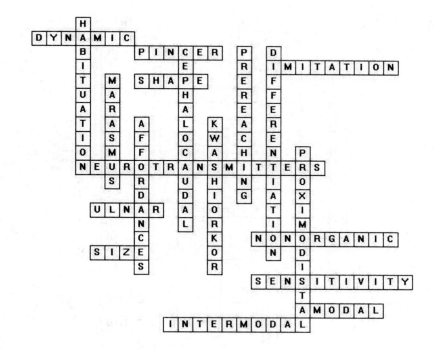

PUZZLE 6.1

PUZZLE 6.2

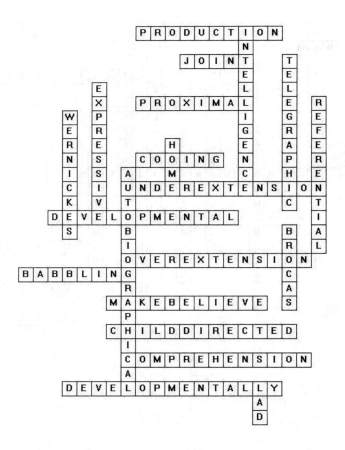

PUZZLE 7.1

PUZZLE 7.2

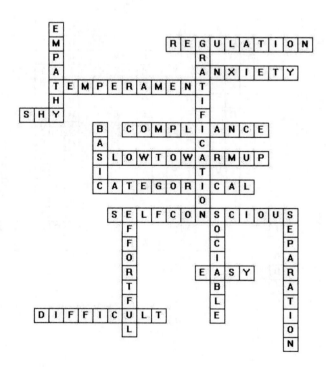

PUZZLE 8.1

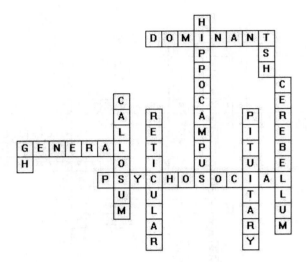

PUZZLE 9.1

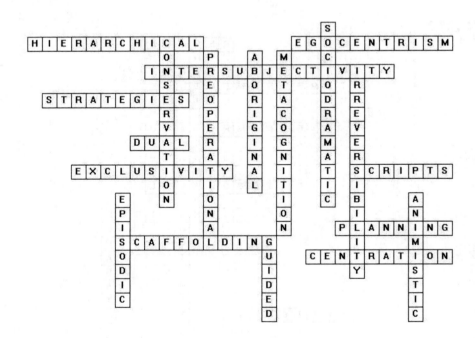

PUZZLE 9.2

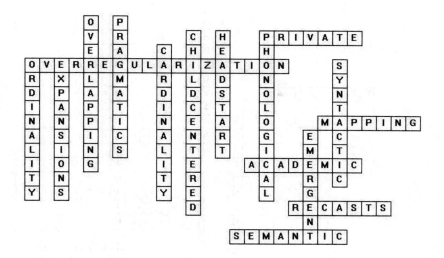

PUZZLE 10.1

PUZZLE 10.2

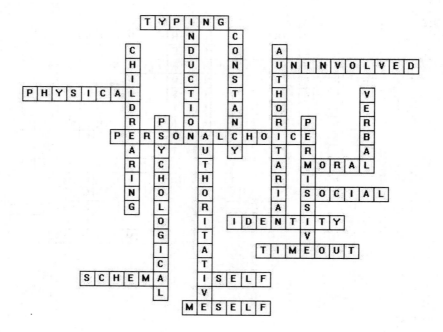

PUZZLE 11.1

PUZZLE 12.1

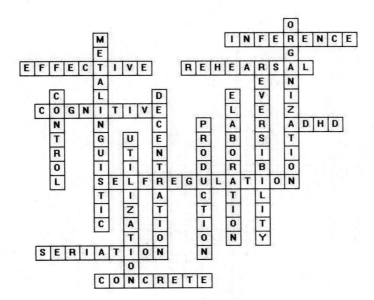

PUZZLE 12.2

PUZZLE 13.1

PUZZLE 13.2

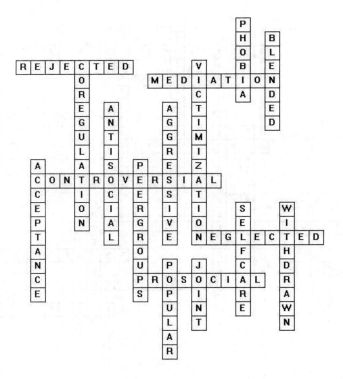

PUZZLE 14.1

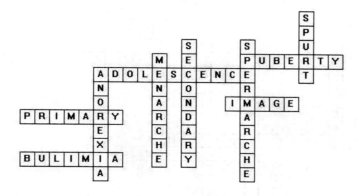

PUZZLE 15.1

PUZZLE 16.1

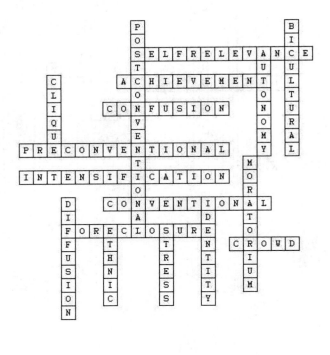

PUZZLE 17.1

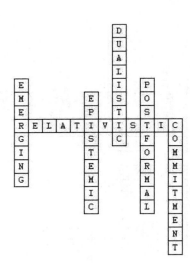

ANSWERS TO PRACTICE TESTS

CHAPTER 1

Practice Test #1

1. c	2. d	3. b	4. b	5. c
6. d	7. a	8. c	9. a	10. c
11. b	12. d	13. c	14. b	15. a
16. c	17. b	18. d	19. b	20. a
21. d	22. c	23. b	24. c	25. a

Practice Test #2

1. c	2. a	3. d	4. b	5. a
6. c	7. b	8. a	9. c	10. d
11. c	12. a	13. d	14. c	15. a
16. d	17. b	18. c	19. a	20. d
21. a	22. c	23. b	24. a	25. d

CHAPTER 2

Practice Test #1

1. b	2. d	3. c	4. a	5. d
6. b	7. d	8. c	9. a	10. d
11. c	12. b	13. a	14. c	15. b
16. d	17. a	18. c	19. b	20. d
21. b	22. a	23. c	24. b	25. d

Practice Test #2

1. d	2. a	3. c	4. c	5. d
6. b	7. a	8. b	9. d	10. c
11. b	12. a	13. c	14. b	15. d
16. a	17. c	18. b	19. a	20. c
21. d	22. b	23. c	24. a	25. d

CHAPTER 3

Practice Test #1

1. b	2. c	3. d	4. c	5. a
6. d	7. c	8. b	9. a	10. c
11. d	12. b	13. a	14. c	15. b
16. d	17. c	18. a	19. d	20. b
21. d	22. b	23. c	24. a	25. d

Practice Test #2

1. c	2. b	3. a	4. d	5. b
6. c	7. a	8. d	9. b	10. a
11. c	12. d	13. a	14. c	15. b
16. d	17. c	18. b	19. a	20. d
21. c	22. b	23. a	24. d	25. c

CHAPTER 4

Practice Test #1

1. b	2. a	3. d	4. b	5. a
6. d	7. c	8. b	9. a	10. c
11. d	12. c	13. b	14. a	15. c
16. d	17. a	18. c	19. d	20. a
21. b	22. c	23. b	24. d	25. b

Practice Test #2

1. c	2. a	3. b	4. d	5. a
6. c	7. b	8. c	9. d	10. b
11. a	12. c	13. b	14. a	15. d
16. c	17. b	18. d	19. a	20. c
21. b	22. d	23. a	24. c	25. b

CHAPTER 5

Practice Test #1

1. a	2. c	3. d	4. b	5. d
6. b	7. a	8. c	9. b	10. c
11. d	12. a	13. b	14. b	15. d
16. b	17. a	18. c	19. b	20. d
21. c	22. a	23. b	24. d	25. a

Practice Test #2

1. b	2. c	3. a	4. d	5. c
6. c	7. b	8. a	9. c	10. d
11. a	12. b	13. d	14. c	15. a
16. d	17. b	18. c	19. d	20. a
21. c	22. b	23. a	24. d	25. b

CHAPTER 6

Practice Test #1

1. b	2. d	3. a	4. c	5. b
6. d	7. b	8. a	9. c	10. a
11. d	12. a	13. c	14. a	15. d
16. b	17. c	18. a	19. d	20. b
21. a	22. c	23. d	24. a	25. b

Practice Test #2

1. c	2. a	3. b	4. d	5. c
6. b	7. a	8. d	9. c	10. b
11. d	12. c	13. a	14. c	15. d
16. a	17. c	18. b	19. a	20. d
21. c	22. b	23. a	24. c	25. d

CHAPTER 7

Practice Test #1

1. d	2. c	3. a	4. c	5. d
6. b	7. a	8. c	9. b	10. d
11. a	12. c	13. b	14. a	15. d
16. b	17. c	18. a	19. d	20. c
21. b	22. a	23. b	24. d	25. c

Practice Test #2

1. a	2. d	3. b	4. c	5. b
6. a	7. d	8. c	9. a	10. c
11. b	12. d	13. c	14. a	15. b
16. d	17. c	18. a	19. b	20. d
21. c	22. a	23. d	24. b	25. c

CHAPTER 8

Practice Test #1

1. b	2. d	3. c	4. a	5. b
6. d	7. c	8. a	9. b	10. a
11. c	12. b	13. d	14. c	15. a
16. b	17. c	18. a	19. c	20. d
21. a	22. b	23. a	24. c	25. b

Practice Test #2

1. c	2. a	3. d	4. b	5. a
6. c	7. d	8. b	9. d	10. c
11. a	12. c	13. d	14. b	15. d
16. a	17. c	18. b	19. d	20. c
21. a	22. d	23. b	24. a	25. d

CHAPTER 9

Practice Test #1

1. a	2. d	3. b	4. c	5. a
6. d	7. b	8. d	9. c	10. a
11. b	12. a	13. c	14. b	15. d
16. a	17. c	18. b	19. d	20. a
21. c	22. a	23. b	24. a	25. b

Practice Test #2

1. b	2. a	3. d	4. b	5. c
6. d	7. a	8. b	9. c	10. a
11. b	12. d	13. c	14. a	15. b
16. d	17. c	18. b	19. a	20. d
21. b	22. c	23. a	24. d	25. b

CHAPTER 10

Practice Test #1

1. a	2. c	3. b	4. a	5. d
6. b	7. d	8. a	9. c	10. b
11. d	12. c	13. b	14. c	15. a
16. c	17. c	18. b	19. d	20. c
21. a	22. d	23. b	24. c	25. a

Practice Test #2

1. c	2. b	3. d	4. a	5. c
6. b	7. d	8. a	9. c	10. a
11. d	12. a	13. b	14. d	15. c
16. a	17. b	18. d	19. c	20. a
21. d	22. c	23. b	24. d	25. a

CHAPTER 11

Practice Test #1

1. c	2. d	3. b	4. c	5. d
6. a	7. c	8. b	9. a	10. d
11. b	12. c	13. d	14. a	15. c
16. b	17. d	18. c	19. a	20. b
21. d	22. c	23. d	24. c	25. a

Practice Test #2

1. d	2. c	3. a	4. d	5. b
6. c	7. b	8. a	9. d	10. c
11. b	12. d	13. a	14. c	15. b
16. b	17. d	18. a	19. c	20. b
21. c	22. a	23. d	24. b	25. c

CHAPTER 12

Practice Test #1

1. b	2. d	3. a	4. c	5. b
6. d	7. c	8. a	9. b	10. d
11. a	12. c	13. b	14. d	15. c
16. a	17. b	18. d	19. c	20. a
21. b	22. d	23. b	24. d	25. b

Practice Test #2

1. d	2. c	3. a	4. b	5. d
6. c	7. a	8. c	9. b	10. a
11. b	12. d	13. c	14. b	15. a
16. c	17. b	18. d	19. a	20. c
21. a	22. d	23. b	24. c	25. a

CHAPTER 13

Practice Test #1

1. c	2. a	3. b	4. d	5. c
6. a	7. c	8. b	9. b	10. a
11. c	12. d	13. b	14. a	15. c
16. b	17. d	18. a	19. c	20. b
21. d	22. c	23. b	24. a	25. d

Practice Test #2

1. a	2. d	3. b	4. a	5. c
6. b	7. a	8. c	9. b	10. d
11. a	12. c	13. d	14. c	15. a
16. b	17. a	18. c	19. d	20. b
21. a	22. c	23. d	24. b	25. a

CHAPTER 14

Practice Test #1

1. a	2. d	3. b	4. c	5. a
6. c	7. d	8. b	9. d	10. a
11. c	12. d	13. a	14. b	15. d
16. b	17. d	18. b	19. a	20. d
21. c	22. b	23. d	24. b	25. d

Practice Test #2

1. b	2. c	3. d	4. b	5. a
6. c	7. b	8. d	9. a	10. d
11. c	12. b	13. a	14. b	15. d
16. a	17. c	18. a	19. c	20. d
21. a	22. b	23. b	24. d	25. c

CHAPTER 15

Practice Test #1

1. a	2. b	3. d	4. c	5. c
6. a	7. b	8. c	9. d	10. a
11. d	12. b	13. c	14. b	15. c
16. a	17. d	18. b	19. c	20. a
21. c	22. d	23. a	24. b	25. a

Practice Test #2

1. c	2. a	3. b	4. b	5. c
6. d	7. c	8. c	9. a	10. d
11. c	12. a	13. c	14. d	15. c
16. d	17. b	18. a	19. c	20. b
21. c	22. a	23. c	24. d	25. b

CHAPTER 16

Practice Test #1

1. b	2. a	3. c	4. b	5. a
6. d	7. b	8. a	9. c	10. c
11. b	12. a	13. a	14. c	15. d
16. a	17. b	18. a	19. d	20. b
21. a	22. c	23. c	24. b	25. d

Practice Test #2

1. c	2. d	3. a	4. a	5. c
6. b	7. d	8. b	9. c	10. d
11. a	12. c	13. c	14. d	15. b
16. b	17. d	18. c	19. b	20. a
21. c	22. d	23. c	24. a	25. b

CHAPTER 17

Practice Test #1

1. b	2. a	3. c	4. b	5. a
6. d	7. c	8. a	9. b	10. d
11. b	12. a	13. c	14. b	15. d
16. c	17. a	18. c	19. d	20. b
21. a	22. c	23. a	24. d	25. b

Practice Test #2

1. b	2. a	3. d	4. b	5. c
6. b	7. d	8. c	9. c	10. a
11. b	12. d	13. b	14. c	15. a
16. b	17. d	18. c	19. a	20. c
21. b	22. a	23. d	24. b	25. a